CW00539855

A STRANGER IN YOUR OWN CITY

A STRANGER IN YOUR OWN CITY

Travels in the Middle East's Long War

Ghaith Abdul-Ahad

HUTCHINSON
HEINEMANN

1 3 5 7 9 10 8 6 4 2

Hutchinson Heinemann
20 Vauxhall Bridge Road
London SW1V 2SA

Hutchinson Heinemann is part of the Penguin Random House group of companies
whose addresses can be found at global.penguinrandomhouse.com

Penguin
Random House
UK

Copyright © Ghaith Abdul-Ahad 2023

Illustrations and maps by Ghaith Abdul-Ahad

Ghaith Abdul-Ahad has asserted his right to be identified as the author of this
Work in accordance with the Copyright, Designs and Patents Act 1988.

First published by Hutchinson Heinemann in 2023

www.penguin.co.uk

A CIP catalogue record for this book is available from the British Library.

ISBN 9781529151534

Typeset in 12.5/16pt Fournier MT Pro by Jouve (UK), Milton Keynes
Printed and bound in Great Britain by Clays Ltd, Elcograf S.p.A.

The authorised representative in the EEA is Penguin Random House Ireland,
Morrison Chambers, 32 Nassau Street, Dublin D02 YH68

www.greenpenguin.co.uk

MIX
Paper from
responsible sources
FSC® C018179

Penguin Random House is committed to a
sustainable future for our business, our readers
and our planet. This book is made from Forest
Stewardship Council® certified paper.

Iraqis and palm trees. Who resembles whom? There are millions of Iraqis and as many, or perhaps somewhat fewer, palm trees. Some have had their fronds burned. Some have been beheaded. Some have had their backs broken by time, but are still trying to stand. Some have dried bunches of dates. Some have been uprooted, mutilated and exiled from their orchards. Some have allowed invaders to lean on their trunk. Some are combing the winds with their fronds. Some stand in silence. Some have fallen. Some stand tall and raise their heads high despite everything in this vast orchard: Iraq. When will the orchard return to its owners? Not to those who carry axes. Not even to the attendant who assassinates palm trees, no matter what the color of his knife.

Sinan Antoon, *The Corpse Washer*

Contents

Contents

Contents

Author's Note

This book is a work of non-fiction based on the life, experiences and recollections of the author. The majority of the stories told here took place in the midst of violence and civil wars, and in many cases the people featured in these stories – both the victims of that violence and its perpetrators – asked for their names to be changed for their protection.

A lot of literature has been published on Iraq and the rise of the Islamic State and sectarianism in the region, and the author is indebted to many writers and journalists for their brilliant books on these subjects. In particular: Charles Tripp's *A History of Iraq*, Samuel Helfont's *Compulsion in Religion*, Johan Franzen's *Pride and Power*, Fawaz Gerges's *ISIS: A History*, and of course the mighty Hanna Batatu and his authoritative work *The Old Social Classes and the Revolutionary Movements of Iraq*.

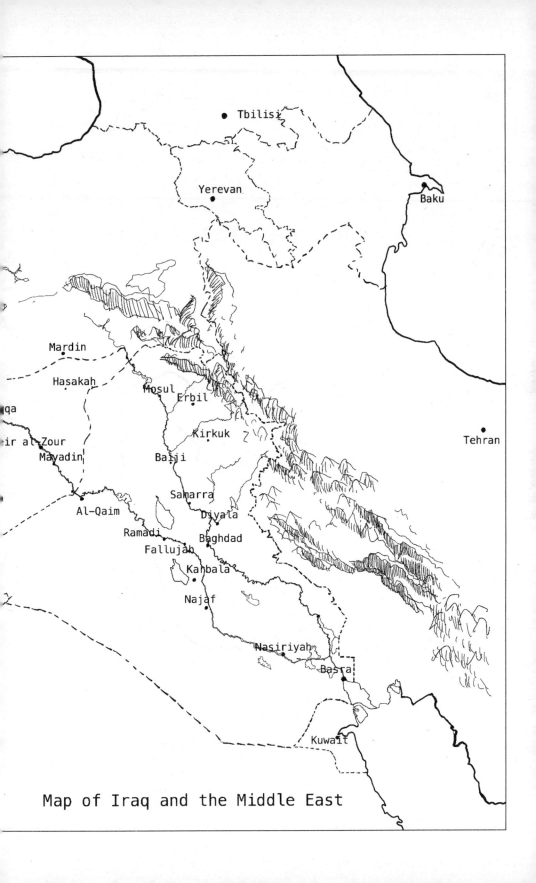

Map of Iraq and the Middle East

Prologue

Hotel room. Baghdad, 2007.

Late at night, I am awake in my hotel bed, listening to the sounds of a city at war: the distant thuds of mortars crashing in the Green Zone, the monotonous din of supply convoys, shrouded in the safety of the dark curfew hours. There are rumblings in the street below, and the howling of street dogs. Dawn will break soon; the clashes will resume. Car bombs will start blowing up in the morning rush hour. The sounds, like the war, have become repetitive, rhythmic and very predictable.

Like insomniacs counting sheep to fall asleep, I play my own game; sifting through the faces of friends from the pre-invasion days, I try to place each one on the sectarian map of a fragmented city. Tonight, I mentally run through a faded school picture, taken on a spring day in 1991, just before the second Gulf War; a group of friends in high-waisted jeans and tucked-in T-shirts, posing in front of the tall, imposing brick facade of the Jesuit-built – subsequently nationalised – school. Scrawny limbs, hollowed chests, childish and naughty eyes, and the first traces of moustaches lining their lips.

I try to imagine their lives in the context of the civil war raging outside my hotel room. Who was a Shia, and who was a Sunni? How many were kidnapped and how many killed? How many members of militias and how many in exile?

Those with easy-to-classify family names emerge first. Ahmad must be a Shia. Raid is a Sunni –he used to be proud of a distant tribal relation to the Great Leader, an association that must haunt

I

him in these days of Shia death squads. Basil was Christian and had long since left Iraq. The game is hard, old memories can't always be translated into the latest sectarian terminology, and I fail to place most of my friends on the new sectarian map of Baghdad.

The poet who I presumed to be a Shia, just because he lived close to the Shia shrine in Khadimiya, turned out to be a Sunni from Mosul. He dallied with radical Islam, grew a long beard, and flirted with Sunni insurgents, before fleeing from Shia death squads into Syria. He could have been a useful contact in these days, but when a few years later I met him in Dubai, he drank his whisky neat and was back to writing poetry. The young boys from the high school picture are now scattered between Dubai, Amman, Liverpool and Toronto. A neurosurgeon, a paediatrician, an architect, a civil engineer and a couple of university professors, a businessman who twice made a multimillion-dollar fortune and twice lost it on the stock market. Alas, none is a vicious militia commander; there are no sectarian politicians and no killers among them. They are useless friends in a Baghdad torn by civil war, where one needs contacts among the different fighting groups to help negotiate the multiple front lines. I have become a stranger in my own city.

———

The hotel bed is narrow with a pale wooden frame, sagging in the middle where two planks are missing. The room is heavy with the dust of two decades of War, Sanctions and Occupation. Two car bombs have left long, thin cracks on the walls; plastic sheeting covers a broken window, and pipes are dripping in the bathroom, where layers of grimy green mould carpet the corners. The hotel was once a fashionable enterprise with the sharp, concrete corners of brutalist architecture, chic seventies furniture and an excellent bakery. The

swimming pool, with its deep blue tiles, was elegant and exception-
ally clean. The cold, over-chlorinated water frothed in little waves
over the edge, and floating eucalyptus leaves would cast twirling
shadows on its blue tiles before being scooped up by a diligent staff
member. A long-life ago, I swam here every summer. A benevolent,
wealthy, formerly Communist grand-aunt paid my entry fees; she
also introduced me to Russian literature and ailurophilia. I used to
sit at one of the white plastic tables by the poolside playing Uno with
other boys and girls. We ate melon, ice cream and sometimes, if we
could afford it, croissant sandwiches. When most of the guests left,
we stayed behind, racing each other in the pool, or swimming endless
laps until it was dark and too cold.

A few days after the American invasion and the toppling of
Saddam's statue in central Baghdad, foreign journalists took over the
hotel, adding its name to a long list of war-zone hotels that stretched
from Saigon to Beirut. The journalists — Americans and British with
a spattering of French and a couple of Italians — were young and
lean, dressed in khakis and scarves. They sat around the pool, drank
Turkish beer and became rowdy and festive. In the post-coital bliss
of war survivors, they caroused and rekindled old affairs from previous wars or embarked on new ones, to be revived later in Tripoli
or Gaza. They reminisced about Moscow in the nineties and Kabul
in 2001, and in their we-liberated-the-city attitude, despaired at the
ingratitude and dullness of the Iraqis, lamenting their previous war
subjects; the noble Chechens, the feisty Lebanese or the beautiful
Bosnians.

One night, sitting around the same white plastic tables, I told a
group of them that I used to come here and swim with friends before
the war; they gave me kind, patronising and unbelieving smiles. How
can there have been life in Baghdad before they had arrived? How
dare I introduce normality into their adventure sphere? We were

designated to be victims or the victimisers in their stories. I felt I was an intruder on their war and a bit sorry that we Iraqis couldn't be more exciting.

After the war I found a job as a translator, accompanying journalists as they travelled around the city and the country, and I cringed every time I had to translate one question, the only one that seemed to matter: Are you a Sunni or a Shia? They asked it in a crass and vulgar way, there was no subtlety about it, just in-your-face directness and urgency, as if everything depended on that single answer. One's character was drawn with stick-figure simplicity. Sunni: oppressor, Shia: victim.

Well, Saddam was a Sunni, they said, and so all the Sunnis must support him, right?

When did 'From Baghdad' become an insufficient answer to the question 'Where are you from?'

Even before the city fragmented and divided, and the civil war raged in the streets, the country was defined by outsiders on binary bases. The sect and ethnicity had become the most important identifier of a person. Social or political classifications, history – none of that mattered any more.

I invented a game called 'Play with Foreigners', dedicated to those who thought they were smart enough to guess one's sect from a few clues. I dangled bits and pieces of personal life for them and watched – in their binary cognition of black and white, Hutu and Tutsi, Muslim and Serbian – their wild hunt, sniffing for sect and identity from Basra in the south where my father was born – aha, must be a Shia! – to Baghdad where I was born – well, could be anything, really – and to the small Arabic town between Mosul and Aleppo in the north where my grandfather was born in Ottoman times – definitely a Sunni, but then??

Later, when the sectarian politics led to conflict, we, the Iraqis, were informed by the Occupation overlords, their pontificates and well-intentioned journalists, that the problem lay in the fact that Iraq was a fake construct – formed when the British lumped together the three Ottoman vilayets (provinces) of Mosul, Baghdad and Basra. They told us that these three groups of incongruous people had fought along ethnic and sectarian lines for hundreds sometimes thousands of years and had always been unable to live together. To remedy all the sins committed by the British colonialists and the Saddam regime, some of the pontificates suggested – and still suggest – breaking up the country; a decade later, Islamic State jihadis wanted to do away with the border altogether.

But then all nations are, in one way or another, a construct, and nationalism is a fictional narrative based on a group of people's collection of myths and symbols. 'Iraq' as a distinctive geographical region denoting the plains south of Mosul and north of the Persian Gulf was there long before the British sailed out of their islands. The people of these three Ottoman provinces – connected by trade, tribal lineage, religion and ethnicity – had been treated as a notional entity since the late Ottoman period and were welded together by centralised bureaucracy from the seat of power in Baghdad. It is true that Mosul had stronger cultural connections to Aleppo than to Basra, which as a port had a distinctive Indian Ocean influence, and that denying the Kurds a national homeland had haunted Iraq ever since its formation. The fact is: in Iraq, as in all other countries in the region, a common identity, imagined and constructed, solidified into belligerent nationalism after a hundred years of a centralised government, the creation of an army that dominated social and political life, the drilling of a national myth into generations of schoolchildren, and the glorified celebration of a myopic version of history.

Within months of the occupation, killings, kidnappings and car bombs had put an end to the press corps' festive euphoria. The hotel turned into a suffocating and depressing holding pen. A trip to the supermarket became an adventure worth telling a story about. Multiple heavy armoured doors and former military mercenaries segregated the American TV network occupying the higher floors from the rest.

The hotel itself aged into an ugly and haggard building. Car bombs abraded its jagged modernist edges, dark mysteries gaped behind fallen ceiling tiles. Windows were covered permanently with plastic anti-blast sheets, and black fumes from the two massive generators stained the whitewashed walls. Rubbish nestled between the coils of barbed wire. Under relentless attack from the oily and fatty Iraqi food, the lean bodies of journalists sagged, and their affairs, like the myths and dreams of the 'Liberation', subsided creaking and crumbling. They were laid to rest by the now murky and stagnant waters of the swimming pool.

PART ONE

*The Leader Necessity
and his Statue*

1

My First War

WAR CAME TO OUR HOUSE on a sunny and cold September morning. I stood on my parents' bed trying to peer out of the window. My mother had her head in the blankets, and my father was propped on one elbow, looking out at the empty patch of land behind our house. What did we expect to see? Tanks and soldiers fighting there? There must have been air-raid sirens, anti-aircraft guns that woke me up and sent me scuttling down to their room, but I don't remember. It was 1980, I was five years old, and the Eight Years War with Iran had just begun.

Later, on the roof of our squat brick house in eastern Baghdad, my father, with honey-coloured eyes, black moustache and thick pomaded hair, carried me with one arm and stretched the other to point at a thin white trail that arced in the pale blue sky. With a big smile, he declared 'Phantoms, F4' with the confidence of a hunter who could spot a partridge at a distance in hazy dawn light. From my vantage point resting on his chest, I looked down at my dear uncle standing next to us, his face furrowed with concern and bewilderment. Downstairs, confusion – and people cowering under a white Formica-topped iron table that had been placed under the stairs. Someone was trying to get an old radio to work. For a while they remained there, squeezed into the safety and comfort of that cramped place, then one after the other – grandmother, mother, aunts and cousins – seeing the silliness of their shelter, left and headed to the kitchen, turning the day into a festive family gathering. Only one aunt remained under the table, whimpering.

Eight years of war cluttered my memory with images, mixed in with scenes from Russian war films, creating a news reel where reality and fiction seemed equally absurd. There must have been tender memories of childhood, images of uncles and aunts, of feasts with colourful dishes cooked by grandmothers who'd brought their recipes from far distant places . . . All these images were swept away, drowned out by the wails of sirens and the explosions of the Scud missiles that shook the houses.

Spring in those years was marked by major infantry offensives, in which human waves of tens of thousands of soldiers crashed against each other. On TV they ran endless loops of a programme called *Images from the Battlefront*. They showed footage of trenches piled with the mangled and burned corpses. We were told that these were the bodies of Iranian soldiers; mowed down, electrocuted or gassed. The screen filled, the images multiplying: blackened limbs hung from barbed wire, mouths stuffed with dirt, bloated khaki uniforms and helmets scattered along a large field. The pictures were always accompanied by the hoarse voice of the narrator assuring us of imminent victory.

After each of these battles, we watched the Leader Necessity on TV, gathering his generals in the gilded hall of one of his many opulent palaces. He took the 'Medals of Courage' from a tray carried by his tall bodyguard, who followed respectfully two steps behind. As he pinned them to the generals' chests, you could see them suck in the well-fed bellies that bulged through crisp military uniforms. The medals collected on the bosoms of the generals, and thousands of black banners blossomed throughout the city. They were hung on walls, tied between trees and lamp posts, each announcing – by the name of Allah the most compassionate and most merciful – the martyrdom of an Iraqi man. Collective grief hung over Baghdad during these days. Men raised their hands in a final farewell gesture to wooden coffins draped in Iraqi flags and strapped to the tops of white-and-orange taxis making their way to the cemeteries outside the city, followed usually by a minibus or a van packed with women dressed in black, weeping and smacking their faces in mourning.

At night, my father crouched next to the old chrome-coloured radio, straining his ear through the jamming static, trying to listen to foreign stations – an act punishable by seven years in prison – to find out what was going on. 'Come to the flavour, come to Marlboros . . . fighting in Palestinian refugee camps in Beirut . . . Iran rejects a peace offer . . .' The snippets of conversation we heard from returning soldiers told us more – artillery shelling in Basra, trenches, and families displaced in the fighting. The dead in that war, all conscript soldiers forced to march to the front, were divided into 'martyrs' and 'deserters'. One set died 'gloriously', and were exalted; the other hunted, summarily executed and despised even in death. We saw the deserters transferred into buses with metal grilles on the windows, hands cuffed to the bars of the seats in front of them, scared eyes in their shaven heads. There was the story of the man who killed his own son, for desertion, and was rewarded with a Medal of Courage by the Leader himself.

On TV and in school, we were told that this war was a continuation of the first battle of Qadisiyyah, when the Muslim Arabs defeated the Sassanid Empire in 636. Thirteen and a half centuries later, and under the wise command of the Leader Necessity, we the inheritors of the legacy of the Muslim conquerors were defeating the wicked Persians in the Second Qadisiyyah, or the Qadisiyyah of Saddam. The Iranians/Persians were the mortal enemies, the regime declared; they were the thread that ran through all our Babylonian, Assyrian and Arab Muslim metamorphoses.

Not only the war but our whole history was explained in the same straightforward linear narrative of phantasmagoria. It ran like this: first God created Adam and Eve in Eden, which was in the south of Iraq, then after a period of confused early humans, the Sumerians emerged, again in the south of Iraq. The Sumerians begat the Babylonians, who begat the mighty Assyrians and eventually metamorphosed into Arabs in a swift natural progression of history. The Arabs became Muslims and went on to conquer the world, defeating the wicked Sassanid Empire in the aforementioned battle of Qadisiyyah, which brought Islam and civilisation to the backward lands of the Persians. After many glorious centuries of unity, evil invaders – Mongols, Turks, more wicked Persians and British imperialists – conspired against us. We had to endure centuries of darkness and oppression, until the Glorious Revolution, led by the Leader Necessity, Saddam Hussein, liberated us and showed us the path to emancipation, progress and victory. Murals decorating official buildings illustrated that history, with the austere bearded profile of an Assyrian king at one end, and the portrait of Saddam at the other, and in between there was a collage of Saladin, Arab warriors and tribal rebels, with a couple of workers and farmers thrown in as a nod to the socialist myth of the Baath Party.

The Leader was the embodiment of our national narrative, tall, moustached; eating watermelons with farmers. Wearing dark sunglasses, smoking cigars and with a pistol tucked in his waistband, he struck the quintessential pose of a Third World dictator channelling Che Guevara and Yasser Arafat. The Leader Necessity title was first mentioned in the writings of Michel Aflaq, a Syrian writer and paramount Arab nationalist, who co-founded the Baath Party. Aflaq, inspired by the writings of German ideologues of the nineteenth century, wrote about the historical emergence of a long-awaited Leader Necessity who shall unify the nation and march on the path of victory and glory. Some say Saddam's press secretary was the first to bestow the title on the Leader, others say the Leader himself chose it; in any case, the Leader, a Historic Necessity, was born.

At school, we stood to attention as the Iraqi flag was raised. I looked with envy at those whose fathers had been killed in the war because they were allowed to wear military uniforms and carry their late father's insignia on their shoulders. The stern teacher, with her blonde-dyed hair, wore an army uniform and fired a volley of dummy bullets over our heads. We strained hard not to flinch as they echoed across the schoolyard. We sang and goose-stepped to the old Levantine song 'The Daughter of the Merchant had Almond Eyes', which had become 'We are the Baathists, March to the Sounds of Cannons and Bombs'. In art class, we drew jet fighters, tanks and stick soldiers emblazoned with the Iraqi flag attacking and destroying Iranian jet fighters, tanks and stick soldiers.

———

The imagery and rhetoric of the state and the Baath Party in those days were that of revolution, radical socialism and Pan-Arab nationalism. None of it meant anything beyond folklore and pageantry. The Leader Necessity, the supreme leader, the ultimate manifestation of the state, and the arbiter of its ideology, had long since emptied the Baath Party of any meaning beyond the implementation of his personal will. Sycophantic party apparatchiks – easily spotted by the style of their moustaches and the short-sleeved safari shirts or military uniforms – parroted ad nauseam the idiosyncratic, incomprehensibly blabbering speeches of the Leader. They were present in every institution and worked to control the masses through denunciations, intimidation and the rounding up of men, who were subsequently forced to 'volunteer' in the fight at the front. There was also a formidable array of security services answerable directly to the Leader, which used exemplary violence to quash any dissenting voices and to guarantee obedience. Pictures of the omniscient Leader Necessity decorated each classroom and every public building. Murals stood watching over us, and walls were lined with his sayings. Every evening an hour of TV broadcast was devoted to 'poetry in the love of the Leader', or to his pearls of wisdom, accompanied by soft music.

One of the cartoons aired on Iraqi TV at that time was a Japanese anime series called *Grendizer*. The hero, Duke Fleed – read: Saddam Hussein – battled the evil King Vega – read: Imam Khomeini – in defence of planet Earth – read: Iraq. Waves of invading UFO flying saucers bombing cities and civilians represented the evil Iranian jet fighters. I took the good vs evil analogy even further when listening to nuns in our primary school speak of the Lord our Saviour: I came to believe that Saddam was either God or Jesus, or maybe both of them. In reality, Saddam – whose titles included the Great Historic Leader, Allah's gift to Iraq, the Saviour, the Inspirer, the Victorious, the Honest, the Creative, the Wise, the Teacher and the Pioneer, the Beloved of the People, the Consciousness of the Nation, Father of all Iraqis and the Tent of all the Arabs – was far more important, and dangerous, than God Almighty. While God rarely strikes the blasphemous with instant fury, using the Leader's name in vain was punishable by long years of torture and imprisonment followed by execution. Nevertheless, people did tell jokes about the Leader, just as they did about God, but these were only whispered among trusted friends and family in hushed voices and with a twinkling of guilty eyes, and only after looking at the phone nervously, since we all believed that the security services used phones as listening devices. He was never mentioned in name but referred to as 'HIM'.

Two or three years after the start of the war, on a late afternoon in winter, I stood with my father among a crowd that had gathered to watch a military parade. Iraqi soldiers in olive-green uniforms and helmets sat on the back of Russian trucks that filed by slowly. Between the soldiers sat the tired, dishevelled and bound Iranian prisoners of war, their heads bowed, their eyes confused; some were very young, others were haggard, old bearded men. The crowd was cheering, but the soldiers, like their prisoners, were silent with dark and morbid looks on their faces. The light was fading quickly, and the sky was turning a purple-blue as the trucks inched their way along, when an Iraqi soldier with a sad face grabbed my waving hand, closed over it with his own big rough one for a second before letting it go. I opened my hand, and in my small palm rested a large copper bullet with a thin red line. I held on to it like a sacred relic for a long time; little did I know that it was a harbinger of the many wars to come.

There were two realities of life during that war. In the background, the war continued after Saddam's gamble to achieve a quick military victory had failed; hundreds of thousands of soldiers slept in trenches or ploughed through the muddy marshes, or were killed or maimed. The other reality was of life in the cities. Apart from Basra and Kurdish villages in the north, right in the middle of battle, for the rest of us, these were the years of prosperity – the years when we went to schools, had jobs; when hospitals functioned and roads were built.

These realities collided when uncles and cousins were drafted into the folly of war; eventually, my father himself was taken as a conscript soldier. Mothers and aunts wept, whimpered, and prayed. The two realities came together again when the two countries fired long-range missiles at each other's cities. One afternoon our apartment building shook when a rocket fell close by. My father and I walked a few blocks: a couple of houses had been turned into a mound of brick walls and broken concrete roofs. The last memory of that war was cowering behind a sofa with my mother and my young brother. Explosions of anti-aircraft fire rattled the apartment, in what must have been the last Baghdad air raid of the war. I imagined the Iranian fighter hovering over the streets in front of our building, ready at any moment to come pouncing at us through the window.

———

Many years later, when I finally visited Iran, I went to Behesht-e Zahra, a cemetery the size of a small town on the outskirts of Tehran. In the martyrs' section, most of the dead had been killed in the Holy War, or the 'Jangi Muqadas', the Iranian name for our eight years of folly. At the head of each grave stood a small aluminium and glass cabinet containing a few items of the martyr's memorabilia; a small copy of the Quran, pictures of Imam Ali and Hussein, plastic flowers, a bottle of rose water, a piece of blood-soaked cloth, and tiny leather pouches carrying verses from the Quran to be worn like a talisman. There were also photographs of the dead soldiers: some black and white, others in colour, faded, re-touched, taken in studios or by a friend in a park or a bus terminal before heading to the front.

Inscribed on the graves were the names of the battles – Ahwaz, Kurdistan, Ailam, Shalamgah – the names of towns and marshes in the south and villages in the Kurdish mountains in the north that delineate the borders between our two countries. I knew these names, they were the names of the spring offensives. In the middle of the sea of pictures of the young and sometimes old men in Behesht-e Zahra, I came across a small plot of earth, surrounded by a metal rail, where an Iranian family with the name Qassim was buried; the father was forty, the mother twenty-seven, the children three, two and one. They were all killed by an Iraqi air force attack on Tehran in our version of the 'War of Cities'. When both Iraq and Iran fired rockets and sent planes to bomb each other's cities. Later I stood in front of one grave scribbling in my notebook when, raising my head, I saw in the altar-like cabinet the bearded face of the martyr, staring at me. I moved, and he moved with me. I stumbled a few steps back, and my heart pounded hard. I was looking at my own reflection in a mirror.

After a million people killed or injured on both sides, the two countries accepted a UN resolution and returned to the same point of departure, minus their losses. But in Iraq, the Leader Necessity believed he had a formidable army now, and that no one in the region was going to stand against him.

2

Mother of all Battles

ON THE NIGHT OF 15 January 1991, I went to bed wearing my jeans, a sweater and socks. My shoes were laid next to my bed. The American ultimatum for Saddam to withdraw from Kuwait expired that night.

Two years after the Iranian adventure had ended in a stalemate, Iraq was financially ruined and under significant economic constraints. Saddam demanded that the Gulf countries cancel Iraq's debts incurred during the war, claiming that he was defending all the Arabs in his war with Iran. When he was ignored and the price of oil went down, Saddam, with his village tough-guy attitude, decided to take a gamble. On 2 August, he invaded Kuwait. The Iraqi state and the ruling elite embarked on the most systematic looting of the country, taking everything from planes to chocolate bars. In the flea markets of Baghdad, pedlars sold used VCRs, tape recorders, mismatched trainers. American Chevrolets carrying Iraq-Kuwait licence plates cruised the streets. On TV we were told how we went to Kuwait to liberate it, and how Kuwait had always been part of Iraq. We watched with disbelief as the hubris and arrogance of the Leader dragged us into war again. Even a fifteen-year-old like me thought a war would end in utter defeat, but the wise Leader chose to gamble to the last. At around 2 a.m, the Americans and their allies began their bombing campaign. I woke up startled by the sound of explosions, and I jumped from my bed and ran out of the room. On the landing,

I met my father and younger brother, and we stood facing each other for a second; outside the skies were shaking. We hurried to the basement shelter, where a few families gathered in the darkness. The men stood at the entrance smoking and pontificating. Cruise missiles and not very smart bombs were falling upon the city while whips of red anti-aircraft fire arced through the sky. The presidential palace and other buildings across the river were already hit and on fire and the sky was flickering with a million sparkling bullets. Within a day, the basement resembled a refugee camp, with bedding, bundles of clothing and families settling on them.

In the mornings with their diffused January light, air crisp and cold, we enjoyed the thrill of surviving another night of massive bombing and took advantage of the few precious hours before the war resumed. We walked around the deserted streets to inspect the damage of the night before – the pulverised telephone exchange, the destroyed buildings – but the saddest sight by far was the bombed-out remains of the old green suspension bridge, built in the fifties and much loved by Baghdadis. It lay on its side, the muddy Tigris flowing over its half-sunken tower and thick tension cables. We stood watching it as if we were mourning a dead relative. By that point, we had been subsisting like scavengers in our own homes for weeks, with no electricity and an intermittent supply of water. We had to carry buckets of water up and down the stairs; we baked flatbread on the kerosene heaters and left pots and dishes to pile high unwashed. Will life ever be the same after this? More than the bombs themselves, we feared that this war would last another decade. At night, the bombs shook the building; we felt them in our spines, shuddering, the sounds that said 'no one can survive this'.

The war ended forty days later with Saddam's defeat. A few days after that, my father and I were in a crowded bus station waiting for one of the few buses that still had petrol, when I saw what crystallised later in my mind as the image of the rout: three Iraqi soldiers, walking slowly, one of them dragging behind him an RPG launcher, like an old rusting pipe. People moved around them, no one cared or tried to help. The three soldiers were the face of a broken nation. The skies too were defeated, shrouded by the smoke from the burning oilfields of Kuwait, and when the rain fell, it dripped thick black lines on the walls and down the streets, gathering in puddles, and ditches, like mascara lines tracked by the tears of a crying woman.

The threats of the American secretary of state, George Shultz, of pushing us back into the Stone Age, seemed to have been fulfilled.

In that boredom, I read and reread Pushkin and Amin Maalouf and drew copies of every frame of the few Tintin books I had. A passion for doodling was the war's lasting gift.

3

The Years of the Sanctions

IF A MILLION MEN WERE killed and injured on the front lines in the eight years of war with Iran, and the first American Gulf War destroyed buildings and bridges and decimated the infrastructure, then the thirteen years of UN sanctions – Sanawat al-Hisar – humiliated the nation and brought it to its knees. Proud families sold their possessions just to survive from one month to the next. First to go was the wife's jewellery, then vases, carpets and other family heirlooms. Furniture started disappearing, along with books and kitchen appliances. In the working-class neighbourhoods on the outskirts of Baghdad and in the south, it was the poor who bore the brunt of these hunger years, when they had to sell their government food rations to buy medicine or baby formula on the black market. As students at the Architectural school, we used to go through drawers and storerooms to scavenge for old drawings, just for the paper. Those who could afford to were leaving the country in droves, seeking work elsewhere; those who couldn't survived through the aid and remittances sent by those who had already escaped, hustled black market goods, or worked three jobs. Infant mortality more than doubled, and 500,000 children died because of the sanctions, according to a UNICEF study conducted in 1999. Long queues formed outside the local groceries for butter, milk or, if one was very lucky, cheese.

Corruption was consuming the state from the inside, turning it into a hollow putrid shell devoid of legitimate authority and unworthy of respect. When a teacher's salary was reduced to $2 a month, and that of a police officer was $5, and when pilots and tank commanders drove taxis to make a living, corruption and embezzlement became a way of life.

Even the Leader's ability to project power and authority was curtailed. Most military hardware had been destroyed; the Kurdish regions had broken away under the auspices of a no-fly zone, with US and British jets patrolling the skies and occasionally bombing air defence units. All topped off by the constant humiliation of the UN weapons inspectors.

The sanctions also weakened the party and its security apparatus. The apparatchiks were still capable of destroying the lives of citizens through reports and denunciations, were still present in every institution, and yet they were no longer capable of totally dominating the people, for although they fared marginally better than the rest of the population, they too felt the impact of the sanctions, and had to resort to corruption and the black market to survive. Their olive-green uniforms became shabbier, and their hold over power and death became more negotiable with bribes.

In response, the Leader Necessity – the omniscient, omnipresent, whose ultimate goal was to achieve total control and hegemony over all Iraqi people – tweaked the national narrative. The old obsolete revolutionary images of pan-Arabism and socialism were replaced by a new set of values based on Islam and the tribe, portraying himself as the pious, father-like, tribal sheikh. He used tribal and religious networks, both as means to extend his control and to appease by expanding his patron–client networks. Replacing socialist jargon with an Islamist one. Saddam was not the only dictator who attempted to harness the power of religion to promote his own version of history and impose his authority, he just did it better than anyone else.

In the late eighties and early nineties, religiosity swept across the Arab and Muslim world in general. During the harsh sanction years, religion became a solace – an alternative support network to the state, with aid distributed through charities and local mosques both Sunni and Shia. It also became a political lever to create 'solidarity and steadfastness' against the 'aggression of the Zionists and imperialists', in the linguistic jargon of our press.

In Saddam's promotion of religion he attempted to achieve two goals: to harness the general religious mood to legitimise his rule, and to counter the narrative of the radical religious opposition movements, be they Sunni or Shia, that called for the toppling of the regime and the establishment of an Islamic republic. So while he promoted his version of Islam, his security apparatus continued to hunt down Islamists.

Of course, Iraq under the rule of the Baath Party and Saddam was never a secular country in the sense that it attempted to completely separate religion from social life; on the contrary, Islamic history and tradition was 'a proof of the greatness and the exceptionalism of the Arab Umma' and 'the inspiration for their eternal message' (according to the official doctrines of the party).

Saddam, bestowed with a halo of quasi-divinity, now collected a whole new set of titles. He became the mujahid, the Defender of the Realms of Islam against the infidels and the crusaders of the modern age, and the Leader of the Faith Campaign. Religion entered the social sphere as it never had before. He built large mosque complexes, promoted the learning and memorisation of the Quran, banned the serving, but not the sale, of alcohol, added the words Allahu Akbar to the flag.

Samuel Helfont brilliantly illustrates in his book *Compulsion in Religion* – based on the archives of the Baath party – how the regime version of Islam, communicated to the masses through a public TV and radio by a cadre of Muslim scholars – approved, vetted and groomed by the party apparatus – was traditional, quietist and extremely apolitical. The vocabulary, symbols and tools changed but the regime's core messages remained: Arabism, anti-colonialism and anti-Americanism.

Strange though it sounds, regime-promoted Islam tried to be non-sectarian. However, even if it was not an orthodox Islam, it was still based on the mainstream generic narrative of Islam, one with a clear Sunni slant, dominant in the Arab world through religious education as well as in popular culture. So while it glorified Imam Ali, it also honoured the Rashidun caliphs, who are of course considered usurpers by the Shia.

But the general religious atmosphere and the regime's continuous attempts to promote an Arab Shia 'Hawza', as opposed to the one in Qum in Iran, or the one dominated by Persian scholars in Najaf, allowed a stern and vocal cleric called Muhammad Sadiq al-Sadr to achieve prominence. He articulated the pain and the suffering of the poor Shia masses during the sanctions, and gathered around him a tight circle of disciples drawn from the same poor classes. While he opposed the regime – not publicly – his fiery sermons were directed at the West, blaming America and Israel for Iraq's sufferings, and calling for the liberation of Palestine in a language not dissimilar to the regime's. Alas, when he became too popular he was assassinated along with two of his sons in 1998. His youngest son Muqtada would later lead a rebellion against the Americans using the same anti-Western rhetoric of his father.

———

The Pious Leader, the Philosopher and the Source of Inspiration bored the nation to death with his long, meandering monologues encompassing religion, traditions and nationalism, and also his 'anonymously' published novels, featuring tragic, heroic figures fending off foreign invasions. He took a personal interest in the designs of a large number of palaces, and grand mosques all carrying his name and built in the new 'Presidential' architectural style that was born under his wise guidance – a mishmash of neoclassical columns, Babylonian gates and a variety of Islamic domes – which, like his eminence, were imposing, magnificent and authoritarian. He examined architectural models of the Grand Saddam Mosque, followed at a respectful distance by his trembling architects. It was supposed to be the biggest in the world with a dome spanning dozens of metres, and to the last days of his rule, he dithered over the final shape of the minarets: should they resemble rockets or Kalashnikov barrels? The hulk of that unfinished structure stands today, a monument to his hubris and madness.

In these years of severe hardship, the Leader's dress code was also becoming increasingly eccentric. Shedding his green military uniform, he appeared in a variety of costumes: white suits, long leather coats with fur collars, sometimes donning a shepherd's astrakhan hat, or a Tyrolean cap complete with a long feather. We saw him on TV, visiting towns and villages, waving his hand slowly to the gathered masses who jumped up and down shouting his name. He reciprocated their love by firing a few shots from a pistol or a hunting rifle. A confident grin was drawn under his thick moustache, but by the last couple of years of his reign his cheeks were already growing sallow and drooping.

Economically, the Leader had to improvise too. Since the early days of his rule, he had established a patronage system that used state resources to maintain his control over – and ensure the loyalty of – different centres of power: his extended family, his clan, the party leadership and the officer corps. In the nineties, with the sanctions and the collapse of the economy, the state was no longer capable of awarding contracts to his clients and distributing wealth among his loyalists. Instead, the Leader created his own parallel economy, in which he was the sole distributor of largesse. By taking the limited resources at his disposal – from the smuggling of crude oil, the black market and whatever he could siphon from the corruption-ridden UN's Oil for Food programme – he fine-tuned and expanded the patronage system. Thus as the sanctions weakened the state and its institutions, the Leader's grip on society was strengthened.

The second component of the new strategy was the tribe. The Leader had always portrayed himself as the quintessential Arab tribesman, comfortable on horseback, most at ease when visiting farmers and nomads. Now the tribes were utilised to extend the power of the regime and to compensate for the weakness of the party and security apparatus. He distributed largesse (mostly in the form of money and cars) to tribal leaders, not only in his own region but also with the aim of extending his patronage networks further across Iraq, in both Sunni and Shia areas. In return the sheikhs delivered the support of their tribesmen and functioned as guarantors of their loyalty. He divided the sheikhs into classes A, B and C, each with its own perks and gifts, with the sheikhs of large tribes at the top, and the so-called sheikhs-of-the-nineties who owed their positions to the Leader and the party at the bottom. He also engineered change within the tribes by expelling those unwilling to cooperate and drawing the more acquiescent ones closer.

'Loyal Tribes', mostly from the central and western regions of Iraq, formed the backbone of the regime's power. Locked in a symbiotic relationship with the authorities, they provided a reliable supply of trusted men to serve in sensitive government jobs and the security apparatus, and in return, the Leader ensured that they occupied a prominent role in the hierarchy of power. Reflecting Saddam's own tribal background, these tribes formed the core of his patronage–clientelism regime, the clan and the tribe benefiting when one of its members rose to prominence in the regime hierarchy, channelling resources to its members. The opposite was also true when a member of a specific tribe betrayed the regime's trust:

the whole tribe felt the pain of collective punishment. This method of collective punishment and patronage ensured the loyalty of such tribes and allowed the Leader to sustain his rule even after military defeats and attempted coups. The names of loyal tribes became synonymous with power – waving such names around public offices guaranteed one a fast track – but they also became a liability and a curse after the fall of the regime.

In the centre of the system of patronage was the Leader, and emanating from him were circles of influence – the extended family, the clan, his home town of Tikrit and its surrounding countryside – and these tight circles provided the regime with its trusted men. The circles then rippled and expanded further and wealth and power depended on how close one got to their sources. They were not exclusive to a sect or ethnic group. Of course, it helped if one was from the Leader's locality and spoke with the right accent, and it was more difficult to access power centres if one belonged to a rebellious locality. But the patronage system was not sectarian, as Sunni, Shia, Kurds and Christians were all willing to compromise, and gained access. This was in part because the Leader did not tolerate any sub-identity, even that of his own sect, that might pose a threat to his total domination.

Other power centres emerged during the sanctions years, like that of the Leader's psychopathic eldest son Uday, and his corrupt and embezzling son-in-law Hussein Kamel, each building their own patron–client network, empowered by the black market economy of sanctions. When these different patronage systems clashed, Infinite Obedience to the Leader was valued above all, and to that end, he wouldn't hesitate to use violence even against his own family. When his son-in-law defected in 1996 after a feud with his son, and fled to Jordan, he was lured back and then shot and killed alongside many of his relatives.

The Leader and his men sapped the life from the country and turned Iraq into a nation of hustlers, selling a carton of smuggled cigarettes for a few dollars on the black market, or just withering in poverty. A fraudulent, fabricated narrative of history served as the backdrop for his brutality, which fossilised social, artistic and economic development and caused a developing emerging society to regress.

4

Baghdad and the Red Room

IN THOSE YEARS I WAS living in a small room, referred to as the Red Room, barely large enough to hold a single bed, a writing table and a trunk. A nook at one end housed the sink, the stove and the toilet. For decoration, I had painted one wall a bright orange-red, which amplified and radiated the hot Baghdad sunlight. The old air conditioner had died, and I had no money to fix it. In the summer of 2002, the room was stifling hot, and I felt the walls were closing in on me. I hadn't paid the rent for six months. As an architect working in private practice, I was paid $50 every few months. In the Years of Sanctions, I was doing ugly work for ugly people who had the money to afford their ugly houses. I wanted to leave the country, to travel and walk through the streets of different cities, but I was a military deserter, and without documentation I could not get a passport.

I wasn't tortured by the Mukhabarat, the regime intelligence service, nor did any of my family vanish into a mass grave, but like the rest of the nation, I was trapped with no hope and no prospects. What if, we wondered, the Leader were to become mortally ill one day? How would our lives change after his death? Would we be ruled by one of his sons? Would that be better than this? Worse? I felt that my life was seeping slowly away in that hot and oppressive place I called home. My only refuges were books and long walks exploring the city that I was confined in.

———

For centuries Baghdad consisted of a string of the old mahalas (traditional neighbourhoods) that sat on either bank of the Tigris. In the early twentieth century the city began to grow – a process that accelerated as oil money poured in. Like a lump of dough, kneaded and pulled in different directions, it absorbed surrounding farms, orchards and neighbouring villages, turning them into charmless suburbs, eventually reaching its current shape: a wide and flat octagonal disc of mud and concrete, divided roughly in the middle by the curling and looping of the mighty Tigris.

Apart from an occasional trip to Basra, Mosul or Kirkuk, I lived in Baghdad for nearly thirty years without ever leaving it; walking for hours daily on its broken irregular pavements with its scorching sun assaulting my head or sitting in its cramped buses and shared taxis that reeked of petrol, tobacco and sweat.

There always seemed to be two cities, two Baghdads: an imaginary city, cursed by its own name and historical myths of opulent palaces, ruby-studded minarets, and the decadence of boozing and whoring sultans; and the real city, which was provincial and charmless, a city so level that it had no horizon beyond the end of the street, with no parks, and no skyline or vista.

Most of the troubles of our modern history seem to stem from the discrepancy between the two. Coup after coup, our Leader stood on a pedestal and aspired to greatness and claimed he would restore this wretched city to its former glory, as he killed and imprisoned droves of people in the process of trying to reconcile the mythical city with the real one.

For decades and centuries Baghdad, like a patient mother, abused by her own sons and neighbours, witnessed wars, strife, floods and pandemics, each leaving its mark on her haggard face.

My Baghdad, from childhood until the war of 2003, was divided between four districts located along the four cardinal points. In the south, I and most of my relatives and friends lived in Karrada, a semi-peninsula formed by the Tigris as it swerves in a great loop, veering nearly ten kilometres west before it bends and turns right again. Up until the fifties, Karrada, a mixed neighbourhood of various sects and religions, used to house the orchards and vegetable gardens serving Baghdad, and the tall eucalyptus trees of its narrow twisting market street almost preserved that green feel of an orchard.

My high school was in the north, in the district of Adhamiya, on the eastern banks of the Tigris. A former cemetery of the Abbasid nobility, for many centuries it was a separate district outside the borders of Baghdad, until the growth of the city and construction absorbed it into the larger metropolis. On the north-west tip of Adhamiya was the shrine of Abu Hanifa, a great Muslim scholar of the seventh century; on the opposite bank of the Tigris was the shrine of the Shia imam Musa al-Kadhem, the two neighbourhoods linked by the bridge of the two imams. During the celebrations of the Prophet's birthday, tens of thousands of people visited Adhamiya and the streets would turn into a festival of light bulbs, coloured ribbons and Sufi music.

The residents of Adhamiya, with its tight-knit alleyways and traditional houses, had maintained a strong sense of community; many had lived in the area for generations and acquired a reputation as tough and hot-blooded. In the fifties and sixties, the area was a hotbed of Arab nationalism, and its youth fought pitched street battles with Communist sympathisers. My grandmother's house was in the east, in a working-class neighbourhood on the southern edge of the great slums of what was known as Thawra and later became Sadr City. I would accompany her to the vegetable market that, with its muddy lanes and heaps of fruits and vegetables, resembled a small village in the heart of the city.

When we were allowed to explore the city on our own, we went

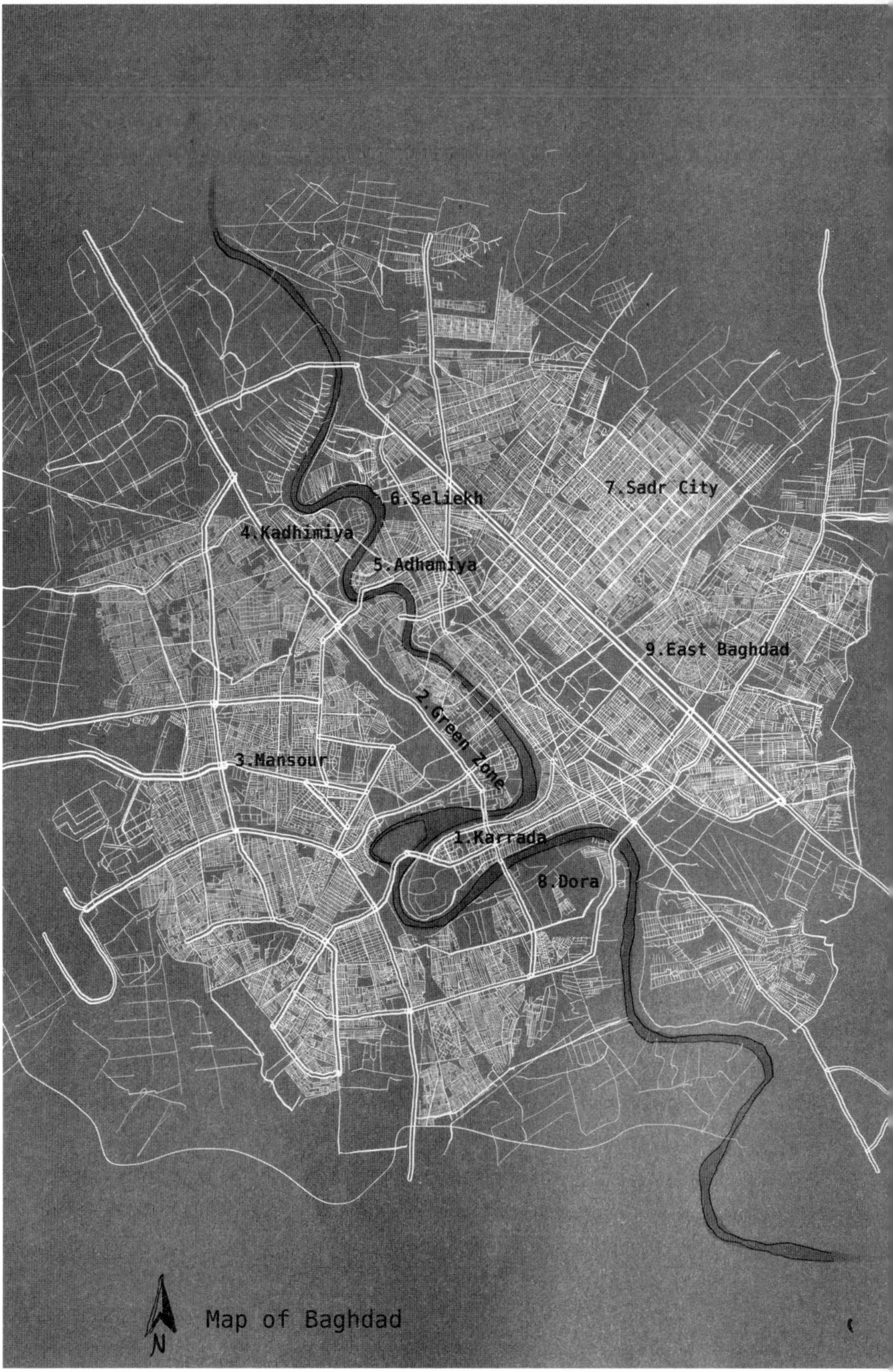

4.Kadhimiya

6.Seliekh

7.Sadr City

5.Adhamiya

9.East Baghdad

2.Green Zone

3.Mansour

1.Karrada

8.Dora

N

Map of Baghdad

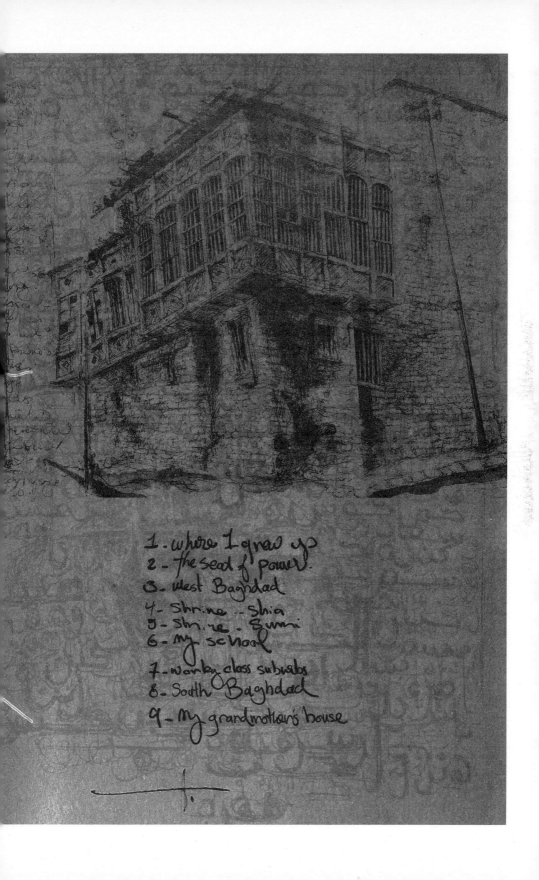

1. where I grew up
2. the seat of power.
3. west Baghdad
4. Shrine – Shia
5. Shrine – Sunni
6. my school
7. working class suburbs
8. South Baghdad
9. my grandmother's house

to the west of Baghdad. My friends and I headed to the upper-class neighbourhoods of Mansour, where there were many fashionable shops and restaurants, and where on Thursdays the streets would be packed with young men and women congregating at ice-cream parlours or fast-food joints.

Further to the west, in the newly built suburbs, distributed among professionals and bureaucrats, lived some of my university friends. Beyond these suburbs lay wastelands and the desert and then the towns of Fallujah and Ramadi.

When I was studying architecture, I tried to explore the older quarters of the city, the nucleus of 'historic Baghdad'. These mahalas were in an advanced state of decay even then, most of them buried under heaps of rubbish and ugly modern concrete buildings moving down a path of continued dilapidation. Unlike the new Baghdad neighbourhoods where I lived and worked, these mahalas – with their narrow alleyways lined with wooden window boxes, casting dark shadows on the people walking beneath, the rickety wooden benches of street cafes, the mosques and the shrines, the smattering of ancient monuments, and a chunk of wall dating back to Abbasid Baghdad – all gave that part of Baghdad a distinctive character shared with other ancient Muslim cities. These mahalas also witnessed the first sectarian riots in the city as far back as the tenth century.

By the time the summer of 2002 was nearing its end, the drip of 'regime change' and 'axis of evil' news that came through my old radio was turning into a constant stream of UN meetings, threatening speeches, along with tens of thousands of soldiers, tanks and armoured vehicles pitching their tents in the tiny state of Kuwait, south of Basra. We held our own meetings in the Red Room with the soon-to-become-famous Salam Pax, and another architect friend, and we had endless discussions over glasses of cheap and poisonous Bulgarian vodka and Iraqi beer. We debated the same thing over and over: is it really going to happen? Is it going to be like the last war? Air raids, bombings, collapsing infrastructure? The Americans were amassing a huge army across the border, but could they invade? How would Saddam and his regime respond? For sure they will burn the country, street fighting will ensue, and the war will last for months, but the Americans said they don't want to fight in summer? Most important was the question, how do you *feel* about the invasion of your country? A Faustian deal? Accept a foreign invasion to get rid of a dictator? Did I want to see the end of the reign of the Leader Necessity? Yes. Did I want the war? No. Was I naive and also opportunistic? Yes. Do I believe now that invading and bombing a nation can bring it democracy and human rights? No.

But that whole debate was flawed from the start: why were the only options for us as a nation and a people the choice between a foreign invasion and a noxious regime led by a brutal dictator? Not that anyone cared what we thought. We were all merely potential collateral damage in a war between the dictator and American neocons adamant that the world should be shaped in their image.

The fear that captured us wasn't the fear of war, though that brought its own anxieties, but the fear of what might come after the Leader Necessity. No one apart from the Leader himself had any delusions about the outcome if there was a war, but no one could even imagine what would follow.

Something unheard of took place in the last few weeks in the life of the Leader's regime. A group of women draped in their black abayas stood in front of the Ministry of Information where all the foreign media was based, demanding to know the whereabouts of their sons and husbands. Earlier that month the Leader had issued an amnesty releasing all prisoners, criminal and political. People thronged to the notorious Abu Ghraib and other prisons to receive their relatives, but many, who had lived for years, sometimes decades, with the understanding that their loved ones had been incarcerated, suddenly realised that they had long ago been executed or disappeared. In terms of numbers, the demonstration was insignificant but for me the mere fact that one could now stand opposing the regime in the light of day and not disappear instantly was far more telling of the change to come than all the armies that had gathered at our borders.

5

Hawassim, the Decisive Battle

IN EARLY MARCH, A COUPLE of weeks before the start of the war, I was in a taxi heading home, when the driver waved his hand at the street and said: 'Look around you, there are streets, people, state institutions . . . I can't imagine how they [the Americans] could undo all of these things and come invade.' Maybe he is right, I thought.

16 March 2003

I am running about like mad stockpiling for the war. The shops are emptying quickly and everyone is stockpiling food. In the streets, members of the Baath Party and the security forces are building sandbag barricades and more and more TV dishes and antennas are springing up on the roofs of the Sheraton and Meridian hotels.

But in the side street Chai-Khana, where I sit under the shade of the huge eucalyptus tree absorbed in a book, the war seems far away, and I can forget what is going on around.

17 March 2003

I ask the people around me, what do they think of an American invasion? And apart from the well-to-do no one is really looking forward to a bombed democracy.

PS What is democracy?

Guards áre building sand barricades around the *Thawra* news-paper at the end of my street.

18 March 2003

A woman and her daughter enter the shop next to my place; they have a look of horror on their faces – all the shelves are empty by now. Do you have salt? asks the woman. No, answers the shopkeeper. Eggs? No. The girl is running around trying to find something useful. The man starts reproaching the woman for not coming earlier. But I just got the money today, we borrowed some from a neighbour, she says. The girl finds a couple of boxes of washing powder. Don't know what she's going to do with them.

We Iraqis are experts in stockpiling. I have bought: 20 cans of tuna, rice, potatoes, 5 crates of water, olive oil and candles and two jerrycans of kerosene.

9 p.m. Not anxious any more: I am afraid, I am scared, I am counting the hours now.

20 March 2003

3.50 a.m. Waiting, every minute I am more anxious, how will it come?

5.30 It came as several explosions, not as I imagined, pretty pathetic. NOT shocked or awed.

I can see from my window a police car racing through the street.

———

After Bush issued an ultimatum, on 17 March, for the Leader and his two sons to leave the country, I thought it was safer to sleep away from the window, and I made my bed on the kilims on the floor. I woke up soon after midnight to the sound of explosions. A long silence followed, and I thought, how disappointing. The explosions were loud, but they lacked that persistent relentlessness, the hammer-like ferocity of the aerial bombardment of the Mother of All Battles in 1991. Around dawn, there were a few more explosions and the 'Hawassim', or the Decisive and Definite Battle, my third and our Leader's last war, had begun in earnest.

The power was cut on the second day, and my room began to smell of a mixture of canned tuna, boiled rice and kerosene fumes from the lantern. A heavy sandstorm that wrapped Baghdad in a red blanket blew through the window and covered the bed, table and food in a film of fine dust. I followed the progress of the war using an old, half-broken radio that I handled delicately, caressing it like a cherished museum piece. Still, the World Service news bulletins were often interrupted by the screeching whistle of static. The reports increasingly bore the tone of 'our boys' out there fighting in this savage desolate desert against the evil army of Saddam. Maybe the reporters didn't know that the bulk of the Iraqi army was made up of conscript soldiers forced to go to the front.

I tried to keep a journal for my two French friends who had left before the war, recording how many explosions I heard every night, what people were saying in the street, and – foolishly – even took pictures using the cameras my friends had lent me. They needed to see and know what was happening, I thought. During the night, when long lines of anti-aircraft fire arced in the skies, I climbed onto the roof of my building and squatted under an old carpet – carpets are known to be excellent protection against hot burning projectiles falling from the sky – and took a few photos of explosions against the backdrop of a black sky.

During the day, I cycled through the deserted streets, and hurriedly snapped pictures of the destroyed and bombed buildings to document the damage of the war before quickly hiding the camera in my rucksack and rushing away, to avoid the prying eyes of party militiamen or security people. There were military trucks in side streets, and soldiers and policemen wearing helmets and carrying machine guns.

One morning, a few days before the fall of Baghdad, I stood in front of a large bronze statue under a dark sky, heavy with the black smoke of fires lit by the government, theoretically so that American pilots flying at 30,000 feet (and armed with the latest technology) wouldn't spot their targets. The statue was of an Iraqi pilot, sculpted according to the aesthetic of Soviet social realism, directing his sombre eyes at the skies, with a helmet under his arm and his right foot on the cockpit of a destroyed Iranian F-4 Phantom jet. Behind the statue stood the ruins of the Air Force headquarters, bombed in an air strike the night before. Only four Roman-style columns still stood, slanting at different angles. I took a couple of pictures, framing the pilot amid the columns and destruction, and cycled away.

On Abu Nuwas Street, I spotted a security officer sitting on a chair under a tree. He was short and scrawny and must have been from the Special Security Branch that was in charge of protecting the presidential palace and party headquarters on the other bank of the river (now known as the Green Zone). Our eyes met. Bad, I thought, for we never meet their eyes; next, they ask for your ID card, and demand to know what you're doing on the streets. All questions to be avoided, especially when one was a military deserter with no valid ID card. That eye contact should have been a sufficient warning to avoid that segment of the street for at least a month. The next day, however, I stupidly cycled past him again. He stood up and swiftly moved from his spot under the tree to stop me. Took my knapsack and started rifling through it. Inside there were two cameras, some rolls of film and, as if all of that wasn't suspicious enough, a David Lodge novel in English. I tried to plead, but even I could sympathise with his claims of capturing a 'spy'; who else would be cycling through a war zone with two cameras and a David Lodge novel? He made me stand against a tree. Was I going to be shot here? I wondered. A white Corolla sedan pulled up, and I was bundled into the back between two plain-clothes officers. We drove in silence to a house that was functioning as temporary headquarters for the local security service. I was made to sit on the floor in a large bare room. Next to me crouched a young man who was whimpering and moaning in anticipation of the pain to come. We were alone, and there were no guards at the door, so I opened my bag and started exposing the film I had shot, one roll after the other before winding them back. When I'd finished, I leaned against the wall and waited for my turn to be interrogated. In the evening, I was led into a small room, where a young officer, burly and bored, sat on a swivel chair, next to boxes piled with manila files. He wore the dark green uniform of the security service. 'I just want you to tell me, when did they [Americans?] parachute you in?' He spoke in a calm and patient tone. In reply, I grinned idiotically. I pleaded that I was just cycling around, but he kept repeating the question and said that I would be detained until all the films had been developed and analysed. I noticed that he was toying with one of the cameras, an automatic Minolta with a collapsible lens that expanded and retracted with a metallic whirl. I politely suggested that he should keep the camera; he looked up at me and asked if I had any money. I had two fifty-dollar bills stashed in my shoes, my whole wealth. I told him that I had only fifty dollars on me, please take it, for the trouble I have caused. He must have known that the end was approaching, and that the Americans were on the outskirts of Baghdad. He took the camera and the money and put me in his car. We drove a short distance before he told me to get out and not to do anything stupid again. I went back to the Red Room and hid there for three days, the last three days of the life of the regime.

6

The Statue

ON 9 APRIL 2003, I stood on the roof of my building, looking at the clear blue sky. The streets were deserted, and the olive-green uniforms and checked keffiyehs of the party militias who usually stood guard around the Baath Party newspaper at the end of my road had disappeared. The city was quiet; the Americans had stopped their bombing early that morning. Only the screech of an A-10 fighter flying low somewhere over the city centre interrupted the stillness and indicated that some units were continuing the fight. In the distance, I saw a helicopter, dark against the pale sky and hanging low over the houses. Unlike the chubby Russian ones that we were used to, which swayed left and right like giant flying rams, this one was nimble, like a mean wasp.

Thirty-five years of the Leader Necessity's rule had dissolved overnight, collapsing in on itself without a trace. Baghdad, that city of fear and oppression, was free for an hour, suspended between the departure of the dictator and the arrival of the occupiers.

I went down to my room to listen to the news bulletin when the neighbour came knocking on my door.

'The Americans are here,' he said with excitement.

'Yes, I heard on the radio that they had reached Hillah [a hundred kilometres south of Baghdad].'

'Hillah?!' the neighbour said with a grin. 'They are here, down in the street.'

I went down, and I saw a few large boat-like armoured amphibi-
ous vehicles spread around the intersection near my flat, as if the
shores of Normandy lay just behind the buildings. They were slung
with the soldiers' large backpacks covered in dust. Descending from
one of these boats were American soldiers, like the ones we'd seen
on TV, in my street, in my own city.

The soldiers spread across the road, knelt on a single knee and
pointed their guns at us, the handful of people who stood watching
them. Behind the soldiers came men dressed in blue vests and carrying big cameras. Their helmets bore the letters 'TV'.

I sat on the kerb looking as the soldiers trained their guns at the
buildings around them. One of the men in blue, tall with a bald head,
and carrying two cameras with large zooms, was moving gingerly
towards us, like a wildlife photographer approaching a herd of wild
animals, not wanting to scare them away and yet not sure if they
might charge him. He squatted a few feet in front of me and trained a
long white lens at me; fuck off, I shooed him away, I won't become an
item of news, another face of a defeated nation. The soldiers climbed
back into their armoured boat trucks and started driving down the
road, past the national theatre and down Sadoon Street. A small
crowd of men and children followed.

The armoured vehicles and the crowd moved slowly, passing in
front of the Vatican embassy, where a papal diplomat, dressed in his
black cassock with a purple sash around his waist, stood observing
the invading armies. He shook his head in disbelief and muttered to
anyone who cared to listen that this was bad, that this was an illegal
occupation. On the other side of the street, a chubby middle-aged
Iraqi man, standing at the entrance of his shop, sputtered insults, but
most of the crowd that followed the Americans was excited. The
old and decaying regime had fallen. The armoured column came to
a stop in front of the Meridian and Sheraton hotels, where most of

the international media had set up base. In front of the hotels stood a large statue of Saddam, his right arm stretched awkwardly into the sky, inviting looks of scorn and spite from the crowd below, like someone still lingering uninvited long after the party was over.

I stood there watching, along with a few other Iraqis and a much larger crowd of foreign journalists, as a handful of enthusiastic men began banging at the plinth base of the statue with hammers and metal rods, succeeding only in cracking the marble cladding. It was taking the men a long time, and the journalists were getting bored, when one of the armoured vehicles, with a large crane on the back, started reversing into the middle of the square. Oh no, don't do it, let the Iraqis at least topple the statue of their dictator. A marine climbed to the top and dropped a thick rope around the neck, and then he pulled out an American flag. No, no, you can't be doing this, I gasped, at least allow the facade of liberation to last for a day. But no, with all the arrogance of every occupying soldier throughout history, he covered the face of the defeated dictator with the flag of his victorious nation; briefly, but long enough to seal the fate of the invasion in the eyes of many. But then, why shouldn't he raise an American flag? Maybe in all the declarations and justifications of the war by leaders and commanders who spoke of liberation and democracy, the act of that marine was the most honest; he understood the war as a conflict between the US and Iraq – he and his countrymen had won. It was his right to plant a flag.

The armoured vehicle pulled, the statue resisted a bit, and then gave way just above the feet. It tumbled into the square with a hollow crash. Like his state, the Leader's statue was only an empty cast with a single metal pillar inside supporting it.

A dozen or so men jumped on the statue, beating it with chains and shoes. That iconic image has played again and again on every report on Iraq ever since, as if those men represented all the nation;

their jubilation was a justification, even if briefly, for the madness that would follow. The head of the statue was dragged through the streets and more men spat on it and cursed it.

I met a friend, also standing in the square. Let's go into the palace, I said; he said it was getting dark. Instead, we walked around the block imagining what would come next: the hopes, the future, and the anxieties.

The UNICEF building, less than fifty metres away from the square where the Americans had established their base, was in the process of being looted. We met a young Iraqi man in the street dressed only in his white underpants.

'Are there any Americans from where you came?' he asked, his voice shaking. 'Oh yes, brother, lots of them,' I answered cheerfully. He turned and started running in the opposite direction, disappearing into the first side street, maybe he was an officer or a soldier.

'This is my money, Saddam stole it from me,' said an old woman, as she dragged a carpet from the Directorate of Dams and Irrigation. The carpet was old and torn and worth nothing, but maybe she felt that this was a piece of the regime, part of Saddam's tyranny and authority, and that claiming it might magically erase her suffering of the last few decades.

———

The next morning I found the garage of my building piled with junk: a desk chair flipped upside down, an old A/C unit, computer cases and a couple of monitors stacked on top of each other, all looted from the Baath Party newspaper offices nearby. A neighbour and her two sons inspected the loot cheerfully. The doorman came into the garage carrying another computer case. For decades, the state had meant oppression and secret police, the Leader and his family living in wealth and the rest of the population struggling. Looting these pitiful items was their attempt to rectify the cruelty of the sanctions, their revenge against the regime.

I decided to walk to the presidential palace. Why? Because I wanted to see where the Leader had lived; maybe the walls of the rooms and corridors where he walked, conferred with his closest aides and ordered the destruction of tens of thousands of his people, might get me closer to him, help me make sense of what he was and why he shaped our lives and our history the way he did. Or maybe it was my own act of desecration of the holy sanctum of power, an act of utter insolence just like that of the people looting. It was still early and I walked the empty streets. Tongues of black smoke poured from the windows of buildings that had been looted the night before. There were American checkpoints, defended by young soldiers and coils of barbed wire; I talked my way through them by claiming that I was a British journalist and that the Iraqi police had confiscated my papers. The combination of the knapsack on my back and my imitation of a World Service accent did the trick and they let me pass. I reached the Jimhouriya Bridge and crossed the Tigris into the presidential palace. To my right, smoke still billowed from buildings hit by rocket blasts.

An armoured vehicle was stationed at the entrance of the presidential palace; next to it was a thick crimson-red puddle of blood. The edges were drying under the sun. I asked the exhausted soldier who sat atop the vehicle behind a machine gun if I could enter the palace, and he waved me along.

I walked through the tall arches of the gate and down the well-paved, clean road, lined with trees and rose bushes. Halfway down I came across a swollen and blackened corpse that lay to the side of the road. I hesitated, I hadn't seen a dead man before, but kept walking.

Next day on another road outside the palace, there were cars frozen in that eternal moment of death in the middle of the road,

riddled with bullets from the marching Americans who shot at them as they tried to flee. Inside the cars, bodies were beginning to decompose. A young woman puckered her face, collecting in a plastic bag the remains of her dead uncle. Black flesh melting into the steering wheel. Was there a putrid smell of death or was that a memory acquired from the scene of a car bomb a year later?

The presidential palace loomed in the distance, a massive stone bulk. A line of US soldiers sat on the ground, resting their backs against its ornamented walls. Giant bronze busts of the Leader adorned the four corners of the palace. His moustached head, wearing a helmet, the shape of the Dome of the Rock in Jerusalem, was peering from above with silent and solemn greatness, ignoring the insolent soldiers who had occupied his palace, continuing to stare at the distant horizon. A young American officer gave me a tour of a massive dining hall, with a beautiful cascading wooden ceiling, now converted into a large dormitory with dozens of metal beds stacked next to each other. I wanted to walk further towards

48

the intelligence headquarters, another symbol of the regime. But the American told me that there was still fighting going on, so I walked back towards the gate, and hitched a ride with James Meek, a British journalist who worked for the *Guardian*. He hired me as his translator.

PART TWO

The Collapse of the State
and the First Civil War

7

Bakunin in Baghdad

BAKUNIN WOULD HAVE REVELLED IN the Baghdad of 2003 where chaos reigned. All was permissible, and everything was possible. Beer and whisky were sold on the pavements or from the boots of parked cars. Mobs of looters ransacked government offices and ministries, apart from the Ministry of Oil, protected by American tanks. They gutted factories, pulled the doors off their hinges and stripped electrical wiring from the walls, and then sold the looted equipment as scrap metal. Weapons and ammunition from looted military camps and depots were traded on the open market. In the months and years to come, these arsenals would sustain civil wars in Iraq and Syria, with some smuggled out to nourish distant wars in Yemen and Somalia. Soviet jet fighters, hidden in the deserts outside military bases to save them from American attacks, lay half buried in the sand like the skeletons of beached whales, stripped of their weapons and metal plates. But there was probably nothing more painful and damaging than the pillaging of the Iraqi Museum. Nearly 15,000 items were looted, most disappearing for ever.

Armed mobs roamed the city looking for plunder, broke into bank vaults and then fought for the spoils in the streets outside. What they couldn't claim, they set on fire, like the National Library, or the TV and radio archives that burned for days. In central Baghdad, I saw the smoke rising from the windows of the Directorate of Nationality: the archives and registries of a century were burning. Yes, destroy everything, I thought to myself with the extreme naivety of the self-righteous, why do we even need the Directorate of Nationality? Didn't Saddam manipulate everything for his own interest? Didn't he deport tens of thousands, and strip millions more of their will to live? Wasn't our whole state a construct of his will? So why not destroy everything, and from the carnage a new country will be born, with no fear or oppression, where everyone will be equal and prosperous?

The Great Leader had dominated our lives and moulded the whole nation in his image for decades, not just the army and police but even schools, farms and factories. So when his statue was toppled and people wanted vengeance for the years of oppression, they not only destroyed the symbols of his power, his palaces, his statues and murals, or satisfied themselves by taking his furniture and sleeping in his opulent bedrooms – they also turned their anger on anything that symbolised the state, because the state was Saddam and Saddam was the state, as he used to say. Even words like citizenship, solidarity,

patriotism were soiled for ever because they were associated with his rule. In that destructive atmosphere many, both foreigners and Iraqis, were willing to tear the very concept of an Iraqi state apart completely.

The poor moved out of their wretched, overcrowded neighbour-hoods and started building on military camps and government lands. These new slums of one-storey concrete shacks with rivulets of oily green sewage and heaps of trash were called Hawassim, after the name of the Leader's last battles – and the same name given to those who subsequently acquired colossal wealth.

———

It was also a time of discovery, of unearthing, literally, a history of horrors committed by the regime and its men. Mass graves were discovered near prisons, or on remote and desolate roadsides, where thousands of men had been buried after the failed 1991 uprising. Bulldozers exhumed what was left of their bodies amid heaps of dry yellowish-grey earth. Women draped in black wailed and scratched their faces in grief over piles of bones and skulls that lay on plastic sheets, as a hot, dry and dusty wind blew. Some could identify their missing one from a picture stashed in a pocket, or an ID card; others hurriedly gathered bones, any bones, to bury and finally have a grave at which to mourn their lost children. In their homes, families hung pictures of relatives who had been executed or long since disappeared by the regime; they were now proud of people who up until a few weeks ago they had striven to hide and disown. In other houses, a rectangle of white appeared on grimy walls where the portrait of the Leader had recently hung.

The history that had been written by the Leader was unravel-ling, and people demanded that a new history be written and the lies be corrected. They wanted compensation and amendments for the oppression, a redress of the wrongs committed against them for decades. And just as these mass graves were exhumed, local conflicts, grievances and struggles were coming to the surface after decades of burial by the monolithic existence of the regime. In late April 2003, I watched thousands of people march to Karbala, their feet kicking up a thick cloud of dust. They were commemorating the Arba'een (marking forty days after the day of Ashura when Imam Hussein had been killed fourteen centuries earlier). It is traditionally a day of sadness and mourning – people weep and beat their chests – but on that occasion, it was also a day of joy, because for the first time in decades Shias were allowed to freely express a religious and cultural identity long suppressed by the Leader. It was an extreme contrast to how the day of Ashura had been observed a few weeks earlier, just before the war, when I had sat in the Khadimiya, the biggest Shia shrine in Baghdad, and watched a few people shuffle quickly in and out.

In May 2003, I met an old man in a poor and crowded suburb of eastern Baghdad. He sat on an empty tin box, with a broad smile drawn across his face. He said the Americans who had brought all these tanks and planes would fix everything in a matter of weeks. They would bring electricity and turn his wretched neighbourhood into heaven. He spoke as if he could see his tiny alleyway already transformed, the sewage flowing next to his feet disappearing, the poverty dissipating, the houses of concrete cinder blocks cleaned up and freshly painted. But weeks and months passed, and the situation was only getting worse. The collective intoxication of Iraqis at the end of the regime wore off quickly, and the people of Baghdad moved from euphoria to frustration and then fury. When they wanted to go to hospitals they found them looted, schools had either been burned down or were occupied by squatters. There was no one in control and all public services had collapsed. Kilometre-long queues had formed outside petrol stations because oil wells and refineries had been damaged in the looting. Electricity failed because there was no fuel for the power plants and because transmission towers and high-voltage cables had been stripped and sold as scrap copper. With no electricity, water pumps and purification plants stopped running, and raw sewage was piped into the rivers. Doctors and nurses carried guns and stood guarding the few hospitals and clinics that had not already been ransacked.

American soldiers, stupefied by the Baghdad heat, stood clueless amid that chaos, and Iraqis – accustomed to decades of efficient centralised bureaucracy – were baffled at the rash and arbitrary way the Americans were running the country. Everything was improvised on the spur of the moment. Sometimes the soldiers tried to stop the looting, but mostly they just stood by; sometimes they tried to control the massive traffic gridlocks, while at others they drove their tanks into the middle of roads causing even bigger snarl-ups. Of course, the Iraqis could not believe that their new colonial masters had no clue, had done no planning and made no preparations for what was going to happen after they invaded the country. Or that the whole adventure was based solely on their might and their powerful weapons and the messianic half-beliefs of Bush and co. When the myth of an American-generated prosperity clashed with the realities of occupation, chaos and destruction followed. Resentment and anger swept the country and all the suppressed rage of the previous decades exploded.

The day after the statue fell, I abandoned the Red Room and my life as an architect. I worked first as a translator and fixer, and was then promoted to news assistant – a glorified translator and fixer – leading a peripatetic lifestyle. For years I moved from one hotel room to another, travelling the width and length of Iraq. In reality, I – the Iraqi who had never left Iraq – was discovering my country for the first time, just as the foreign journalists were. My only advantage was that I spoke the language.

With my daily fees, an enormous fortune compared to the meagre salary I was paid as an architect, I bought a camera and I started taking pictures of the chaos unfolding around me. One picture got published, then another, and by 2004 I was hired as a stringer for a wire agency.

Around that time I published my first article in the *Guardian*. I wrote how Saddam and I spent our first night in an American prison cell. The Leader had been taken earlier that day, and the American journalists I was translating for thought it unwise to show up in the Leader's home town the day he had been captured by their government, so I volunteered to go and do some vox pop. On my way back that night we were stopped at a checkpoint north of Baghdad, and the American officer thought the driver and I looked suspicious – well, I did have a beard. An hour later we were blindfolded and taken to an American military base and locked in a prison cell. We slept on the cold concrete floor, and next day when we were led out I laughed at the irony of it all: we were in a former Iraqi military base, which the Americans were using, and I, who proudly spent years dodging my Iraqi military service and avoiding capture, was finally locked in an Iraqi military prison by my own supposed 'liberators'.

8

The Viceroy

WE WERE TOLD, MUCH LATER, that the adventure of the Iraq War was based on the myopic vision of a band of American neoconservatives, who – in their desire to project American power in a unipolar world – argued that regime change here would bring democracy not only to Iraq but the whole Middle East, pivoting it closer to the US – and that the oil wealth of Iraq would pay for its reconstruction. Some still use the same argument to preach war with Iran.

The origins of the plans for a regime change in Iraq dated to the nineties, when under the constant lobbying of Iraqi exiles the neocons passed the Iraq Liberation Act. However, Saddam's fate was sealed after 9/11, regardless of any weapons of mass destruction he may or may not have possessed.

The UN Security Council bestowed posthumous legitimacy on the illegal war by granting the Americans 'occupying power status' with all the happy connotations the word 'occupation' has in the Middle East. After some weeks of faffing about, a new American administration was established, led by Paul Bremer, a close ally of the neocons in Washington. He became the viceroy and the ruler of the country and was given sweeping legislative and executive powers reminiscent of a British proconsul of the Indian Raj. The new occupation authority – called the Coalition Provisional Authority, the CPA – was staffed by young, naive zealots who held unchallenged powers to reshape Iraq the way their masters wanted. They represented the worst combination of colonial hubris, toxic racist arrogance and criminal incompetence. Many would later write books about their heroic struggle in the lands of the Arabs. Some of these CPA officials were put in charge of ministries, upending existing administrative systems. Others ran whole cities or provinces.

In Baghdad, the presidential palace, former government buildings and neighbouring streets became the Green Zone, the centre of the delusional administration. Access to the Americans in these chaotic days when blocks of dollars were handed out without oversight generated another wave of 'Hawassim' and established the model of corruption that the new state would be based on. Contracts were inflated for projects that were never built, and in some cases, there was graft within the CPA itself. Fortunes were made, corruption institutionalised. Long queues formed outside the gates of the Green Zone; they included the sincere who wished for American help in forming an NGO, the maverick tribal sheikhs who wanted recognition and financial subsidies, and opportunists looking for any niches they might exploit.

Many Western writers and journalists have argued since then that Bremer's first two fatal decisions – the disbanding of the Iraqi army and all security apparatuses, and the banning of members of the Baath Party from public jobs, both of which left hundreds of thousands of men without pension or salary – helped instigate the insurgency that would consume the country. These Western pontificates lamented the stupidity of Bush and the neocons. If only, they said, they had done their homework and planned for the post-invasion Iraq, things could have been so different. But to be fair to Bush and the neocons, the occupation was bound to collapse and fail – both logic and history tell us that – because a nation can't be bombed, humiliated and sanctioned, then bombed again, and then told to become a democracy. No amount of planning could have turned an illegal occupation into a liberation.

The illegal war that was based on a lie not only destroyed Iraq, causing the deaths of nearly a quarter of a million Iraqis and a few thousand Americans and unleashing a sectarian war that would engulf the region, but it permanently crippled democracy in the Middle East. So, democracy was another victim of the criminally incompetent administration. 'Do you want democracy? Didn't you see what democracy did to Iraq?' became the repeated refrain of dictators and potentates throughout the region.

9

Of Exiles and Militias

FOLLOWING THE AMERICAN ARMY, CAME the exiles: politicians, religious leaders and rogue businessmen. Most of them had spent decades in the claustrophobic and paranoid circles of émigré communities in Beirut, London and Tehran, where they lived in fear of the long arm of the regime's lethal security apparatus, and nurtured feelings of bitterness and anger at the Iraqis who they saw as having compromised by living under the regime.

The people of the inside – isolated from the outside world and accustomed to the regime's propaganda – saw the exiles as foreigners in their own country, if not outright traitors who had sided with the Iranian regime during the eighties war, and who had worked closely with the CIA after the first Gulf War in 1991. The locals pointed out that the exiles had lived in the comfort of Western countries, while it was the people who remained in Iraq who suffered under the sanctions, and the brutality of the regime. The fact that the exiles formed a pathetic opposition to Saddam, and were notorious for their petty feuds and rivalries, did not help their credibility. Sometimes, they had cooperated with the regime to settle the infighting among themselves.

Upon their return to Iraq, the exiles wanted to avenge comrades and relatives killed and imprisoned by the regime. With the anger of the self-righteous, they demanded the restitution of their rights, and the wholesale punishment of those they accused of having served the regime. Just like the mobs that looted and set government buildings on fire because they associated the state with Saddam, the exiles – and the Americans – failed to see how dangerous and devastating it was to go about dismantling the state in an attempt to dismantle the legacy of the Leader Necessity.

A large majority of the exiles belonged to Islamist Shia parties, ones which promoted sectarian, communal politics. Although numerically small and with only marginal influence in wider society, the exiles had close working relationships with the new rulers of Iraq, the Americans, compared to the people of the inside who were just discovering the meaning of free press, congregation and politics. Many, like Ahmad al-Chalabi, had worked with the neocons since the nineties and had played an influential rule in shaping public opinion to support the war, even manufacturing fake evidence of weapons of mass destruction.

The sectarian vision of the exiles prevailed when, after weeks of haggling with Viceroy Bremer, they settled on the charade called the Iraqi Governing Council, made up of twenty-five members chosen to represent all the components of the Iraqi society on the basis of sectarian and ethnic criteria.

One hot July morning, in the auditorium of the convention centre, we waited like the audience of a school play to meet the new leaders of Iraq. Twenty-five men and women, all carrying self-congratulatory smiles, emerged and took their seats in a wide semicircle. The members had failed to choose a president for the council; instead, they settled on an absurd presidential council of nine, who in the months to come would play a silly game in which each would pretend to be the president of Iraq for one month.

The Governing Council, of course, could not govern: the real authority lay in the hands of the viceroy and his teams of minions and the American army. It was an advisory body with no power, a joke, riddled with petty feuds among its members who squabbled over stolen state properties.

More dangerously, however, the Governing Council solidified the sectarian rhetoric into a form of government. The Iraqis were shown that their future political system would be based on 'Muhassasa', the allocation of state resources and division of the spoils of power along sectarian and ethnic lines. The Muhassasa would enable a coalition of corrupt, imbecilic, religious, warlords to rule the country for the next twenty years and create one of the most corrupt nations on earth.

———

The void created by the war and the subsequent destruction of the regime was filled by the exiles, especially the Shia religious parties, who set about building a new national myth founded on sectarian identity politics, replacing the artificial nationalistic constructs of the Leader Necessity.

Essential to the new narrative was the 'madhloumiya', the injustice and oppression, real or imaginary, inflicted on the Shia community since the time of Ali and his son Hussein, 1,400 years earlier. This new narrative went like this: because the Leader of Necessity was a Sunni, all Sunnis were, by association, if not culprits in the regime's crimes, at least beneficiaries of its rule. The rest were victims. This interpretation required wilful obliviousness to the fact that the regime was based on family and clan networks and not on sectarianism. Not all Sunnis were supporters of the regime; many of them had opposed it and plotted against it, just as many Shia and Kurds had collaborated with it.

That narrative set one segment of society against the other. If one was 'madhloum', oppressed, then the other was by definition a 'dhalem', or an oppressor. The victims demanded reparations from the oppressors in a political system misconceived as a zero-sum game, turning issues like transitional justice, accountability and history into divisive, future conflicts.

'The [exiled] parties constructed the society as a case of a victor and vanquished,' I was told in Basra by a union leader and civil rights campaigner who had spent years in Saddam's prisons. 'The victors were now the Shia, whose religious practices were banned under Saddam, and the vanquished were the Sunnis who were all labelled as Baathists although many if not most of the Baathists in Basra, for example, were themselves Shia.'

What was posited as Shia empowerment meant the downfall of not only the people seen as loyalists to the former regime, but also the targeting of their tribes and villages. A family name that had once opened doors became a curse on a whole community.

Unlike the Shia and the Kurds who had developed a clear religious and ethnic identity over centuries of opposition to the centre, the Sunni Arabs of Iraq had never had a communal identity as Sunnis. They were always associated with the state, as the followers of the dominant and official state religion. Their identity was regional, of towns and cities and tribes. In the new Iraq, the farmers of Diala, the desert tribesmen of Ramadi and the wealthy mercantile classes of Mosul were all lumped together, labelled 'Sunnis', squeezed into a corner and told to come up with a collective political identity.

A belligerent 'Sunni' identity emerged, based on opposition and resistance to the new order. The Sunni parties that were established could not formulate any ideology beyond a rejection of the current political process and the post-US invasion changes. To oppose the sectarian voice of Shias, the Sunnis created their own. On the one hand, they spoke of bringing back an Iraq of the strong state; on the other, they played the same sectarian politics that they claimed to oppose. Tragically, their reaction to the Shia communal politics only bred further sectarianism. At the same time, the Sunnis who did join the political process were seen as collaborators for working with the occupation and many were killed by Sunni insurgents.

———

Abu Hashem was one of those returning exiles. A few days after the British took over Basra, he and other exiled militia commanders and intelligence officers left their base in south-western Iran and headed to the Iraqi border in a column of military jeeps. Ostensibly their task was to prepare the ground and organise the logistics needed for members of the Shia exiled armed force to move back into Iraq. Their main objective, however, was to test the British response to their presence.

'Until the last minutes before crossing the border into Iraq, we didn't know what would happen. Will the British open fire on us? Will we respond and shoot back at them?'

It was a time of confusion: the Americans and the British, who were their enemies, had toppled the regime of Saddam that Abu Hashem and his comrades had opposed and fought against for decades.

'In exile in Iran, we were always told that our struggle was against the Great Satan [the US] and their British allies, so are we going to fight them now that they are in Iraq?' Abu Hashem told me when we met a decade later in Basra. 'Some in the republic [Iran] thought that a weak Saddam was less dangerous than an American army stationed across the border. The more ideological members of the regime thought that a fatwa declaring jihad should be issued and that we should start fighting the Americans. In the end, the more pragmatic voices in the intelligence community prevailed, and they adopted a "wait and see" approach.'

A convoy of jeeps crossed the border and drove to Basra

unopposed, and Abu Hashem and the other exiled leaders realised that not only were the British not going to shoot at them, but that they were going to be their new allies, depending on them to run the city and to provide the charade of normality in progress.

Born in 1940 in the northern suburbs of Basra, Abu Hashem grew up in abject poverty in a community of peasants. They lived in mud huts with no running water, and sewage flowing through open canals. There were no schools and no clinics, and their lives, in the last decade of the monarchy, were dominated by the feudal tribal sheikhs, who treated them like serfs, and the traditional Shia clergy which demanded the 'khums', one-fifth of their income as a religious tax. The revolution of 1958 that toppled the monarchy and brought a benevolent dictator with leftist leanings changed their lives. Feudal lands were confiscated and distributed to the peasants, a school and a clinic opened in the nearby town, and the power of the clergy was tempered by a string of new progressive laws. Like many of the poor Shia youths, Abu Hashem drifted towards the revolutionary ideologies of the Iraqi Communist Party which had a large following in towns and villages in southern Iraq in the fifties and sixties. He remembered marching in the streets, shouting revolutionary slogans and eagerly reading the *Party* newspaper. By the mid seventies new revolutionary ideas were spreading in the regions, articulated by a young generation of Shia clerics who rejected the old traditional 'quietist' school and called for the establishment of a just Islamist rule. The Iranian revolution and the fiery speeches of Imam Khomeini helped convert many from Communist and leftist parties into radical Islam. First it was Abu Hashem's brother who fled to Iran to join an armed group composed of Iraqis exiled by the regime and led by Iranian revolutionary guards fighting against the Iraqi army in the eighties war. Abu Hashem joined his brother after the failed uprising of 1991. For a decade he slipped back and forth across the border leading a small unit that attacked and killed Iraqi soldiers and security forces, until he stepped on a land mine and lost his right leg. Unable to work in the field, he became an instructor with the Iranian intelligence service, the Itila'at.

Then in 2003, and after years of fighting and secretive struggle against the regime, Abu Hashem finally settled in his home town of Basra and opened a bookshop. He watched as the exiled religious parties dominated the new security services and police that were formed by the occupying powers. He watched as in the streets a plethora of Shia militias were multiplying, with names like 'Revenge of Allah', 'Battalions of the Master of Martyrs', some splitting from the larger parties and militias, some formed by radical clerics, and all supported by the Iranians. They took over public buildings, and spread their men through the streets. These militias, along with tribes and criminal cartels, came to dominate every aspect of life in the city, from smuggling crude oil to controlling the port. The story was repeated all over Iraq: as the British and the Americans deluded themselves about the progress they were making in bringing democracy to Iraq, the militias and the religious parties became dispensers of justice and patronage, the gate through which any major transaction was completed. You needed a militia on your side both to get your brother into the police force and to help you start a smuggling business.

Many of the commanders of these militias were men like Abu Hashem, former exiles returning from Iran.

'In Iran, I was one of those armchair experts whose whole theory proved to be wrong. I used to say that the people of Iraq would despise the exiles like us, and throw all of us in the dustbin because they'd see us as puppets in the hands of the Islamic Republic. Just as Saddam had his clients among the Iranian opposition, so we were working for the Iranians,' Abu Hashem told me. 'I was proved wrong when I found out that even the most insignificant of those exiles, those who had nothing to do in Iran but loiter, was now considered an eminence and had found bases, gathered men and started getting positions in the government. They saw a void and they filled it.'

I met many of those returning exiles; they were all humble, poor, estranged from their own society. Many spoke with a distinctive Persian accent, which for us people of the inside – fed for decades on the regime's anti-Iranian, anti-Persian propaganda – was a shock. Their first acts were to lay their hands on public properties, turning them into their 'party' headquarters, and using the money the Americans were dishing out to build their power centres. Suddenly public buildings, schools, Baath Party headquarters, walls and electricity poles were all adorned with Islamic party names and pictures of different ayatollahs.

10

The Rebellion

IRAQ, DESTROYED AND OCCUPIED, HUNG between a state
and no state. The initial guarded optimism of the Iraqis – who were
promised liberation, prosperity and freedom with the removal of
Saddam – shattered with the first car bomb. It became evident that
the long-awaited peace was not coming – and that the occupation
had unleashed something much worse.

Iraqis said, how can the Americans fail? Look at their tanks and weapons, America is the greatest nation. No, Americans never fail. It must all be a plot, a conspiracy, they assured each other. Just as they stood in disbelief in front of the burned-out National Library and said, no, we Iraqis can't have done that, it must be the Kuwaitis acting in revenge for what we did in 1991, so they stood in front of the carcasses of car bombs and swore by the Almighty that they had seen American helicopters firing rockets. They were in denial that the country they knew was gone.

When the violence began, it was sporadic and random. A hand grenade tossed at a passing American Humvee, a home-made land mine on an arterial route, or an RPG targeting a supply convoy. The spokespeople in the Green Zone dismissed these incidents as 'desperate acts of former regime elements' (the FRE in the acronymic lingua of the occupation authority) – even when Humvees were set alight in downtown Baghdad, and IEDs ripped through tanks and armoured vehicles, even as bands of young men fired mortars at American positions in eastern Baghdad.

The Americans responded violently to these attacks, often shooting at nearby civilians indiscriminately, setting up checkpoints and raiding towns and villages searching for weapons and insurgents, alienating more people and adding to the numbers of men taking up arms against them. The 'liberation' was looking like a real occupation.

The violence that targeted the Iraqis, however, was planned and organised. In Baghdad, the Badr brigade, one of the Shia militias formed in Iran, instigated a campaign of assassinations a few weeks after the occupation, targeting the former military pilots who had fought against their Iranian masters in the eighties war, as well as former military scientists and Baath Party officials. As a result, men in several middle-class neighbourhoods in west Baghdad, where many of the former army officers lived, armed themselves with machine guns and stood guard at the entrance of their streets to protect their areas.

Another layer of violence was the competition between different armed Shia factions over power and resources, like the fighting between militiamen following Muqtada al-Sadr and those from the Badr brigade – the biggest of the exiled Shia militias – over the control of the shrines in the holy city of Karbala and their lucrative income. It was the first time I reported on street fighting. I saw a group of impoverished young men in a deserted market, one of them guiding a deaf and mute man carrying an RPG launcher on his shoulder. Bending down and holding the deaf man by the waist, he pushed him into the middle of the street and pointed in the direction of the firing. *Whooosh* went the rocket, and the deaf man turned with a big grin on his face, oblivious to the shooting around him.

My work as a translator and photographer began to change in nature. What started as interviewing Iraqis trying to come to terms with the change in their society gradually turned into war reporting and photography, dodging bullets, hiding behind street corners and taking pictures of young men firing at American tanks and Humvees, along with the occasional interview of a turbaned cleric issuing threats and ultimatums.

By early summer 2003, violence was taking a pattern, and a rebellion by both Sunnis and Shia fighters against the occupying forces had begun. Both attacked the Americans and the newly established Iraqi security forces, as well as civilians working with the new government.

In villages, towns and the suburbs of Baghdad, cells were formed to resist the Americans. Some fought out of nationalism, others a sense of injustice, still more for tribe or religion. Hundreds of cells with hundreds of motives. At first, the men coalesced around the traditional trusted networks of tribe, family and neighbourhood. (For when one evolves into a resistance fighter who does one trust?

Who does one buy weapons from? And who does one send as a message courier? The answer is the same: cousins and family and neighbours that form a support network.)

Over time, the cells merged and became 'armies', 'battalions' and 'organisations' with a clandestine secretive structure under a quasi-military command. Their ideology was simple, jingoistic, nurtured in the isolationism of the tribe, mixed with Iraqi military chauvinism and the fluff of religious edicts about the righteous battle against invaders. The cells collectively called themselves the Resistance and probably for a fraction of a second in the first year of the occupation, they *were* resistance with all the connotations of that word, before they descended into banditry and sectarian mass killings. These bands of fighters could not defeat the Americans militarily; however, they ensured the failure of the American adventure in Iraq. Any community or institution that tried to defy them was attacked through intimidations, assassinations or mass killings. Religiosity, already prevalent in the society since the Faith Campaign in the nineties, acquired a sectarian anti-Shia tone, and began to augment the tribe, family and neighbourhood as the rallying cry for the 'Resistance'. It helped expand the networks of trusted fighters, organising around mosques and galvanising the grief, energy and anger of young men, and channelling it into the war.

———

Ahmad joined the Resistance in its early days. He was living with his grandmother in the neighbourhood of Seliekh in Baghdad, not far from my high school, when the Americans invaded. Stocky with wavy hair, a round kind face and the body of a wrestler, he had left his family home in Diala province and enrolled in high school in Baghdad, but rather than studying he was spending long hours in

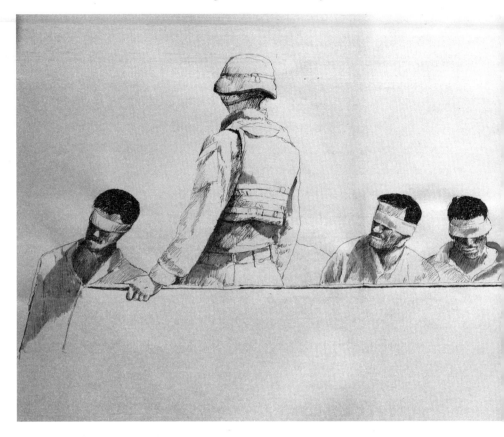

the local gym lifting weights. There he had heard of a young imam
in the local mosque, who was taking advantage of the new religious
freedoms brought with the occupation and preaching a hard form of
defiant militant Islam, something effectively quashed by the previous
regime. Ahmad also heard that the imam was organising 'a protection force' for the neighbourhood, so he gathered a few of his gym
friends and went to meet the charismatic imam. None of them was
religious, but they were fired up by the imam's long sermons about
their duty to defend their country against a foreign occupier and the
threats to their community from the 'Iranians' – a reference to the
new Shia political parties.

Ahmad and some of his friends joined the Resistance and were given the task of planting small home-made land mines in the street. He didn't tell his family back in the village in Diala about any of this, but the new life as a mujahid was very exciting. He would stay awake all night and sleep during the day; he stopped going to his high school, which he had never really liked. They collected money to buy weapons, which were available cheaply in the markets after the looting of army depots.

22

Karbala

THE TENTH DAY OF THE Islamic month of Muharram marks
the last day of the battle of Karbala, and the martyrdom of Imam
Hussein, the grandson of the Prophet Muhammad. It is a grave and
momentous event for the Shia, commemorated with processions of
chants, flagellations and chest-beating. These religious commemora-
tions had been banned since the late seventies by the former regime
for fear that they would be used to vent political grievances.

Tuesday 2 March 2004 saw the first large-scale Ashura commemoration in Iraq in decades. Tens of thousands travelled to Karbala, to
the golden-domed shrine of Imam Hussein. Bands of men dressed
in black marched to the shrine, prostrating themselves in its courtyard. They wailed, chanted lamentations and ceremonially struck
their chests. Drums beat to the rhythm of men shouting 'Haydar . . .
Haydar', echoing the thump . . . thump . . . of their palms beating
their naked chests. Others were swaying left and right and flagellat-
ing their backs with chains. The crowds reached an ecstatic climax
of fervour with the devotees hitting their heads with swords and long
knives, as blood gushed down their faces. I worked until dawn taking
pictures and then collapsed on the floor of the hotel room I shared
with a few other journalists. I fell asleep, exhausted physically and
emotionally. I was startled awake by the sound of the first explosion,
then a second and a third.

I ran into the street and saw hundreds of people weeping and screaming as they fled. I stood in their midst, unable to focus. I heard another explosion – it was close, near the shrine of Imam Abbas. I ran there and stopped at the edge of a pool of blood. Body parts were strewn across the street, and the injured were wailing. Most of them were Iranian pilgrims, their black mourning clothes turned ash-grey by the dust and smoke. They were crying 'Ya Hussein, ya Hussein' – his martyrdom fourteen centuries earlier and their deaths were conjoining. I told myself I had to start taking pictures. But I couldn't, I was paralysed by a sickening feeling that I was intruding on people in their most intimate moment, when they were injured, hurt and dying. I went through the motions of taking pictures, of a man pushing a cart with an injured woman lying on it. Another man, angry, shouted at me to stop. I obeyed, relieved, and just observed. I am paralysed by fear and shame even as I write these lines fifteen years later.

The group which claimed responsibility called themselves al-Tawhid and al-Jihad, a group of foreign and local militant jihadis, some of whom had spent time in Afghanistan. They were led by a young Jordanian fanatic named Abu Musab al-Zarqawi who was so ruthless and murderous that he occupies a distinctive spot in the pantheon of blood-soaked maniacal murderers. Zarqawi's plan was simple: attack the Shia to instigate a civil war by provoking the Shia to retaliate against the Sunnis, which would push the whole Sunni community to join his jihad. The irony lay in the fact that it was the American toppling of Saddam – whose security services had hunted out any militant Islamists, Sunni or Shia – which had enabled the jihadis to spread their militant ideology among the Sunnis just as the radical sectarian Shia movements were spreading among the Shia.

I subsequently witnessed the aftermath of many car bombs; they are all welded in my head into one news reel of charred human remains mixed with shreds of tyres and crumpled debris. A smell of burned concrete and plastic hangs in the air.

12

A Street in Baghdad

EARLY ON THE MORNING OF 11 September 2004, I received a phone call from a fellow photographer. 'Big plume of smoke rising from the other side of the river, I think it's in Haifa Street.' Our lives at this point resembled those of ambulance drivers: we sat in our hotel rooms and waited for the inevitable signs of an exploding car bomb, a cloud of smoke, or the staccato of a gun battle; then we, a group of wire reporters and photographers, would race there before the Americans and Iraqi police cordoned off the area, often arriving before the ambulances and fire trucks, and tried to capture a newsworthy picture. Often of smoke – preferably flames but smoke will do – rising from the guilty car bomb, or of the dead scattered around and the injured limping away with blood covering their faces. We persisted in the habit until the jihadis resorted to the double-explosion technique: wait until a large crowd of civilians gather around the site of the first explosion and then send a suicide bomber into their midst. The casualties from the second attack would often surpass that of the first. On that day, however, I was tired and part of me was hoping that the area would be cordoned off by the time I arrived. But there was no sign of the Americans or the Iraqi police when I got there, and I followed a large crowd of young men and boys as they ran towards the rising cloud of smoke. 'Run fast, it's been burning for a long time,' someone shouted at me.

Haifa Street is a wide thoroughfare parallel to the Tigris, lined with multi-storey residential buildings on each side. Developed during the boom years of the 1980s, property there was largely allocated to university professors and other government functionaries. Behind the buildings are some of the oldest quarters of Baghdad, with their densely packed alleyways and a very belligerent population, which had resisted the Americans from the earliest days of the occupation. Bands of fighters laid their land mines in Haifa Street, took cover in its long concrete arcades, and used the balconies as high-rise sniper positions.

I was a few metres down the road when I heard the sound of explosions, and saw another cloud of dust appear near where the first thick column of smoke was still rising. The crowd turned on their heels and ran back towards me. In the sky, I saw two black helicopters flying very low in a big whooshing circle. A municipal worker in orange overalls stood in the middle of the road sweeping the dust with a wooden broom, seemingly oblivious to the chaos, the men and children running in panic around him. I cowered behind a shop wall with a few other onlookers. 'It's a sound bomb,' said a man who had his face close to mine, reassuring himself. We could hear screaming and shouting bleeding down the street. I came out of my hiding place and walked towards the smoke. I saw a large American armoured vehicle, spewing fire and smoke from open hatches and doors. Across the street, people were screaming, wailing and gesticulating, gathered around a group of injured men. It was early in the morning and many were still in their pyjamas. One young man, beating his head and chest, shouted over and over, 'Is that you, my brother? Is that you?' A burly man sat upright, dazed, and looked around. The back of his blue T-shirt was torn and covered in blood. Next to him two men were lifting an unconscious boy who had lost the lower half of his right leg, the stump leaving a trail of blood mixed with a creamy liquid. His left leg was badly gashed. The two black helicopters had reached the far end of the street and turned, and were heading back towards us; the crowd dispersed and ran for shelter among the buildings. I ran too. There were two more explosions, and a cloud of dust and hot air rose, engulfing the street and the injured men we had left behind. I crawled away and hid behind a concrete prefab kiosk that stood on the pavement. A trickle of blood was dripping down my face, and I tried to keep the lens of my camera clean. Six of us squeezed into the inadequate shelter of the kiosk – one burly man held the arm of the man next to him, closed his eyes and cried, his face distorted with fear. Next to them sat a young man in his early twenties, wearing a pair of army boots and a tracksuit, his legs stretched in front of him but his right knee bent downwards at an unnatural angle. Blood soaked his tracksuit bottoms and gathered in a pool underneath him. Slowly, he leaned his torso forward to peer round the kiosk into the street, where the injured lay wrapped in a shroud of dust and smoke. He pulled his head back, looked at me with big sad eyes, and then turned to look back at the street again, where one of the injured, unrecognisable through his baseball cap and mask of blood, was leaning up on one arm, his eyes and mouth wide open, before falling face down. Next to him, a man with a clipped moustache and short cropped hair lifted himself very slowly and sat upright. His face was criss-crossed with lines of blood, his ripped shirt soaked in it. His right arm hung loosely from his shoulder, as if his shirtsleeve was a sack filled with sand. With grave concentration, he looked first at the boy in the baseball cap, now flat in the road, then at the two bodies lying next to him, then turned his head and stared at the far end of the street, before slowly lowering his torso and resting his head on one of the corpses. He stretched out his left arm, fingers widespread, and his eyes pleaded for help that was not coming. Time seemed to have stopped, the street was quiet and deserted but for the few huddled men injured and dying together.

Behind the kiosk, a young TV reporter in a blue V-necked T-shirt rested his back against a wall, holding on to his arm of missing flesh and exposed bare bone and looking at his bleeding leg. He had been doing a live report from the scene when the helicopters fired their rockets into the crowd of bystanders.

'How are you doing?' asked his cameraman, who leaned next to him, bleeding from his head and fumbling for his phone.

'I am not good,' answered the reporter.

'Bring a car please – we're injured,' yelled the cameraman into his phone.

The helicopters circled again overhead. I wanted to flatten myself on the pavement, to be invisible, to hide under the others. The young man with twisted knee was emitting a faint moaning sound, his face flat to the ground, stubbing his nose. His eyes wide open fixated on an infinite dot on the pavement. He must be OK, I thought. As long as he is not screaming in pain, he must be OK.

As the helicopters wheeled away again, some of the people ran to the nearby buildings. The cameraman held the reporter up and he limped away, the right leg of his white jeans a dark crimson red. He died not long after. I ran to the entrance of a building, someone grabbed my arm and took me inside, where locals were practising whatever first aid they could manage. 'Take pictures!' he told me. 'Show the world the American democracy.'

When the helicopters finally left, we found more bodies scattered in the street. A young boy lying in the base of a palm tree, as though his torso sprouted from its trunk. On the other side of the armoured vehicle, a young boy in white dishdasha lay on his face, washed by the rays of a soft autumn sun that filtered through the smoke and the trees. When they carried the man with the twisted knee to an ambulance, his body sagged like a hay-stuffed scarecrow. 'No, this one is dead,' said the ambulance driver. 'Get someone else.' Thirteen were killed, and sixty injured. The Americans, having fired their rockets into the crowd of civilians who had gathered around the burning armoured vehicle after it was attacked by an IED, issued a statement claiming that they were firing at the armoured vehicle to destroy it and prevent insurgents from using it.

23
Fallujah

BEFORE THE WAR, FALLUJAH — A SMALL town sixty kilometres to the west of Baghdad, straddling the strategically important
Amman–Baghdad highway – was known for its grilled minced meat
kebabs, the best in Iraq, some argued. Its residents were prosperous,
religiously conservative and tribal – and they rejected the presence
of US troops in their city.

On 30 April 2003, less than two weeks after the fall of Baghdad, American soldiers opened fire on a group of unarmed civilians

who were demanding that the occupying forces leave their city, killing thirteen people. The town erupted in anger, and the relatives of the dead vowed revenge. They attacked convoys travelling on the highway, a major supply route for the US and coalition forces, fired rockets at nearby US bases, and gave shelter and refuge to anyone willing to fight the Americans.

On 31 March 2004, armed men ambushed and killed four American armed security contractors as they drove through the city. A mob then set the bodies on fire and dragged the charred and mutilated corpses through the streets, before hanging them from an overpass. In retaliation, the Americans attacked the town, collectively punishing the civilian population, to drive out the insurgents. The battle was inconclusive, and a ceasefire was agreed, but the destruction and the killings created more anger and resentment and led to more men joining the insurgency. By November 2004, Fallujah had become the epicentre for the rebellion and a symbol of resistance against the Americans. Several insurgent factions, jihadi and Islamo-nationalist, had made the city their base. The Americans surrounded the city, and prepared for the second Battle of Fallujah.

The factions were under the nominal command of an old and charismatic cleric called Abdullah al-Janabi, who had lost three sons in the fight against the Americans over the previous year. A trusted go-between arranged for a letter signed by the cleric guaranteeing us a safe passage. I joined forces with a French photographer and his Iraqi Kurdish translator, and we spent a few days in the town at the eve of what became known as the Second Battle of Fallujah.

We were taken to a safe house: an empty, still-under-construction, one-storey brick building, with bare concrete floors and cardboard covering glassless windows. We sat on the porch outside, waiting for the amir (the commander of the unit), listening to the sounds of distant explosions. A group of fighters sat cross-legged in a semicircle facing us. Some of them had their Kalashnikovs on their laps; others rested them against the wall; and they all carried small copies of the Quran. They wore trainers and tracksuit bottoms, and stared at us suspiciously.

They were members of al-Tawhid and al-Jihad, a precursor to al-Qaeda in Iraq, and already notorious for bombings, attacks on civilians, kidnappings and beheadings. They were led by Abu Musab al-Zarqawi.

The group of fighters included five Saudis – who called themselves People of the Peninsula – three Tunisians, and one Yemeni. The rest were locals from Fallujah. Most of the foreign Arabs were young men travelling outside their country for the first time, who spoke in a classical Arabic that I'd only ever heard in historical TV dramas. They came from different places and different backgrounds – teachers, labourers and students – but they all felt oppressed and humiliated by the regimes of their homeland, and the Western powers that propped them up. They were united in their hopes of fighting the infidel American occupation and were still intoxicated by the 'victories' of the 9/11 attacks. Osama bin Laden and the romantic stories of the jihad against the Soviets were their inspirations. They formed a new generation of religious warriors who would inflict so much havoc and destruction on the region in the decades to come. We chatted, and after a while, they dropped their suspicions. Who are you? What do you do? Why the big cameras? Why are you not Muslims? . . . they asked us with the excitement of first-time travellers. Another fighter came onto the porch; he was in his late teens, short, thin, and dressed in a white T-shirt and a pair of long white serwal underpants. He was still groggy from his afternoon sleep and stood rubbing his eyes and listening to the conversation.

'What are you doing?' he asked the Yemeni fighter.

'We are preaching to them about Islam,' he answered.

'Why? They are not Muslims?'

'No, they are not.'

The teenager looked puzzled and confused, then asked the Yemeni with disbelief, 'But then why don't we kill them?'

'We can't do that now,' he said with a broad smile on his face. 'We are in a state of truce with them.'

When the young men were not reading or praying, they spoke about death with a glimmer in their eyes. Not with fear but anticipation, maybe even yearning. They told each other stories about how the martyrs won't feel the pain of death, how their bodies won't rot or decompose but smell of musk and amber, and of course the heavenly rewards of virgins and the other perks of the afterlife.

I asked one of them, a young teacher from Saudi Arabia, why he was here. He went inside and came back with three thick volumes, one of them called *The Management of Savagery*, the manual of the new jihadi movement. He started reading me paragraphs in which the author quotes verses from the Quran that urge Muslims to the jihad, or the fight for the sake of Allah. He stopped, took a deep breath, and opened the second book to read about the importance of martyrdom. After twenty minutes of a tedious lecture delivered in a monotone, he said: 'You know, I am not the best one to answer your question.' He pointed at another fighter, an older man who had a thick beard and spoke with a soft melancholic voice. His name was Abu Ossama, and he was from Tunisia.

'We are here for one of two things: victory or martyrdom and both are great in the eyes of Allah,' Abu Ossama said. 'The most important thing is our religion, not Fallujah and not the occupation. If the American soldiers came to me and converted to Islam, I wouldn't fight them. We are here not because we want to liberate Iraq, but to fight the infidels and to make victorious the name of Islam.' The Saudi man, irritated by the flies persistently hovering over his face, squashed one with his hands. Abu Ossama looked at him angrily and said: 'Why do you kill the fly? It didn't do you any harm; you should be more patient.' He turned to me and continued to explain his jihadi theories: 'They call us terrorists because we resist them. If defending the truth is terrorism then we are terrorists.'

———

In the afternoon, we heard the sound of heavy machine-gun fire. Someone identified it as an American 50-calibre gun. The young Saudi withdrew and returned with a machine gun, ammunition belt wrapped around his chest and a small box of extra bullets. He threw a white-and-black keffiyeh over his head and went to investigate the sound. A young Tunisian followed him, holding an RPG launcher and carrying a few rockets on his back.

The safe house was in the neighbourhood of Julan, in the north-west of Fallujah. The nearby train station and its railway tracks formed the northern front line of the city. I followed the two men who walked openly through the empty streets, but before reaching the station they climbed down into a newly dug trench, about a metre deep. The Saudi grabbed a piece of cardboard and held it in front of his face, presumably to confuse any American soldiers on the other side, who would be wondering why a piece of cardboard was climbing into a trench in Fallujah. After tripping twice and drop-ping his machine gun, he put down the cardboard and rested his back against the wall of the trench. Then he opened his pocket-sized leather-bound Quran and read for a few minutes. He closed the book, and pointed his machine gun at the horizon. Clicked, once, twice, but nothing happened. Tried to fiddle with the safety catch, but it was jammed. He raised his head, looked at me and asked: 'Do you know how this works?'

The two young fighters waited for half an hour, and when no Americans showed up, they decided to leave. Back at the house, the 'amir' of the group had arrived, and brought with him two trays of rice, topped with pieces of mutton and chicken, along with small plates of okra and aubergine stew. After praying, the young fighters sat around the trays, scooped rice, exchanged jokes and laughed; they resembled a group of students on a school trip. It was easy to forget how these were men ready to commit extreme violence for their ideology. The commander fretted around them, asking them if they had enough supplies of fruit and bananas, and if they ate well. They might be jihadi fighters keen to die, but at the same time, they were his foreign guests.

He was middle-aged and heavily built, with soft brown eyes, a grey beard, and a moustache clipped well above the lips. He was a quiet and confident retired military officer, who had once owned a thriving workshop for electrical generators. He told me that when the Americans first entered Iraq, he rejoiced at the toppling of Saddam, who had oppressed Sunni Islamists like himself. He had soon changed his mind.

'As time passed, and the occupation became more visible, patriotic feelings inside me grew greater and greater. Every time I saw the Americans patrolling our streets, I felt ashamed and humiliated.'

After the massacre of the demonstrators, he joined other locals from Fallujah and nearby villages and towns, and began attacking nearby US bases or their convoys travelling on the highway. 'We just wanted them to leave our cities,' he told me. 'I used to take part in an attack once a month, setting an improvised bomb, or firing mortars, and then I would go back to the workshop. In a few months I realised that as long as the Americans were occupying my country, jihad was my only way to get them out.'

He closed his workshop, sold his business and used the money to sponsor a group of fighters. The Americans, with their habitual ignorance, had lumped all the fighters in Fallujah together, labelling them as disgruntled Baathists and jihadis. However, as early as 2004, a cleavage was emerging between local Iraqis who fought to 'liberate their lands' and foreign jihadis who were there to fight a religious war. The amir said he was not a religious extremist; he was fighting for nationalist reasons. He adopted militant Islamic-jihadi rhetoric because that helped him attract aid, funds and foot soldiers, like the young idealists from across the Arab world who sat eating rice and meat.

'The world is convinced that we, the people of Fallujah, are happy to kill the innocents – that's not true. Even when we execute collaborators and people working for the Americans I feel sad for them and sometimes I cry, but this is a war. What we want is for the Americans to leave, and then everything will be fine. The Kurds will stop talking about seceding from Iraq, the Shia will stop talking about settling scores with the Sunni. Then each province can elect a shura council, and these councils can elect a president. That is the election that we see as democratic, not the American one.'

———

After the evening prayers, I heard a beautiful voice drifting from the house, reciting verses from the Quran and choking with tears. 'If your fathers, your sons, your brothers, your wives, your tribe, your fortunes and your trade are dearer to your hearts than God, his prophet and the jihad in the name of God . . .' came the chant.

The room was dark and bare, half lit by a single battery-powered fluorescent light. A prayer mat was laid in the middle, next to a Kalashnikov and an ammunition pouch. A large poster of Mecca hung on one of the walls, and a pair of old trainers stood guard by the door. On the prayer mat sat the Yemeni fighter, Abdullah. A small Quran in one hand and prayer beads in the other, he continued his chanting: 'Be fearful of God then, he will never talk to the wrong-doers.' Sometimes his voice would be drowned out by the sounds of explosions rocking the city. He finished his prayers, held his hands high, palms outwards and called upon God for help in the coming battle: 'Oh God, you who made the Prophet come out victorious in his wars against the infidels, make us come out victorious in our war against America. Oh God, defeat America and its allies everywhere. Oh God, make us worthy of your religion.'

After prayers, a light shower of rain began, and he sat alone cleaning the guns, dismantling each weapon into small pieces, soaking them in petrol before wiping each piece with a little rag. 'In Yemen, you learn how to clean a gun as a child,' he told me. He was tall, lanky with a dark complexion, black eyes and a thin beard, wearing an Adidas jacket and a red keffiyeh. Back in Yemen, he had spent six years studying sharia at the Iman University in Sana'a (a religious institution established by Abdul Majid al-Zindani, a Salafi cleric, maverick politician, and a very wealthy businessman who, among his many other celebrated achievements, claimed that he had invented a cure for cancer, Aids and poverty).

Abdullah's first attempt to come to Iraq was in April 2003. The Leader had invited Arab volunteers to join the jihad against the Americans, and the Yemeni president, Ali Abdullah Saleh, willing to rid himself of the mounting numbers of jihadis in his own country, had turned a half-blind eye to the flow. Meanwhile, the Syrians, who feared they were next on the Bush target list and therefore were keen to see the Americans fail in their adventure in Iraq, allowed the traffic of foreign jihadi fighters to pass through their country largely unmolested.

He was travelling with a group of would-be jihadis – all fellow students from Iman University. The police at the airport became suspicious when they saw the group, dressed in their jalabiyas and turbans, the uniform of religious students and clerics. An officer asked him what he planned to do in Damascus. 'I told him I was going for work. When they asked me what kind of work, I said to work for the salvation of my soul, and they knew I wanted to come to fight.' He and his friends were turned away by the police and prevented from boarding the flight. He pointed to his cheap cotton grey trousers and said he learned the lesson and exchanged the turban and jalabiya for Western-style clothing.

For a whole year he tried to forget about Iraq and jihad. He went back to his studies and his family. But when the scandal of the prisoner abuse at Abu Ghraib broke out, it was like 'an electric shock' that woke him up. His wife, a religious student herself working on her master's degree and heavily pregnant, urged him to leave everything behind and go to Iraq for jihad. 'She told me, if they are doing this to the men, imagine what is happening to the women, imagine your sisters and me being raped by the infidel American pigs.'

He had spent the night crying, and spent the next day visiting friends and acquaintances to borrow money for another attempt to reach Iraq. Through his contacts in the university, he was given the name of someone in Aleppo, northern Syria, who would help smuggle him across the border.

'I didn't tell anyone in my family, I just told my wife, I borrowed a car from a friend, and we went out to do some shopping. She bought me two pairs of trousers and a shirt. We then went to my father's house. I told my mother to forgive me if I had done anything wrong. She said, why? I told her, nothing, I just want forgiveness from you and Dad. She asked me if I was going to Baghdad. I said no, she hugged me and cried.'

He wiped his face with the corner of his keffiyeh, and complained of the cold and rain, before continuing his story. He and his wife went back home, and after dinner the children went to bed early, not knowing that this was their last night with their father. Only the smallest of his children remained with him. 'My favourite daughter came and sat in my lap, and slept there, then she woke up, opened her eyes and said, "Father, I love you."' He began to weep silently and this time did not try to blame the weather. 'You know these memories are the work of the devil; he is trying to soften my heart and bring me back home.'

When he arrived in Damascus, another 'jihadi brother' told him that the Syrians had tightened the border security and that it would be some time before they could cross. He joined a community of would-be jihadis, crammed into small apartments in the suburbs of Damascus, Aleppo and Homs. After a month, he heard that some of his friends had been arrested and came to suspect that the cleric who was running the smuggling network was himself working for the Syrian intelligence service, helping the government round up jihadis in response to American pressure on the Syrian regime. He fled, and travelled through Syria on his own. One day, in a small mosque in Aleppo, he met a cleric called Abu al-Qa'qa' who promised to help him. The cleric handed him on to another group, who placed him in a safe house with other jihadis for two weeks, while they checked his credentials. They told him that to avoid infiltration by security services, any would-be mujahid had to be vouched for by someone known in the jihadi circles in his home country before he was allowed to cross the border into Iraq. 'They were suspicious of me in the beginning until they called my teacher in the Iman University in Sana'a and he vouched for me.' From Aleppo, the group of men were taken to a village on the Syrian side of the border. They waited for their moment while the smuggler bribed the border police. 'It was a terrifying journey; if we heard American helicopters we had to lie still in the desert.'

After crossing, the men spent two nights in a village on the Iraqi side of the border, before being taken to another village for military training. 'Most of the brothers with me had never used a weapon in their lives. I knew how to use a Kalashnikov – every Yemeni knows how to fire a weapon from when he is a small boy.' A few days later, they were told that there was a battle in the town of Hit, 181 kilometres to the west of Baghdad. There, he joined other Arab fighters in a trench, but before they could take part in any fighting a ceasefire was secured by the town elders. He and the other foreign fighters were driven through the night in a minibus escorted by two cars, one of them a police car. He had arrived in Fallujah six weeks earlier and spent a few days with other fighters, before they were dispatched among the different armed factions, and that's how he had ended up in this house with the al-Tawhid and al-Jihad. He had been given the honour of leading the prayers because of his beautiful voice, a role usually reserved for the amir of the unit.

I tried to ease the pain of his longing for his family by saying that I would come and visit him in Yemen one day after the war; his face contorted and he replied with a tinge of anger that the only place he was going to from here was heaven. He explained that he did not love death for the sake of death, but because he perceived martyrdom as the ultimate pure worship of God. He produced his copy of the Quran from his pocket.

'Before flying to Syria, I bought seven copies, wrote the name of my wife and my five children on each and left the seventh empty; I didn't impose a name for the newborn on my wife. She called me the night I was preparing to cross into Iraq and told me she had inscribed the Quran with the name of the new child. She called him Shahid [martyr].'

That night, the sounds of explosions were growing louder and more frequent. After one particularly loud and close explosion, we all went outside where other fighters had gathered. Red and purple clouds rose from the streets.

'Spread around – I don't want to see more than three together,' the amir shouted. We could hear American drones buzzing in the sky. We tried to hide under the trees. The amir and some of the fighters wore overalls made from a reflective plastic material, resembling fishermen's waders, to 'confuse the American thermal cameras', they said. In the darkness, we were then led into a mosque where we spent the night listening to the heavy bombing, shrapnel hitting the outside wall. The next day we moved to a new safe house: the fighters feared that the Americans had located their first one.

The amir headed to the train station, walking up and down the railway tracks, gripping a pistol, inspecting the trenches and other defences, and assigning the men to their different spots. The Yemeni was positioned in a shelter made out of cinder blocks and corrugated-metal sheets. He crouched there, reading from his small Quran. Others lay behind berms and occasionally opened fire when they heard the Americans approaching. Dust and empty casings flew. In the deserted street, a pickup truck mounted with an anti-aircraft cannon sped swiftly past; clashes had erupted along the city perimeter. One young Iraqi man, designated as the unit's martyr, had been tasked with exploding himself next to the Americans. He ran down the street brandishing his gun in one hand and firing intermittently.

The amir asked me to leave while a path out of the city was still open. 'We made a mistake by making Fallujah an American no-go zone; we are besieged here. This will be a great emotional victory but a bad strategy, it will be very easy for the Americans to come and kill us all,' he told me before leaving. We drove at night, along a dry irrigation canal, slipping through the American lines. The battle would rage for two weeks, killing an estimated 700 civilians. The residents became refugees, and this was far from the last time they attempted to defy the authority of central government.

زائرة إيرانية قتلت بتفجير إنتحاري في الكاظمية

14

The Collaterals

THERE WERE MANY WAYS TO die in Baghdad: killed by car bombs; taken out by militias working in tandem with security forces to target Sunnis; targeted by Sunni insurgents killing Shia and those deemed to be US collaborators. Translators and contractors and government employees were under fire. Journalists and even cleaning women working for the Americans were kidnapped. American retaliation meant the fairly indiscriminate killing of civilians; civilians also died at the hands of militias and insurgents when they found themselves in the midst of the fighting – always the collateral damage of war. (Or not so collateral as the WikiLeaks video of the killing of an Iraqi cameraman showed.) In the lawlessness and chaos that engulfed the whole city, criminal gangs overlapped with the insurgents and militias kidnapped doctors and business people. No one ever knew for sure who was doing what killing. Those who could afford it fled to the safety of Amman and Beirut. The levels of fear, anxiety and violence that Iraqis went through on a daily basis could not be measured or reported. Life was shaped by a cycle of violence and counter-violence, by sectarian politicians spewing hatred from pulpits and TV channels, by the ugliness of American occupation, and the racism of foreign soldiers and mercenaries, and of course by the insurgency.

In the midst of all of that violence, random death and war, Iraqis continued to go to work and send their children to school. Traders sold their wares from carts as they always had and often died in the IED attacks; a day or two later, other traders appeared in their place. People jostled in crowded markets until mortars or car bombs ripped through them . . . When the blood had been washed away, they returned to the same markets again. We were playing a game of Russian roulette. My favourite tea house, consisting of a few metal tables and wooden benches that sat on the pavement under the shade of a large eucalyptus tree, was bombed three times; each time I told myself, it can't be bombed again, and went back to sit on its rickety benches. It was not even a year after the toppling of the statue and the regime when people started uttering the unthinkable, that maybe life under Saddam had been better. How could they even think it? Had they forgotten the wars and the secret police and the suffocating dictatorship? The answer was that at least then we knew the parameters of fear, and we knew how to survive. In the midst of this chaos, no one knew anything any more. What were the new boundaries? Not to be seen with the Americans? Not to get a job with the new police and security services? Is it even better not to work at all than work with the new government? Is it worth trying to avoid driving through potential IED sites? But where are those sites this week? And how can you make sure that mortars fired by kids won't fall on your house?

People were so desperate for anything resembling security that there was general approval for the interim prime minister, Ayad Allawi, when rumours spread that he had personally chopped off the hand of a captured insurgent and was carrying out death sentences himself. Maybe, they said, here is someone who will finally be able to deliver security.

The reality of life in Baghdad was much worse than anything we could portray in snippets of news and articles. The real misery and bewilderment of the people could never be captured and translated

into words. Journalists themselves were regularly getting killed –
I woke one morning in Beirut to read about the kidnapping of an
American journalist. The translator was shot and killed; there was
a picture of his feet sticking out of the back of a pickup truck, an
image that will haunt me for the rest of my life. He was a childhood
friend, a father, who loved Western music. I was as angry at him as
his killers – why did he have to do this dangerous job? The euphoria
and excitement of working with Western journalists in the early days
of the war was gone, replaced by paralysing fear. As for the son of
the prominent Sunni politician who lured them into the ambush, I
have never wished for someone to be punished as I wished it for him.

Later, when the number of American soldiers killed in Iraq
climbed to 1,000, there was a flurry of coverage in the Western media.
A critical benchmark had been reached, they declared, but what was
the critical benchmark for the number of Iraqi civilians killed? How
many had died by then? To this day there is no accurate number,
of those killed through the sanctions, in the war and in the violence
that followed.

15

The Shrink

THE CLINIC OF BAGHDAD'S MOST celebrated psychiatrist was on the first floor of a dilapidated building in the neighbourhood of Hafid al-Qadi, one of Baghdad's oldest districts: home to gangs, brothels and some of its most charming and crumbling streets and buildings.

The stairwell leading to the clinic was dark and reeked of urine, the steps chipped and uneven. Plaster peeled from the ceiling in large chunks and the walls were smudged dark by hundreds of hands groping their way through the gloom. The doctor's nameplate was of shining copper but the lettering and the list of his degrees had long faded and were barely readable.

In his cramped waiting room, people crowded around a small metal desk, where a young woman –struggling in the darkness – was looking for patient history and appointments through three big ledgers of names and details. An old TV sat idle in the corner, and a piece of cloth separated the waiting room from a small foul-smelling toilet lit by a candle.

A door led to the doctor's examination room. Inside, beneath the doctor's UK diploma, a tall, thin woman in her forties and her sister, younger and heavier, sat on threadbare green chairs. The headscarf of the tall woman had slid to the back of her head, and she held on to her sister's arm tightly. Her eyes remained fixed on the floor.

The doctor, gaunt and in his sixties, had a soft, reassuring smile, and very pleasant and gentle manners, a grandfatherly figure. The only source of light in the room was from the window behind him illuminating his head, turning his white hair into a glowing halo. He glanced at the card in front of him and whispered something to the male nurse who left the room quickly.

'So, Fatima, tell me what's wrong?' the doctor asked the tall woman gently.

'Doctooor,' answered the sister, stretching her vowels, 'she is not sleeping very well; she talks badly to everyone, and she remembers old quarrels and fights with everyone.'

Fatima was still looking at the floor.

'My daughter,' said the doctor, 'do you think people are talking about you? Every time you go to bed you hear someone whispering in your ears?'

'Yes,' answered the sister. 'She won't eat any food cooked in the house – she says we are trying to poison her.'

The doctor nodded, and started writing something in his notepad. 'She is suffering from acute depression,' he said. 'Fatima my daughter, do you tell yourself that maybe if you died things will get better?'

Still staring at the floor, she spoke for the first time: 'Yes, but then I look at my kids and say no.'

'Doctor, every time there is a knock at the door, she starts screaming and fighting,' said her sister.

'Why is that, my dear?' asked the doctor in his soft and reassuring voice.

'It is all these things around us, the Americans, the booby traps, no security, I can't let the kids go and play outside because of car bombs and fighting.' And then she raised her head for the first time and looked at the doctor with large dark eyes and said: 'Doctor, you are a learned man, why can't you stop these car bombs and explosions?'

The doctor laughed and looked at the ceiling, raising his palms. 'But how can I? I am like you, scared of these things.' He called to the nurse: 'Mustafa, prepare for an ECT.'

The nurse entered the room, and went to the balcony and soon there came the muffled roar of a generator. A faint current of electricity caused the few bulbs to flicker. The nurse returned and opened the door to a small room. Inside a white trolley stood next to a leather bench, and the smell of burning plastic filled the air.

'Doctor, I don't want to do this again,' Fatima pleaded.

'But you want to get well, right?' said the doctor, as he led her to the other room. The sister was holding her arm firmly.

The nurse and the sister laid Fatima on the leather bench. Two wires protruded from a brown wooden box on the white trolley, attached to a plastic and metal headset that was soaking in an aluminium bowl filled with water. The nurse fixed the headset to Fatima's temples, and the doctor activated a switch on the wooden box. Her eyes shut tightly as she went through epileptic spasms, shaking and trembling. Her sister held her feet, mumbling verses from the Quran, and the nurse put his thumb under her chin to stop her from biting her tongue.

They repeated the treatment a few times, until Fatima's eyes rolled in their sockets and showed milky white. The doctor returned to his desk, inspecting the card of another patient as Fatima lay unconscious.

'The conditions in the surrounding environment, the fear, the anxieties of war and violence and the deteriorating security situation, they increase the pressures that chip away the resistance of patients,' he told me with his kind and gentle smile. 'Some people have a low threshold of tolerance, people like Fatima, who will break faster than others.'

The stocky woman reappeared, leading Fatima who was

sleepwalking holding on to her sister. The doctor opened the door for them and looked at the crowded waiting room.

'The pressure, the war and the economical situation – all these factors are the causes why I have more patient visits these days.'

A new patient was already waiting for him on the threadbare green chair.

16

Hameed

THE FIRST TIME I MET Hameed was in October 2005 during the constitutional referendum. The Sunni communities had all but entirely rejected the political process, and the proposed constitution itself had hardly taken their views about the future shape of the state into account. There were two main currents of thought among the Sunnis. On the one hand, politicians and local armed groups wanted people to vote on the new constitution to prove that the Sunni community had numerical weight in the country, and that they clearly rejected the constitution. On the other hand, jihadis and more radical factions saw the whole political process as illegitimate, and any form of participation in it as akin to collaboration with the occupier.

I wanted to visit one of the Sunni communities on polling day to see how the debate was playing out. A friend suggested that I go to the district of Tarmiya, where a local commander, Hameed, was keen for the voting to take place, and also willing to see me.

Tarmiya sat along the highway that connected Baghdad to the north of the country, not far from the massive Taji military base, used by American and Iraqi forces. An array of local rebel groups and jihadi organisations (including al-Qaeda) were active in the area, turning Tarmiya into one of the most dangerous spots in Iraq. The attacks and kidnappings on the highway had contributed to the sense of siege in the capital.

To secure the highway, the Americans had surrounded Tarmiya

with concrete walls and watchtowers and regularly conducted night raids to search out the elusive insurgents. The main road into the district passed through an elaborate American checkpoint – a mini fortress with a hundred-metre concrete corridor of blast walls, metal barriers and coils of razor wire. Alongside the Americans stood masked Iraqi soldiers drawn predominantly from the south of the country. They searched cars and their passengers, checking ID cards against a list of wanted men. A masked informant standing with the soldiers scrutinised faces to identify known enemies or unknown outsiders.

The locals called the checkpoint the Rafah crossing, a reference to the Israeli army checkpoint in Gaza.

We avoided the checkpoint by entering via the alternative 'Mujahideen road', used by the rebels to slip in and out of the area without being detected. It consisted of a network of narrow dirt tracks that snaked through farmland along the banks of irrigation canals, with long reeds providing ample cover.

I arrived in the early afternoon and was taken to meet Hameed, the most senior rebel commander in the area. It was the month of Ramadan, and he apologised for not serving me water or tea. We sat in his large but simply decorated living room; he wore a white dishdasha and sat on the sofa, one leg folded underneath him. Above his head were two portraits, one of his late father wearing the traditional Arab dress of a keffiyeh and a cloak, the other an old black-and-white portrait of a young officer, with a pencil moustache and an earnest look. He said it was his brother, killed in the Iran–Iraq War.

Hameed was a former officer in the General Security Apparatus serving in Basra before the war. He told me that his journey into the insurgency began three days before the statue of the Leader was toppled; and just as British troops were breaking through the last of the Iraqi army defences, he had shed his green military uniform and joined the civilians fleeing the fighting in Basra.

Dressed in a dirty dishdasha to disguise his identity as an officer, he began the slow and dangerous journey to his village north of Baghdad. In the midst of the chaos of war, he walked for hours, along with the hordes of people trudging along a highway clogged with defeated army units, deserting soldiers and civilians displaced by the fighting. He hitched rides on the backs of trucks or in overcrowded buses and took shelter with acquaintances and relatives at night. By the time he reached Baghdad, the Americans had toppled the statue and brought down the regime he had spent two decades serving. He roamed the streets lost and defeated. 'I couldn't go back home, I was too ashamed. I was an officer – how could I sleep next to my wife while my country was occupied?' he told me.

He went to a cleric he knew who had been preaching jihad against the invading Americans before the war. 'I was weeping like a child, I begged him for weapons, asked him to direct me on the jihad he preached.' But the cleric shooed him away and told him that the situation was too dangerous for talk of jihad now. He walked with a bayonet in his pocket, looking for a way to restore his honour. He saw dead bodies and bullets and shell casings scattered in the deserted streets. On the northern outskirts of Baghdad, not far from his village, he came across another group of desperate and defeated men – Syrian volunteers who had been encouraged by the regime to join the jihad against the Americans before the war, and were left to fend for themselves after Baghdad was occupied. They had a rocket launcher, a few rockets and some Kalashnikov rifles between them and they too were looking for Americans to fight. Hameed joined them, and they lay on a footbridge that spanned the main highway north of Baghdad and waited for the Americans to pass. The next morning they saw a convoy approaching. Hameed moved to the edge of the bridge, a rocket launcher on his shoulder. He was a security officer, and had never fired a rocket before. He mumbled a short Quranic verse and fired, the rocket whooshed in a wild circle and exploded far away from the convoy. The attack had failed, but his honour as an officer was exonerated, and his pride restored. He left the Syrians and walked to his village in Tarmiya, where he sat in his home, and, like many, hoped that things would get better and that the long decades of endemic cycles of wars and violence that had plagued Iraq for so long would give way to development, reconstruction and prosperity. Instead, he and his fellow tribesmen found themselves ostracised by the new regime. Many became jobless after the disbanding of the army and security services, or were fired from their government posts through the De-Baathification process. They had clearly been identified as FRE, or former regime elements. He saw the chaos and destruction around him, believed it was all part of an American plot to destroy Iraq, and decided to join the insurgency.

He organised a local group of fighters, initially consisting of cousins, relatives, and a couple of neighbours. They called themselves the Anger Brigades, and he adopted for himself the *nom de guerre* of Abu Theeb or Father of the Wolf.

They issued manifestos and communiqués in a religio-nationalist language, similar to that used in the Faith Campaign, mixing jihadi speak with nationalist rhetoric. The American aggressors were now infidels, and the old Iranian enemies became the new Shia apostates. One of the foreign fighters Hameed had met after the fall of Baghdad had taught him how to build bombs and land mines, rigging old Iraqi army artillery shells with a few cables, an electrical fuse and a remote-controlled detonator. A few months later, a former Iraqi army general laid the military plans for the group, attacking American and Iraqi military convoys as they travelled in and out of Baghdad along the main highway north of the city. He showed them the best spots to plant their improvised bombs, and set up their ambushes, advising that they should be at least two kilometres away from their village to spare the people the wrath of American retaliation. Along with these attacks, Abu Theeb and his men began kidnapping, at gunpoint, those who they accused of collaborating with the occupation forces.

He was particularly nostalgic about these early days of the jihad. 'In the beginning, we had a pure jihad,' he told me. 'Everyone was fighting the Americans in those days. Men who spent years as military deserters under Saddam became zealous fighters; something like fire was inside us. We would go out to fight for days leaving our families and wives behind, because when the infidel conquered our land, it was like seeing our women raped in front of our eyes and our religion being insulted every day.'

Like every insurgent I have met, he marvelled at how they, a group of farmers and peasants, could stand up to the all-powerful American army. 'By God, this is America with its might and glory, hit by a bunch of barefoot fighters, dressed in dishdashas and carrying rusty weapons. But then we were pure men.' He said they couldn't have done it without Allah's help, and to prove it he told me a story of how one day he was driving back home with a sack of mortar shells in the boot of his car. An American patrol stopped him: one soldier checked his ID card, another walked round the car to inspect the boot. 'I prayed to God and said, "God, if this fight is for you then you help me now." The soldier poked about in the boot, pushing the sack filled with mortar shells without opening it. They let me go. That was God's work. Every time we hit an American target, it was a sign that God was with us.'

———

Hameed was born into a family of farmers in the late sixties. Their village – green and lush, with orchards of pomegranate, orange and palm trees, and many irrigation canals – sat on the banks of the Tigris, tucked away from the bleak highway with its drab workshops and factories. Each village in the area was inhabited mostly by one clan, and these village clans would trace their origin into a shared – sometimes real, sometimes imagined – common tribal ancestry.

Rural farming life in the confines of a tight community, where everyone was basically a cousin, was simple. Order stemmed less from the dogmas of the Leader, the Struggle and the Party than from tribal customs and codes of honour: kinship bonds and loyalty to family, hospitality to strangers, and the relentless pursuit of blood feuds based on any perceived slight to honour and reputation.

Hameed's father, an illiterate farmer, insisted that all his sons and daughters finish their education. He used to walk to his fields and orchards carrying a short-wave radio and would sit late into the night debating politics with the other villagers. When Hameed's eldest brother was 'martyred' in the Iran–Iraq War in the eighties, the father refused to mourn. He was proud that his son had given his life to defend the watan against the aggressors.

'Watan' is a word that means the nation, the state and the homeland all in one. Between the identity bonds of small local village and all-embracing watan was a tribal identity. Hameed belonged to al-Mashahdeh, a Sunni tribe that claimed descent from the Prophet Muhammad. It was a 'loyal' tribe, whose proximity to the regime had been far more profitable than its connection to the Prophet's family.

When Hameed finished his law degree in the late eighties, his 'loyal' tribal surname guaranteed his entry into the National Security Academy to become an officer in the Directorate of General Security, one of the dozen or so security organisations that formed the backbone of the regime's security system and was responsible for a litany of human rights abuses. Tall, broad-shouldered, with a handsome face and soft brown twinkling eyes, he was the archetypal image of a proud – moustached – and feared officer.

The first cracks in his nationalistic belief system appeared after the invasion of Kuwait in 1990 and the disastrous war that followed. This was not a war to defend the nation against foreign aggression – as he saw the war with Iran – but a reckless adventure that led to the destruction of critical infrastructure, the imposition of crippling sanctions, and the crushing defeat of the army he and his fellow officers took so much pride in. Those killed in that war could not be celebrated as martyrs of a just war like his brother had been.

In the weeks after the defeat, spontaneous uprisings erupted in Basra and other Shia cities in the south as well as in the Kurdish areas in the north. The uprisings were chaotic and disorganised and descended into bloody reprisals against Baathists and supporters of the regime, and many were killed and their bodies mutilated. The Leader Necessity responded with ferocious brutality: thousands were summarily executed, and their bodies dumped in mass graves. Many more were tortured and imprisoned. Hundreds of thousands fled to Iran and Turkey. Scars from that crackdown remained visible for years to come, and so did the small but persistent acts of defiance and opposition to the regime. The oppression and fear continued, and as a member of the state security service Hameed was a proud officer, but he hated being a tool of that oppression.

The long years of the sanctions that followed further shook his belief in the system. The economic collapse and deprivation had led to vast corruption. He saw how his fellow officers were routinely supplementing their salaries with bribes just to survive, while the high-ranking commanders were turning their positions into fiefdoms, and greedily siphoning off as much money as they could. His image of the state crumbled, and his pride and nationalism splintered into a thousand pieces.

'I hated the government,' he told me. 'I realised that all they were telling us about the nation and the Leader was false. They had no pride or honour, and I wanted to leave.'

He decided to take some time off from the 'service' and enrolled in the newly opened Saddam University for Islamic Studies in Baghdad to get a degree in jurisprudence and Islamic law. Hameed's drift towards religiosity was part of the general mood in the nineties, nurtured by the regime's Faith Campaign. His religious studies did not turn him into a radical, but they provided the basic religious identity and rhetoric he built on in later years. Gradually, as the country continued to deteriorate, his religious views shifted from the 'state-sponsored Islam' to a more puritanical and radical Salafi Islam, which he kept a secret, for the regime was prosecuting any religious movement, both Sunni and Shia, that challenged the regime's control and hegemony. Alas, he could not hide in his religious studies for long, and finishing his degree in the late nineties, he reluctantly returned to his security job in Basra.

Hameed wasn't fighting because he had lost a salary but because in the new narrative of Iraq, shaped by the Americans and the former exiles, he had become a non-entity. Worse, he was held responsible for all that had gone before. He fought to reclaim the state as he imagined it to be: unified under strong government rule, and not fragmented and occupied. But unlike other insurgents, he did not believe that nihilistic, destructive violence in itself was an adequate goal. He used violence to reclaim his community's position, in an attempt to be accepted as partners if not masters in the new Iraq. He thought that his fellow rebels should pursue political paths as well as armed rebellion. His adversaries, however – the Americans, the Shia militias and the more radical elements of the insurgency – would not let him implement his vision.

When he finished talking to me about his journey, the room was getting dark and it was time for Hameed to break his fast. We sat on the floor, ate a simple meal together, and then he ushered me into the small village mosque attached to his house. The mosque was packed with his relatives, and I stood next to him and pretended that I was praying; kneeling and standing, pushing my forehead against the carpeted floor, hung with a faint musky smell of old socks, lulled by the smooth voice of the cleric reciting the Quran. After the prayers, I felt bad – Hameed had been open with me, telling me the secrets of his long fight, and yet I was pretending to be what I was not. So with a stupid shy grin, I told him that I wasn't religious and did not pray.

'If you want to hear the story of this area, and want the people to talk to you, you must wear what we are wearing [a white dishdasha] and come to the mosque to pray with us,' he told me with a big generous smile on his face.

Hameed was the first of many people who protected me in two decades of civil wars. Whether I was shivering in a frost-covered olive grove in northern Syria, or in the back of a pickup truck crossing rugged mountain roads in Yemen, or crouching in an armoured Iraqi army Humvee moving slowly towards ISIS positions in Mosul, there were always people like Hameed who, often against the advice of their own community, wrapped me in a cloak of protection and helped me see the things that I was not allowed to see, revealing a version of events that I was not supposed to witness. Some did it out of hubris and pride, others were concerned about the choices made by their communities and wanted to tell their version of events, but many protected and helped me out of sheer fellow feeling. Their position was far more precarious than whatever I had to contend with in the short period I was with them. Targeted by the same forces they were trying to protect me from, many were killed, kidnapped or forcibly disappeared.

———

After prayers, we sat in Hameed's garden, where white plastic chairs were arranged in a big square on the thick grass lawn enclosed by bitter-orange and citrus trees. Men trickled in, smoked, drank tea, chatted, asked for the latest news and generally groaned about the current state of affairs. Things were not going well, many had lost their jobs, and a tit-for-tat conflict with a powerful neighbouring Shia tribe that lived on the other side of the highway – a precursor for the religious and sectarian war that was to come – was hurting the people much more than the American occupation. Going to Baghdad had become a risky enterprise; Sunni fighters had been kidnapping Shias travelling on the highway out of Baghdad heading north, now Shia militiamen reciprocated by kidnapping Sunnis heading into Baghdad.

A large number of them dressed in the Salafi style, with their ankle-length dishdashas, and had bushy unkempt beards. Most of them had converted to Salafism after 2003, for it had been a very rare phenomenon in the Iraq of the Leader, when Salafis – ultra-conservative revivalist Islamists, who advocate a return to the traditions of the Prophet and his pious companions – were hunted down, imprisoned and even executed.

The men discussed politics, and everyone had an opinion on the upcoming constitutional referendum – should they participate or boycott? Participation would be seen as an endorsement of the occupation, argued those who opposed. But others regretted the Sunni boycott of the political process in the previous elections: they argued that the Shia dominated the state and its security services because the Sunnis were still holding on to the slogan of 'What was built on falsehood is false', meaning that anything that came after the occupation was illegitimate.

Hameed told the men that they should participate in the referendum: they could reject the constitution, but showing up in large numbers would prove the weight of the Sunni faction to the Americans. For a Sunni rebel commander to argue for political participation was a precarious position to take; it was also a very dangerous thing to say in public since al-Qaeda, which had established a foothold in the country after the US invasion and eventually became the strongest Sunni faction, had declared that anyone participating was an apostate who should be killed.

Late that night, Hameed's nephew – very young, slim and angular – came to the garden, flushed with excitement at finishing a 'job'.

When Hameed heard the details of the 'job', he was outraged. The young man had planted an improvised bomb on the main road of the village, frequently used by children going to school and men and women travelling to their farms. 'I thought we had agreed that we don't put bombs amid our families?' Hameed told his nephew.

When the guests had left, Hameed turned to me and began complaining that foreign al-Qaeda jihadis were spreading through the area, radicalising and recruiting young men like his nephew. They did not care about the civilian casualties as long as they could attack the Americans. 'When al-Qaeda came to this area, I was the first to oppose them,' he said.

Earlier that year a group of Syrians visited him, identifying themselves as members of al-Qaeda in Iraq, and asked for his cooperation and support to establish a foothold for their organisation in his area.

'They [Syrians] told me that they had support and money and wanted to open a new front here. I said, what about the village? Do you want this to become a new Fallujah? They went to the clerics and said, "Denounce this man Hameed; otherwise, your blood will be spilled." They wouldn't hesitate to kill and slaughter anyone standing against them.'

Al-Qaeda, with its global connections and money pouring in from all over the Arab world, quickly became the most feared insurgent group in Iraq. Hameed said it initially gained supporters among the Sunni community because of its ferocity in fighting the Americans, and its meticulous planning. The force was mostly made up of foreign Arab fighters, who came to Iraq with bundles of cash and dreams of martyrdom. The group registered their presence with the bloodiest attacks against both civilian and military targets. He said that many of the local insurgent groups accepted their position under the umbrella of al-Qaeda simply because they needed money and weapons. They did not necessarily accept its ideology, and thought – wrongly, tragically – that they could maintain their independence.

Al-Qaeda – known then as the al-Tawhid and al-Jihad – decided to target the Iraqi police and army and other Iraqi institutions. The goal was to prevent the Americans from achieving their essential strategic goal of establishing an Iraqi state that could lead the fight against the insurgency. 'They were clever,' Hameed said. 'They attacked all the centres of the new Iraqi state, preventing the Americans from creating a puppet state that they could control. The Iraqi resistance was focused on fighting the Americans only and couldn't see that larger strategic goal.'

Al-Qaeda labelled everyone who worked with the Iraqi government, police or army as 'kafirs', infidels, along with the entire Shia community. Hameed and other commanders found the strategy to be folly in the extreme, and it created a rift between local and foreign fighters. 'Al-Qaeda believes that anyone who doesn't follow their interpretation of the Quran is a "kafir", infidel, and should be killed,' said Hameed. 'This is wrong.'

By attacking Shia communities, al-Qaeda earned the wrath of Shia militias (like the Mahdi army of Muqtada al-Sadr, the Badr brigade and the Ministry of Interior Commandos, a paramilitary unit closely associated with the Badr brigade), who retaliated for the attacks on the Shia with indiscriminate violence on Tarmiya and other Sunni areas. Scores of Sunni men were kidnapped and executed by the paramilitaries and militias who were arresting men based on their tribal name. More than three hundred Sunni families sought refuge in Hameed's village after fleeing Shia areas in Baghdad.

'Every time al-Qaeda attacks a Shia mosque we are making all the Shia our enemies,' he said. 'We are cementing them against us. We have lost more men to the Shia than we have lost to the Americans. Those Shia are murderous.'

Another rift with al-Qaeda came after its call for the establishment of an Islamic state (caliphate) based on the Taliban model in Afghanistan, which had already started taking place in towns and villages where al-Qaeda was dominant.

'The resistance includes nationalist elements: by calling for the establishment of an Islamic caliphate they will alienate not only the Iraqi resistance factions but also our supporters in Syria and the Gulf countries. The last thing these countries want to see is a Taliban state as a neighbour.' Clashes had erupted between al-Qaeda fighters and Iraqi rebels, although on a limited scale, after al-Qaeda executed a group of Iraqi fighters who they claimed were spying for the Americans.

'They called for my blood when I once said from the pulpit that you can't build a nation on car bombs.' (Hameed's religious education meant he would sometimes give the Friday sermons.) 'There aren't many al-Qaeda fighters in this area, no more than fifteen, but they're still a problem. What can we do with them? We can't hand them over to the Americans or the Shia government, that's not allowed in our religion.'

If he couldn't hand the al-Qaeda fighters to the Americans, he could at least thwart their plans. That night when everyone left the garden, he called an American officer stationed nearby. He handed me the phone and asked me to translate. Pretending that I was a local English teacher, I relayed Hameed's message – that a land mine had been planted on the main road, with a detailed description of the spot.

Two days later, during the referendum, Hameed and his men provided security for a local school that was being used as a polling station. Some men stood on the roof, others were scattered outside. The al-Qaeda fighters didn't attack, perhaps deterred by Hameed and his gunmen, or trying to avoid a confrontation for the time being. Hameed also ensured that the new constitution was rejected in his area, stuffing ballot boxes with referendum sheets already marked with a clear 'No'.

After the referendum, a friend of Hameed's drove me out of the district. He was a short and thin Salafi preacher with an enormous bushy beard and very short white dishdasha, revealing his spindly legs and giving him a slightly comical look. Driving along the 'Mujahideen road' out of the village, we came across an American patrol. The soldiers surrounded the car and asked us to step out and raise our hands. If they found my cameras, I would be in serious trouble – journalists working among the insurgents were regularly detained for long periods. The American soldiers, however, were more interested in the Salafi cleric. 'We found bin Laden,' one of them said laughing. The whole platoon lined up for pictures with him, pointing at him with their machine guns, and making monkey faces, like children playing with their new pet animal, before they let us go.

———

A decade and a half later, in the ruins of the city of Mosul, after the defeat of the Islamic State militants, the last incarnation of that Sunni rebellion, a former military scientist who had worked under Saddam, explained the dynamic and the mentality that formed the logic of the Sunni insurgency. 'Resistance did not come out of love for Saddam. Many of us hated him, and we used to talk about him in whispers. Saddam had wasted our lives according to preordained rules and regulations. You finish university and join a "Brave" platoon to go and fight in one of the "Glorious" battles of the "Great" Leader and come back wrapped in the nation's flag as "Martyr". You died bureaucratically. We were hungry for change, and people were optimistic to see a new dawn after he was gone. Instead dark nights came, in which death became chaotic and random.

'We hated the American occupation. The Americans were Israel, and we have a genetic hate towards Israel. With the Americans came the Iranian interference, so we had to oppose the new situation, we had to contrast ourselves to the Shia expansion and "Sunnism" became the opposition. Some of the Baath Party members and their followers who were once secular eventually joined al-Qaeda and later the Islamic State. They joined not because there was a so-called marriage of convenience or a conspiracy between Baathists and the jihadis – this is a myth and a misconception. They joined to find a position of authority for themselves. They didn't lack the money, but they missed the power. The party was everything to them, and it was now gone, and with it, their authority and status.'

17

Saddam's Trial

I SAW THE LEADER NECESSITY in person twice. The first time was in 1988 when I stood, a thirteen-year-old, with thousands of other schoolchildren from across Baghdad, lining the airport highway, dressed in white shirts and holding yellow and blue ribbons in our hands. We waited under the scorching sun until the motorcade passed. We waved our ribbons furiously and watched our Leader standing tall and handsome in the back of the Presidential Mercedes convertible. Next to him the king of Saudi Arabia was old and frail. Both held their hands in the air.

The second time I saw him was when he was led in front of a panel of judges to be charged with crimes against humanity, in the former Baath Party headquarters in the Green Zone, converted into a special court to try the former president and his aides.

The Leader was captured by the Americans on 18 December 2003, and spent more than three years in American custody where he was described as perceptive and gentle, taking diligent care of his plants while he tried to convince the Americans that he could end the insurgency.

I sat at the back of the court with a handful of other journalists. The curtain was pulled back, and light swept in through the thick double-glazed floor-to-ceiling windows that separated us from the defendants and the judges. A portly court bailiff wearing a pair of jeans and a shirt shouted in a loud and screeching voice: 'Defendant

Saddam Hussein al-Majid.' A guard opened the door of a steel cage as another opened the big wooden door in the side of the court chamber.

Saddam, shorter and thinner than I remembered from our last encounter, was dressed in a dark grey suit and a white shirt. His black hair was combed back, his salt-and-pepper beard thick and neatly trimmed. He was holding a copy of the Quran stuffed with papers, and walked into the court slowly and deliberately. He entered his cage and sat on one of the big leather chairs. 'Ya Allah,' he said as he sat, with the air of one settling down to the day's work.

There he was, the omniscient, omnipresent, larger-than-life conqueror and Leader, the man who haunted our lives for three decades. Sitting a few metres in front of me.

The prosecution team with their red-trimmed robes were arrayed along one side of the room; on the other sat the defence team with green-trimmed robes. Five judges, wearing black robes, sat behind the raised wooden bench, beneath a Quranic verse inscribed on the marble wall: 'If you judge, judge with justice.'

It was the twenty-fourth session of the court and seven months into the trial. Saddam was officially being charged with crimes against humanity.

The chief judge began to read the charges: 'I accuse Saddam Hussein al-Majid that when you occupied the position of the president of the republic . . . you ordered an organised attack using different weapons on the town of Dujail . . .' He continued reading for fifteen minutes.

The list of charges included wilful murder, forcible deportation, imprisonment and deprivation of physical liberty under severe conditions – in violation of international law – torture, and other inhumane acts that caused great suffering or serious physical or mental injury.

'How do you plead – innocent or guilty?' asked the judge.

Saddam walked to the dock within the cage and stood before the microphone. The judge, a frail old Kurd who resembled a grumpy schoolmaster, moved quickly, anticipating one of the long political monologues the Leader was famed for. 'Just answer guilty or not guilty.'

Saddam did not comply. 'I cannot give a short answer to your lengthy argument. Do you want me to answer you here in front of public opinion with two words? For me, your accusation won't shake one hair on my head. I don't care about you; I care about the people . . . I cannot answer you with a "yes" or a "no". You have made a long speech, and I cannot say "guilty" or "not guilty". You are in front of Saddam Hussein, the president of the Republic of Iraq . . . I am the president of the republic by the will of Iraqis, and I respect their choice. I do not recognise the agents who were brought here under banners and given titles and became political officials . . .'

After several minutes of reminding the court who he was, he sat down in silence.

Watching the court proceedings, you got the feeling that the verdict had long been decided, and the judge was simply trying to impose some order on a farce.

A fair trial might have shed light on our history, answered questions like: Why did we fight Iran? Why did we invade Kuwait? But the Americans and their Iraqi lackeys settled on a form of victor's justice, which served no greater truth, and inadvertently turned Saddam into a hero in the Arab world and Iraq, appearing as a dignified old veteran carrying his Quran and watching frantic little men jump around him. Rather than close the chapter of his rule, the show trial allowed him to live on, memorialised in that moment, with his bearded portrait adorning posters and stickers on car windscreens from Sana'a to Kabul. The trial was a favourite reality TV show in the Arab world. Saddam's speeches provided an intoxicating brew to hopeless Arabs looking for any form of heroism, even if it came from a dictator who had led his people to destruction.

On 22 December 2006, the first day of Eid, the former Leader was delivered into Iraqi custody and executed. The execution was filmed by one of the men on the gallows. The grainy images showed Saddam standing tall refusing to have his head covered – Long live the nation, Long live Palestine – then before he could finish his shahada, the right of every Muslim, the gallows trapdoor was opened, and the heavy body swung as the executioners began chanting the name of the Shia cleric, 'Muqtada . . . Muqtada . . .'

Later, his body was flown by helicopter to the house of Prime Minister Maliki, who was celebrating his son's wedding. The grotesque pettiness of Iraq's new masters ran rampant as the shroud was pulled back to allow guests to photograph the corpse.

18

A Civil War is Born

2004, Najaf, Pass.

IN FEBRUARY 2006 AL-QAEDA'S JIHADIS bombed the Shia al-Askari shrine in Samarra. In the following days the Mahdi army militiamen, along with Ministry of Interior commandos, fanned out across Baghdad, kidnapping and killing hundreds of Sunni men, attacking Sunni mosques and driving thousands of Sunni families from their homes. For the international media, this was the watershed moment when the civil war began. However, the gradual slide into civil war had actually begun more than two years earlier. When the violence acquired a sectarian character; when insurgents began to execute Iraqi soldiers not only because they worked with Americans but because they were Shia; when the frantically stoked 'us' versus 'them' scenario of 'Sunni jihadis' and 'Shia collaborators' became a reality, enshrined in myth and ideology and propagated by a sectarian political discourse. Amorphously felt differences solidified into physical and psychological lines of fissure.

Maybe the expression of sectarian identities wouldn't have led to civil war had it not been combined with the calls to avenge a madhloumiya, whether it was the oppression of Shias during Saddam's regime or the victimisation of Sunnis under the new one. The cycle of madhloumiya combined with violence and toxic sectarian rhetoric enabled the demonisation of entire communities.

As always in times of upheaval, Baghdadis reverted to smaller structures to survive, clustering around clans in secure neighbourhoods or the mahalas. When the state failed to protect or provide for its citizens, the 'tribe', 'family' and 'sect' emerged as alternative power structures and a replacement of the larger state. Even before the Americans had installed walls separating districts, terrified locals had barricaded their own streets with tree trunks, barrels and concrete blocks, turning neighbourhoods into small isolated communities to better protect themselves. A few young men, often the tough street kids, stood guard, wielding Kalashnikovs and pistols to stop strangers from entering their areas. They clustered around the local mosque or the clan. A cleric, a former officer or a well-known thug became a 'Leader' and led these gangs of toughs. The locals simply referred to them as the 'gunmen'. The role of these 'gunmen' evolved from protecting the neighbourhood against outsiders to purifying it of the enemy within. They pointed out the 'strangers' living in their midst, and 'collaborators' were denounced, killed or driven from their homes. Cleansing a neighbourhood of collaborators expanded to the expulsion of all who belonged to the other sect. The process spread throughout the city, dividing it along sectarian lines to be negotiated with extreme caution. A family name could help you pass a checkpoint or get you kidnapped and killed.

But rather than a simple binary division of Sunni and Shia, the civil war was inclusive of a wide range of localised schisms and fault lines, feuds based on class or geography or long-dormant tribal feuds.

A battle-hardened corporal in the Iraqi special force named Hayder once explained it to me.

'Civil war in our area started with a football match,' he said, laughing. His village, al Madain, was a farming community south of Baghdad. The landlords were from a local Sunni tribe; the farmers were Shia from the south of Iraq, who had moved to the area back in the fifties to work the land. The children of the landowners and the farmers played football together. After one match, in 2004, a fistfight broke out, and a Sunni boy was beaten up. Shortly afterwards, three cars with no licence plates arrived and snatched a Shia farmer, whose family grabbed their guns and went after the kidnappers. Clashes erupted between the two communities. Outsiders moved in to capitalise on the communal strife; Mahdi army militiamen came in support of the Shia, and al-Qaeda came ostensibly to support the Sunnis. Hayder was a child when the fighting broke out then; his family were Shia. He wanted to join the fight but was not allowed. Instead, he loaded ammunition magazines and ferried mortar shells to the men who were doing the fighting.

Within a year, however, the original conflicts had usually been forgotten, and fighters were simply drawing a direct line from the violence in the streets of Baghdad and Fallujah and Najaf to the eternal Sunni–Shia struggle over the legacy of Imam Hussein and the interpretation of Islam.

The Americans, who like all conquerors aimed to simplify their occupation of a society by breaking it into components, later used one component (Shia) to fight the insurgency of the other (Sunni), thus exacerbating the problem of sectarianism.

Neighbourhoods in east and west Baghdad fell under the de facto control of militias and insurgents respectively. Each area had a distinct identity, expressed with its own symbols, posters and slogans, and its martyrs. You did not need to cross a checkpoint or a physical barrier to know if you were in a Sunni or a Shia district, but it became crucial, even for local Baghdadis like myself, to arrange for someone to vouch for you or to accompany you before visiting one of these areas: outsiders were not welcome. I started collecting letters of accreditation from different organisations and rebel groups with such august names as the Supreme Council, the Army of Muhammad, the Battalions of 1920 Revolution.

———

Firas had lived all his life in Ghazaliya, one of the new suburbs in west Baghdad that was built in the seventies during the oil boom years. By the new sectarian definitions of the city, he was a young Shia man, although – like most of his friends and neighbours, some Sunni and some Shia – the sectarian identity had played no significant role in his life beyond celebrating certain holidays and not observing others.

Things began changing towards the end of 2003: the usual gatherings of neighbours in gardens and on street corners had become toxic, and a source of friction, with arguments like 'Shia are collaborating with the Americans . . . Sunnis are killing innocent Shia . . . No, they are killing the collaborators . . . Saddam was a dictator . . . At least he wasn't a foreign occupation . . .'

As in other neighbourhoods in west Baghdad, close to the towns

126

of Fallujah, Ramadi and Abu Ghraib that had fallen under the control of Sunni insurgents, gunmen established a presence from the early days of the war, and soon after, fear settled in. Those who dared to criticise or oppose them were killed or driven out. People started treating Firas and his fellow Shias as outsiders, as though Firas was himself an Iranian agent. When a few Shia men were kidnapped and killed, and he himself received death threats, he decided to leave. Through a friend at work, he found a Sunni family that was moving out of the now Shia district of Shu'ala across the highway. The two families agreed to exchange houses.

The highway and a wasteland in front of his new house had become the front line between Ghazaliya and Shu'ala, infamous as a dumping ground for bodies. 'Sometimes they shoot them on the spot: old men, young men, some in dishdashas, some in pyjamas, they bring them and dump them in front of everyone. Even if they are Sunnis it doesn't make me happy to see them – I tell myself one day I will end up like them,' he told me when we met.

———

On the other side of the highway, in Shu'ala, Firas's new neighbourhood – a working-class suburb in north-east Baghdad – the Mahdi army militia, along with units of the Ministry of Interior commandos, had driven most of the Sunnis out of the area after kidnapping and killing a few of them. Militiamen blocked the roads leading in and out of the area, and sprayed graffiti on the doors of other Sunni businesses. One of the men who led the cleansing campaign in Shu'ala was Abu Karrar, an intelligence officer in the Mahdi army. He was in his mid-forties, a heavyset, wide-shouldered man, with sinister looks, who had been a corporal in Saddam's army.

'I have men everywhere, ready for any attack from them,' he

told me. 'Them' from Abu Karrar referred exclusively to the Sunnis. 'We have eyes all over Baghdad, even in the Sunni areas we have our agents — we send people to open a cigarette stall and report for us. We investigate the suspects, and then we get them.' He told me how a few days earlier he had received a tip-off from a fellow Shia about a Sunni 'terrorist' group who 'were killing our Shia brothers'.

'What did you do to them? Did you interrogate them?' I asked.

'We don't need interrogations or trials – the informants had sworn by the Quran. We took them to the Seda and finished them there.'

Seda was a dirt berm on the edge of Sadr City north-east of Baghdad. Bodies often ended up there.

Abu Karrar explained that the Mahdi srmy was not only killing the enemy, they were also providing services, like getting gas cans from the plant and delivering them to the people for a nominal price. 'We give the people what the government is unable to provide: services and protection, and the people support us because they are tired of the killing, we can protect them, the police, the commandos even the traffic police help us, they give us tips about strangers coming to our areas.' Listening to Abu Karrar talking about the Mahdi army one might get the impression that he was running a humanitarian NGO, but in the realities of civil war, he and the other commanders were little more than freelance criminal gangsters running their own death squads. Using the pretext of fighting Sunni extremists to enrich themselves – with the average ransom for a hostage standing at $5,000 and sometimes reaching up to $20,000 – being a militia commander was becoming a very lucrative job, especially when the average salary of a government soldier was $500 per month.

He walked around the neighbourhood with a swagger, that of an important man, and kept a pistol tucked in his trousers. The civil war had given men like him a purpose and a meaning. By the end of the war those men, or at least the ones who survived, had become wealthy from the expropriated property and protection money they extorted from the people. Many attached themselves to the ruling religious parties; some were elected to parliament. They became part of the new patronage networks of the new Iraq, investing their money in the property markets in Dubai, Amman and Erbil.

19

The Spy

FEW COULD NAVIGATE THE FRONT line of a civil war between Sunni insurgents and Shia militias like Fadhel. He came from a family of farmers who had benefited from the Land Reform Law of the seventies. They moved out of their small mud house on the outskirts of (Shia) Najaf and took a loan from the Agrarian Bank to buy a farm in the rich fertile area of Yusifiya, south of Baghdad, an area inhabited by a few Sunni tribes. At that time, it was a matter of moving from one province in Iraq and settling in another. A decision that initially seemed inconsequential. Fadhel went to school with Sunni and Shia kids and in the early nineties joined the Iraqi army and became a corporal in the military police. A year after Baghdad fell, the family started receiving threats, which they ignored at first. Where would they go? They had been living there for three decades. Then a neighbour, also a farmer from the south, was kidnapped; his body was found dumped in a ditch. Fadhel's family along with another half a dozen Shia families left. Their farm had become part of what was called the 'triangle of death', where jihadis kidnapped and killed Shia, foreigners and soldiers. The family moved to the Shia suburbs in east Baghdad, squatting in a government compound. Fadhel and his brother then joined the Mahdi army militia to exact revenge on Sunnis and defend fellow Shias.

'We had fifteen dunams of the best lands. I was born there and worked there all my life: they told us, you Shia are not from here, go

130

away,' Fadhel told me when I met him in 2006. 'I joined the Mahdi Army not because I want to dress in black and kill, but because I want to serve my imam and my people.'

He was twenty-six years old, lean and well muscled. His face was framed by an oily flop of hair and a very thin goatee. He was addressed as Sayed, an honorific given to the descendants of the Prophet. He showed me a big square laminated card identifying him as an 'Amir Faseel', or Platoon Commander, in the Mahdi army, a unit of around thirty-five fighters. He had fought against the Americans in Sadr City and Karbala and twice had been seriously injured.

As militias and insurgent checkpoints mushroomed all over Baghdad and the city began to divide along sectarian lines, Fadhel's childhood in south Baghdad became his most important asset, when a man's accent and his ID card were more valuable than his gun.

'My ID card is registered in Yusufiya [a Sunni town], and I can speak in their accent, so I can come and go to Sunni areas without anyone knowing that I am a Shia.' Meanwhile, his Mahdi army laminated card assured him of safe passage through Shia checkpoints.

Because of his ID card, accent and military training, Fadhel became a commander of a strike unit, whose main job was kidnapping the Sunnis allegedly involved in attacking Shia areas. He and his men were one of the many Shia militia units responsible for the scores of bodies dumped in the streets every day, shot and killed execution-style.

'We receive intelligence, and we go grab them, we go deep into their areas, and look for them. These days, the Sunnis are changing their names, sending their women to do shopping. The Sunnis have lost, this is a victory for the Shia. We didn't start it, they did,' he told me.

Fadhel rented a small flat in Dora – once a mixed area with Sunnis, Shia and a sizeable Christian community, now one of the main battlefronts of the sectarian war – and began making friends. 'I live with them, pray like them, I even insult the imams and the Mahdi army.'

He spoke about his main 'achievements' with a big smile on his face. A month earlier, he had identified and kidnapped a group of three Sunni men who were involved in killing Shia. 'We first informed a nearby Iraqi army checkpoint that we were from the Mahdi army, and we were arresting terrorists; we attacked them, put them in the boot of the car and drove them back to Sadr City.'

In Sadr City, the vast Shia slums, home to two million people and the stronghold of the Mahdi army, Fadhel said a separate 'committee' interrogated the men and ordered their execution.

He explained the mechanism of the kidnappings: 'We ask the families of the terrorists for ransom money, and after they pay the ransom, we kill them anyway. This money we use to buy weapons, or provide services for the people.' Just like his Sunni counterparts, the kidnap money was providing one of the primary reasons for the raging civil war.

Baghdad was no longer my city; it did not matter that I had lived there for three decades. I obtained several fake ID cards, with different tribal and family names on each to be used in different parts of the city. But knowing which gunmen manned each checkpoint was itself a challenge. I needed contacts on both sides of the front lines, sometimes I had to travel with two people, each with their own set of contacts, to help us negotiate Sunni insurgents or Shia militia checkpoints.

20

The Wedding

IN THE MIDDLE OF THAT civil war, Akram and Zainab fell in love.
They saw each other a couple of times, spent long nights talking on
the phone and decided to get married. They decided this should be
as soon as possible, their families said yes, and all was set. However,
there remained one problem: Akram was a Sunni, and Zainab was a
Shia, and they lived either side of the front line. Zainab's house was
in Gray'at, and Akram's was in Seliekh.

Seliekh, a neighbourhood in north-east Baghdad had a mixed
Sunni and Shia population. A significant portion of its residents
migrated from Sunni villages in the provinces of Diala and Ramadi,
in the fifties and sixties. The children of the migrants enrolled in
schools to become government employees or serve in the army and
police; they formed the nascent urban middle class that thrived in
the seventies and eighties with government subsidies, loans and easy
access to employment.

Gray'at, on the other hand, retained the feeling of a village-like
community of Shia farmers, with palm groves, flower nurseries and
fish restaurants sprawled along the banks of the Tigris.

Once upon a time, people in the two neighbourhoods lived hap-
pily side by side. Sunnis and Shia moved freely from one area to the
other. There were no barricades or front lines, no risk of men getting
killed because they showed the wrong ID card at a checkpoint.

In the post-2003 sectarian landscape, the Shia community in

Gray'at were revelling in their new-found religious identity, exhibiting Shia banners and slogans. Simultaneously, the residents of Seliekh, especially those who served in the army and police, were feeling the discriminations of the new government. Insurgent activities in Seliekh led to American and Iraqi army raids that picked up young men randomly, many of whom were brutally tortured. The fact that both neighbourhoods sat to the north of Adhamiya, an epicentre of Sunni jihadi insurgency, exacerbated the tensions between the two communities.

In Seliekh, the radical and charismatic imam who had recruited Ahmad and his gym friends to form a small insurgency cell attacking the Americans began telling the people of Seliekh that these slogans and banners were signs of Shia attempts at dominance, and therefore – according to his logic – Iranian expansionism. The young gunmen responded by delivering death threats to the Shia families living in the area. These families were not foreign settlers or outsiders but part of the fabric of the area. The community was terrorised by the killings of alleged 'collaborators and spies' in the middle of the market. Many were driven out, often forced to sell their houses dirt cheap to the same people who threatened them. Identifying a Shia family became a lucrative source of income for the commanders. Some of the Sunni families tried to stand up to the gunmen, protecting their Shia neighbours or hiding them in their own houses, but the gunmen succeeded in 'cleansing' Seliekh of its Shia residents.

The Mahdi army militia began manning checkpoints in and around Gray'at and kidnapped Sunni men as they left Seliekh and drove to work. The bodies of the kidnapped would appear in sewage canals a day or two later. In the space of a couple of years, a siege mentality evolved and the quiet, peaceful neighbourhoods of Seliekh and Gray'at were surrounded by sandbag fortifications and barricades of palm trunks and metal boxes. Lethal skirmishes erupted between the two sides every few days, and mortar fire was regularly exchanged across neighbourhood boundaries.

———

In modern times a mixed marriage between Sunnis and Shia was the most common and normal thing: class, education, family background and suchlike were far more important factors in approving or preventing a marriage. But in the midst of a civil war, marrying into the other community was akin to treason. 'Some of my cousins objected to me marrying a Shia woman, but most of my family were fine with my decision. We Iraqis never had sectarian discrimination before,' Akram, a tall, burly man with a thin moustache and smart eyes, told me. A few months before his wedding, the family had accepted a Shia suitor who had proposed to Akram's sister. The young man, who lived in a Sunni area, was killed by gunmen a few days later.

In the middle of chaos and civil war, how does one organise a wedding? According to Iraqi law, the marriage should be conducted in the district courthouse where the bride and the groom were registered – and which was in Adhamiya, at that time one of the most dangerous areas in Baghdad. It was a risk for Akram to go there alone: 'outsiders' – even Sunnis – were in danger of being kidnapped by the local gunmen. Taking a Shia bride and her family with him was suicidal.

He had to devise a plan.

'First, I had to get Zainab into my neighbourhood, so we sent the women from my family to escort her; women can move easier than men and they weren't stopped at checkpoints. They crossed the front line into Gray'at and brought her in.'

Marwan, a local Sunni insurgent from Adhamiya and an old school friend of Akram, escorted the wedding convoy to the courthouse. The market street of Adhamiya was deserted; it had turned into a venue for clashes between Sunni insurgents and Shia army soldiers and commandos, targeted by car bombs, IEDs and mortars.

'We arrived at the courthouse, my bride and her relatives yellow with fear. Marwan stood outside keeping an eye on the street, everything went well, and we got married.'

Akram thought the worst was over, but the bride's family had a request: according to Shia traditions a marriage must be blessed by a sayyid, a Shia cleric descended from the Prophet's family. They wanted Akram to cross the river from Adhamiya to Khadimiya, where a holy Shia shrine was situated. Like every other Shia area, it was heavily guarded by militiamen and commandos.

'I tried to reason with them, but they said, we went with you to Adhamiya, you come with us to Khadimiya.'

Another military-style operation was organised and Akram found himself in the office of a Shia cleric.

'When he asked for the marriage certificate and realised that I was a Sunni, I was sure I wouldn't make it back to my home, but the sayyid calmed me down.'

Now both Akram and his wife live with his family in Seliekh.

'Every time she wants to go and see her family, I walk her to the edge of Seliekh, and she crosses the front line alone. I come back after a few hours and walk her back home. I am afraid that a day will come when the only place we can live together is somewhere outside this country.'

———

In the abandoned streets of Seliekh a few men huddled around bonfires, at night. Smoking and drinking hot tea, attempting to guard the area against the incursions of Shia militiamen. Every man was required to either take part in these vigilante groups or contribute financially. Very few dared to leave the area at all. The fighters called themselves mujahideen, but the locals simply called them 'the Gunmen'. They slept during the day, and woke up sometime in the late afternoon, locked inside their fortress-like neighbourhoods; there was no work to be done. Their only job was looking for infiltrators and shaking down residents for contributions; at night they spread across the area waiting for the other side to attack, constantly on the phone to their network of lookouts and spies. In the dynamic of civil war, they had evolved into a mafia and a protection racket, enriching themselves with the stolen cars and confiscated houses of Shia residents, protection money disguised as contributions and kidnappings for ransom. The war fuelled an economy of its own.

At dusk in a deserted Seliekh street, not far from my old high school, small electrical generators were humming, and light glowed in a few windows, but most of the walled houses were dark with no signs of life. There was little evidence in this part of Baghdad of a civil war raging; no destroyed buildings, pockmarked facades, and no wailing women in black. There were no signs that this mundane street – which ran between the river Tigris on the left and a major highway on the right – was prime real estate in the geography of civil war, used by Americans, militiamen, commandos, death squads, jihadis and civilians.

Earlier that evening, a car had made the deadly mistake of passing twice in the street. It was intercepted on its return by men who stopped the driver at gunpoint, forced themselves into the car, and drove it and its passengers away, all within a few minutes.

'It's OK, it's OK, we will just check their IDs and take the measures,' bellowed one of the gunmen from inside the car to the bystanders who stood watching.

'I am sure they are members of the Mahdi army,' said one of the brave men standing in the street.

'The man sitting next to the driver was wearing a black shirt – did you see him?' said a third, displaying the micro-xenophobic civil war mentality.

Within five minutes, the street was quiet again.

———

The friend who took me to Seliekh, a man who had loved to spend his evenings drinking ouzo in other parts of the city, had found himself forced to stand with other confused young men waiting aimlessly for the outsiders to attack.

'They came to me one evening and told me, you have to come out with us and protect your neighbourhood. I told them I didn't want to, I don't like shooting others. They said, then you are a collaborator. I can't say no and I don't want to kill Shia. I know these people are not protecting the neighbourhood: they go around shooting at Shia houses, they kidnap Shia people who have been living here for years. I am between two fires, my Sunni neighbours who would kill me if I don't go out with them into the street, and the Shia militia.' He paused before correcting himself. 'No, three fires – there are the Americans too.'

21

The Baghdad Morgue

IT WAS A SWELTERING AND humid day in May 2007, and twenty men gathered in the courtyard of the Baghdad central morgue, next to a white plastic sign that pointed to 'The Refrigerator'. Inside sat a clerk, his computer monitor turned towards the men who pressed their faces against the metal bars of his window and watched in silence as pictures flickered on the screen: a man with a swollen face blackened with bruises; an older man, maybe in his fifties, with a white beard and an orange-sized hole in his forehead; a man lying on a green stretcher, his arms twisted unnaturally beneath him . . . The slide show went on, and occasionally someone at the back pushed forward to try and get a better look. The silence was often broken by someone mumbling 'No God but the one God' or 'God is great.' Some of the men covered their noses with paper tissues, others wrapped the ends of their keffiyehs around their mouths, and everyone smoked to cover the stench of death that mixed with the heavy odour of sweat and tobacco. One young man in his early twenties, with a few days' beard, stood in a corner and sobbed silently into his scarf, drops of rain fell from a grim and cloudy sky.

Women gathered some short distance away, forming small circles, wailing and beating their chests. One young woman had removed her black headscarf and was pulling at her hair.

So many dead bodies were being found in Baghdad – forty on 'quiet' days. They were mostly Sunni men kidnapped and murdered by Shia death squads – dumped in sewage plants, irrigation ditches or thrown onto the side of the roads, hands tied and a bullet in the head, often showing signs of torture. Police picked up the unidentified corpses and brought them to the morgue, where people came to enquire about their missing relatives. The numbers were so large that it became impossible to let all the people into the fridge to identify the corpses, so the officials improvised and came up with the hellish slideshow.

Every morning, pickup trucks, minibuses and taxis carrying empty coffins lined the concrete blast walls surrounding the morgue in the compound of the Ministry of Health, waiting to ferry the claimed corpses to cemeteries. Slogans calling for unity, brotherly love and patriotism were painted on the blast walls, while the trash of plastic bags and bottles collected at their base, caught by the coils of razor wire. A huge mural of Muqtada's dead father stood at the entrance. Armed family members sometimes waited in the vehicles clutching their weapons, because reclaiming the body was itself a risk. The Ministry of Health was under the control of Muqtada al-Sadr, staffed by members of his militia, the same organisation that was responsible for so much of the killing. Being killed while attempting to retrieve the body of a relative was not uncommon.

In the days that followed the February 2006 bombings of the Shia shrines in Samarra, which had unleashed retaliatory attacks against the Sunnis in Baghdad and Basra, the head of Baghdad's morgue declared that up to 1,300 people had been killed in sectarian fighting. He was summarily removed from his job and had to flee to Jordan.

Captain Abu Ahmad, the chief security officer for the morgue, looked with a very cold smile at the official permission from the Ministry of Health, allowing me access to the morgue. 'No, you can't go inside and take pictures. Why do you want to go inside? Those inside are all terrorists, Sunni terrorists. If you want to see innocent victims go to the hospitals and see the victims of Sunni terrorism on Shia civilians. And if you're not careful you might get kidnapped and end up lying with them.'

Even in death the people of Baghdad were segregated along sectarian lines, although they were all killed by similar men in their different incarnations as Shia militia or Sunni insurgent.

22

Migration, Part 1

EACH DAY, THE RASAFA PASSPORT office in east Baghdad served a different neighbourhood, accepting a hundred applications only. If a resident of that specific neighbourhood failed to submit their papers on the allocated day, they would have to wait another month for their next turn. Tens of thousands of Iraqis were trying to flee the country each day, running away from jihadis, militiamen or just trying to find work away from the murderous atmosphere in Iraq. The violence had left very few options for the people of Baghdad. They could stay at home, keep a low profile and only venture out if it was strictly necessary. They could try to leave Baghdad and stay with relatives in another city. The safest option was to pack up, sell what could be sold and join the millions of Iraqis in the diaspora spread across neighbouring countries.

The passport office, like all government buildings, was surrounded by high grey concrete blast walls. Outside the walls, people congregated around tea sellers, photocopying machines and dozens of men promising a passport for a hefty price.

A skinny, Kalashnikov-toting teenage policeman stood guard at the entrance, a tooth gap between two slabs. Another policeman sat on a bench behind a bundle of razor wire. First, the crowd of people crammed inside the cold and filthy yard had to obtain a passport form. There were young men in tight jeans, women in black abayas holding their children, professional middle-aged men and

women: all had merged into one mass of bodies trying reach a small
window at the other end of the yard. They shoved and pushed; a
woman elbowed her way to the window, a man swore and shouted.
Outstretched arms frantically waved files, fists clutched at the metal
railings of the window, everyone desperate to submit their papers
and leave. A thick cloud of fear and anxiety filled the air – the pos-
sibility of a suicide bomber blowing himself up amid the crowd, a
recurrent pattern these days, especially in Shia neighbourhoods in
east Baghdad.

A woman in her late thirties, hijab wrapped tight around her face
and dressed in a long coat, squeezed herself against the metal railings and shouted to the two officers in plain clothes sitting behind
the window.

'I have been here since eight in the morning, may Allah protect
you, I can't wait another month, for just one form.'

A man standing next to her said contemptuously, 'Eight . . . heh,
I have been here since six and one of the officers is a friend of my
cousin.'

'No more forms today,' said one of the two officers, from behind
the grille. They left the room, carrying a few spare forms under their
arms, to be distributed later among relatives and people willing to
bribe their way up the bureaucratic queue.

For the lucky ones who had got a form, the day had just begun:
a day to be spent inside the dark and muddy corridors of the new
Iraqi passport office in the democratic, post-Saddam bureaucracy,
where the heavy smell of urine hung in the air.

After completing the form, it had to be stamped at one window,
then at another window people queued for an officer to check that
all their supporting documents were in order. Affecting a look of
severe condescending boredom, he scribbled a 'yes' on each form.
The process was continually interrupted by fellow officers ferrying

files to be signed for absent dignitaries, who would get their passport delivered to them within a few hours without having had to show their faces at all. After the signature, the mass moved to another queue outside the registration window, and then to another outside the computer room, where they were each issued a reference number. On that specific day, the computer didn't work, and two women were allocating numbers manually. Eventually, applicants reached the final window where two officers took the applications, completed another form and a collection receipt, and told them when their passport would be ready.

The officers kept shouting at the people to organise themselves. A Christian man, in his late sixties, stood with his three daughters, stretching out a hand filled with forms towards the officer, who ignored him as he fiddled in his pocket looking for cigarettes.

'Can you write in the Profession section that I was an English-language teacher?' the man said anxiously, but in a very clear and loud voice.

'There is no Profession section in the new passport,' replied the officer eventually without moving his eyes from the papers.

'But if I apply for a visa to Australia, how would they know that I am a teacher?' asked the man.

'There is no Profession section,' the officer repeated.

'Don't worry, haji,' said a young man in the queue, 'no one is giving Iraqis a visa.'

A few minutes later, the Christian teacher, grumbling but happy he was leaving, was given a slip to collect the passports in six weeks.

A burly young man, wearing thick glasses, submitted his form.

'Name?' asked the officer.

'Omar,' replied the young man. A Sunni name.

'Family name?'

'Al-Samarra'i.' A very Sunni surname.

Someone from the queue said, 'It's better to change your name now.' Another said, 'Why are they still giving the Sunnis passports?' Eyes were staring at him as if he were a specimen of a harmful creature that was not supposed to be seen in public.

The day ended with no suicide bombs, and at least another hundred Iraqis joining the queue to escape their country.

———

At least three versions of an Iraqi passport existed in the public sphere at this time. There was the old version from the days of the former regime, which the Iraqi government initially cancelled but then restored, but which no country apart from Syria accepted. Then there were the 'S' series passports issued after the invasion, hand-filled and easily forged, and no longer recognised by the EU, UK and the USA. Finally, the jewel of all passports, the much-coveted 'G' series, meeting the standards of international passports, with digital numbers and watermarks accepted more or less everywhere (should one be so lucky to obtain a visa), and very hard to forge, unless you knew someone in the passport office. Someone like Abu Ahmad.

Abu Ahmad was a very energetic, short, big-bellied officer in the Directorate of Nationality and Passports. When I first met him, he was dressed in a pair of jeans and was carrying two mobile phones and a big file of documents: ID cards, passports and photos of half a dozen people. He spoke about passports with the zeal of a wine connoisseur. 'I love passports, I love watching the process of making one, and I tell you, I have been working in the Passport Directorate for fifteen years, and this G passport is the best. It is even better than the Jordanian; you can carry one in your pocket and walk like a lord to any immigration desk around the world.'

He told me that it took six weeks to issue a passport, but with so many people trying to leave, he could help issue a passport in one week. He said if it weren't for people like him, far fewer people would have successfully left the country.

In 2007, men like Abu Ahmad, and his partner, were very important people, and not just for cutting short the bureaucracy. As the civil war in Baghdad escalated, crossing from one district to the other became virtually impossible. People found themselves cut off, and unable to visit the passport office where their names were registered because they were suddenly in the land of the other sect. Abu Ahmad, a Sunni himself, found a very lucrative business with fellow Sunnis unwilling to venture into passport offices controlled by the Shia Ministry of Interior.

'We help our brothers, by God – others charge $600 but I only take $500.' His conversation was interrupted often by calls from clients demanding news of the progress of their documents.

———

In the aftermath of the First World War and just before the formation of the state of Iraq, my paternal grandfather migrated from a small Arab village in what is now southern Turkey into Basra. Armed with a high school diploma from an American missionary school, he first found a job as a tutor to the family of a tribal sheikh and then as a clerk in the British-run port in Basra. After a few years he saved enough money to make the journey back to his village, now across international borders, and come back with a child bride, my grandmother.

My maternal grandfather, a native of Madras (Chennai), first came to Iraq in the last year of the Second World War, as an officer in the British-Indian expeditionary force that recaptured Basra. In the northern city of Kirkuk, he met the Iraqi-born daughter of a British engineer, who had come on the heels of the first British invading army in 1914, survived the Kut disaster, and lived the prosperous life of a colonial settler.

After Indian independence and the foundation of Pakistan, my maternal grandfather resigned his military commission and moved from Lahore to Kirkuk with his wife and newborn son. He found a job in the British-owned Iraqi Petroleum Company in Kirkuk. Two families of many sons and daughters were born in Iraq. They grew and established roots in the country, forming part of its nascent lower-middle class, working as teachers, engineers and government employees. They were conscripted as soldiers in the regime's armies. Cousins and cousins of cousins multiplied. Their exodus from Iraq – that land of opportunity that had attracted their grandfathers a hundred years earlier – began with the hardship of the sanctions years and culminated after the US invasion. Within three years of the toppling of the statue, almost every single one of them had left the country. Scattering all over the world, from Canada and the US to the UK, Germany, Switzerland, UAE and Australia. I, connected to Baghdad with that umbilical cord of the war, never managed to stray away from the city for more than a few months. I travelled the world first on a piece of paper issued by the occupation authority and later on a newly minted Iraqi passport, and each time returned to my city to witness another phase of destruction.

———

We Iraqis never expect to be treated like lords by any immigration officers around the world, for as long as the passports we carry have the word 'Iraq' embossed on the front. We feel fortunate if we are allowed into a country with the minimum of hassle and harassment from authorities. At Amman airport in 2008, I saw a dozen Iraqi families squeezed between their bags and bundles, some sitting on the metal benches, others sleeping on the floor with their children. They had been denied entry and were waiting to be sent back to Baghdad. Other Iraqis approaching the immigration desk avoided looking at them – it was a bad omen to exchange glances with such unfortunates. It had become all but impossible for young men to enter Jordan; those lucky enough to pass the obnoxious immigration officers underwent further interrogation by plain-clothes security officers.

Once Iraqis received their passports, the life of endless queues recommenced. Iraqis, like the citizens of other nations ruled by Great Leaders, learn how to queue from a young age. They queue outside bakeries, state-run stores for a ration of cheese, and in long lines to pay respect to Baath Party dignitaries. They queue outside conscription centres and their parents queue outside military morgues to receive their bodies. Once during the sanctions my father and I stood in a queue for hours to receive the Leader's largesse: one chicken per family. Note that a queue in Iraq does not take a linear form, but more like a large huddle of people from which arms and legs protrude. Now in their attempt to leave the country they queued outside Western embassies for visas, asylum, reunion, clutching letters from relatives and waving university certificates. They queued outside the UNHCR for papers identifying them as refugees and granting them protection from deportation. They queued for aid and food. In Damascus in the winter of 2008, there were around twenty Iraqi men and women queuing outside the entrance of the Church of Abraham in the Christian suburb of Jaramana. The church, thanks to its diminutive but highly energetic mother superior, had become a centre for helping Iraqis: food was distributed twice a week and shelter was sometimes provided. But on that sunny day, no one in the crowd knew why they were standing there.

'Do you know why we are queuing?' asked a young man.

'I don't,' replied an old woman holding her family's passports.

Other voices joined:

'They said it's for asylum seekers.'

'I heard it's for Australia, but only for people with relatives there.'

'Just queue – do you have anything else to do?'

Inside was a scene familiar to Iraqis: a crowded room, a man with a big moustache, who wrote the names, passport numbers and phone numbers of the people in a small neatly lined notebook. The nun later told me that the church guard, the moustached man in the room, didn't have any work to do so she had asked him to register the names of Iraqis in case the church received more aid. The crowd willing to register had grown so big that she had had to stop the registration two days later, fearing that the Syrian police would think she was organising a demonstration. People were becoming so desperate to leave, to get hold of an aid package, to find some hope, that they were willing to queue for hours to register in a church guard's ledger, on the off chance that someone some day might call them and offer aid, or a chance to be resettled in another country.

In an alleyway behind the church, I met Mona, a short Christian woman in her thirties, with thick black hair and a sharp nose. She had been an engineer in the Dora refinery in Baghdad. She had left Iraq a couple of months earlier after Sunni insurgents came to her house and accused her of collaborating with the Americans.

'Yes, Americans did come to the refinery, but what was I supposed to do? Tell them not to come? Who am I? I am just a small employee,' she told me, spitting her words in quick bursts.

She pulled out her mobile and showed me pictures of her office, complete with desktop computer.

'I had $600 a month, now I'm here eating my savings and waiting. But even if I have to beg in the streets, I am not going back to Iraq.'

It was an all-too-familiar refugee story: violence, sectarian threats, car bombs. Whatever their current suffering, it was still much better than what they saw in Baghdad.

———

Two weeks later, I was following Imad, a chubby 23-year-old Iraqi guy, along a path zigzagging between apartment blocks on top of a hill on the eastern outskirts of Beirut. The sun was a large orange disc sinking quickly in the dark waters of the Mediterranean and the first stars had appeared in the sky. We went to his flat, sparsely furnished with a table, two chairs, a TV set and a DVD player. Three mattresses occupied half the floorspace; the kitchen and toilet filled a small nook on the other side of the room. Five of his friends were already sitting there, waiting for him.

'We gather here every Saturday night,' he told me as we all shook hands. For the rest of the week, some sleep in the restaurants where they work or squat with other friends. 'Someone cooks Iraqi food, another prepares a shisha [water pipe], and if someone wants to masturbate, they can do it in the kitchen.' One young man, Samir, played a DVD of Iraqi songs.

Puffing the smoke of the water pipe and drinking cheap whisky mixed with mango juice, they told me their stories. They were all Shia young men, mostly from Sadr City, and they were all in Lebanon illegally. Imad had fled in 2004, travelling to Syria first and then crossing to Lebanon. 'The Lebanese won't give us visas, and it only costs $100 to cross,' he said. 'I get $300 a month working as a labourer, and every three months I manage to send $100 to my family in Iraq.' They knew the parameters. 'We avoid going out on Saturday nights, because the Lebanese police have checkpoints, and we only stay in east Beirut.'

Samir had been in Lebanon, illegally and without a passport, since 1996. In 2006, he handed over $2,500 to a smuggler who promised to get him to Europe. He was arrested in Turkey and spent a few weeks in jail in Syria until they sent him back to Baghdad.

'I spent a month in Sadr City, but I didn't leave my street. One morning I was talking to a friend; that same night they told me terrorists had killed him. When another cousin was killed in a car bomb, I knew I had to leave.'

By the end of the month, he was back in Lebanon. Over the empty whisky bottle and as the sad Iraqi music throbbed in the background, all the men talked about was reaching Europe. They discussed routes and prices, exchanged names and phone numbers of smugglers. There were various options, ranging from the deluxe with a $10,000 visa to Germany, to the cheap $2,500 one which involved crossing the mountains between Syria and Turkey on foot, from there to Greece, and then by truck to anywhere in the EU.

A business in Iraqi passports had also flourished: those who were not willing to walk through the mountains and couldn't afford a $10,000 visa resorted to buying old Iraqi passports with a visa already issued in another name.

'You get an old Iraqi passport with, let's say, an old German visa, you change the picture, and you use the passport to apply for a visa to another country,' I heard from Sa'eed, another rotund Iraqi guy who was planning an escape route. He explained that embassy officials tend to look more favourably on Iraqis who had already travelled abroad.

'All I want is to reach Europe. I don't care where, anywhere. I am not going back to Baghdad,' Samir said as he walked me down the hill late at night. 'I know this guy; his name is Abu Ali. He told me he could help me reach Turkey for $500. I will give him a call first thing in the morning.'

Within a few years a new route would open, and bigger and larger crowds of refugees would fill the streets and alleyways of Damascus, Beirut and Istanbul.

23

The Sunnis Defeated

IN 2007, BAGHDAD WAS BECOMING increasingly a Shia city; the Sunni residents had been driven from many of the mixed neighbourhoods, maintaining a presence in Adhamiya, Seliekh and some mahalas of old Baghdad in the east. But they had held on to a number of districts in the west of the city and 'cleansed' them of their Shia residents. Fighters and ammunition reached these areas from the Sunni cities of Fallujah and Ramadi. But in general, few Sunnis dared to venture out of their areas. Meanwhile, al-Qaeda and other jihadi groups continued to terrorise the city with car bombs, kidnappings and beheadings.

One afternoon in early spring, I called Hameed, the insurgent commander from north Baghdad, on his mobile phone. He was staying with relatives in the south of Baghdad. I asked if I could come and see him.

'No, it's too dangerous for you – there are a lot of al-Qaeda fighters here, you'll be kidnapped.'

'Can you come to my hotel in Karrada?'

'No, it's very dangerous for me, lots of [Shia] militia checkpoints on the way.'

The haggling went on.

'Maybe we meet on the Jadiriya Bridge?' I suggested.

'No, still dangerous.'

'Mansour?'

'Dangerous for you.'

Finally, we agreed that I would send a Shia driver to pick him up and bring him to my hotel. I sat waiting for him in the dining room. It was empty and depressing. Most of the journalists had either stopped coming to Iraq altogether or stayed in more secure places after jihadis had attacked the hotel with car bombs. The elegant white seventies furniture was stained and grimy, the red velvet upholstery dark grey and threadbare. The windows had been shattered so many times that they remained permanently covered in plastic sheets, blurring the outside world. Hameed arrived an hour later, dressed in a polo T-shirt and a pair of jeans. He had gained weight, but his handsome face was sallow and looked much smaller without his thick black beard. His eyes had lost their spark, encircled by thick dark shadows. He looked like a defeated man.

'It is not a good time to be a Sunni in Baghdad,' he said in a low voice.

I had never seen him so anxious and paranoid. He kept looking towards the door. He told me he had fled his village after the al-Qaeda commander in the area issued a death sentence against him. Al-Qaeda was now the biggest and most powerful jihadi faction, demanding total obedience, and frequently assassinating other Sunni commanders if they dared to oppose them. Hameed had been taking a stance against the al-Qaeda jihadis since they entered his area soon after the fall of the regime, opposing their indiscriminate sectarian attacks on civilians.

He said the Sunni district where he was staying was surrounded by Shia militia checkpoints and his youngest brother had been kidnapped a few days earlier. He believed that he was next on a militia list. He slumped in front of me, despairing and angry.

'We Sunni are to blame,' he said. 'In my area, some ignorant al-Qaeda guys kidnapped poor Shia farmers, killing them and throwing their bodies in the river. I told them: this is not jihad. You can't kill all the Shia! This is wrong! The Shia militias are like rabid dogs, why provoke them? I am trying to talk to the Americans; I want to give them assurances that no one will attack them in our area if they stop the Shia militias from coming.' After all the years of the civil war, Hameed was still capable of making a distinction between Shia civilians and militiamen, a distinction very few other commanders would make.

And here was a man who had spent the last three years fighting the Americans, who was now willing to talk to them, not because he wanted to make peace but because he saw the Americans as the least of the evils facing him, when compared to the Shia militias and al-Qaeda.

Many Sunni leaders found themselves in the same dilemma. They had allied themselves with the extremist jihadis of al-Qaeda in Iraq in the hope of defeating the Americans. But the jihadis had other aims; among them, the establishment of an Islamic caliphate and the domination of all other factions. To this end, they had begun a war of extermination against the Shia population, massacring thousands

of civilians. Shia militias retaliated, and soon insurgent commanders like Hameed found themselves outnumbered and outgunned, as
they tried to fend off attacks by organised militias that were backed
by the Shia-dominated security forces. Their doomed alliance with
al-Qaeda and foreign jihadis had dragged the whole Sunni community into the civil war.

A week later, Hameed invited me to a meeting with several insurgent commanders. I was asked to wait in the reception room of a Sunni
political party. A thin taxi driver with dark shades picked me up. We
drove a couple of blocks through the upscale neighbourhood of Yar-
mouk, to a house that had recently been vacated forcefully by its Shia
owners and confiscated by the local Sunni insurgents. The taxi driver
came in with me; it turned out that he too was a commander. We sat on
sofas in the dusty living room. The house had been vacated in a hurry;
cardboard boxes were stacked by the door, some of the furniture was
covered with white sheets, and a few cheap paintings lay piled against
a wall. Hameed had been meeting with several commanders (of groups
with names like the Fury Brigade, the Battalions of the 1920 Revolution and the Mujahideen Army) to discuss the strategies they had been
pursuing in their original war against the Americans, as well as the civil
war with the Shia, and what options they had left. I arrived towards
the end of the meeting. Hameed had suggested encouraging young
Sunni men to enlist in the army and the police to redress the sectarian
balance, and also to offer the Americans a ceasefire, in an attempt to
stop the Ministry of Interior's commando raids on his area. Al-Qaeda
had rejected all these measures; now he wanted other Iraqi insurgent
commanders to support him. A heated discussion was raging – to compromise and participate in the political process, or oppose and fight?
These discussions had been going on in one form or another among
Sunni politicians, insurgents and tribal leaders since 2003.

A man with a very thin moustache, a huge belly and a red keffiyeh wrapped around his shoulder, who held a copy of the Quran in one hand and a mobile phone in the other, said: 'We have to fight to liberate our country from the occupation of the Americans and their Iranian-Shia stooges.'

'My brother, I disagree,' Hameed said. 'Look, the Americans are trying to talk to us Sunnis, and we need to show them that we can do politics. We need to use the Americans to fight the Shia.' As he pleaded his point, he looked nervously at the others – openly expressing ideas like talking to the Americans could easily see him labelled as an apostate and a traitor. Many had been killed for saying much less. 'Where is the jihad and the mujahideen?' he continued. 'Baghdad has become a Shia town; our brothers are being slaughtered every day! Where are these al-Qaeda heroes? One neighbourhood after another will be lost if we don't work on a strategy.'

'If the Americans leave, we will be slaughtered,' agreed the taxi driver-commander, who sat cross-legged on a sofa.

The big-bellied man waved his hands dismissively. 'We will massacre the Shia and show them who we Sunnis are! They couldn't have done anything without American support.'

When the meeting was over, the taxi driver-commander went out first to check the road, then the rest of us followed. 'Don't look up, we could be monitored, Shia spies are everywhere,' said the big-bellied man. The next day the taxi driver-commander was arrested by Ministry of Interior commandos.

———

By December 2007, Hameed's fears were coming true. The Sunnis had been squeezed into a corner, fighting two sides at once. But by then, he had disappeared – taken by Shia militias? Sunni jihadis? His body was never found.

Like Hameed before him, Abu Aisha – a mid-level Sunni commander – had come to understand that the threat from the Shia was perhaps greater than his need to fight the occupying Americans. A former NCO in the Iraqi army, he had fought in Baghdad's western (Sunni) suburbs, but unlike Hameed, he was a follower of the extremist jihadi-Salafi Islam and his solution was different. Deep lines crisscrossed his narrow forehead, and his eyes half closed whenever he tried to answer a question. He tended to evaluate every answer for a few seconds before he spoke and seemed clinically paranoid. He claimed involvement in dozens of attacks against US and Iraqi troops, mostly planting land mines but also ambushes, as well as countless executions of alleged Shia spies. He tended to volunteer jihadi tips mid-conversation.

'We have stopped using remote controls to detonate IEDs,' he said. 'Only wires work now because the Americans are jamming the signals.' He proudly showed me grainy images on his phone, of dead bodies lying in the street, their hands tied behind their backs. He claimed they were Shia agents and that he had killed them. 'There is a new jihad now. The jihad now is against the Shia, not the Americans.' He quickly qualified his statement by saying that in Ramadi there was still jihad against the Americans, just because there were no Shia to fight there, but in Baghdad he and his group only attacked the Americans if they were with Shia army forces or if they were coming to arrest someone.

'We have been deceived by the jihadi Arabs,' he admitted, referring to al-Qaeda and other foreign fighters. 'They had an international agenda, and we implemented it. But now all the leadership of the jihad in Iraq are Iraqis.'

Abu Aisha described how the Sunnis were reorganising. After Sunni families had been expelled from mixed areas throughout Baghdad, his Sunni area in the western suburbs was methodically preparing to defend itself against any militia attack.

He listed neighbourhoods in Baghdad: 'Ameriya, Jihad, Ghazali-yah . . . all these areas are becoming part of the new Islamic State of Iraq, each with an amir in charge'. A forerunner to the caliphate of the Islamic State that would be created many years later.

Of his own efforts he said: 'Each group is in charge of a specific street. We have defence lines, trenches and booby traps. When the Americans arrive, we let them go through, but if they show up with Iraqi troops then it's a fight.'

Sunni areas in Baghdad were virtually empty of Shia. Shops could not open without the permission of the local commander; even mosque preachers were appointed by the insurgents. The Iraqi insurgency which had begun with local cells fighting the Americans, for a variety of reasons, was consolidating into larger organisations trying to hold on to territory and resources.

———

Abu Aisha introduced me to Rami, a formidable-looking man with a thick neck, wide shoulders and a broken nose. He had been a commando in the Republican Guards before the 2003 war, and later joined the insurgency. We met in Seliekh in northern Baghdad at the end of December 2007. Groups of men gathered at street corners, eyeing strangers with suspicion.

'Some of them are insurgents,' Rami told me, 'but most are just unemployed men, too scared to leave the area.'

We sat in his car talking, next to a line of barricades and small berms built to block the side streets, making it easier to defend in case of raids by Ministry of Interior troops. A convoy of two cars whizzed past us. 'Ah, they are brothers on a mission,' Rami noted. Like every man of fighting age, he was required to carry arms and be part of a local vigilante group protecting the area at night, but now he pays $30 a week to a local commander to be exempted. 'I used to attack the Americans when there was jihad. Now there is no jihad. Go look around Adhamiya [the notorious Sunni insurgent area]: all the commanders are sitting sipping coffee; it's only the young kids who are fighting now. And they aren't fighting the Americans any more, they are just killing Shia. There are kids who carry two guns each and roam the streets looking for their prey. They will kill for anything – for a gun, for a car – and all that can be dressed up as jihad.'

Rami himself has stopped fighting, turning arms dealer instead. He makes a handsome profit selling weapons and ammunition to those still willing to fight.

Until a few months earlier, the insurgency had been dependent on weapons and ammunition looted from former Iraqi army depots, but with Sunnis besieged in their neighbourhoods, fighting daily clashes with the better equipped Shia militias and Ministry of Interior forces, they required new sources of weapons and money. As Rami explained, 'If you have money, you have weapons.' He said he gets most of his supplies from the new American-equipped Iraqi army.

'We buy ammunition from the [American] officer in charge of the warehouses; a small box of AK-47 bullets costs $450. If the guy sells a thousand boxes, he can get rich and leave the country.' His point of contact was an Iraqi interpreter working for the US army in Baghdad. 'He had a deal with an American officer. We bought new AKs and ammunition from them. The American officer would divert a small truck loaded with weapons when it came across the border from Jordan before it even reached an Iraqi base.'

The difficulty was in travelling across Baghdad and crossing multiple sectarian front lines. 'I have to pay a Shia taxi driver to bring ammunition to me. He gets $50 for each shipment.'

According to Rami and other commanders I talked to, money

for the war had three main sources. Some arrived as donations from wealthy Sunni businessmen or financiers in Iraq, Jordan and the Gulf countries. Another source was dues raised from the local residents, with each household paying around $8 a week. 'And when we go through lots of ammunitions because of clashes,' said Rami, 'they pay an extra $5.' But increasingly, 'Ghanima', or spoils of war, was becoming the main resource fuelling the civil war. 'Every time they [insurgents] arrest Shia, we take their car and sell it. The money is used to fund fighters and buy their ammunition,' Abu Aisha had told me.

The mosque sheikh or the local commander collected the money which they distributed among the fighters; some get fixed salaries, others are paid by 'operations'. The money left over was used for ammo purchases.

'It has become a business; they give you money to kill Shia, we take their houses and sell their cars,' said Rami. 'The Shia are doing the same.'

Rami, Abu Karrar, Fadhel and hundreds of the so-called 'commanders', both Shia and Sunnis, had begun the fight for a variety of reasons: religious, national, protecting one's neighbourhood, sect, tribe or family. These men, who had killed, maimed and destroyed for what they believed in, had after a few years of fighting become nothing more than criminals exploiting the opportunities available to them in the chaos of civil war. And that is probably one of the most lasting legacies of civil wars. I would see it again and again in Iraq, Syria, Yemen and beyond.

24

The Schoolteacher

THE SHIA ALSO LIVED IN fear: they feared car bombs, jihadi suicide bombers exploding in the middle of their packed markets, attacks
on religious processions or at the funerals of victims of earlier bombings. They also feared the militias controlling their neighbourhoods,
ostensibly to protect them from Sunni jihadis. These had come to
resemble mafia organisations, enriching themselves from the wreckage of the civil war, while oppressing the people and dominating their
lives in the name of religion, the sect and leader.

The biggest of these militias was the Mahdi army led by the Iraqi
Shia cleric Muqtada al-Sadr. He was the youngest son of a prominent ayatollah, Muhammad Sadiq al-Sadr, assassinated by Saddam in
1999.

Muqtada and especially his father's network of disciples grew
up inside Iraq and not in exile in Iran like other Shia factions. Their
brand of militant Shia Islam had evolved during the sanctions, with
a distinctive anti-American, anti-Western message not dissimilar to
that of the regime. They were beneficiaries of the regime's Faith
Campaign just as their Sunni opponents were. While they opposed,
and resisted, the Americans, they remained locked in a power struggle with other Shia parties, especially the returning exiles, over both
the recourses available and on who could authentically claim to represent the Shia. The struggle had both social and political dimensions.
The Sadrists despised the exiles for their servile attitude towards the

Iranians, but also because Muqtada's followers were mainly poor, urban, working-class Shia, descendants of migrants who came to the cities in the fifties and sixties, while many of the exiles came from prominent old families of privilege. The exiles in return dismissed Muqtada's religious qualifications, called his followers the riff-raff of the slums, and whispered – in none-too-low voices – that his father had been a tool in the hand of the Saddam regime. (Many more militant splinter groups would schism from the Sadrists in the coming years.)

Since their early battles against the Americans and the British in 2004, the Mahdi army had evolved from bands of disorganised fighters into a well-structured organisation. Their offices were spread across Baghdad and most of the southern cities. In their biggest stronghold, the poor suburbs of Sadr City – formerly Saddam City, and renamed after Muqtada's father – they wielded more authority than the state, imposing religious codes, extorting money and providing protection. Each office was headed by a cleric appointed by Muqtada. The office supervised the activities of Mahdi army units in the area, which were led by local field commanders.

'We have intelligence units, commando strike units who train twice a week at night on street fighting, and we have explosives experts from Saddam's army who manufacture our IEDs to plant in different places in Baghdad. The most important thing is the belief: weapons can come and go, but faith comes only from God. We are trying to build our force on the same lines of organisation as Hezbollah [in Lebanon],' Abu Karrar, the intelligence commander had told me.

Living in the shadow of the Mahdi army was Ustad Ali, a high school English teacher in a boys' school in Sadr City. One winter morning in 2008, he stood in the middle of the Year 9 class, holding a textbook in his left hand and resting his right palm on the filthy rickety wooden desk. On one side of the blackboard behind him, the conjugation of the verb 'play' was scribbled in white chalk; on the other side, the words: 'Long live Sayed Muqtada. Long live Muqtada . . . Muqtada . . . Muqtada.'

In his heavily accented English, rounded by Hollywood-flavoured vowels, Ustad Ali read from the textbook: 'The great seventh-century Arab warrior Khaled bin Waleed went to fight the enemies of Islam.' He paused, looked at the bewildered faces of his young students, and asked them: 'Do you know the meaning of the word ENEMY?'

Two students raised their hands.

'Yes?' He pointed at one.

'It is "adou",' said the young student. 'That is right,' said Ustad Ali and lowered his eyes to continue reading, but he was interrupted by another student, who shouted from the back: 'Just like Amreeka.'

Ustad Ali, tall and lanky, with a very kind face, wore a slightly oversized brown suit and seemed to be smiling perpetually even when he was angry. A Tintin-like whiff of hair sprouted from his head, and he had a thin, well-trimmed beard, a signifier – according to the new sectarian aesthetics – that he was a devout Shia. He was the school principal, as well as the English teacher. If he wasn't teaching or busy with school administration, he was found in his small, dim office reading a book on politics or Shia theology.

'The schools are in a disastrous situation,' he told me when I went to see him after the class. 'I have students in the ninth grade who don't know the English alphabet.' (In Iraq, students start learning English from the fifth grade.) He looked at the teachers crammed on the sofa in his office, and leaned forward, whispering in my ear: 'The young teacher over there doesn't know the difference between N and Z. Education in Iraq is catastrophic; the real disaster will emerge when this generation grows up, a generation that only knows fear and sectarianism, whose heroes are ignorant extremists. You know, during the baccalaureate exams last year, militiamen came and wrote all the answers on the board, and no one could say anything. Some of the students threaten that if I don't let them pass the exam, the militias will know what to do to me. People are scared. If the father is scared, and he is the victim of violence, and if life in the street is controlled by militiamen and if the students don't leave their neighbourhoods because Baghdad is divided into cantons, then how can you expect a proper education in Iraq? As a teacher I think the worst thing that is happening is that the student defines himself only by his sectarian identity, he is a Shia from Sadr City or from Bayaa. There is no "watan", no nation, any more.'

Ustad Ali grew up in the slums of Sadr City, and graduated from the Teachers Institute in the early nineties. When the Saddam regime was toppled, Ali's life changed. The Shia militia, eager to exact revenge on beneficiaries of the former regime, went around threatening, and in many cases, killing former school principals who were perceived as members of the Baath Party or as sympathetic to Saddam. Ali, a devout Shia, was appointed headmaster, replacing the former headmaster – a Baath Party member – who fled the area fearing for his life. Salaries increased but poverty had yet to disappear.

'I can't blame the students,' he said. A gloomy look settled on his cheerful face. 'Some of my students are eager to finish school to get to work, selling petrol on the black market. Before 2003, my salary was $3; a teacher had to beg a student for a cigarette. Now my salary is 300,000 Iraqi dinar [around $300], but a gas can that used to be 50 cents now costs $10. I dream that one day I can buy my kids proper clothes, not the threadbare second-hand clothes I get them now. I dream of having a life with dignity. And the worst is the electricity blackouts; they make us all live in darkness – physical and psychological darkness.'

After recess, I accompanied him back into the classroom. It was a warm spring day, and the students were shabby, tired and scared. Whenever they heard an explosion, they jumped. They were all Shia; the fifteen Sunni students had left at the beginning of the civil war, replaced by thirty-five new Shia students whose families had been driven out of Sunni neighbourhoods.

'Who wants to read the dialogue?' Ali asked them.

Only one student, in a blue-striped shirt, raised his hand.

'Why has no one else prepared his homework?' Ali said.

A student sitting in the second row answered: 'Ustad, the electricity always goes off and doesn't give us the opportunity to study.'

Another student said that he and his family had had to walk to Karbala for the commemoration of the killing of Imam Hussein.

'My students,' Ali pleaded, 'what is more important? To walk to Karbala or to do your homework?'

What a stupid question, I thought, and coming from a religious Shia teacher, no less. It would have been like asking me when I was in high school whether it was better to study or commemorate Saddam's birthday. To commemorate, of course! I would have answered.

'To commemorate the Arba'een,' the students answered predictably.

'NO, NO, NO,' said Ali. 'Imam Hussein does not want you to flagellate; he wants you to study, to read. He said in one of his sermons: "I came to reform my nation" – how can the imam reform a nation with a bunch of illiterates?'

Silence . . . I looked at the name of Muqtada scribbled on the blackboard behind Ustad Ali. He knew that these words had not materialised on their own. One of those little students had a brother in the militia, or he himself was a member.

'Husham,' Ali said.

A boy at least three years older than the student in the blue-striped shirt, stood up.

'Husham, why don't you know the letters in English?'

Husham remained silent. Later Ali told me that Husham worked as an 'attag', combing rubbish dumps to collect plastic bottles and metal cans to sell for recycling.

'If we don't study, my sons, Iraq will stay like this,' Ali told his students. 'Iraq will continue to be violated.'

'But we are occupied by the Americans,' one of the students said.

After the class was over, we went back to Ustad Ali's office. He closed the door and sat on the window ledge smoking.

'How can I fix my school if the head of the education directorate is a cleric you must always address as "your eminency"? How is it possible, when he constantly tells me "this is haram" and "that is not allowed"?'

The militia that appointed him as a headmaster control the streets and they decide how the school should be run. Some of their gunmen were his own failed students. And after a few years of the war, Ali the religious and devout Shia, with his beard and the book of the Sermons of Imam Ali on his desk, found that the tyranny of the dictatorship had not ended. It had only changed its shape.

'For thirty-five years we lived under the tyranny of Saddam. I was living in fear all my life, whispering and looking around. When we were liberated from Saddam, we breathed air freely. But we didn't know that the price was the occupation, and after that, the turbaned clerics using the name of Imam Ali came and climbed to power over our shoulders. We are an ignorant nation led like sheep by the edicts of the clerics.'

When we left the school after our interview, Ustad Ali was surrounded by three young teachers for protection. Because a year earlier, when he was walking out of the school in the afternoon, a black car with four gunmen drove by. They shot him three times, twice in the back and once in the leg. He spent months in his house recuperating, and realised that someone must have heard him air his criticisms. Still limping, he stood at the threshold, looked around nervously before hopping along a path of bricks laid across the sewage-and-mud lake in front of his school. He jumped into his car and drove away quickly.

Another day of teaching done.

25

The Sadda

THE DISAPPEARED, THE KIDNAPPED, THE murdered and their murderers congregated in a place called the Sadda, which had entered Iraqi mythology as the place of no return. 'They took him to Sadda' was a much deployed euphemism.

The first time I came across it was by mistake, in October 2009. I was in the company of a militiaman and an official from Muqtada's office; they were driving me to the outskirts of Sadr City to a place called the Tin City – a slum on the edge of the slums – to show me some of their charity work. We drove along a berm road also called Sadda – the word means dam in Arabic, a reference to the old embankments built to protect Baghdad from the seasonal floods of the Diala River (one of the tributaries of the Tigris that forms the eastern boundaries of Baghdad). We passed an Iraqi police outpost, a ramshackle construction made of a few blue-painted blast walls and concrete slabs. One policeman came out of a prefab watchtower, looked inside our car, saw the militiaman's gun, and waved us through quickly, before rushing back to the safety of his shelter.

We had taken a wrong turn, and shortly after passing the checkpoint, we came across a patch of wasteland, with what looked like sticks and mounds randomly scattered across it, then we saw a second patch and a third. At first I had no idea what these sticks and mounds were, until the militiaman escorting us turned to the driver and told him joyfully:

'Wallah, this is so good! A nice fresh soil here - one could bring someone and kill him here, huh?'

And I realised that these were graves. We drove for another twenty minutes, and the road took us through a field littered with hundreds of objects, like a big scrapyard. This was the Sadda I had heard so much about.

A few days later I came back, without the militiaman this time. Organising the journey was a mini-military operation involving both Sunni and Shia friends as a precaution against being kidnapped by insurgents and/or militiamen. The place was deserted. Two kinds of people came here: the killers and their victims. I walked across the uneven earth, studded with hundreds of bits of debris and scrap metal. The carcass of an air cooler, the bumper of an old car, a bucket of paint, metal of all shapes and sizes, plastic bottles, broken pipes, a fork missing a prong. They all sprouted from the dark soil, and each marked the grave of someone killed in the civil war.

A gust of wind blew, the barren earth awoke, and dust rose in columns that walked across the fields. Green and yellow Shia flags fluttered in swirls and the breeze whipped up an overwhelming stench of the dead bodies buried under the thinnest layer of soil. Dogs limped between the graves and everything was coated in the same brownish-red.

On a parallel road, life went on; garbage trucks were going up and down, dumping their loads in nearby fields. Tankers emptied their sewage into a vast lake where a handful of local kids splashed and swam, seemingly oblivious to the ghosts of the men lying so near.

PART THREE

A New State

26

Hassan

CIVILIANS WERE STILL DYING, BUT by 2009 the worst of the killings had eased and the first stage of the civil war was over. Neighbourhoods that had been homogenised by militiamen and jihadis were now segregated from each other by American-built walls designed to control the warring communities. Day and night, flatbed trucks ferried construction materials across the city, as though sleeping giants had woken to turn invisible fault lines into front lines, marked by kilometre-long stretches of concrete slabs and coiled barbed wire.

Car bomb attacks still killed scores of people, but fewer bodies appeared every morning in ditches or in the wastelands on the out-skirts of the city.

In the space of four years, the Sunni rebellion had been defeated: Baghdad became a Shia city. Tens of thousands had been killed or 'disappeared', and hundreds of thousands more fled the country. The Sunnis who stayed remained sequestered in their areas. The Sunni gunmen and rebels who had thrown their support behind the jihadis of al-Qaeda, turning the fight against the Americans into a civil war, came to realise that they couldn't fight the Americans, the Iraqi army and the Shia militias all at the same time. They reached out to the least evil of their enemies, the Americans, and struck a deal, fighting against their former jihadi allies for the price of keeping the Shia mili-tias out of their areas. In return, the Americans promised to incorpor-ate the Sunnis back into the army and give them the employment they had lost with the occupation. One of those 'turncoat commanders' explained his recent change of allegiance to me: 'The Americans will leave one day but if the Shia occupy an area they will stay.'

During the civil war, so many men had been killed in Adhamiya – the last Sunni enclave in east Baghdad – that the local cemetery ran out of space. The residents, too scared to leave the safety of their area to take their dead to the Sunni cemeteries outside the city, turned a small park behind the shrine of Abu Hanifa into a make-shift graveyard. Soon, that new cemetery was filled with hundreds of new graves. On Fridays, families walked between white concrete gravestones, each carrying a colour photograph of a young man and adorned with plastic flowers. It was as if a plague had hit the area and only killed men of fighting age. In one corner, an old man in a white dishdasha and a red keffiyeh was sprinkling rose water from a plastic bag on his son's grave. Drawing on a cigarette, he said that his son had been killed because he was called Omar. Two women, both in black, stood behind another gravestone. One was the wife of the dead man, the other his mother, but grief had rendered them both old and haggard. Most of the men had been killed by Shia militias, but some were killed by their fellow Sunnis: the collateral damage of car bombs and land mines, or just caught up in random gun battles that raged across the vicinity.

The commander assigned a few of his men to accompany me through the area. We visited my old high school where the young men told me that the street in front of it, with its tall eucalyptus trees was a favoured dumping ground for executed victims. Near the school, there was a working-class market street where we used to take refuge whenever we skipped school. Grocery shops and car mechanics lined the market, and rickety wooden benches overflowed onto the cracked pavement from the antiquated tea houses. During the sanctions years, men sat drinking thick black sweet tea and withered away their days of unemployment.

I remembered a small and filthy cafe with two or three metal tables and rusting stools, which had served kahi – a baked flaky and layered pastry topped with clotted cream and soaked in sugar syrup – in the morning, and oily fried rolls stuffed with minced meat and cheese for lunch. We would stop there for a cheap and filling meal in those days of hardship. But on that hot day, the market was deserted, and the cafe's metal shutters were twisted and riddled with bullets. The cafes had closed long ago, and their wooden benches piled on top of each other like the dead bodies that had littered the city. A dog hobbled across the empty street towards the high concrete wall that surrounded the area, separating it from the highway beyond.

———

I knew that Hassan, an old friend of mine, had lived in the neighbourhood across that highway. He was the wittiest of my high school friends, with a filthy lacerating tongue that spared no one's mother or sister. His moustache, large forehead and the brown briefcase he carried, along with his crumpled shirts and sagging trousers, gave him the look of a middle-aged teacher when he was just fifteen years old.

On a spring day in 1992, a year after the grand defeat of the Mother of All Battles, a few of us ran away from school and spent the afternoon at his house. We must have been dodging one of the 'spontaneous' victory marches common in those days, when we waved flags and chanted slogans expressing our love of the Great Leader, and celebrated our glorious victories against the Americans, the imperialists and the Zionists. We ran away by climbing a brick wall and slipping through a gap in the metal barrier on top. We walked in single file under the shade of large eucalyptus trees, following Hassan. We walked through the market and then we crossed the highway. Hassan's house was in a newly built neighbourhood with grid-like streets. It was a typical two-storey brick home with a small front garden and a palm tree. We spent the afternoon in his spacious living room with its heavy seventies wooden furniture. Bright sun seeped through the thick curtains, and a fresh flowery smell filled the room. We poked around in drawers, opened cabinets and looked at photos; someone pulled out a cardboard box stacked with videotapes, neatly numbered and labelled. Hassan told us it was his father's film collection. We started playing them randomly, hoping for some nice old seventies German porn; instead the screen flickered with horrific images of dead Iranian soldiers on the front lines, and military parades. The Great Leader's long blabbering speeches, poetry, songs and dances glorifying him and his two sons, was the soundtrack. In one tape, the newscaster was declaring in a heavy guttural voice our victory in one of the battles in that folly of a war. The tapes were a bibliothèque of the macabre and dull broadcasts of Iraqi state propaganda. Why? Why record this? we asked in bewilderment. These

were the programmes that sent every Iraqi rushing to switch off the
TV while muttering – in a low voice – a series of curses directed at
the Great Leader and his mother.

'My father says we need to collect these archives now; one day,
he says, this will all be part of our history,' Hassan told us then. At
that time, his prophecy sounded as distant and inconceivable as space
exploration might have sounded to a group of friends in the Middle
Ages gazing up at the stars.

———

How do you go about finding someone in a city ripped apart by a
foreign invasion and a brutal civil war? I was becoming increasingly disorientated while travelling through Baghdad, with roads
closed and districts divided by walls and checkpoints. I thought if I
retraced my steps through the market, across the highway, I might
find Hassan's house, but the militiamen escorting me wouldn't go
beyond the deserted street and the safety of the high concrete walls
surrounding the area. They said that the other side of the highway
was under the control of the Shia Mahdi army, from where they still
occasionally lobbed mortars at their Sunni neighbours. In any case,
the militiamen pointed out, the bridge connecting the two sides of
the highway was blocked by coils of razor wire and barricades. So
to reach the houses just across the street, we had to leave the Sunni
area, drive down the highway, make a U-turn, and drive back again,
passing through multiple checkpoints where more gunmen stood
'protecting' their neighbourhood.

The highway that I used to travel on every day on my way to
school was now lined with tall concrete slabs, numbered by the
American units who installed them. Openings in that concrete tunnel
marked entry points to neighbourhoods on both sides of the highway.

These meaningless checkpoints, manned by young men in a variety of impromptu uniforms, consisted of a few slabs of concrete, broken chairs, barrels, bricks and more coils of barbed wire, as well as the obligatory garlanding of windblown trash. It seemed that every man in the city was manning a checkpoint of his own.

Hassan's neighbourhood was divided into blocks of identical squat two-storey houses, distributed among government employees. It had no sectarian identity before the war, but according to the very unreliable sectarian map of my high school friends, I had presumed that Hassan was a Sunni, and I was also told by our friends that he had become an army officer.

Disorientated, I drove through many streets accompanied by a 'Sunni' friend and a 'Shia' driver, asked many people, until I was directed to a house where an army officer was living. I approached with great trepidation – did he survive the carnage of the civil war? In Iraq, the missing are presumed dead until they reveal themselves. On the wall outside the house hung a black banner, a death notice – had I arrived too late? Death was no more ever a surprise in Baghdad, but the name on the death notice was not Hassan's. A young man in the street pointed to another house where another officer lived. I knocked, and no one answered; I hammered at the door, but the house was deserted. I was about to leave when a haggard and dishevelled man opened the door. The benefit of looking like a forty-year-old when you are fifteen is that when you are forty, you look the same. Hassan brought me inside. We sat in the same living room; he was bewildered at the return of a ghost from two decades ago. Happy? Maybe, but tinged with a sense of betrayal that he had been left alone all that time. How dare I come from a distant past to trouble the monotony of the present? The once elegant living room was now old and worn, thick with the dust of decades of neglect. Some of the furniture was piled in the corner covered in white sheets.

The musty smell of an antique shop hung in the air. Hassan talked like someone silent too long. Words, sentences tumbled from his mouth, describing his life of the past few years, only stopping to shake his head in disbelief and release loud shrill laughter. It was his life and not his father's video archives that had documented the miseries of the last two decades of Iraq's history.

———

Shortly after Hassan graduated from high school in 1993, his father, a highly respected English-language teacher and translator at a foreign embassy in Baghdad, was disappeared by the security services. Some said he had had too many foreign contacts; others said he was denounced for telling a joke about the Great Leader. For years, Hassan looked for him in prisons and hospitals, begged favours from connected people, and was rebuffed and warned many times to keep silent. As Hassan fell into despair, his mother became sick and died, still waiting for her disappeared husband. Alone in the big empty house, he was a pariah, avoided by family, ostracised even by his closest friends.

Hassan continued his studies at the medical school in Baghdad, and one day he saw a nephew of the Leader Necessity walking across the yard, followed by an entourage of cronies. Hassan ran after him, begging him for help in locating his father.

'I had tried everything, and I thought, if they take me away, I have nothing more to lose anyway: my mother had died of her sadness and my father was missing,' he told me. A few days later he received a phone call, summoning him to the infamous Abu Ghraib prison. There he met his father for the first time in many years. He had been sentenced to death, but the sentence had been commuted to life in prison. 'I am still indebted to that man for helping me,' Hassan said.

As the Americans amassed their armies in Kuwait in early 2003 and the war drew closer, the Leader issued an amnesty, emptying the prisons. Hassan's father staggered out of jail, dazed, along with the wretched, the innocent, the poor and the criminal who flooded out of the gates. He was a broken man, and shortly after fell ill and became bedridden. While the bombs rained on Baghdad, and the American land invasion commenced, Hassan nursed his father, feeding and washing him. He had studied medicine on a Ministry of Defence scholarship and had graduated with a military rank; now he found himself in an awkward situation. The Americans had disbanded the former army and were forming a new one – should he join the new army or stay away? What choices did he have?

He joined and was assigned to a military hospital in the Taji base north of Baghdad, becoming a surgeon in the middle of a war. 'I performed more amputations in a year than doctors in England would do in a decade,' he said. Hassan was everything his American supervisor had wished for; young, professional and untainted by the ethics of the old regime's army. They sent him for specialised training in the US and UK and he quickly rose to the rank of captain, but bad luck never abandoned him. In his journey from Baghdad to his military base, he had to travel through the district of Tarmiya, where Hameed and other insurgents were laying their ambushes for men like Hassan, who they considered collaborators. One day, the bus driver had asked the passengers if there were any Shia among them.

'I decided to trust him and said yes,' Hassan told me. I kept listening to his story, but allowed myself a brief inner smile: it was only then that I realised that my sectarian map of my friends had failed again, and Hassan was a Shia.

The driver, who was a Sunni, took Hassan's ID card and hid it under his seat. They were stopped at a random checkpoint a few kilometres away from the base, and gunmen boarded the bus and demanded ID cards. The Sunnis handed them over.

'And where is yours?' the gunmen asked Hassan.

'He is my cousin,' the Sunni driver said. 'He doesn't have one.' The gunmen let him go, and his life was saved, but the reality of being a citizen of Iraq ensured that his exposure to near-death experiences continued.

'One day in Sadr City, I looked at a car across the street, a new-model Toyota that I wanted to buy. I thought, what a beautiful car, then it just exploded right in front of my eyes. People were screaming, they ran – and I just stood watching it burn and laughed.'

He was bitter at everything he had been through. He was tired and he just wanted to run. 'I can sell the house and go anywhere.'

He ended his narrative with a plea. 'Please get me out of here. I have seen nothing but misery in this life.'

27

The New Leader

IN THE MONTHS THAT FOLLOWED, every time I travelled to Baghdad, I called on Hassan. We met in the evenings after he finished his shift at the military hospital and drove to one of the new 'trendy' restaurants that were opening in the fancy parts of the city. Life was edging towards normality despite the car bombs and the assassinations and the everyday violence. But can life ever be normal in a segregated city? Where Sunnis and Shia huddled in their separate and walled neighbourhoods and where only a year earlier one street had lobbed mortars at another? When neighbours denounced neighbours, when people were forced to sell their houses for a fraction of their value and join the trail of refugees? The civil war had violated our society and left it shattered and broken.

Hassan drove, cheerful and laughing, as in the old days, his conversation punctuated by a torrent of filthy jokes. Like the city itself, Zain's moods swung violently from disapproval to euphoria and back to despair. He was also enjoying his privileges as an army officer: the power, the pistol that lay between us in the car, the military badges that granted him VIP access through bottle-necked checkpoints, where he spoke to the soldiers in the condescending manner befitting an officer of his rank. He even sported an officer's moustache, fashioned after a style popular during the war with Iran: thick, well trimmed on the upper lip, with its ends sliding down the edges of the lower lip giving him a sinister angry look.

Hassan belonged to the new well-armed army that was projecting confidence and power in the streets after the American withdrawal, and he relished his power. It was a mongrel organisation, a mixture of Shia sectarian nationalism, the trappings of Saddam-style authoritarianism, and American gadgetry and trinkets. Gone were the days of wiry, puny, underfed, scared soldiers in mismatched uniforms. Now they stood manning the hundreds of checkpoints spread throughout the city, dressed in new uniforms, furnished with all-American paraphernalia: kneepads, M-16s, wraparound sunglasses, night-vision goggles fitted onto helmets. Their officers went back to the Great Leader era for inspiration, spewing the same old nationalist jargon – but now Shia-flavoured – dressed in eighties dark green uniforms, adorning their chests with badges and regalia, and their faces with distinctive Iraqi moustaches, and carrying proudly the tyrannical attitude that came with it all.

The Americans had packed up their bases and flags, along with their stories of men and women killed, tortured and imprisoned, and departed. Amid the lamentations and the cries of joy that declared the 'End of the War', a new Iraqi state was emerging. Flimsy and shaken, but confident in the new national narrative and awash with oil money. (It was our seventh or eighth attempt since the formation of the Iraqi state in 1921, at recreating our national myth – depending on how many coups you count.) With the new state came a new strongman, Prime Minister Maliki, who emerged as the Steadfast Leader, promising to unite the country and set it again on the path of glory and victory. The humiliation and destruction that the occupation had unleashed were so vile that even those who came to power on the back of American tanks were now distancing themselves from them and Maliki channelled all that through boisterously nationalistic rhetoric as he consolidated his power. For his detractors, his nationalistic rhetoric was a thin disguise for purely sectarian politics.

In 2008, I stood in the courtyard of the Iraqi National Museum and watched as hundreds of soldiers carrying brand-new American guns took their positions in and around the building. Armoured vehicles blocked roads for miles around, and a helicopter buzzed overhead in the dusty Baghdad sky. Outside the gates, dozens of black SUVs and pickup trucks mounted with heavy machine guns waited like loyal dogs; people pressed against the metal railings waiting for a glimpse of the Leader; banners were unfurled pleading for the dispensation of his charity. In the centre of that universe of men, guns and steel walked the Iraqi prime minister thronged by three rings of tough bodyguards, dressed respectively in dark grey suits, khaki outdoor outfits and commando fatigues. He attempted to move with the grace of the wise sombre Leader, inspecting glass cabinets filled with Sumerian seals or Islamic bowls, and listening to the eager museum official explaining the scenes in an Assyrian motif carved on limestone. After reviewing each glass cabinet, the Leader posed, shifted his gaze nervously and quickly from the artefact into the accompanying lens of the Iraqi state TV camera, broadcasting his confident image to the nation.

That scene – the dignified Leader, moving slowly and gazing gravely through the TV camera – had been repeated many times over the earlier decades. We were wearily familiar with it. All our previous leaders had attempted to borrow legitimacy from Iraqi history. In the lobby of the museum, newspaper clippings showed a previous dictator, Abdul Salam Arif, walking the same corridors during the inauguration of the museum building in 1963, with fewer armed guards. Saddam did the same, although his newspaper clippings were not in evidence. All over Baghdad, Abu Israa, as Prime Minister Maliki was fondly known, represented the hope that a strong leader was finally born out of the destructions of civil war and occupation. He was applauded for leading a military operation against the Mahdi army militias in Basra. The operation almost disintegrated into total failure, but was recovered by the intervention of rapid US and British troop reinforcements. Nevertheless he could point to the operation as proof that he was a non-sectarian Iraqi leader. His success later that year in local and parliamentary elections was a sign of his popularity. But in Iraq, a nation that still yearns for the brutal days of Saddam and calls them the days of safety and security, the lines between 'strong' and 'authoritarian' are often blurred.

Maliki – like the prime minister before him and the one after him – belonged to the Islamic Dawa Party, one of the Shia exiled groups that returned from Iran. In 2006 he was chosen as a compromise candidate, after the Americans vetoed the former prime minister, accusing him of enabling sectarian militias.

In the Shia southern suburbs of Beirut, I met an Iraqi Shia cleric who knew Maliki during their years of exile. The cleric had fled Saddam's persecution in 1979, crossing first into Iran and then moving to settle in Damascus, where Maliki was based as the head of the Islamic Dawa Party.

'Maliki was very honest and very well organised, and unlike other opposition figures he didn't build personal wealth,' the cleric said. 'He ran the branch of the Dawa Party in Syria by himself, overseeing the activities and looking into all the details personally. He did not delegate his responsibilities to aides.' He was perceived to be weak and without a power base, but Maliki managed to outflank everyone: his Shia allies and foes, the Americans and even the Iranians.

After his election, Maliki concentrated power within his Office of the Prime Minister to become the highest authority in the land. His advisers ran 'a government inside a government', bypassing ministers and the parliament. His son-in-law and other relatives became rich business tycoons. In his role as the commander-in-chief, Maliki appointed loyal generals as heads of military units without parliamentary approval, created at least one intelligence service dominated by his clan and party members, and placed two large and well-equipped military divisions – the Anti-Terrorism force and the Baghdad brigade – under his own direct command and not that of the Ministry of Defence. He also inflated the size of the Ministry of National Security, headed up by one of his chief allies. He used all the resources at his disposal, deploying the highly politicised and corrupt judiciary to go after his political opponents. Through corruption, cronyism and intimidation and the exploitation of state resources, Maliki managed to rebuild the system of clientelism and patronage of the late Great Leader, creating a parallel state that has continued to this day, maintaining his status as one of the strongest politicians in the country even after he lost power.

'Iraq is ruled by institutions that are not covered by law or the constitution,' a senior official working in the Council of Ministers told me in 2009. 'They have their own prisons and intelligence services, working for the benefit of the government, not the state.' Squeezed into an elegant blue suit, the official bounced up and down in his plastic chair as he outlined the security apparatus of Iraq: 'Constitutionally, we have intelligence units in the Ministry of Defence and Interior, but then we also have the Ministry of State for National Security, run by a Maliki ally. According to the constitution, this should have a staff of no more than twenty-six people; currently they number more than a thousand. Maliki has his own intelligence unit, and military units that work directly under his command as the commander-in-chief. The prime minister is running everything through his advisers, and nothing happens without his approval or the Office of the Prime Minister.' The official, who was a senior bureaucrat, could not tell me how many intelligence services Iraq had, maybe seven, but could be eight, he wasn't sure.

Then he looked away at his jacket nervously and said after a long silence: 'They changed their rhetoric, now they talk about law, order and nationalism, but the reality is that they are the same sectarian people.' After some further contemplation, he revised: 'No, it's not about sects any more, it's about the party, the interests of the party.' While claiming to represent the Iraqis and acting as if he was defending the sect, Maliki's corruption and consolidation of power hollowed out his own party of any ideological significance, turning its members into faithful clients dependent on his patronage, just as Saddam did with the Baath three decades earlier.

And so, six years after the toppling of the dictator, a few hundred thousand Iraqis killed, a brutal insurgency, trillions of dollars wasted and five thousand dead US soldiers, the country was being rebuilt on the same model of a concentration of unaccountable power, shadowy intelligence services and corruption.

'The problem is the people, they want a strong person,' Mahmoud Othman, an independent Kurdish member of parliament once told me. 'People are used to that image, because Iraq went through decades of centralised authority and because people who want electricity, water and sewerage and are suffering from unemployment think that the authority of a strong man can solve all these problems. People think that all these apparatuses – intelligence, national security, counterterrorism and a lot of institutions centralised around the commander-in-chief – is what made the security situation better. They are wrong.'

In meetings with tribal leaders, the scenes were very similar to the days of the old regime. Sheikhs in their traditional tribal finery cheered for Maliki, jumped up and down waving their hands, and recited impromptu poems praising the wisdom and bravery of the Leader. One tribal sheikh who had attended such meetings with both Saddam and Maliki described it for me. 'The sheiks chanted

"Yes, yes, to Maliki, the leader", some waved banners and, just like Saddam, Maliki went on talking for hours, without a coherent message,' the sheikh said, half giggling. 'These are all the signs of the day when the dictator emerges.'

Maliki used the same old authoritarian tools to shape his own version of Iraq: like Saddam and the Baath, he proved capable of shifting the national narrative to fit his own purposes and needs. He spoke about sovereignty and nationalism and the great eternal Iraq, but his was an exclusively Shia nationalism, mired in sectarian myths and symbols and alliances and enmities.

An Iraqi journalist close to some government officials explained the situation further. 'People shouldn't blame Maliki – the security situation creates from the leader a dictator. And that's normal and logical, to surround yourself with friends and family, because you don't trust the others.'

The Iraqi Shia cleric who I had met in Beirut confirmed this view. He explained how Maliki and his colleagues suffered from the conspiratorial mentality common among small and highly secretive opposition groups. 'The Dawa Party, in its secretive organising and methods of working, is very similar to the Communist Party; they don't trust anyone and surround themselves with people they've known for a long time. Maliki, like all of us, is the product of life in exile. They have suffered for so long in exile that now they trust no one.'

In fairness, Maliki was not alone in building patron–client networks for himself and his party and his clan: all the party bosses did that – Shia, Sunnis and Kurds alike. The quota system initiated by the Americans after the war meant each group had been awarded a set of ministries and government institutions. These became personal fiefdoms used to distribute state resources, jobs and wealth to the party loyalists through a patronage system.

But Maliki was the most powerful.

In the garden of a newly opened restaurant in Baghdad, I met three Iraqi intelligence officers, working for the newly formed Iraqi National Intelligence Service (INIS). The INIS was founded by the Americans shortly after the occupation, run by a former general from Saddam's era, with American support and considerable funding. The organisation maintained a high degree of independence from Maliki's government, which in turn accused it of being more loyal to the Americans than to the Iraqi state. The officers were veterans of the former regime's intelligence service, the Mukhabarat, and were recruited to the new service because of their professionalism and experience.

After the initial pleasantries, which included a light frisking for wiretapping devices, we sat down. One of the officers, the most senior, sat next to me while the other two sat opposite silently, scanning the garden with motionless faces. I was at first very bemused by the theatrics until the senior man told me that the officers had been gathering intelligence and monitoring military activities inside Maliki's government. To all intents and purposes, spying on their own.

'We have our own eyes and follow what they're doing there,' the senior officer said in a conspiratorial tone. 'Maliki is running a dictatorship; everything goes through his office and advisers. Maliki is surrounded only by his party and clan members; they form a tight knot that is controlling Iraq now.'

A waiter approached us, and the officer fell silent; one of the two men at the far end of the table ordered tea.

'We compile reports on their activities, the generals' and military units' movements, and their corruption, the positions they are taking in the government and the contracts they are obtaining . . .' he listed efficiently. Then, falling back into tones of desperation, '. . . but we don't know what to do with all these reports, because we don't trust the government.'

The waiter arrived with a tray and cups of tea, and the conversation changed immediately. 'Nice weather for sitting outside in the gardens.' 'Yes, but the sound of generators is too loud.'

After the waiter left, I asked the senior officer if he was scared of something.

In his conspiratorial and self-important way, he said, 'We are all being monitored, we monitor each other.' Then added laughingly, 'But Maliki's people are too young in the world of Mukhabarat – they are just learning.'

It was unclear to me whether the officers were spying on Maliki as part of their official job or if they were freelancing out of sectarian or political interests.

In a low, desperate tone, the officer said: 'I hate him.'

Why?

'While Maliki uses nationalist rhetoric on TV, in reality he is the same sectarian person; he is not building a country, he is building a state for his own party and his own people.'

It would not be long before that rotten entity collapsed before the forces of the so-called Islamic State, but in the meantime people tired of war and sectarian killings rejoiced at their new strong Leader.

28

The State of Corruption

MALIKI'S BLOC CAME SECOND IN the 2010 elections, having been beaten by the secular mixed list of Ayad Allawi. But both the Americans and the Iranians had agreed to support Maliki's bid to serve a second term – the Iranians because he had become their chief ally, and the Americans because they, already planning to withdraw their forces, did not want to disturb the status quo. After the votes had been counted, the chief judge, a close collaborator of Maliki, declared that the government could be formed by the biggest list created *after* the elections and not before. This allowed Maliki the opportunity to buy further MPs into his list, and thus be declared victorious. Adnan al-Janabi, a tribal sheikh and member of parliament, described it to me as the day Iraq saw democracy die.

Maliki's second term in office was further steeped in mistrust and paranoia, and constantly imagining a Baathi or a Sunni *coup d'état*. He was the Prime Minister, Supreme Commander of the Armed Forces, and, for a while, both Minister of Interior and Minister of Defence. The anti-terrorism force answered to him alone, and the Baghdad brigade, his praetorian guard, was the best-equipped army unit in the country, and controlled all access in and out of the Green Zone. Not one single senior army officer, security official or government official was appointed without his or his close circle of advisers' personal approval. He also bought the loyalty of those officers by allowing them to turn the army into one inflated machine of corruption.

These appointments became a form of patronage used to buy loyalties among the army, security forces and independent state institutions. Through a mixture of intimidation, corruption and political intrigue, he also spread his tentacles through the judiciary, the anti-corruption commission and the press, turning them into tools used to hunt down his opponents in a zero-sum game. Rather than starting a reconciliation process with former Sunni insurgents after the defeat of al-Qaeda, Maliki used his new powers to go after his senior Sunni politicians and the (Sunni) former insurgents who had turned against the jihadis by allying themselves with the Americans and the government. Instead of rewarding them with promised jobs and military posts – as he did with Shia militiamen, who were incorporated into the security forces – he cut their stipends, jailed and sometimes assassinated their commanders.

———

In their fortified Green Zone sat the new Iraqi elite: politicians and generals, sectarian warlords and provincial tycoons, rich and corrupt double-chinned buffoons. They and their sons, cousins, and clans, their militiamen and guards, and their guards' military units, formed a new class of a few thousand men which had a monopoly on the wealth of Iraq, soaked deep in a cesspool of extortion. Bribes ruled everything, from getting an ID card, to joining the army or signing a multimillion-dollar government contract.

'They – politicians and warlords – don't take bribes any more, they become "business partners", you take your first payments, pay them and then fulfil your project, or not, it's up to you,' a friend told me.

Hundreds of billions of dollars of oil money had been squandered since 2003, and there were hardly any new development projects to show for it. Just the same old potholed streets, miserable schools and decaying hospitals. Ministers occasionally fled the country with millions of dollars. A colonel in an exquisite and expensive suit sat smoking a nargile while 'facilitating' the issuing of passports and other government documents in exchange for the proper bribe. His son, a stocky young man who doubled as his father's gatekeeper and bodyguard, sat beside him with a notebook and an American pistol.

'To be appointed as a military commander in charge of a neighbourhood or a military unit – you buy your post by paying a big bribe and then a monthly salary.'

To whom? I asked.

'To the political party, bloc, minister or commander that will appoint you, up to $300,000 per month. You get the money back by detaining people and negotiating with their families, taking a cut from your soldiers' salaries, or by issuing special permits for trucks to move in or out of the neighbourhood.'

———

Um Tahseen's children had been killed, by everyone.

She and what was left of her family lived in one of the poorer parts of Seliekh, in a small brick house of two rooms separated by a curtain. They slept, cooked and ate in one room, and received guests in the second, which had two rickety green sofas and a TV, and was stuffy with the smell of sewage, cooking oil and fried potatoes that seeped through the curtain. On the walls hung four large portraits of her murdered sons, each picture framed with yellow and pink plastic roses and green ribbons. The eldest fell foul of Sunni gunmen when they ran the neighbourhood: he ignored their religious regulations and wouldn't join them, or stop drinking. Three other sons were kidnapped by different Shia militias from neighbouring areas when they left for work and were never seen again.

Um Tahseen was probably in her sixties, thin and wiry. Her face was wrinkled, her nose arched, and her left eye was turning white. She was confused, she talked about her sons as if they were alive, then held her orphaned grandchildren and began to cry, shouted at her young daughter to bring tea, and then remembered that her youngest son had just been released from jail and started praising God and his Prophet for keeping him alive.

'Wallah, we sold everything and begged money from everyone until we got him out,' she told me. 'For three years I didn't hear anything, for three years we thought he was dead like his brothers, then one day prison officers called us, they said you can go visit your son if you pay. I went to Mayson, my neighbour; I told her I need money to go visit my son in prison. We waited, they brought him, his hands and legs tied in metal chains like a criminal. He wasn't my son, he was someone else, I didn't recognise him from the torture. Your mother dies for you, my dear son, I wailed and cried. I picked dirt from the floor smacked it on my head, they dragged me out and wouldn't let me see him again.'

Her right eye was bright as she recounted how she, a poor lone woman, rescued her last remaining son. 'I had lost four, I told them, I won't lose this one. I told them I would pay; we paid one, then two, then five million Iraqi dinars. They would call us from the prison – we have to send them phonecards, and they call us – they said your son is being tortured, he will die if you don't pay, and we paid and paid. What can I do? He is the last I have. I said I would sell myself in the streets, just bring him back to me. First, they asked for sixty papers [a paper is slang for a hundred-dollar bill], then they said thirty. I begged them and they still said thirty. I told them I don't have that sum, so we settled on twenty. We went to the mosque, our intermediary gave the money to the officer, and they brought him out two days later.'

What the officers in prison didn't tell Um Tahseen was that the judge had already signed his release papers months earlier, but the officers wouldn't release him until they'd received a bribe.

I wanted to meet the son, but she told me she was hiding him. Usually, whenever government forces raided an area, those who were released are detained again. She called him, and we talked on the phone, he said he would come and see me.

The mother disappeared behind the curtain and came back with a small bottle of Pepsi. Two kids peered around the curtain, a son and a daughter of two dead brothers. Above the TV, there was a picture of the Shia shrine of Imam Ali, and calligraphy of the name of Fatima his daughter and the mother of Imam Hussein. My sectarian compass was confused. Shia militias had killed three of her children, her youngest son was tortured by Shia officers, so why does she have these Shia symbols on her wall? When I asked her, she told me that Fatima had lost her sons too. Um Tahseen belonged to the pre-sectarian age.

The son's name was Sari; his baby face was puckered with fear and confusion. He lifted his shirt to show me the thick red lacerations on his back, the edge of each scar had a pink line where the skin tissue had bubbled. His mother turned her head and let out a soft cry. 'For two weeks I was tortured, the torture started at midnight and went on to the morning,' he said. 'They used different methods; there were the hanging and beating, or the beating on the kidneys. I still urinate blood. They wanted me to confess, but I didn't.'

———

A few days later, a friend of mine who was a low-ranking intelligence officer in the Ministry of Interior took me to meet one of his colleagues, a fixer who conducted negotiations with officers on behalf of the detainees' families. His name was Rafiq, and he was standing on the pavement outside the shop where he held council every night, drinking ouzo with his friends and receiving visitors. He was tall and erect with a clean-shaven head, dressed in a fitted black roll-neck sweater and slim trousers. He shouted into his phone, waved his hands to passing neighbours with elaborate theatrics and laughed stridently, showing his big yellow teeth and the self-confidence of a man with authority. His neighbours walked by quickly, throwing out a quick greeting, avoiding his squinting eyes and pugnacious laughter. They loathed him, a Shia in a Sunni neighbourhood, a denouncer, an agent, and an officer in one of the most feared security apparatuses in Iraq – the Ministry of Interior Intelligence Unit. They knew that every time they passed in front of him, his piercing eyes registered them in that big ledger book that he would open later to examine them closely. And that when he needed prey, they or their brothers or cousins would be detained and disappear for months if not years. But they also needed him. He was their negotiator and mediator. They knew that when someone was arrested, they should come to him, and from him seek intercession. He would fix a visit, get a phone smuggled in, reduce the torture and eventually arrange a bribe to get the prisoner released. Each service had its price.

Rafiq was their saviour, their tormentor and the symbol of the new Iraq: confident, brutal and corrupt. When I met him in the last week of December 2011, he was just closing a $5,000 deal with the family of a detainee. He promised them that he would send their son some blankets and food and assured them that the beating and torture would stop. The money was a down payment, the first of many. Further negotiations for a bribe to release him would follow.

Rafiq and his network were part of a flourishing industry in which Sunni neighbourhoods – surrounded by high concrete walls and army checkpoints – were treated like tax farms The threat of kidnappers, militias and insurgents was replaced by that of 'official' arrest, yet the outcome is the same: pay money, keep fingers crossed, get released.

'Everyone is rotten,' said the officer who had introduced me to Rafiq. 'Rafiq loves money – it is his religion and his sect – and that's why he is very useful for us. At least there is someone to negotiate with, unlike in the days of sectarianism when we paid the money and they killed our sons anyway.' The officer, who was a Sunni, was part of Rafiq's network; they worked together.

We sat in a yellow taxi to talk. His eyes twitched and darted everywhere like two flies trapped in the car – they scanned me, the vehicle and the world beyond: the pedestrians, the two men playing backgammon on small wooden stools, the man selling tea from a stall by the kerb.

'We are neutral; we don't do Sunni and Shia any more. We are professional – detain people, hang them from the ceiling, beat them until they are motionless corpses. Shia and Sunni, no difference. Now the system is just like under Saddam: if you don't pose a threat to the political class, you can walk with your head high and not fear any-thing, but if you come close to the seat of power, then the wrath of Allah will fall upon your head.'

Here his theatrics commandeered his face, he turned his lips down, and his eyebrows fell as, faking pain and sadness, he said:

'Look what happened to the poor bodyguards of [Vice Presi-dent] al-Hashimi – they have been tortured for a week now. They took them directly to our unit, and they were interrogated severely. Even an old general was hanging from the ceiling.' A week ear-lier Maliki had moved against the Sunni vice president, arresting his bodyguards, who made televised confessions likening their boss to a terrorist attacker.

I asked my friend, the low-ranking intelligence officer, if he could help get access to one of the Iraqi jails. What if, I suggested, he arrested me, but then returned the next day to release me, saying it was a case of mistaken identity. He set me straight. 'I can arrest you, and I will charge you for that, but even if I came the next day and we proved that it was a case of mistaken identity, and I and you swear by the Quran that you were innocent, you will still have to go through the same process of torture and paying bribes. It's not about your guilt or innocence, but about how much money they can get out of you.'

29

Hassan and Maliki

HASSAN AND I DROVE TOWARDS a fish restaurant in the river-side street of Abu Nuwas, newly opened amid much fanfare from the government, the Americans and the press alike, and heralded as a sign of the coming peace. From an elevated highway, Baghdad spread in front of us, flat and depressive. Sirens blared as convoys of officials traversed the city, their importance measured by the number of armoured SUVs and pickup trucks mounted with machine guns in each convoy. One could even guess the sect of the gunmen by the way they dressed and carried themselves.

There were a few signs of Baghdad's new wealth flashing past as we drove: brand-new cars, new restaurants, massive advertising billboards and even the odd shopping mall. But beyond these cosmetic enhancements, Baghdad remained a begrimed and wretched city. Layers of grey covered everything from the crumbling buildings to the cracked concrete walls. Sewage and filth was everywhere, despite the shuffling municipal cleaners dragging the dust around the streets. Old, dilapidated buildings circa the 1970s and 80s, built during oil-boom years, were 'rehabilitated' and given a new facelift by covering their old facades with fake aluminium cladding. Underneath lay the same tired and disintegrating concrete. Baghdad's architecture was like its political scene, a shiny masquerade covering a festering core ready to collapse at the first real challenge. The day before, despite the usual roadblocks and police and army sirens announcing their presence throughout the city, eleven explosions had gone off in the space of two hours. In one street, police officers gathered around the mangled wreckage of a car bomb; men swept glass from their shops, a grocer selling fruit and vegetables was covered in a thin film of explosives dust.

'When does a country turn into a dictatorship?' I asked Hassan after we finished our fish. Fat grey rats darted between the tables feeding on leftovers and rubbish thrown by the waiters.

'I don't care,' he snapped with irritation, after listening to me narrate the failings of the new regime. 'And no one in the security forces really cares. An officer is paid four million dinars [$3,500], he makes another four through bribes and that's just the junior officer. Everyone is connected through a network of contacts to Maliki and his office and his son now – do you think anyone would like to jeopardise this for some politician thrown in jail, who himself is deep in corruption?'

He went on looking straight at me.

'I am really amazed at those who compare Maliki to Saddam,' he said. 'Did they forget how life was under Saddam? Did they not remember what happened? Was it possible for me, an officer, to sit and talk to a journalist under Saddam? Of course, Maliki has problems but that's nothing compared to what we had before. Is there anyone better than him? He is the best of the worst. All the other politicians are in it for the sake of money; at least he is building a new state.'

Who was responsible for creating this new state, I wondered, a lie that the tired and weary people wanted to believe after years of wars – America? Iran? The inept, corrupt political elite?

—

It is 2011 and young men are marching in the streets of Arab capitals to denounce military councils, brutal dictators and emergency laws enshrined for decades, while in Iraq we were at the mercy of draconian terrorism laws and a new dictator.

This time Hassan and I met in a fancy Kurdish restaurant in Baghdad that was catering to the new middle class by charging exorbitant prices for mediocre food. A waiter in white plastic surgical gloves brought us two small bowls of lentil soup and thick hot discs of flatbread.

Hassan was still serving at the hospital attached to the military base in Baghdad. There was a high-security prison at the base that he had to visit twice a week to check on the prisoners. He repeated the horror stories I had heard from other officers: prisoners hung from their wrists for days, floggings with thick cables, electrocution, and nails pulled out.

'Sometimes they put the prisoners in the "corner" position. They put them in a corridor facing a wall, and everyone passing by has to hit them, a slap, a kick, an insult, to degrade them and break them,' he said over the plates of salads and grilled meat in front of us. 'I know that some of them are innocent but what to do? Better to pretend that you're with the gang rather than attract attention to yourself.' Then he changed the subject and said: 'I am sitting on a ticking bomb, you need to help me get out. If I don't join the network of corrupt officers in the base, they're threatening to transfer me to a front-line division. I tell them I don't want to steal, but they can go ahead. They are involved in all kinds of corruption, selling off anything from food and provisions to diesel and fuel trucks that don't even arrive at the base – only documents signed and the trucks are sold on the black market. And that's the tip of the iceberg – my unit is supposed to have two hundred men, but we are just eighty, where are the rest? They are ghost soldiers, existing only on the payroll, and this is nothing compared to the corruption of senior army officers in charge of ammunitions and weapons contracts.'

The corruption, Hassan says, was a way of appeasing officers in order to win their support, but it was also a way to control them. When the prime minister or his men wanted to get rid of someone, they could always accuse him of corruption.

'The corruption is consuming the army, and the problem is not the young officers but the old generals. Sometimes I feel I am a stranger in this country – all these [security] badges and I am still scared; how do the normal people live in this fear?'

Hassan's moods swung wildly, from enjoying his perks as an officer, to despairing at the corruption surrounding him. He clung to hopes of travelling, leaving Iraq, but he knew them to be delusions, because he did not want to take the risk of leaving whatever privileges he had behind. We drove back in silence through empty streets, and I thought of reminding him how he had defended Maliki only a year earlier but stopped myself and instead told him how, during the Ottoman times, Sarkisian Janissaries used to sell the posts of the governor of Baghdad, chief of police or the judge to the highest bidder. Those who ruled Baghdad treated the city people as nothing more than a tax farm and its people as milk cows. The word 'khawa' came from that time, denoting protection money extorted from ordinary citizens by anyone from street thugs to the chief of police.

While the Arab Spring was gathering momentum, in Iraq, in the lull that followed the first civil war, the little dictator was continuing with his project of building a parallel state that would ensure a perpetual rule for the Shia. He vowed that never again would the Sunnis be allowed to mount a challenge in Iraq.

PART FOUR

In Between Two Wars

30

The Sunni Spring, Syria

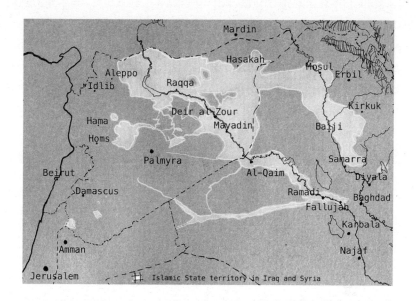

Islamic State territory in Iraq and Syria

DECEMBER 2011.

There are demonstrations in Tunis. They began last week, and are still going on. I tell myself if they continue for another week I will go to the embassy and apply for a visa. I know it's a futile feel-good exercise. If travelling to Europe on an Iraqi passport is hard, then it makes travelling to Arab countries almost impossible – they see us Iraqis as either Shia militiamen working for Iran or Sunni jihadis, members of al-Qaeda.

I applied and waited, and in the meantime, the Tunisian regime fell and demonstrations erupted in Cairo, and still I waited. I fretted,

I begged for weeks, and ended up watching the fall of President Mubarak on the TV in my hotel room in London while drinking four bottles of Cava. To celebrate or to commiserate?

I had been waiting for this moment all my life, not just as a journalist, but as an Arab. I dreamt of these revolutions against the dictators and their corrupt kleptocratic regimes that had looted, oppressed and stifled their nations for decades. Finally, here it was – the moment when the region would be liberated, by its own people, and the age of sectarian civil wars would be over, giving way to a new era of hope and enlightenment in the Arab world.

When an uprising broke out in Libya, most of the journalists were crossing into the rebel-held city of Benghazi from Egypt. I still had no Egyptian visa, so instead I used my belatedly issued Tunisian visa to travel to the Tunisian–Libyan border. A Libyan contact I had met in a cafe in west London arranged for me to cross the border with a group of Berber tribesmen. Within a few days of crossing illegally into Libya, I was captured, and imprisoned in a tiny dark solitary confinement cell of the Foreign Intelligence Service in Tripoli.

When the Syrian uprising began, I crossed into northern towns, watched hundreds of civilians bravely demonstrating and calling for the end of the regime, but I also saw how small bands of fighters were taking a leading role in the uprising, and how the same sectarian rhetoric that had destroyed Iraq was seeping into Syria. Using old communal prejudices, and amplified by the thrumming sectarian rhetoric championed by clerics based in the Gulf, and pouring from Arabic satellite TV channels, sectarianism quickly gave rise to tit-for-tat kidnappings and killings.

By the end of 2011, the Syrian uprising had turned into an all-out civil war. Different armed rebel groups captured towns and villages across large swathes of the country, driving out government troops which retaliated with indiscriminate shelling and aerial bombing.

Thousands of Syrian men were detained and tortured by the regime's brutal security forces and yet they could not break the rising tide of the rebellion. Even the suburbs of the capital Damascus, and parts of the city of Homs, a major commercial centre, had fallen into rebel hands. It seemed that the end of the regime of Bashar al-Assad was in sight.

While the majority of people opposing the regime were ordinary civilians – demonstrating every Friday, with slogans denouncing dictatorship, corruption and demanding democracy – the undisciplined armed 'Kata'ib' battalions became the de facto revolutionary forces ruling the 'liberated' areas. Given the grand name of the Free Syrian Army, the battalions had a handful of defecting officers and soldiers, but the majority of its fighters were workers from the poor rural areas and city suburbs, as well as street thugs.

We in the Middle East have always had a healthy appetite for factionalism. Some attribute it to individualism; others blame the nature of our political development, or our tribalism. Some even blame the weather. We call it 'tasharthum' and we loathe it: we hold it as the main reason for all our losses and defeats from al-Andalus to Palestine. Yet we love it, and bask in it, and excel in it, and if there is one thing we appreciate it is a faction that splinters into smaller factions. But even on the level of previous civil wars in the Middle East, the Syrians seem to have reached new heights. After all, the Palestinians in their heyday had only a dozen or so factions, and the Lebanese, God bless them, pretending that it was the ideology that divided them, never surpassed thirty different factions.

In Istanbul, I asked a Syrian journalist, an activist, why there were so many battalions. He laughed and said, 'Because we are Syrians,' and went on to tell me a story I have heard many times before. 'When the Syrian president, the head of the military junta at the time, signed the unification agreement with Jamal Abdul Nasser in

1958, basically handing the country to the Egyptians and stripping himself from his presidential title, he passed the document to Nasser and said I give up my role as president but I hand you a country of four million presidents.'

Officially – or at least this is what many would like to believe – all the battalions were part of the Free Syrian Army, but the FSA never managed to develop a centralised command structure that would allow it to coordinate attacks and move units on the ground.

Outside Syria, a set of players was conspiring to direct events in ways amenable to them. There were the Saudis, who had never liked Bashar, but were wary of more chaos in the Middle East. The Qataris, who were positioning themselves at the forefront of the revolutions of the Arab Spring, using both their formidable TV networks to mobilise support and their wealth to advance the interests of their Muslim Brotherhood clients, in Syria, Libya and Yemen. Turkey, which was caught off guard at the start of the Arab uprising, was intent on using the war in Syria to further its own regional influence. And of course there were the Americans, British and French who thought that toppling Bashar would help contain his ally Iran, and break land routes to Hezbollah in Lebanon. While all these powers voiced their support for freedom of the Syrian people, and shared the goal of toppling Bashar, each was serving their own strategic goals, and backing their own set of clients on the ground: the Qataris were backing the Muslim Brotherhood and Salafi brigades; the Saudis – who were competing with Qataris – backed battalions that opposed the battalions backed by Qataris. The CIA were training and equipping one set of battalions while the US State Department was funding others. Even the jihadis had their own sources of funding. And it was only natural for Iran, and its clients – Hezbollah and the Iraqi Shia militias, and later Russia – to come to the aid of their ally Bashar.

As the civil war progressed, the Syrian countryside became

dotted with hundreds of these small battalions, many consisting of nothing more than a man with a connection to a financier, along with a few of his clansmen. They became roaming fighting groups, moving from one battle to another, attaching themselves to one or other larger formation before fragmenting again, ever desperate for funding and a fight and the spoils that would follow. The numbers of those itinerant fighters swelled as the war progressed in the already impoverished Syrian countryside: fighting became the only job available for the poor labourers and seasonal farmers.

Beyond the desire to depose Bashar, and sometimes vague notions of democracy, there was no shared coherent ideology bringing all these armed factions together. As a result, the rebellion was increasingly tinged with an Islamist, sectarian tone. Almost every single battalion adopted a religious (Sunni) name and espoused a rhetoric exalting jihad and martyrdom, even when these same brigades were manned by fighters who hardly prayed.

'Religion is the best way to impose discipline,' one commander told me then. 'Even if the fighter is not religious he can't disobey a religious order in battle.'

Sectarianism became the other major component of the uprising, using the narrative of injustice (madhloumiya) harboured by the majority Sunnis towards the minority rule of Bashar and his Alawite clan, to appeal to those Syrians who had not yet joined the uprising, and to garner financial support from the Sunni Arab regimes and Turkey.

Eventually that sectarianism would become a monster bigger than any oppressive Arab regime.

31

Enter the Jihadis

INTO THE CHAOTIC WORLD OF the Syrian civil war – with its brutal atrocities, feuding battalions and war-profiteering commanders – entered the jihadis as early as the summer of 2011. For the first few months they kept to themselves, maintaining a very low profile, while focusing their efforts on reorganisation, reviving old networks and building new ones, especially in the eastern region of Deir al-Zour. Two years earlier, across the border in Iraq, a coalition of Sunni tribesmen and former insurgents had turned against the jihadis and driven them from the cities, blaming them for starting a civil war that had heaped disasters upon civilian Sunni communities. But in Syria, the jihadis slipped comfortably into the hyper-sectarian narrative that was shaping the uprising. They portrayed themselves, just as they had in Iraq, as defenders of a Sunni population against the onslaught of an 'apostate' Alawite regime and its Shia allies of Iran, Lebanese Hezbollah and Iraqi militias. They also harnessed the image of a disciplined force protecting the people from the criminality of other rebel battalions.

Unlike in Iraq where fundamental Salafism – and its violent off-shoot of jihadi-Salafism – had had little presence before the American invasion, these ideologies had, in Syria, made inroads into the poor and tribal eastern regions since the early nineties, when migrant workers in Saudi Arabia and other Gulf countries returned home carrying the ultra-conservative teachings they had encountered in mosques and preaching centres there. Later, the Salafi Dawah (call) movement was amplified by a group of radical Syrian preachers, also based in the Gulf and funded by wealthy religious charities. Those preachers used the new medium of satellite TV to disseminate radical teachings, which offered simple narratives set in an imaginary glorious and puritanical past. They found a willing audience in rural and impoverished regions left reeling by the transformation of Syria's economy from state control to capitalism through neoliberal policies, which benefited the regime's cronies, corrupt officials and the urban upper-middle classes.

The 2003 American invasion of Iraq catalysed the explosion of jihadi-Salafism in Iraq, Syria and the broader Middle East. Eastern Syria – where tribes, just like the Euphrates and the desert, flowed into neighbouring Iraq, unimpeded by modern borders – became the gateway through which thousands of Syrians and other foreign jihadis flooded into the cities of Fallujah, Ramadi and Mosul, to fight their holy wars against the Americans. Al-Qaeda in Iraq – later renamed as the Islamic State of Iraq, or ISI – established safe havens in Syrian villages and deserts where many of its senior leaders took shelter during American and Iraqi military operations.

Osama (his real name) was only seventeen when he ran away from home to join thousands of other Syrians who heeded the calls from local mosques to cross the border and fight in Iraq. Like many other volunteers, he was driven at first by a mixture of religious, nationalistic and tribal allegiances. After the Americans occupied Baghdad, he went back to his village in Syria, carrying with him the bitterness of another Muslim defeat at the hands of a Western power. He followed the news of the war closely; the images of the prisoner abuse at Abu Ghraib and the stories of torture he heard from relatives across the border in Iraq filled him with fury at the hypocrisy and the injustice of the new world order. Only the news of the

Islamic mujahideen resisting the mighty American army gave him hope. They seemed to be the only people capable of channelling his feelings of anger and humiliation into coherent action. He maintained contact with some of those he had met in Iraq and drifted closer to their jihadi ideology: resistance was no longer tribal or national but religious. But in Syria, under the rule of the Baath Party and its brutal security apparatus, any Islamist political affiliation, let alone radical jihad, was a dangerous affair. Many of Osama's 'jihad brothers' were detained and imprisoned by a regime that played a double game for years: allowing the jihadis to infiltrate the borders to fight the Americans and destroy the US project in Iraq while keeping a tight lid on their activity inside Syria.

When the uprising started in March 2011, Osama was serving as a corporal in the army. Nevertheless, hiding his face behind a scarf, he joined the youths in their demonstrations in the streets of Deir al-Zour and Mohassan, and when some of his relatives were killed by the regime's forces, he defected and joined one of the Free Syrian Army battalions.

When I met him in the summer of 2012 he told me how rapidly disillusionment had followed. 'When they fought, they were great, but most of the time they sat in rooms doing nothing but smoking, gossiping and chatting on Skype.'

Osama, whose face formed a perfect circle around a kind smile and a stringy beard, said that another reason for his disenchantment was the bickering, infighting and corruption of some of the Free Syrian Army commanders. Deir al-Zour was one of the main routes for smuggling weapons from Iraq, and many of its commanders made fortunes selling weapons at exorbitant prices to other units deep in the country. 'No one knows how much money they are getting or where this money is going. Men are dying fighting, and the commanders are hoarding weapons and money for another day.'

Then in late 2011, two of his old acquaintances from the days of Iraq contacted him and told him that they had joined a devout group of fighters based in the nearby village of Shahail. They were led by a pious leader who travelled across the region, recruiting and organising men into new battalions.

'They were committed men, virtuous, and they obeyed their leader and never argued; usually in the Free Syrian Army, if you have ten people they split and form three groups.'

One day, the pious leader, a lanky Saudi who covered his hair with a red keffiyeh and carried a small Kalashnikov imitating the style of Osama bin Laden, visited Mohassan, where Osama was staying. He gave a long sermon during the funeral of a local commander, telling the hushed audience that jihad was the only path to true revolution against the infidel regime of Bashar. He also told them that the Syrians were not only the victims of the regime but also of the hypocrisy of the West, which refused to help or arm them. Osama decided to join his group.

'He is a very good man,' Osama said. 'He spends his days teaching us, you can ask him anything, and he will answer you quoting verses from the Quran. We spend our time in useful activities; if you want to read the Quran, you can read; if you want to study bomb-making, he will teach you. Even the chores are divided equally among us.'

The small town of Shahail became the de facto capital of al-Qaeda in Deir al-Zour. The Jihadi fighters drove around the village in white SUVs with flags fluttering. At first, Osama said, there were only ten people, and they knew each other from the time they'd spent fighting the Americans in Iraq – dozens of young men from the town had been killed fighting the Americans in Iraq. The handful of Jihadis then reconnecting with other brothers. 'Under the regime, it would take us a year to recruit one man, but now thanks to God, we are working in the open and many people are joining us every day.'

Osama then told me that his group was very cautious about not repeating the Iraqi experience. 'The commanders admit they made a lot of mistakes in Iraq and they are keen to avoid it [here].' After spending a few months working in the shadow of other battalions and spreading their networks on the margins of the civil war raging around them, the jihadis came to the surface when Abu Muhammad al-Julani, a veteran of the jihad in Iraq, announced the formation of Jabhat al-Nusra. Julani had fought alongside the founder of al-Qaeda in Iraq, Abu Musab al-Zarqawi, then served under his successor, the infamous Caliph Abu Baker al-Baghdadi, and had sworn allegiance to Ayman al-Zawahiri, the then head of al-Qaeda. Yet he still maintained in his statement that al-Nusra was part of the larger Syrian mujahideen fighting the regime and not any international jihadi organisation. In the streets, however, people still referred to them as al-Qaeda, or sometimes just the Tanzeem, the organisation.

Organised, motivated and disciplined, al-Nusra jihadis soon became the strongest rebel faction. They led hundreds of attacks against government forces, capturing military bases, accumulating a large arsenal of weapons and expanding their territory. The nucleus of the original jihadi commanders, many of whom came from Iraq, grew when commanders began to defect from the battalions under the umbrella of the Free Syrian Army and join them. So did hundreds of young fighters, who were paid a regular salary and forced to abide by the strict religious order of the organisation. The jihadis also provided social services, and ran Islamic courts. In times of chaos, any kind of court seemed better than the lawlessness of warlords.

———

One late afternoon, a few days after I met Osama, in the Syrian town of Mohassan, where I was waiting to enter the besieged city of

Deir al-Zour, I went for a walk with two activists. The brutal heat had eased a bit, and a sweet smell rose in the air as the people began watering their gardens and fruit orchards. It all felt very normal, and the war very far away. We passed a government building comman-deered by one of the many battalions in the town. There was nothing uncommon about the fighters standing outside – their mismatched uniforms, trainers and long shaggy beards were all standard-issue for revolutionary fighters – apart from a couple of them dressed in a dark-coloured, Afghan-style, shalwar kameez. I raised an eyebrow and turned to one of the activists walking beside me – a thin man with the defeated melancholic looks of a village intellectual. He told me the men belonged to a battalion called the Ghuraba'a (strangers) of Mohassan and walked on. After a few days in the town, chatting to fighters and civilians, I came to realise that the Ghuraba'a were the town's worst-kept secret. Everyone knew they were jihadi fighters; passers-by joked with them about IEDs and suicide bombers. At the same time, the activists, who were in essence my guides into the revolution, refused to admit that jihadis were part of the fight against the Assad regime.

Most of those activists – not only in Deir al-Zour but all over Syria – as well as many Western journalists and diplomats, would argue for a long time that there were no jihadis in Syria, even after the jihadis themselves had announced their participation in the fight. They insisted that only the Free Syrian Army was battling the regime to create a free and democratic Syria. They dismissed all the reports of the jihadis' presence in Syria as a disinformation campaign dis-seminated by the Assad regime. The regime, of course, had labelled all civilian demonstrators and armed rebels as terrorists from the start, portraying itself as the defender of a secular Syria, and pushing the line that the only alternative to Bashar would be radical Islamist rule. Later, when the jihadis emerged as the strongest faction in the civil war, the activists and their supporters would alter their position, claiming that the presence of the jihadis had been a deliberate ploy by the regime, used to destroy the democratic revolution from within. They pointed out that many of the Islamist leaders – along with other political detainees – had been released from prisons just after the uprising had begun. One reason for these denials was the fear that the opposition might lose US and Western support if the presence of the jihadis in their midst were made public. Another was a sense of sheer denial; again and again, I was told by both rebel commanders and activists that Syrians are not like Iraqis, that they wouldn't allow the jihadis to expand and grow in power.

The relative easiness of the jihadis' journeys from Europe, Asia and the Middle East into the new training camps erected openly along the border with Turkey had turned Syria into the new jihadi safe haven that soon eclipsed that of Yemen, Iraq and Afghanistan.

'In the beginning, we were very few, but now, mashallah, there are many "muhajiroun" [immigrants] joining us and bringing with them their different experiences in the war,' the commander of the Ghuraba'a later told me. 'Yemenis, Saudis, Iraqis and Jordanians,' and with a big smile, he added: 'Yemenis are the best in their religion and discipline, and the Iraqis are the worst in everything, even in their religion.'

———

I first met the foreign jihadis in Syria in the city of Aleppo one afternoon in December 2012. I was with Captain Hussam, a former government officer who had defected to the rebel side. He was doing one of his usual ammunition delivery rounds to front-line units. On the back seat of his old Lada, there were two hand-held military radios:

one for the Syrian rebels and one for the foreigners, which babbled in a variety of languages but mainly Chechen. When he arrived at one of their positions he saw three short Tajiks, two Turks, a Pakistani with a thick beard, a young Saudi and some tall blond Chechens, huddled together in the entrance of an apartment building. They were quiet, tired and looked confused.

The Saudi looked ill. He wore a dirty black T-shirt and a black prayer cap; his eyes were small and beady. He asked me: 'What do the foreign news and the outside world say about us? do they know that we are here? do they know about the fighting in Aleppo?'

He said he was from the Peninsula (a name used by jihadis to refer to Saudi Arabia) and had arrived a week earlier, and was fighting the jihad. When he turned to the Turk next to him, I noticed he spoke perfect English.

We saw a family hurrying down the street towards us, ignoring orders to go back. 'Soldiers, soldiers,' the father said and rushed down the road, avoiding looking at the bearded and heavily armed foreign fighters. A Chechen with a pale face and wispy ginger beard issued a retreat order in Arabic, but only two of the Chechens, one Turk, the Pakistani and the Saudi spoke Arabic, the rest needed a translation. A barrage of four languages bounced back and forth – Russian, Chechen, Turkish and Arabic – before the men walked in single file, hastily but orderly, past the piles of smouldering garbage and twisted plastic bottles.

Omar the Chechen issued an ultimatum to the Syrian rebel commanders: if they didn't muster a large number of men to reinforce their rear, the Muhajiroun would pack up and leave. There had been forty Muhajiroun a few days earlier; by the end of fighting that day they were down to thirty, losing ten men in two days.

That night they left for another front in the city.

Jihadis flocked into Syria from all over the world, some bringing their wives and children with them, and the world was watching. Every time I flew to the south of Turkey in the first three years of the war I came across a group of foreigners, wearing brand-new trainers and backpacks, heading to Syria. Some were veterans of other jihadi wars with no home to go back to, but most were first-timers, who became the backbone of the Islamic State.

Unlike their previous adventures in Iraq, Afghanistan or Yemen, when their trips were arduous and dangerous, crossing many borders, changing passports and dodging the scrutiny of secret services — now their journeys were a mere comfortable flight into Istanbul and from there into southern Turkey. From there, their handlers would lead them on the short walk across the border into Syria, where they stayed in a small town called Anadan. In the hilly countryside of olive groves the men were arranged into smaller groups with at least one Arabic speaker in each group. It is estimated that up to 20,000 foreigners arrived via this route, men and women who would later join the Islamic State caliphate.

After ten days of basic training on how to work together, communicate and the basic principles of urban warfare, they would be dispatched to join different jihadi Syrian groups, like Ahrar al-Sham or the al-Qaeda affiliate Jabhat al-Nusra, or, like the Chechens, form their own fighting units simply referred to as the Muhajiroun.

They were cagey and secretive, and had little respect for the Syrian FSA fighters. When the Syrians asked them where they were from, a blond Frenchman answered that he was Moroccan, the Chechens said they were Turks and the Tajiks said they were Afghans. The Syrians referred to them collectively as the Turkish Brothers.

Of course, the irony of the Syrian war was how the two mortal enemies of the past decade, this band of foreign jihadis on one side and the Americans on the other, were now trying to defeat a common enemy.

32

The Sunni Spring, Iraqi Version

UNLIKE SYRIA, IRAQ WAS A democracy, at least according to the constitution, with a free media, elections and parliament. Yet it suffered the same illnesses that afflicted other oppressive Arab regimes: the failure of the state to provide its citizens with a dignified life, corrupt kleptocratic political elites, oppressive security services involved in atrocious human rights abuses. All these illnesses were exacerbated in Sunni areas where in the decade since the toppling of the statue, the Sunnis had become a defeated class, subsisting on the margins of an oppressive state, and treated as second-class citizens at best if not outright suspects and enemies. They retreated, and had no reason to be loyal to that state. The army for them was Maliki's army, and the Shia government Iranian stooges. But the Sunnis in Iraq, humiliated and defeated as they were, saw hope in the events of the Arab Spring in neighbouring Syria.

When in December 2012, the government of Nouri al-Maliki issued a warrant for the arrest of the bodyguards of the Sunni finance minister, a charismatic doctor from the town of Fallujah, a tipping point was reached and demonstrations erupted. The residents of Ramadi and Fallujah took to the streets after Friday prayers, shouting 'Allahu akbar', and pelting the police and army with stones. Their grievances went beyond the arrest warrants; they included oppression at the hands of blatantly sectarian security forces, draconian anti-terrorism laws targeting their community, the dysfunctional parliament and the corruption of their political representatives. All signs of the failure of the political system.

In Fallujah, police opened fire, killing a few people, and masked men retaliated by capturing and executing four soldiers, mutilating their bodies and hanging them from a bridge. In Ramadi the demonstrators pushed through police lines and confronted government troops on the outskirts of the city, burning police cars and building barricades. By the end of that Friday, called the Friday of Anger – a name borrowed from other Arab Spring demonstrations in Yemen and Syria – the demonstrators started building the Dignity and Steadfastness sit-in camps and declared the birth of the Herak al-Sunni (the Sunni movement). Protest camps sprang up in other Sunni towns and cities. They refused to leave until the government, who they denounced as 'agents of the Iranians', yielded to their demands, which included the release of all female Sunni prisoners, easing the anti-terror laws that targeted their community and an end to the De-Baathification process.

Maliki, who since the departure of the Americans a year earlier, had shed any pretence of being a national leader now became blatantly sectarian, consolidating his power, and moving against all those he perceived as forming potential threats. This included not only prominent Sunni politicians and Sahwa (Awakening, the name given to Sunnis who fought against the jihadis) leaders who fought al-Qaeda, but also writers, independent-minded bureaucrats and former allies, Sunni and Shia alike. Maliki borrowed from the rulebook of other Arab tyrants, heaping improbable accusations on the demonstrators, calling them terrorists and foot soldiers of al-Qaeda and the Baath Party and part of an international plot. He rejected their demands, and sent the army and special police units to surround their sit-in camps. More protests erupted. In Baghdad, Sunni neighbourhoods were locked down on Fridays to prevent demonstrations, and residents from Ramadi and other Sunni cities were all but barred from entering Baghdad. By painting the demonstrators as jihadi Sunnis trying to take power, Maliki succeeded not only in preventing the Shia – who lived under the same corrupt regime – from joining the demonstrations, but managed to portray himself as the strong man capable of defending the Shia. A sense of a country divided started to settle in once more.

March 2013.

In a small white tent in the middle of the Dignity and Steadfastness protest camp in Ramadi, the Dignity student union was holding its first Dignity photography exhibition, documenting 'the atrocities of the Maliki regime against the Iraqi people'.

The pictures – downloaded from the internet, printed on A4 paper and hung from string – showed the Sunni (madhloumiya) injustices, grievances and hardship suffered at the hands of the Americans and the Shia ruling parties. It was also a catalogue of the craftsmanship of the new Iraqi security forces: mutilated bodies, tortured faces, knees with drill holes and mangled limbs. There was a picture of black-clad men manning a checkpoint in the middle of a street but it was unclear to me if they were Shia death squads trying to kidnap Sunnis or Sunni insurgents kidnapping Shia. At the far end of the tent stood a plump man, looking at the pictures with curiosity and a bit of nostalgia. He had a large balding head and wore a tattered sagging pale blue dishdasha. His leather sandals were old and worn. He seemed lost among the excited young students and activists, who were drawing banners, preparing for speeches and filling out forms. One of the activists introduced me. Abu Saleh took my hand and led me out of the tent. Still holding my hand, we strolled through the camp, built on a stretch of the highway that linked Iraq to Jordan and Syria.

Blocking the traffic was the demonstrators' way to try and pressure the government, turning Ramadi's most prized asset, the highway, into an impromptu symbolic square like Tahrir in Cairo or Maidan in Kiev. The camp consisted of two rows of large tents, of the type usually reserved for weddings and funerals. At the entrance of each tent hung a banner carrying a message of support for the demonstrators, and the name of the tribal sheikh or the wealthy businessman who had paid for it. Every clan and tribe in Ramadi had its tent, but doctors, engineers, students and other professionals built their own 'non-tribal' tents. After three months of protests, the camp had acquired the air of a country fair, with patriotic music blaring from a dozen loudspeakers and Saddam-era Iraqi flags and coloured ribbons fluttering from lamp posts. Stalls selling cigarettes, tea, soft drinks and sandwiches stood between the tents, along with lavatories and washing areas for ablutions.

Abu Saleh led me to a half-empty tent that belonged to a tribe not his own. He hesitated for a few seconds at the entrance, his eyes darting around the tent, scanning the faces of men sitting inside before we entered and took two seats in a corner. Around us, men sat on white plastic chairs, drank tea, smoked and spoke loudly, denouncing the government and lamenting the days when proper men ruled the country – Saddam and his Baath Party – not those good-for-nothing Iranian agents. Excitement and bravado throbbed in the air. Abu Saleh was excited too. He was sitting in public for the first time in many years thanks to a truce between the various factions in Ramadi. After the years of Intra-Sunni civil war, everyone had a feud with someone, but if the Sunnis wanted to come together united in their opposition to Maliki and his government, all blood feuds had to be suspended. 'The Sunnis had not united like this since the fall of Baghdad [in 2003],' he said. 'Even the tribal sheikhs who fought and killed our cousins and brothers have joined us, the politicians have joined us and now we have the legitimacy of the street.' He told me how these protest tents had brought different Sunni factions together: Baathists, nationalists and Islamists, as well as remnants of the former insurgency, and the American-funded Sahwa militias that fought them. Even some members of al-Qaeda in Iraq (they had changed their name to the Islamic State in Iraq but people still referred to them as al-Qaeda) had representatives. All were united in their hatred and opposition to the current political system, although each party thought they could use the others to achieve their own specific agenda. Regardless of the truce, Abu Saleh remained alert and nervous. His face contorted and his eyes chased after every new person who entered the tent until proven harmless. In Ramadi, blood vendettas lasted for generations and wouldn't usually respect a truce. Many of the boisterous men sitting around him were his former enemies and victims. They had feared him and his men when they had roamed the city in black sedans, kidnapping and killing anyone they deemed a 'collaborator' with the Americans or the Iraqi army. He had killed many, he forgot how many, but he was sure that their families didn't forget and would at some point exact their revenge.

Before the Americans invaded the country, and the killings turned Abu Saleh into an important 'gunman', he was a young man who 'hadn't killed a chicken, let alone a man'.

He grew up in a poor family that had moved from their village and settled in the town of Ramadi. He had worked since childhood: on farms and orchards along the Euphrates; driving a taxi; smuggling sheep, chocolate and Pepsi between Iraq and Jordan during the sanctions years.

When the Americans invaded, he was intrigued at first, then puzzled and eventually infuriated. He rebelled against the new order not out of religious zeal or nationalism but out of a tribal solidarity. He joined a small band of fighters with some of his cousins. They fought the Americans, an enemy a hundredfold superior in numbers and weaponry. The first time he thought he had killed someone was after a firefight with local police. He saw bodies scattered out of a pickup truck he had ambushed and felt disgusted.

In 2004, Abu Saleh started meeting members of al-Tawhid wal-Jihad, led by the Jordanian Abu Musab al-Zarqawi, who were fighting the Americans between Ramadi and Fallujah and in the deserts beyond. Jihadi-Salafism offered him a straightforward black-and-white interpretation of the religion, and view of the world (and who the enemy is).

The al-Qaeda jihadis dominated the war and the Sunni rebellion. Many other fighting groups came to adopt their murderous tactics. Abu Saleh acquired a new identity, and his resistance became a jihad. What was not permissible in war according to the tribal codes, like the killing of women and children, became permissible in a total religious war that divided the people into two camps, the believers and the enemy. In their twisted logic of war, kidnapping the 'rejectionist Shia' became the primary goal, their ambushes targeting more civilian trucks and cars and fewer of the 'infidel occupier'. And if any of the believers happened to be standing by and killed in a car bomb then they were a permissible sacrifice, martyrs.

Even before the Americans killed Zarqawi, in June 2006, friction between Iraqi factions and the foreign Arabs dominating al-Qaeda had already emerged. Like any group of bandits they started feuding among themselves over loot – al-Qaeda was accused of not sharing the spoils of war – and matters of leadership – the Iraqis were furious that foreign Arabs dominated the leadership positions – and finally, over the al-Qaeda total war which had led to the defeat of the Sunni communities. They came to blame gunmen like Abu Saleh for destroying the community.

The same xenophobic impulse that drove them to fight the foreigner and the 'other' was now pushing the local tribes to fight the jihadis, as they were seen as nothing more than another oppressive occupation.

In 2007 Sunni tribesmen in Ramadi rose up against al-Qaeda and then turned to hunting other groups. Some of Abu Saleh's men joined the hunters; others were hunted. He fled into exile in Syria, lived in Damascus, supported by the charity of former comrades and financiers.

'We made huge mistakes; the worst was the random killing: if we didn't like someone we just bundled him in the boot of a car and disappeared him,' he told me. 'To be honest, we reached a point when people hated us; only your own brother would support you. If you had come three months ago, our morals were at zero.' He spoke softly, sometimes justifying, sometimes just confessing. He stayed in exile until the truce between the Ramadi tribes was signed.

———

I stood next to Abu Saleh, atop a flyover that spanned the highway-cum-square and watched as thousands of men stood in long, neat lines performing the Friday prayers in the middle of the road under a hot, bright sun. Under their feet, a mosaic of coloured prayer mats. They were surrounded by the much hated and feared security forces in American Humvees mounted with machine guns and Shia banners. Local police in riot gear stood nearby too. This was the umpteenth Friday demonstration since the uprising started.

'The stupidity of the government gave us back legitimacy and brought the people round to us. Even in 2003, we didn't have this much support from the people. This is an opportunity that we have to exploit; people here are still sensitive to using words like "mujahideen" or "resistance" but call us the honourable nationalistic factions,' Abu Saleh told me.

After prayers, the men gathered at one end of the camp in front of a podium in the shade of a flyover, their voices thundering with the chants familiar from Tunis, Cairo, Homs and Tripoli: 'The people want to topple the regime.' Only here the people were Sunnis and the regime Shia: a recipe for civil war.

A range of dignitaries addressed the crowd, some wearing the white turbans of the Sunni clerics, others in tribal attire of white dishdashas and red keffiyehs. They clutched microphones and gave long, fiery speeches denouncing the corrupt sectarian government of Nouri al-Maliki. The crowd chanted reciprocally, becoming more vehement and more sectarian, condemning not only the government but the whole Shia community. A young cleric with a very shrill voice climbed the podium, rousing the crowd with a speech of pure sectarian rhetoric lamenting a lost glory. He told his audience that the latest conflict with the government was another phase in the historical war between Arab, and by extension Sunni, and Shia Iran that stretched from the time of the Muslim conquest of Persia to the glorious Eight Years War of Saddam. The crowds responded with chants of 'Baghdad is ours, and we won't give it back', waving Saddam-era flags. Concert-size amplifiers beamed loud patriotic songs from the days of the war with Iran. The whole atmosphere was an absurd re-enactment of eighties nostalgia in which the cleric and other speakers combined the Baathist narrative of the Iran–Iraq War – that the audience were well accustomed to hearing – with the sectarian, delusional and xenophobic rhetoric of 'the Iraqi Shia were nothing but the Iranian enemy in a new disguise'. The frenzied message that came from the podium was that the Sunnis, resurrected from their defeat, would resist and stop at nothing to reclaim their historical capital.

Very few among the thousands of men who waved the flags of Saddam and chanted war songs every Friday were Baathists. The yearning for the past and Saddam were the standard practice of people imagining a perfect and distant past that contrasted with their miserable present leveraging the nationalist narrative for their own sectarian use.

'The people waved these Saddam flags to spite the Shia in Baghdad and not because they want the Baath Party to rule them again,' said Abu Saleh.

And yet the camp in Ramadi, like the camps in other Sunni towns and cities, with all its sectarian rhetoric and opportunist leader, was the closest that the Sunni community had come to a political manifestation of their communal will in the past decade. A rare moment of political maturity, in a decade of failures. After years of rejectionist policies and armed resistance, it seemed that the Sunnis – if there was ever such a homogeneous identity – were adopting peaceful means of protest to participate in the state as normal citizens.

———

Heavily armed bodyguards pushed through the crowd; they looked impressive and dressed like American special forces, in shades and flak jackets. They climbed the podium interrupting the rabid cleric's speech; in their midst stood the soft-spoken finance minister and the deputy prime minister. The crowd surged and flocked to the podium shouting 'Welcome to you, welcome'. Another relic from Saddam's time – when the Beloved Leader used to visit towns and villages, the people greeted him with the exact same chant. The finance minister stood in front of the crowd declaring his resignation, three months after the arrest warrant against his bodyguards had ignited the demonstration in the first place. More chants followed. Abu Saleh, who was watching the minister, said: 'The politicians who joined the political process have finally realised what we were trying to tell them ten years ago – the best way forward is to end this whole political system and start from the beginning.'

After prayers and speeches, packed lunches were served to the demonstrators. When the demonstrations first started, tribal sheikhs and dignitaries would compete with each other to throw massive lunch feasts each Friday, but as the protests dragged on, costs mounted, and it became clear that many people came to the camp just for the free lunches, so the organising committee decided to switch to the more humble lunch boxes.

———

The night descended quickly, and the square went quiet, reclaimed by the desert surrounding it. Brilliant stars shimmered in the sky, and dusty winds tore away flags and ribbons. In one tent, men sat in silence, drinking small cups of bitter coffee and listening to Ali al-Hatem, a lean and dandyish scion of one of the oldest and most prominent sheikhly houses in Ramadi. He stood at the entrance of his tent, dressed in tight-fitting dishdasha and coloured keffiyeh in the modern Emirati style, a relic of the many years he had spent floating round Dubai. Amber prayer beads were wrapped around his wrist like a bracelet. He was giving a long interview to the Fallujah TV channel, threatening an outright rebellion if Maliki failed to respond to the protesters' demands. Under the camera lights, his jawbones cast deep shadows.

His outspoken manner of speech, elegant Bedouin accent and the romantic fatalism of a prodigal son returning to lead his people out of their misery had made him a favourite among the young protesters disillusioned with corrupt politicians. Ex-army officers, Baath Party members and former rebels and insurgents chose him as the nominal head of the Council for Tribal Revolutionaries. He was becoming a threat not just to Maliki but to other prominent politicians and tribal sheikhs who were all vying for the leadership of the Sunni community. Ali al-Hatem was an unusual candidate for the role of a revolutionary leader, for he was not the outsider he liked to portray himself as, but a maverick politician who until recently had been a close ally of Maliki's – one of the so-called 'Maliki Sunnis' – running on Maliki's electoral list and failing to win a seat in Ramadi in the elections of 2010. Both his great-grandfather and grandfather loomed large in tribal history, had signed peace treaties with the British and the Americans respectively, effectively surrendering the city and later coming to benefit widely from lands and contracts awarded to them by the foreign occupying powers. Not that there was anything unusual about a tribal sheikh flipping his political alliances and switching sides – it was almost a compulsory trait.

A few tents away, another prominent sheikh – and rival of Ali al-Hatem – was also holding court. Abu Risha was a notoriously shrewd opportunist, whose brother's alliance with the Americans in fighting al-Qaeda had elevated a family of smugglers to one of the wealthiest clans in Ramadi, eclipsing that of Hatem. Abu Risha, an ally of Maliki and commander of the main faction of the pro-government tribal militia, couldn't afford not to be seen as part of the protest camps, if he wanted to maintain his influence in Ramadi. Alongside Ali al-Hatem and Abu Risha were other sheikhs of dubious background, all joining the camps while at the same time denouncing each other as clients of Maliki. The early moment of Sunni unity was disappearing quickly.

———

I spent the night in the house of Khaled al-Qaraghuli, a sad-faced teacher, dressed perpetually in shabby black trousers and a thread-bare shirt. He was one of the first organisers of the demonstrations. A man who could barely make ends meet, he had spent most of his and his wife's meagre salaries on the camp. It was the closest thing to a political struggle that he had ever witnessed in his lifetime, and he had stayed every night in the tents waiting for the government troops to barge in. But a few months later, and at the height of the cacophony of flags, shouts and songs, he and other activists were sidelined by the traditional powers of Ramadi. He stopped going to the camp, and lost hope in the ability of the demonstrations to achieve anything.

'At the beginning, the demonstrations were spontaneous. The people had genuine and clear demands; they wanted to release the prisoners, and end the oppression, but with every Friday the demands were increased and now they want to topple the regime. Today, the protest camps are used by the tribal sheikhs and politicians to further their personal goals,' he told me in the true depressive tones of Arab intellectuals. 'All those demonstrators that you saw today were brought to the camp by their tribal sheikhs; all the tents belong to the tribes, not the intellectuals or professionals. When we started the demos, we tried to follow the example of the Arab Spring, but unlike in Tunis or Egypt, here it's the tribes that have come to dominate the demonstrations and not the youth or the intellectuals. Here in Ramadi it's the turbans of the clerics and the aqal [the headgear] of the sheikhs that control the streets,' he said.

None of the factions that had gathered in the camp, trying to use the demonstrations to cajole for their share of spoils, had any popularity in the streets, beyond the direct client–patron system that each had built. The Islamists were seen as the cause of the radicalisation of the rebellion, and the drift towards the horrors of al-Qaeda. The gunmen of the insurgency factions were blamed for the military defeats. The politicians were mistrusted and seen as corrupt opportunists, as many had one foot in the government and another in the camps. And no one had any faith in the sheikhs but their cousins. The Baathists and the former army officers had no coherent idea beyond a simple time machine to take them back to the helm of power. Each of these different factions had their own vision of what the Sunnis should do and be, and these visions rarely accorded. A conflict brewed behind all the banners and chants, over who could lay claim to the new Sunni uprising.

At the heart of the matter lay the issue of Sunni identity: what constituted a Sunni and what was the Sunni project? Unlike the Kurds who had a clear ethnic identity and the Shia who developed their own political–religious identity through centuries of opposition to mainstream Sunni ruling powers, the Sunnis had been associated with the state throughout the modern history of Iraq and had no collective identity of their own but rather sub-identities of tribes, clans and villages (Ramadi, Fallujah, Dulaim, Shamar . . .).

Meanwhile, the jihadis in their desert camps near the Syrian border were moving steadily eastwards, while everyone insisted that they didn't exist any more.

———

Early next morning I left Ramadi. The highway beyond the camp was besieged by army and special forces pickup trucks mounted with machine guns; further along the road to Baghdad there was an army or a police checkpoint every few kilometres, hoisting Shia flags and banners from concrete watchtowers and tanks.

The checkpoints were to be negotiated with the utmost care.

Every soldier and officer carried in addition to his weapons the power to humiliate, intimidate and disappear anyone at whim. Men with Sunni family names were treated with disdain and suspicion by the predominantly Shia soldiers who hailed from the south. It felt like a foreign occupation army trying to project its power in hostile territory. On Fridays, the rules were more strict: those identified as Sunnis who couldn't produce a Baghdad-issued ID card were barred from entering the city. Not only had I to show the right ID card, but it was very important to hide my notebooks and camera; a journalist visiting Ramadi was in the eyes of the security state equal to aiding 'terrorists'.

On the outskirts of Baghdad, anti-aircraft guns were placed on a bridge facing the west. Who were they supposed to protect the city from? The hordes of approaching Sunnis? A border was drawn between the communities, normalising the communal divisions. Not all borders of the Middle East were made of concrete and barbed wire; sometimes they could be softer, like the flag of a specific party displayed from a window, or the stencilled face of a leader on a street corner, a subtle change of accent, a difference in the colour of a keffiyeh: they all marked a territory, delineating and reinforcing a myth separating people.

Most of these boundaries are trivial and crossed a thousand times every day without notice. But every once in a while, one of these subtle borders starts to sharpen, and solidifies into a boundary. When that happens there will be no shortage of men willing to die on either side to defend the sanctity of that newly precious border. Orators like the rabid mullah on the podium will rise and give speech after speech telling the men how that border between Ramadi and Baghdad had existed forever, even before Saddam and maybe since the early days of Islam. Historical narratives will be churned, misrepresented and, if needs be, created to give significance to that border, significance

that only increases with every drop of blood shed to defend it. Stories will be told about how we are different from them. We are the noble warriors, and they the peasant farmers. Even if everyone was currently a wretched taxi driver who could hardly support his family.

A Sunni narrative was being created, and it demanded its border, but that was leading to confusion in the Sunni mentality itself. How can you draw boundaries that will separate the country that you claim to rule and that belongs to you in its entirety? And who will draw these borders, and where?

A Sunni tribal sheikh, a veteran politician, who had spent most of the past few years campaigning against Maliki's hold on power, was furious with his fellow Sunnis. 'The Sunnis have lost the compass. They can't see an Iraq that they don't rule.' He was also furious with the use of sectarian rhetoric. 'Of course the people of Ramadi can afford to use such sectarian language, they have no Shia around them, they can talk like that, but what should I do? I am a Sunni, and my tribe are Sunnis surrounded by Shia, how will we survive if there is a civil war? The Sunnis will not be able to form any structure that can last, and the moment they start forming it, they will start fighting among themselves. Yet at the same time no one can defeat them militarily – not Maliki and not Iran.'

In Baghdad, the prevailing view among the Shia was that the camps represented an existential threat, nothing more than a staging ground for a new round in the civil war. People drew a line connecting the sectarian chants to the car bombs that rocked Iraqi cities on a daily basis. In a small cafe in the old city, I overheard a man explaining to his audience how the camps were filled with ex-Saddam special forces waiting to breach the walls of Baghdad.

While the Sunnis saw the camps as a way to put pressure on the government – the height of their political organisation – Prime Minister Maliki, and even the moderate Shia politicians, called the camps the headquarters of al-Qaeda and the Baathists and labelled all of them Daesh (the Arabic acronym for the Islamic State in Iraq and al-Sham).

33

The Jihadi Begin Building a State

MEANWHILE, BY THE SUMMER OF 2013, in neighbouring Syria the jihadis had become the most formidable contingent among all the rebel groups battling the regime. Continuing their military advance in eastern Syria, they captured towns and military bases, wheat silos, factories, fleets of government cars, and the most precious spoil of the war: large oil and gas fields.

The wealth generated by the civil wars in Syria – and later in Iraq – would transform the jihadis from a band of impoverished warriors striving to raise the flag of jihad and create a pure Islamic 'ummah' in rugged mountains and parched deserts into a wealthy mafia-like global conglomerate.

Using a network of friendly businessmen in neighbouring Turkey, they exported oil, wheat, olive oil and other raw materials from the numerous warehouses under their control in northern and eastern Syria. While other groups fragmented, feuded and sometimes sold their weapons instead of using them, the jihadis created a central administration and ran all their resources through 'Bait al-Mall', a central treasury. They invested their wealth in property and weapons, and recruited more fighters, capturing a large share of the civil war market, so to speak, all the while ensuring the loyalty of their subjects through religious discipline and a ruthless punishment system. That wealth, especially the oil and gas fields, became a significant point of contention, leading to the inevitable clashes with other battalions and tribes building their fiefdoms, as well as among the jihadis them-selves. It created a multi-faceted civil war, in which everyone fought everyone else.

In the heart of these disputes, or mini-wars, lay the age-old dilemma that had bedevilled all rebel movements, especially those with a puritanical fanatical ideology: how to maintain unity when they become mired in the realpolitik of civil war, and the fight to acquire more wealth and assets.

I went back to Syria to look into these jihadi organisations and the conflict brewing between them. The border crossing from Turkey was a straightforward business. But in the Syrian town of Tal Abyad, we were told that our path east was barred by another jihadi entity who had cap-tured a neighbouring town. They called themselves the Islamic State in Iraq and Syria, ISIS. They had recently split from al-Nusra – the Syrian franchise of al-Qaeda – and were even more fanatical, and dominated by many foreigners. But after a few days waiting in yet another room filled with fighters and reeking of stale cigarettes, sweat-soaked blankets and stinking socks, my fixer and I went to meet the ISIS commander and ask for his permission to use the road to travel east.

We were led into a small room in a former government build-ing and were told to wait for the commander. I was sure the door would be locked and we would be taken hostage; instead, we were served tea, and a few minutes later, a tall man in a shalwar kameez entered the room and greeted us. He was polite and spoke courte-ously but asked to see our papers. We handed him our passports, and he handed them to another fighter who sat behind a desk and meticu-lously copied all the details into a big ledger. The tall commander sat next to me on the sofa, telling me about their dreams of an Islamic state that shall impose justice, unify the Muslims and do away with the fake borders of the national states, which were imposed on us by the colonialist infidels.

I don't remember much else of what he said in the meeting because I was terrified and trembling with fear. I do remember, however, one detail very clearly: when we left and sat in our car, a young fighter – he couldn't have been more than twelve years old – came close to the window and stared at me. I remember his eyes very vividly; they were filled with anger, ferocious anger, and his small fingers were wrapped tight around his Kalashnikov. I thought that the only thing stopping him from shooting us was his unwavering obedience to his commander: should the order come, he wouldn't hesitate a second.

The next day, armed with ISIS permission, we left Tal Abyad and headed to the east; we passed a checkpoint manned by a dozen or so ISIS fighters, all with long flowing hair and thick beards, who sat on a large boulder on the side of the road. Their commander spoke with a Saudi accent, smirked at us arrogantly and waved us through after a few threats and insults. Little did I know that many journalists would be kidnapped when passing through this and other ISIS checkpoints just a few weeks later.

———

Wheat fields lined both sides of the road, and the horizon was framed by black fumes from wells where crude oil was refined in hundreds of pits, scattered across the region. Our first destination was al-Shadadi, a strategic town surrounded by oilfields and home to the state oil company; it sat astride the road connecting the cities of Hasseka in the north and Deir al-Zour in the south, and also Iraq in the east.

A coalition of rebel battalions had captured the town a few weeks earlier, but al-Nusra took control, expelling all the other factions. Their commander, the town's 'emir', resided in the oil company's sprawling brick-and-concrete compound, built in the seventies architectural style of assertive nationalism. Outside the compound gate, a large crowd had gathered, trying to bring their grievances and the unfulfilled promises to the attention of the town's new rulers. It was a typical scene from any government building in Iraq or Syria, with men shoving, yelling and waving thick files of papers in the air as they tried to push through the metal barrier. Barring their way was a scrawny young doorman, or 'bawab', a person of utmost importance in these sanctums of bureaucracy. He wore an oversized shalwar kameez, and his face was wrapped menacingly in a black scarf. He held the sceptre of his power: a chain attached to a metal barrier. Every now and then someone managed to muster enough volume and muscle, or successfully deploy their Very Close Personal Connection to get past him. On those rare occasions, he would give the chain a yank, causing the metal barrier to lift ever so slightly, forcing those allowed in to bend double to get underneath. Once inside, those lucky enough to pass the first hurdle were met by a short man with broad shoulders who sat on a big fake leather swivel chair in the middle of the car park. He questioned the people thoroughly before directing them to the different departments using a machete that he waved around like a delicate conductor's baton.

The sharia judge of al-Nusra approached the barrier, holding another man by the hand. The judge was a tall thickset man, dressed in a spotless white dishdasha that stopped halfway down his shins. He had dreamy smiling eyes and a long beard that fanned across his chest. The crowd parted, and the metal bar was raised to its maximum height. The scrawny gatekeeper welcomed him and swiftly ushered them in. Two men who had been waiting outside the barrier for some time tried to push through behind the judge, but the gatekeeper pushed them back and lowered the gate.

Seeing how the jihadis were enjoying all the same privileges awarded to the previous rulers of the town – the Baath Party apparatchiks – a man standing in the shade of a corrugated-metal sheet, said: 'We got rid of one despot [Bashar] and replaced him with another.'

'Like in every place, there are good people and bad people,' interjected a young technician dressed in a white shirt and heavy worker's boots. He said he had given the Nusra his oath of allegiance and had been allowed to keep his job in the compound. 'When a group of people become big and successful, they have people who want to join them just for personal benefits,' he added. 'Of course, there are some Nusra commanders who are here just for the position. But the foreign mujahideen, they are good and decent, and they are only interested in the fight and not any personal gain.'

'Why is it permissible for you to take all the wheat silos, and it's not for the others?' demanded the man under the corrugated sheets.

'Because we are the best to rule, and we can take care of the wheat,' the technician answered calmly.

'Wallah, al-Nusra takes a cut even from the air that we breathe here,' the man said. In a few months such backchat would be punishable by death, but for now the jihadis hadn't yet shown that face.

Half an hour later, the 'emir' walked out of the building, accompanying the judge and his guest, the machete man following them at a respectable distance. The group of three chatted amiably, smiling and laughing before the emir walked back into his compound. When it was our turn, the machete-wielding guard ushered us inside, and the emir started explaining the appeal of the Nusra to the people of the newly captured town.

'Go ask the people in the streets – is there a liberated town or city elsewhere in Syria that is ruled so well and efficiently as this one?' he boasted. 'There is electricity, water, bread and security. Inshallah, this will be a nucleus of a new Islamic caliphate that will spread all over Syria,' said the emir, who was thin and strongly built with a farmer's big hands and small alert eyes.

He told me that since al-Nusra had taken over the town, they had been providing services and delivering aid to the people. There was also a small clinic that treated all comers regardless of whether they had sworn allegiance to the Nusra or not. Finally, order and the promise of swift justice were delivered according to sharia law by a handful of newly appointed judges.

'God has chosen us to provide security to the people, and we do it for nothing,' he said. 'We have vowed to sacrifice ourselves to serve the people. If we leave, the tribes will start killing each other over the oil and the loot. We have to show force in dealing with the tribes; even now, one to three people are killed every day because of feuding over the oil. We also protect the silos of wheat. All the silos are under our protection. We kicked out the FSA from these facilities, and now this wealth is for all the Muslims to enjoy.'

Then he delivered his final line: 'We want a single Islamic State, a state without borders and without passports; we want to undo the disgraceful Sykes–Picot treaty.'

The hills outside al-Shadadi were dotted with oil pumps that resembled giant long-legged birds dipping their beaks into the earth. Most of the wells were not functional after fighters and local tribesmen looted motors, stripped away electrical cable and other machinery; but the few that remained operational – controlled by tribes, FSA battalions or the jihadis – were generating a large revenue, turning the wells into the most lucrative spoils of the civil war. Throughout the day, oil tankers, pickup trucks with large drum barrels stacked in the back, and even a school bus gutted from inside and converted into a tanker drove to these wells along dirt roads that skirted the hills, leaving long trails of black oil sludge behind them.

Al-Nusra's most valuable asset lay in these hills: a gas refinery run by a young Nusra emir, whose title was shortened from 'The Emir in Charge of the Gas Refinery' into the 'Emir of Gas'. He wore an old dishdasha frayed around the edges and sat on a green mattress on the floor of his office, conspicuously eschewing the desk and its computer and preferring the simplicity of his warrior life.

He was almost skeletally thin, his handsome face framed by long black hair, parted in the middle and wrapped lazily around his ears, giving him the air of a mischievous playboy. When the rebels first captured the refinery, it was run by a joint committee that represented all the battalions in the area, but the emir decided to kick them out because of 'their petty thefts'.

'The Free Syrian Army are poor, and they have no funding, so they steal stupid things, anything,' he said contemptuously of the FSA battalions around him. 'We don't need this petty money; we are only taking the big assets and use the revenue to help the people.'

The refinery lay idle; a tentative deal was reached to start pumping to the government refineries in Homs, but that collapsed when other factions objected.

'Most of the fighters are against pumping to the government, but this is something related to the leadership and it will decide, not the fighters.'

The emir explained to me why the Nusra had become such a powerful economic entity even when most of the world was supporting their FSA rivals. The most significant difference, he said, was organisation. For example, all their captured loot went into Bayt al-Mal, the centralised treasury, which oversaw wealth distribution to the different battlefronts.

Like a shrewd businessman, he said: 'If your money is scattered around you can't succeed, but if you centralise your resources, you can do much. We don't get any of the aid the FSA gets, but we are not rich and powerful, because when we seize cars or weapons, we don't keep anything with us. It's all sent to the Bayt al-Mal. As for me,' he hastened to add, 'I am as poor as I was before joining the revolution.'

He said he had been a law student when the uprising started, and back then he identified himself as a Salafi, though he had disapproved of the jihadis and their tactics and fought under the FSA banner for a whole year. When al-Qaeda first emerged in the east, he thought they would harm the revolution.

'I used to disagree with them over the implementation of their policies. Even now, they commit mistakes on the ground, and their setbacks in Iraq and Somalia were because of similar mistakes. They focus too much on the sword rather than the Quran and preaching. I thought it was not in our interest to have al-Qaeda in our midst, it would harm our struggle and our revolution against Bashar, and I thought we shouldn't declare our animosity to America now. I said we could be jihadis but raise the flag of the FSA.

'What changed my mind was the chaos and corruption of FSA. I used to think that my fellow fighters were like the Prophet's companions, like Omar and Abu Baker. But after I went with them into four battles and saw how they fought and argued over the loot and spoils in the middle of a battle, my outlook changed, and I became more realistic. I contacted some of my friends who had joined the Nusra, and they told me how things were different.

'Their religious leaders explained to me that we should not fight blindly, that the flag of the FSA is the flag of the infidel secularism and that America is our enemy, whether we declare it or not. America will always fight us and will never be satisfied.

'We are not fighting against Bashar only; we are fighting the system of the Arabic states. We can't topple Bashar and hand it to FSA to establish the same apostate secularist state.'

A few weeks earlier, a feud with a local tribe over a couple of oil tankers had led to the murder of a Nusra commander. The jihadi fighters retaliated by surrounding the tribe's village and taking the male population as hostages, executing a dozen men accused of the killing and levelling their houses to the ground.

Then, to explain their logic, the emir turned to a group of young men sitting around him and told them: 'Do you know why the Americans and Israelis are winning and we Arabs always lose? Because we Arabs are emotional. We in the Nusra are an international organisation, and it is not built on emotions. We are ready to kill our brother or cousin if he was proven to have committed apostasy.

'Hitting that rebellious tribe – that was a pre-emptive stroke: they are weak, they have a bad reputation; kill them, and you will teach more powerful tribes a lesson, they will start fearing.'

A couple of years after our meeting, the emir abandoned the crumbling jihadi dreams and went to Europe to seek asylum; he was later identified by fellow Syrians and arrested by the German police. He is still awaiting trial.

———

All the jihadis that I talked to in the first two years of the Syrian war had one fear: the Sahwa, or the Awakening, the Sunni militias in Iraq made up of former insurgents and tribesmen, recruited by the Americans to fight and eventually defeat al-Qaeda there. A model later repeated to varying degrees of success, and failure, in Yemen, Somalia and Afghanistan. For the jihadis in Syria, the Sahwa had become a paranoia. They were convinced that the Free Syrian Army battalions, especially those equipped and funded by the Americans, would turn against them. Sometimes they unconsciously referred to the battalions as Sahwa.

'They used to tell us that this FSA will turn to Sahwa and fight us, which I thought was an exaggeration; now I know that it will happen for sure,' the Emir of Gas had told me. 'After Bashar falls, I see the battalions divided into three parts. Some will go back home to their previous lives, some will join us in establishing the rule of sharia, and a third part will become a Sahwa and turn and fight us.'

While it had taken the Americans months of intricate negotiations, facilitated by massive sums of money, to convince a few Iraqi tribal leaders and insurgent commanders to turn against the jihadis, in Syria almost every other marginal tribal elder and his many cousins flirted with the idea of forming their own Sahwa militia, hoping to capitalise on America's fears and paranoias.

Clashes between the battalions/tribes and al-Nusra were not uncommon, especially in eastern Syria, but these fights were over resources rather than ideological differences.

Eventually, the threat that almost destroyed al-Nusra came not from the battalions but from within the jihadis' own ranks. In April 2013, the future Caliph Abu Baker al-Baghdadi declared in an audio recording that al-Nusra had all along been a branch of his own Islamic State of Iraq, and that it had been established with his blessing. Henceforth, he added, the two organisations would merge into the Islamic State of Iraq and Syria. The future caliph ended his speech by declaring that anyone who refused to swear allegiance to ISIS would be considered an enemy.

In his book *ISIS: A History*, Fawaz Gerges draws a vivid history of the rise of the Jihadi movements and its subsequent conflict with al-Nusra and tells how Abu Muhammad al-Julani – the head of Nusra, whose financial and military achievements posed a threat to the jihadi leadership in Iraq – issued a counter-statement. He stated that he had already given allegiance to Ayman al-Zawahiri, Osama bin Laden's deputy and the overall supreme leader of all the global jihadi movements, thus defying the ultimatum of Abu Baker al-Baghdadi.

Baghdadi's 'merger' — which was nothing but an aggressive take-over to bring all the Nusra assets under his leadership — rocked the jihadi world, from its leaders in the mountains of Afghanistan to the deserts of Yemen and Somalia, causing jihadi to slaughter brother jihadi. In Syria, the jihadi civil war was the fiercest, and the Islamic State fighters, with their ranks swelled by the foreign fighters, captured territory and assets from their rival jihadis.

The conflict between a Syrian-based jihadi organisation and an Iraqi one was reminiscent not only of the decades-old feud between the Iraqi and Syrian branches of the Baath Party but also a continuation of a historical competition between Iraqis and Syrians long pre-dating the 'creation' of the modern states by the French and the British. On both sides of the Euphrates and in the great expanses of the Syrian desert, geography, history and socio-economic conditions had led to the creation of distinctive political identities that had often competed and clashed from the earliest days of Islamic history.

I met a senior al-Nusra commander in the town of Miyadin on the banks of the Euphrates. He sat pondering these difficult times, baffled and confused. His confident jihadi manner of speech had deserted him; instead, his sentences were fragmented and often left hanging in the air.

'I expected clashes with everyone,' he said. 'With tribes, with the Free Syrian Army, with anyone, but not with other jihadis. No, no! I never thought that day would come. Yes, in the beginning, they [the Iraqis] did give us weapons and send some of their leaders to help us; may Allah bless them for that. But now we have become a state, we control massive areas, and they [ISIS] are just a faction. They don't even control land in Iraq, they were defeated there, and we have been sending them weapons and vehicles to strengthen their spear against the Iraqi rejectionist government. So now they want us to be part of them — that I don't understand,' he said in a tone of disbelief.

248

'The foreign mujahideen blame us for starting this "fitna" [strife] by refusing the orders of the senior leader [Abu Baker], and the majority of them have joined the Islamic State. That's why Julani issued a statement giving allegiance to Zawahiri – to outflank them. We sent a letter to him in Afghanistan and we are waiting for the answer,' he said, before adding that this strife had 'broken our spine, many of our fighters became lax. They say, why should we fight if there is dispute among the emirs?'

Zawahiri later stated that Baghdadi's announcement of ISIS 'was a clear violation of the orders of the al-Qaeda leadership . . . to not announce an official presence in Syria'. He also called Baghdadi's decision catastrophic because it triggered fitna within the jihadist camps: 'The announcement caused a sharp split within the same group which led to infighting . . . and a stream of blood.

'ISIS said that the Nusra had become soft; they deal with the infidel FSA battalions and coordinate with them and fight together,' the commander said. 'The reality is that most people who have accepted the presence of al-Nusra in these areas did so because they saw us as people like them, fellow Syrians. Some even adopted our ideology. Now many have retreated because they see us as an al-Qaeda front.'

Citing the old Arabic proverb that the people of Mecca know its mountains better than the outsiders, he said, 'We know better than the outsiders who are here to fight and kill, we have to learn from the mistakes of Iraq that caused the defeat of al-Qaeda there and turned the tribes against them. They want to come here and repeat these same mistakes. We see ourselves starting where our Iraqi brothers ended in Iraq. We are all fighting a jihad, but we have to learn from their mistakes. If we had followed Iraq's path, the tribes would have turned against us. These tribes are very dangerous; they were all with the regime until recently, and when they saw us liberating this area, they turned against the regime and joined the revolution. Some of them are making 5–7 million Syrian pounds from the wells, and they can quickly turn into a Sahwa.'

A few weeks earlier, the commander and his men had tried to take over the Omar gas field that was still under the control of the government. But it was tribes and some FSA battalions that fought back and not the government. The tribes didn't want the field to fall under the control of the jihadis before they had agreed on how to share its wealth. So a meagre government force of a few dozen soldiers remained there surrounded by a rebel army of a few thousand.

'We need to take the oil wells from the tribes,' insisted the commander. 'I told the tribal elders, you see that oil that flows under the earth? We are ready to let our blood run like it, but we won't let you keep it; this is the wealth of Syrian people.'

Rather than the concern over the well-being of the nation, the real issue here was the growing wealth of the tribes; the more wealth they acquired, the higher the risk that they would become too powerful to defeat.

The hard edges of Syria's front lines – dogmatic, revolutionary, Islamist or murderously sectarian – almost melt away outside the oilfields. New lines emerge pitting tribesmen against battalions, Islamists against everyone else, and creating sometimes surreal lines of engagement, where rebels help maintain government oil supplies in return for their villages being spared from bombardment and being allowed to siphon oil for themselves.

34

We Are Coming to Baghdad
and Other Delusions

BY THE END OF 2013, war was becoming inevitable in Iraq. The message was spreading: a reconstituted insurgency would attempt to take Baghdad by force.

Members of the former insurgency, Baathists and former army officers along with Ali al-Hatem, the maverick tribal sheikh, agreed that an actual revolt was needed. The peaceful protests had fizzled out, and nothing much was achieved by the camps, where the podium had become a platform for people wanting to vent their anger.

The coordination committees that were in charge of the peaceful demonstrations started preparing men for war, organising them into small cells according to their tribe; each tribe contributing a certain number of men to be trained to 'defend the camps of the attacked'.

In the charged sectarian atmosphere of the post-Arab-Spring Middle East, reactionist countries – Iran, Saudi Arabia and other Gulf nations – worked to thwart the revolutions of their opponents, defend their client regimes and seek to defeat their opponents by sponsoring their own set of uprisings. The Sunnis of Iraq sought the support of the Sunni regimes in the Gulf.

Abu Saleh, the former insurgent I had interviewed in the pro-test tent, told me that he and other Sunni leaders had met with representatives of 'charities' from the Gulf in the Jordanian capital, Amman. These were essentially fronts for wealthy figures who funded them during the early years of their insurgency against the Americans, and were willing to support a new Sunni uprising again. And just like in neighbouring Syria, the funding from the Gulf countries to aid the rebellion would become a source of division and conflict between the Sunni. Each of the so-called leaders – prominent Sunni businessmen, politicians and tribal sheikhs – was marketing himself as the sole leader of the protest while denouncing the others so that he could exclusively receive all the financial aid pouring in from Qataris, Emiratis and Turks.

In Beirut, a veteran – Sunni – Iraqi politician told me how he had warned the Qatari foreign minister against meddling with Iraq's Sunnis. 'I told him the Sunnis of Iraq are not the Sunnis of Syria – we are a minority. Any war will lead to the destruction of the Sunnis.'

———

A year later, in March 2014, all that was left of the Dignity and Steadfastness camps were piles of twisted and rusting metal poles, heaps of shredded canvas and mottled and soiled plastic banners. A big black Shia flag with the words 'Ya Hussein' in red was planted on top of one of the mounds of debris. Another cycle in Iraq's civil war, with yesterday's oppressed becoming today's oppressors. The soldiers who had planted the flag sat nearby in their makeshift camp, buttressed behind armoured vehicles and sandbags. The highway was littered with mangled remains of armoured vehicles, destroyed in recent clashes between the fighters and the army. IED blasts had gouged deep holes in the bridge leading to the city where two tanks stood at either end with turrets facing opposite directions. One was an ancient Russian T-72, spewing black fumes from its engine, the other was a new American Abrams, purring softly. Between them, they seemed to tell the story of our wars. Further down, beyond what was left of the camp – beyond the tanks, the coils of barbed wire, and the masked informant standing at a checkpoint pointing at locals who would be taken out of cars, handcuffed and lined against a wall – lay the city of Ramadi, largely captured by a coalition of armed factions with only a small part still under government control. The city hid partially behind a curtain of tall palm trees that swerved along the Euphrates; it was looking deceptively quiet and calm in the early-morning haze. A distinctive odour – a mixture of charred concrete, putrified garbage and gunpowder – betrayed the war raging inside. A few cars drove slowly, in single file, down deserted streets that constituted a no man's land controlled by no one. In one street hel-meted soldiers appeared from a tank; in another, fighters with faces wrapped in keffiyehs peered from behind a street corner, both sides violating the city. Old and tired Russian-made helicopters staggered through the sky, bringing supplies by air to the small regiments of soldiers left surrounded in the government building. Columns of smoke rose and formed low clouds and the monotonous sound of a lone machine gun rang in the distance.

The war had begun six months earlier when government troops raided the house of a foul-mouthed and little known member of parlia-ment. He was one of the rabid sectarian orators of the protest podium. His brother was killed during the operation to detain him. Two days later, the troops dismantled the camp; in response, armed Sunni fighters calling themselves Tribal Revolutionaries clashed with the army, kill-ing eleven soldiers and policemen. The army withdrew to the outskirts of the city, leaving only a small detachment of special forces soldiers in the governor's building. That same day the fighters also captured the city of Fallujah and a new Sunni armed rebellion was born.

Different armed groups came under the banner of the Tribal

Revolutionaries: former military officers, Sufi religious orders, a smattering of jihadis and former insurgents. Within a few days, however, a long line of pickup trucks flying black banners and carrying Islamic State fighters smoothly captured the town of Fallujah, expelling other factions. To avoid a repeat of their internal wars, the ex-army and tribal rebels issued a statement expressing regret . . . and left Fallujah to the Islamic State to concentrate on Ramadi, believing that they could contain the jihadis.

Over six months of heavy fighting, the army sustained heavy losses. They shelled cities indiscriminately, sent young Shia volunteers to the front to die. At the same time, thousands of Iraqi soldiers deserted, abandoning their units mid-battle. The insurgency was spreading into the religiously mixed areas around Baghdad where most of the sectarian killing in the last bout of civil war had taken place. Nouri al-Maliki portrayed the battle as part of the global war on terrorism and went on a massive shopping spree for weapons and ammunition from the US, Russia and even Iran. The brother of an MP who was detained by Maliki told me that he was planning to stand instead of his brother in the next elections. He was excited about the prospect of war. 'This war will be good for us, it will help us in the next elections,' he said. 'The government will see what the Sunnis are made of.'

I walked through Ramadi with a local activist, as a few people ventured into the main street, walking gingerly to the market to watch their city getting destroyed one more time. Men stood by their garden gates, chatting with the few remaining neighbours; they enquired about each other's health, offering tea and their political analysis of the war to anyone who listened. When the war and the killing came too close to their street, and shops burned and buildings shuddered into heaps of concrete, these men would pack up their lives and their families and move to the house of a cousin or an uncle: women, children, blankets and gas cans piled into the back of pickup trucks or squeezed together in cars, joining that endless trail of refugees criss-crossing the Middle East. Was that a well-practised routine? Did these people just accept the war as their fate and resign themselves to their destiny with a shrug of the shoulder? A black BMW sedan drove by; inside sat two men, their faces covered by scarves. They wore flak jackets and black shades; Kalashnikovs rested between their knees. They drove slowly, checking out the group of men standing in the market before speeding away.

Who are they? I asked.

'Probably military intelligence,' answered a visibly scared barber.

'Or Sahwa,' said his friend.

'No, Sahwa only wear green camouflage uniforms – they must be the mujahideen,' another man said. He was carrying a suitcase and planning to leave the city entirely.

'Islamic State?' suggested someone.

'No, Islamic State fighters don't wear shades,' reasoned the barber.

'No one knows. Everyone is a civilian and everyone is carrying weapons, you will never know,' Suitcase Man retorted, before slamming the door of his car and making his escape.

From the market, we headed to a small cemetery, a no man's land between the warring factions, dominated by snipers. Brave locals were collecting the dead and burying them, regardless of who they were. There were a dozen freshly dug graves waiting for the new arrivals, as well as two dozen graves draped with flags and flowers; these were the martyrs, my companion explained. Scattered around them were unmarked graves with no names, no flags and no flowers – I was told these belonged to pro-government Shia militiamen killed in the fighting. Forty-five graves in total in this small patch alone. At least there was one place left where Sunnis and Shia could coexist together.

Abu Saleh was fighting somewhere in the city, but no one knew where. So I decided to spend the night in Ramadi, in the flat of the activist, situated in the middle of the old market. Books, notebooks and papers lay all over the floor; on the sofa, a fat white cat slept while the war raged on. With the help of the activist, I tried to make a list of all the different factions fighting in Ramadi. Fourteen in total. The Shia militias and the army were two; the rest were all Sunnis. This was a Sunni–Sunni civil war. A convoy of armoured vehicles drove down the street; soldiers cleared their path with flashlights and bursts of machine-gun fire. We saw a group of men standing in the shadows underneath the flat – who were they? IS? Military councils? Sahwa volunteers? And what were they waiting for? A few minutes later, a big explosion rocked the neighbourhood, followed by a series of smaller explosions and heavy gunfire. The activist pulled back the curtain and watched as people ran quickly into their homes. 'The soldiers will retaliate soon,' he said. An hour later, there was knocking at the doors warning the residents: soldiers were beginning to conduct a sweep of the area. Quickly, life returned to the dark streets, as men abandoned their houses and ran, everyone in flip-flops and dishdashas, but a few clutching plastic bags and preparing for a long exile. We decided to leave the flat. The activist's hands were shaking as he tried to open a can of food for the cat. He had been in an Iraqi jail once before, and he didn't want to go back there. We followed the line of men running away under cover of darkness, jumping over puddles of mud and sewage, their backs always against the walls. Running parallel to the street the soldiers were coming from. Everyone was looking for a safe house, a relative who would host them for the night.

———

We returned to the activist's flat the next day. The night before, two of his colleagues had been detained by the military intelligence, accused of having had contact with the rebels. He thought it was only a matter of time before they'd come for him. I helped him pile notebooks and hard drives into bags and the white cat into a box and leave.

The old souk during the day was narrower than at night. Many shops remained open, piling their goods and merchandise in front, the streets were crowded, and in the middle, the constant flow of thick oily dark refuse, a sure sign of life. The sounds of war and explosions still filtered through the din of the covered market, but it was as if the city had decided to confine its wars to the boulevards, highways and public squares. Here in the darkness and filth, it brought its feuding sons together. In the middle of one covered street sat two policemen, bored but unmolested in a city of rebels. Their post was no more than a pile of concrete blocks and a tangle of razor wire. They looked sad rather than scared, like kids missing the fun outside.

'They don't want to hit the Sahwa because they don't want to open an internal front,' the activist told me as we carried his notebooks and cat through the narrow streets. Then I saw Abu Saleh walking through the covered market; he had lost a lot of weight and what remained of his hair was cropped short. He was wearing a clean white dishdasha and had a small boy with him. In the chaos of the market where people mingle and shout, a spy or a government agent would struggle to tell if he was there to meet someone, pick up explosives or detonators or just buy some clothes for his young son.

He beckoned me to follow him into a shop selling aluminium kettles. He left the boy with the shop owner, and we sat on a pile of boxes in the back. He told me that after our meeting in the tent a year earlier, he had abandoned all hope of a peaceful solution and re-formed his fighting group. He was now in charge of the rebel-controlled sector of the city.

'The oppression became unbearable. After what happened in the last war we thought we would live together in this country, but the detentions, the marginalisation – it all targeted one component of this country, the Sunnis. It's like they want to castrate us. We came to the political process, we supported the politicians, but then even those politicians were detained. We took to the streets. We demonstrated peacefully, and you saw what happened. Yes, some of the people who came to the camps were al-Qaeda, but the majority just wanted change. Now the fighting is better and the people are supporting us more than when we fought the Americans. The Americans were fighting for their interests, and you knew that America would pack up and leave eventually. Our enemy now fights over belief and ideology; these people are trying to eradicate us. It's a war on our sect and beliefs. Just tell anyone in the street "America" and they wouldn't mind. Say "Iran" and they will revolt. The commanders are military officers, the plan comes from our past wars with the Americans and Iran; like the crawling of ants, we take an area, we secure it, we move forward. Gradually, the war will reach the walls of Baghdad.

'There is a fundamental difference in the way we work now from the old days. We made mistakes and we paid dearly by losing the popular support, and we were almost wiped out. We won't display the same attitude – even if honestly we don't think everything we did was wrong. Now I stop myself and try to be more moderate, at least towards the people around us. For example, we don't execute prisoners now – we exchange them or set them free. In 2005/6 not only the prisoner, but his cousin and his cousin's cousin would also be killed. Once the local support is lost, one is finished.'

He stood, shook my hand with his firm grip, picked up his son and walked out of the shop. There was something sad and wretched about him. He and his men had done it all before, they carried the anger, the fury and the sense of injustices wreaked on them, and they fought and they killed. They became outlaws and criminals and were defeated – and now they are back at it. Would he reach the walls of

Baghdad or was he just destroying the city once more while creating a space for IS to expand?

———

The image of a unified Sunni community collapsed with the outbreak of the fighting. Many of the Ramadi tribes joined the Maliki camp, either lured by money or because of their feuds with the tribes that had joined the rebel camp. Each sheikh was playing his own power game, against or with Maliki, and in return, Maliki, using state money and resources, was playing them all against each other.

The myth perpetuated by everyone in the camp – that Ramadi, a city embedded in the heart of the desert, inhabited by fierce tribes- men who would pick up arms and avenge Sunni grievances and restore their dignity – turned out to be a folly. Ramadi, a micro- cosm of the Sunni community, was nothing more than a collection of many clans and families, tribes and political power centres, each with its own set of interests, allegiances and grievances. Sectarian ideologues – the jihadis and the Shia militias – spoke of one war that stretched in an arc – sometimes described as the Shia arc and sometimes the Sunni – from southern Lebanon to Syria, Iraq and Iran. A clash between two masses of people and two monolithic ideologies. But the war was made of smaller conflicts, each fuelled by its own motivations, each striving for different goals: a summa- tion of all the conflicts between its peoples. And that has been the tragedy of the Sunnis over the past decade, shrouding their local feuds in bigger wars.

For the men shooting at each other from behind berms and walls, their wars were local. Along the road leading to one of the many front lines outside the city, Saddam-era flags were planted on oil drums; next to them teenagers from pro-government tribal militia stood guard with brand-new weapons. They flew the Saddam Iraqi flag and not the new Iraqi flag because even if they were fighting alongside the government, they were still proud Sunnis. Weapons, a major source of income, were found in abundance in Ramadi. With the army in retreat, Maliki sent money and weapons to tribal sheikhs who claimed they were willing to fight the rebels. Few were willing to do any actual fighting, though, and many of their men sold their brand-new machine guns to the rebels themselves. The price of a machine gun dropped by 50 per cent.

———

In the land of the pro-government Albu-Fahd tribe in the countryside outside Ramadi, a high sand berm separated their men from the rebels. A tribal fighter in mismatched military uniform and a red keffiyeh manned a sniper position. He was sitting on a broken metal chair with bits of cardboard overhead, looking through a small hole at the lush green fields ahead bisected by irrigation canals.

He pointed at distant mud houses and said, those are the Albu-Faraj tribe, they are Daesh. Here in the countryside of Ramadi, IS and the rebels were not an invading force that came from outside but local tribesmen. The berm separated two tribes, one fighting for the government, the other against. Unlike in the city, in the countryside there was no confusion with the front lines, they matched tribal and clan territories. Certain clans and villages joined the rebels, or at least were unable to resist, while others joined the government, or at least took money to oppose the rebels. Some clans who were in dispute with each other over land or blood simply joined opposing sides, each using one power against the other.

Behind the fighter, in a small shed, an Iraqi army soldier slept on a camp bed. The army despised the tribal fighters and dismissed them as militiamen. Their American tank and an armoured vehicle stood majestically nearby.

The commander of the tribal fighter, still limping from the bomb that had killed his two brothers and a cousin a few weeks earlier, walked up and down the front line. 'From 2007 I fought in these fields,' he said. 'We liberated it once from al-Qaeda when the Americans were here, and now they are back, but this time it's harder. During the American times, I could pick up the phone, and they'd send me weapons; now I have to beg twenty times before anyone will send me some ammunition.' He paused to shout at a young fighter who was firing at no one just to impress his commander.

'Now because they call themselves the tribal revolutionaries, people are confused, and not everyone wants to fight them.' Looking at the slouching soldiers, he said: 'I made sure this unit stayed here – I don't care for the soldiers, they are useless, but I need the tanks. If they take them away the front line will be overrun quickly.'

On the way back to Ramadi I watched the sun setting on the Euphrates that flows between green orchards and palm groves; berms and fortifications now surround many. One local tribal sheikh said to me: 'Look, this is the Euphrates River – now it resembles one of the front lines we had in the war with Iran. Now we have it at home.'

———

In Baghdad, Omar al-Shahir, a journalist who grew up in Ramadi, told me to stop asking why there isn't a unified Sunni leadership after a decade of war. 'Why do you ask me, where are the wise Sunni leaders? Why don't you ask me, where are the wise Iraqi leaders? The Kurds and the Shia are equally divided and obnoxious,' he said with agitation. His bulging eyes were staring at me. 'There isn't one leader that represents the Sunnis; they are all miserably fragmented.

The Sunnis committed their worst act the day they allowed Shaker Wahaib [a low-level ISIS commander who was filmed executing Syrian truck drivers] to appear on their streets. The only good deed that this province achieved is that one day in 2008 they kicked out al-Qaeda, and now they have allowed them to come back. All their achievements have collapsed, and the war will destroy them again.'

I was committing the same mistake as those committed by the people in the Dignity camp: addressing all the Sunnis as if they were one homogeneous people.

Partly to blame was the etymology of the Iraq conflict. Since the American invasion, it has been based on wide definitions of the Sunnis (Baathists, regime loyalists, jihadis, insurgents, etc.). These terminologies not only shaped the coverage of the war but also created the impression that the Sunnis were a monolithic body in their devotion to Saddam, rebellion against the Americans, and opposition to the political process of post-2003 Iraq. It was a myth perpetuated by the Americans and the exiled politicians, and the Sunnis bought into it, and in their defiance decided to associate themselves with Saddam to spite the Shia.

The idea of uniformity, of a strong tribe ruled by a powerful sheikh in Ramadi or elsewhere in Iraq, was a fallacy. A process of the erosion of tribal authority that was an inevitable by-product of modernity was exacerbated by the last three powers that dominated Iraqi politics: Saddam, the Americans and Maliki. All three powers chose to deal with troublesome Sunni sheikhs in the same way. Either coerce with offers of money, influence and contracts, or depose by jail, exile or murder, replacing the troublesome sheikh with another. The new sheikh's authority would be contested because he lacked legitimacy in the eyes of his people, thus starting a process of fragmentation. All three powers missed the paradox that the moment a tribal elder is successfully coerced is the exact moment that he loses respect and influence among his tribesmen. When the tribesmen look at the extremely wealthy tribal elder flooded with money, they no longer look at him as a representative of their collective tribal will, but as someone enriching himself and his direct family by using them.

'The problem with the sheikhs started from Saddam's times when he created the sheikhs category A, B and C, and Maliki followed the same footpath,' Rafe'a, a tribal sheikh, told me, whose own Albu-Fahd was once one of the biggest tribal families but had fragmented into half a dozen sub-clans.

The camp and the subsequent rebellion was also about the issue of the redistribution of wealth among the Sunnis themselves. Many of the protests were as much against other Sunni powers as they were against Maliki. Those who had used the power and wealth of their government positions to enrich themselves and their tribes.

'When the women in our tribe fight, they curse each other by saying "May Allah increase the number of sheikhs in your family", because feuds and wars will follow,' Sheikh Rafe'a said. The sheikhs would go on to build lavish villas with gilded marble cornices, furnished with pools and zoos, drive in fleets of SUVs, and a few of them would develop an appetite for spending hundreds of thousands of dollars in gambling and nightclubs.

35

The Collapse of the Brave New Army

SPRING 2014.

By late spring and after a few months of fighting in Ramadi and Fallujah, the army had started to crack, which would lead to its eventual rout in Mosul. It was becoming apparent that it was incapable of achieving any military victory. So Maliki and other politicians sent Shia militiamen to bolster the army, thus further inflaming the sectarian tensions.

In a garden restaurant in an upscale Baghdad neighbourhood, under tall palm trees decorated with purple and blue lights, I met with Hassan again, recently promoted to the rank of major. He was anxious and fluctuated between anger and depression. Holding his head in both hands, he told me that the army was suffering 150 casualties a day. That the medical corps was overwhelmed and that the government was imposing a total media blackout. I asked him why a country with more than a million men in its security forces would need to send militiamen to the front lines?

'The main problem is not the dead and injured, but the desertion. Whole units are deserting en masse. Soldiers openly defy commands, abandon their weapons and walk away when ordered to attack; they are even threatening to shoot their commanders. This is why the government is sending militia volunteers. Why do you think the government is giving soldiers an extra 500,000 Iraqi dinars in bonuses? They want them to stay but they won't, and I don't blame them. They don't receive the support they need, they are sent without adequate food, ammunition or medical supplies. Units run out of ammunition because the army is using one supply route that is being bombed frequently. If I know this and I am just a junior officer, shouldn't our brilliant commanders know this too? This is a government killing its soldiers.' Yet, Hassan still described himself as loyal to Maliki and thought the cause of corruption was the older officers.

'Corruption is eating the army. Officers steal everything: fuel, money assigned to feeding soldiers, ammunition, salaries, and I am not even talking about corruption in the big contracts. So what do you think the soldiers should do? Die for their corrupt officer or run away? I would run myself.'

In the all-embracing corruption culture of the Iraqi state, the depravity and cronyism of the security services had reached surreal levels. Officers were assigned to lead units either because of their loyalty to Maliki or after paying exorbitant bribes, often both.

Young men willing to join the army or police would have to pay a couple of thousand dollars in advance to get a job that paid a salary of around $750 a month, a very well-paid job in a country where most of the youth were unemployed. Many were ghost soldiers, whose names appeared on the military payrolls, but either they had gone back to their civilian lives – with a small percentage of their nominal salaries – or they did not exist in the first place, their salaries simply pocketed by commanding officers and politicians.

Passing through an army or a police checkpoint was a daily ordeal; a young soldier had the power to humiliate and, if he wished, to detain at will and disappear young men in a quagmire of torture and prisons.

'The army has become an investment project. You join to make money,' one Shia politician told me in Baghdad.

After the collapse in Mosul and Tikrit, I met a former military intelligence officer who had served in the Iran–Iraq War until the fall of Baghdad and was then recruited by the Americans when they reformed the Iraqi intelligence service.

'In my lifetime as an officer, I have seen an army collapse like that three times. It happens when the soldiers don't trust their political leadership. The soldier knows when he is being sacrificed for politics. In 1988, everyone knew the war would be over; Iraq had accepted the UN ceasefire; the Iranian leadership was stubborn. It was then that we saw the Iranian army collapse. Every day we took dozens of Iranians as POWs; they lost the will to fight, they knew the war was over, why should they be killed? The same thing happened to our army in 1991 in Kuwait – tens of thousands of Iraqi soldiers just dropped their weapons and ran away; again, they knew the war was continuing only because Saddam was stubborn and refused to leave Kuwait. Now it's the same; this is a corrupt army sending southern Shia boys to fight in Mosul and Ramadi for what? Maliki was deceived by his generals just like Saddam was by his – they kept telling him yes, yes. And when the war broke out, the army collapsed.'

PART FIVE

The Islamic State and Second Civil War

36

Fall of Mosul

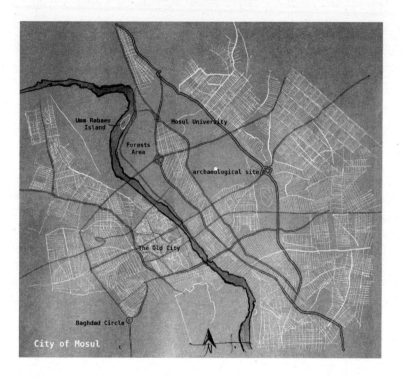

ON 6 JUNE 2014, BANDS of IS fighters attacked a prison on the outskirts of the city of Mosul, to liberate some of their leaders.

Other IS units were targeting Mosul's police and military installations, which fell to them quickly. Defensive lines were collapsing as fast they were formed by the retreating army and police units. Soldiers were deserting en masse when they saw their officers running away, fleeing across the bridges to the eastern side of the city.

Wassan, a young doctor with an affable, cherubic face, ran out of the maternity ward of the Jimhouriya hospital, down the stairs and into the emergency room on the ground floor, and began attending to the injured filling the room. She had just graduated from the medical school, with no experience whatsoever in treating trauma casualties, but whatever she lacked in experience she compensated for with passion and commitment. The government had imposed a curfew, but clashes continued, and by the evening the hospital wards and corridors were overflowing. They ran out of beds and casualties were laid on the bare floor. Wassan stayed at the hospital that night, ignoring her father's incessant phone calls, alternately pleading, demanding and cajoling her to come home.

In the morning, mortar shells started falling near the hospital, and Wassan – along with other doctors and patients in critical condition – piled into ambulances and were evacuated across the bridge to another hospital on the east side of the city.

There, they heard that the government complex on the western side of Mosul had fallen to Islamic State fighters; the governor, along with senior generals, had abandoned the city.

Her father called again to tell her he was taking the family to safety in Erbil, in the autonomous Kurdish region. He threatened that if she didn't come back home immediately, they would leave without her. 'Just leave my passport at home and go,' she told him. 'I have sworn an oath to help the patients.' She hung up.

A few hours later, all signs of government authority had disappeared from the eastern side too. On the afternoon of 7 June, three days after the clashes had begun, gunmen entered the hospital, their faces concealed and machine guns in their hands. Wassan's father arrived shortly after and took her home. When she thought of all the injured left behind, she began to weep. Four hours later she was back at the hospital, working, along with the few other young doctors who had stayed at their posts, under the command of the new rulers of the city.

———

Ahmad, a stocky and energetic engineer, had owned a thriving computer business in Mosul in 2014. He was visiting friends in Erbil when his wife called him to say that something was happening in the city. He drove back quickly and found the roads blocked by checkpoints, and the situation tense. When he reached home that night and heard about the clashes between the militants and government troops, he thought nothing of it at first. Clashes were frequent in Mosul. The militants were the de facto rulers of the city after dark, levying taxes, imposing protection rackets and controlling the roads in and out of the city. Like all business owners, he had to pay them to be left alone, as well as the usual bribes he had to pay to the army and the police.

Next day, rumours were spreading, and when the government imposed a curfew, he realised the situation was serious. Then came the unbelievable reports: the rebels were in control of the western part of the city, the governor and all high-ranking officials had fled. The army was in disarray, officers had abandoned their soldiers who were deserting in droves. Mosul had fallen.

'We started seeing the poor soldiers running through the streets, some in their underwear. They begged us to tell them how they could leave the city. In my street, I showed two soldiers the way out. Some of my neighbours said we should attack them, take their weapons, but I said no, those two soldiers hadn't harmed us. Truly, the people of Mosul did not harm the soldiers. Those who fled survived, but those who were captured [by the rebels] were killed. No one could believe that the army that had oppressed us for so long and that had treated us so badly had vanished so quickly.'

———

Kifah, a tall, thin and handsome special forces soldier, was stationed in Mosul when the city fell and witnessed the humiliating rout of tens of thousands of Iraqi soldiers and policemen. He retreated with his unit in a column of armoured Humvees, one of the very few units that withdrew in order, retaining their weapons. The rest were dropping their guns and uniforms in the streets, donning civilian clothes and running. Kifah was operating the machine gun on his vehicle when the convoy reached the city gates and saw – contrary to Ahmad's claims – the locals were throwing stones and bricks at the retreating soldiers. 'I wished, with all my heart, that one of the civilians would hit me with a stone, so I could turn my machine gun and mow them all down, but they didn't mess with us [special forces], just with poor unarmed soldiers,' he told me when I met him two years later.

Kifah and his unit retreated along the Mosul–Baghdad highway, coming under fire twice and losing one man.

'We saw dead soldiers scattered along the road, no one stopped to collect them or bury them,' he said. 'I am telling you everything – the good and the bad.'

They stopped that night at a sprawling air base in Tikrit, 170 kilometres north of Baghdad.

The base, which sat in the middle of the desert, surrounded by large berms and fortifications, had been home to the Air Force Academy since the days of Saddam. When the Americans took control of it in 2003, they renamed it 'Camp Speicher'. That name stuck even after the Americans handed the base back to the Iraqi government.

Thousands of young air force and army cadets were already at the base along with retreating soldiers from broken units. Chaos prevailed, and no one was in charge.

The next morning, some officers tried to organise a defensive line, scrambling the few armoured vehicles to go out and secure the area surrounding the airbase. Meanwhile, all over the Sunni heartland, towns and villages were rising up, expelling security forces even before ISIS forces arrived.

'A general came to the base in the morning and ordered us to organise an attack to clear the neighbouring villages, but the men ignored him. The men said: General? What general?' Kifah recounted. 'We knew the area had fallen, our special forces battalion said we wouldn't go, and the soldiers disobeyed the general's orders. When the general ordered one unit to close the gates of the airbase to prevent soldiers from deserting, other units mutinied, and they fought each other. Relatives were calling the soldiers on their mobile phones, urging them to desert. You must imagine the collapse of morale at this time,' said Kifah. 'Those [Sunnis] who had relatives in the area slipped away, and we [Shia] remained. We were a handful of special forces soldiers, along with thousands of young cadets from the army and air force. Most of the cadets had just joined, and had not yet received military training. Yesterday they were civilians, and today they were in a huge base surrounded by the enemy. They were panicking and began leaving. Where are you going? we asked them. Oh, we will hand ourselves over to the tribes, they replied. Why? We have Humvees in the base, and there are weapons and tons of ammunition.

'I said to my corporal, why don't we try to collect weapons and arm those men? There were no officers with us, so I tried to form my own unit. I told them we could leave in a large convoy – if anyone shot at us we would fire a thousand bullets in return. I fired in the air trying to stop them from leaving until one of my men came and said stop firing, they will rip us apart. So they breached the gates and left. You know how our Shia people march in Ashura processions, in their thousands? They marched like that abandoning the base.'

Kifah and other soldiers left the camp in a convoy of three trucks, coming under fire repeatedly until they reached the outskirts of Baghdad.

'We didn't see who was attacking us, just bullets fired from bushes and villages hitting our cars.'

When he reached his home in Baghdad, like tens of thousands of other Iraqi soldiers and policemen, Kifah deserted.

———

A few kilometres down the road from Camp Speicher, the cadets were rounded up by dozens of militants and executed.

Islamic State propaganda videos documenting the mass killing showed how the young cadets, who were promised safe passage by neighbouring tribes, were herded into lorries and pickup trucks like cattle. A single gunman guarding scores of them. They were filmed 'repenting' for joining the army, denouncing the prime minister, the Shia clergy and begging for their lives. They were marched to a complex of former Saddam palaces on the Tigris riverbank, or to neighbouring fields, spat on and humiliated by men and children alike. They were made to kneel or lie on their stomachs in rows. A man carrying a Kalashnikov, his head covered, walked behind them, firing a single bullet into the back of each head. The gunman moved up the line and fired, and another died. Sometimes they fired more bullets into the corpses to make completely sure they were all dead. The official count said 1,700 men were killed on that day, although Kifah and others say the number is higher.

'People won't like to hear this because those who died are considered martyrs now, but they shouldn't have left a base filled with weapons, they could have resisted. I say may they rest in peace, but it's hard to comprehend: a truck packed with young cadets – sitting, crouching – and one man with a stick or a single gun guarding them – why didn't they fight back?' Kifah said.

What came to be known as the Speicher massacre became the catalyst for the rage that followed. The trauma of that massacre sat high in the pantheon of Shia grievances, and this time definitively real and not imagined.

The Speicher massacre also set the barometer of brutality in this war. This was a different war from the sectarian civil war of a few years earlier when Kifah protected his Sunni neighbour against threats from Shia militias and the neighbour reciprocated by getting them out of a jihadi checkpoint in west Baghdad. In the previous war, a medic, a journalist and any non-combatant would have been exempted the harshest of treatment, but in this brutal war whose rules were laid out by the jihadis themselves, no one expected or gave clemency. The soldiers knew the treatment they would receive if captured by the jihadis, and they responded in kind.

After Mosul fell, Kifah sat in the house, spending his days lying on the sofa and watching TV, until one afternoon when he learned that his father, a university teacher in his fifties, was volunteering for the front. We are two men in this house, he told Kifah, and one of us should go and fight. Kifah rejoined the special forces.

That massacre, along with the edict of Grand Ayatollah Ali al-Sistani urging young men to volunteer to help defend the country, mobilised tens of thousands of men to join the fight against Islamic State.

37

The Shia Mobilise for War

SUNNI TOWNS AND VILLAGES IMPLODED in revolt, leaving government forces across the country in disorder. Within a week, Islamic State fighters had reached the gates of Baghdad, at the head of a long trail of massacres and destruction. The formidable army and security services that Prime Minister Maliki had used to implement his sectarian policies crumbled, whole divisions just vanished, weapons and armaments worth billions of dollars fell into the hands of IS militants, and it is estimated that of the 250,000-strong army and federal police, only 50,000 remained in service after the fall of Mosul. The defeat also exposed the wide discrepancy between the army's active fighting force on the ground and the numbers of ghost soldiers who only existed on payroll slips. Many of the Sunnis, alienated by years of discrimination, stood watching Maliki and IS fight each other, delusionally believing that they could tame IS, and waiting for the right moment to move in and take their place, forgetting how a few years earlier they had repeated the exact same mistake with al-Qaeda. Although there were also those with clearer vision and fears, like Adnan al-Janabi, the tribal sheikh and MP.

'This will lead to a chaotic and fragmented Sunni war. What is your programme?' I ask the Sunnis. 'Maliki is corrupt, and his army is sectarian, fine, but what is the plan? A Sunni region? And who will lead it – IS?'. Al-Janabi told me when we met in Baghdad after the fall of Mosul: 'Whatever happens, the Sunnis of Iraq are the biggest losers. In Syria, the Sunnis can win if they expunge the foreign jihadis from their midst, but in Iraq, the Sunnis will lose whatever happens. They are a minority against the Shia, and now they've allowed the jihadis and IS into Sunni regions,' he said, a weary look in his milky grey eyes. He had a face lined by deep wrinkles that sometimes made me feel as if each crevasse represented a different Sunni crisis from the past decade.

Following Sistani's fatwa urging Iraqis to join the fight against the militants and protect the holy Shia shrines, tens of thousands of men – mostly young, mostly from the poor Shia south and Baghdad suburbs – flocked to recruiting centres, military camps and militia headquarters to volunteer in the war. With little or no training, they were chanting and singing as they were shipped to the front in buses and open trucks, like cattle led to the slaughter. Just as the Iranians used to do in their war with Iraq in the eighties.

The whole of Baghdad was gripped by war mania. Militiamen, hardened by years of wars in neighbouring Syria, started patrolling the streets in civilian cars, many sporting green bandanas and bushy beards, armed with pistols and machine guns. Dozens of Shia and pro-government TV stations broadcast endless streams of patriotic songs accompanying propaganda pictures of fierce-looking Iraqi soldiers jumping and marching and shooting.

Driving through Baghdad behind a military police truck ferrying the coffin of a 'martyr' draped in the Iraqi flag, I felt like I was back in the days of the Iran–Iraq War again.

I met with many militia commanders while trying to secure permission to go to the front. Some were well known, part of the landscape of the civil war since 2003; others had gained notoriety in the war in Syria; plus a couple of colourful figures who used the fight against Islamic State to legitimise whatever militia/gang they had already been running.

Most of these meetings lasted a few hours, spent largely with me expressing my utmost respect for the commander and his valorous men, and the commander, sitting under a large portrait of one Shia cleric or another, looking at me suspiciously and talking about himself, the victories of his militia and how he could single-handedly defeat those IS rats. The meetings always ended with the solid promise that the commander's secretary would call me the next day to take me to the front. No calls came, and I kept trying.

———

One very hot afternoon in July 2014, I went to the compound of one of those militias, Kataib Hezbollah, or Hezbollah Battalions, to meet the commander and to plead again for access to the front. Kataib Hezbollah was formed by Abu Mahdi al-Muhandis back in 2007 to 'resist' the American occupation, and later played a crucial role fighting in Syria under Iranian command.

The militia's compound was guarded by men in clean, crisp beige uniforms. (Gone were the tracksuits, flip-flops and T-shirts that had been the earlier iterations of war-wear.) The concrete blast walls surrounding the building were decorated with pictures of men killed in the civil war in Syria. All the men in the pictures wore identical military fatigues and struck a similar pose. I wondered if all their headshots had been photoshopped onto the same body.

The posters were adorned with words like 'Oh Zaynab, you shall not be taken prisoner again' – a reference to the Damascus shrine of Zainab (sister of Imam Hussein), the protection of which was ostensibly why the militias took part in the Syrian civil war.

The compound housed a mosque, a radio station, aid distribution office and a lecture hall that on that hot afternoon was packed with a large crowd of cheerful young men, keen and excited to be volunteering for the front. The prospective fighters clutched plastic shopping bags filled with their belongings, and many of them wore coloured Bermuda shorts. They were loud and boisterous as if they were on their way to a picnic and not another war. Perhaps they were too young to remember the last one. Some had already adorned their heads with the green bandanas bearing the militia's logo. Again, there was something reminiscent of images of the Iran–Iraq War, but then it was Iranians who used to wrap green bandanas around their heads.

The militia's chief 'recruiting officer' was tall and broad-shouldered with a thin beard and short-cropped hair. He clutched a yellow pad in his strong arm and walked among the rows, taking names and details.

'Previously, we chose only people who were committed to protecting the sect and observed their religious commitments – men who prayed and fasted – but now we are accepting anyone,' I was told by the officer, who a few weeks earlier had been commanding a unit of fighters in Aleppo. 'We fought the Americans, and now we are fighting Daesh in Syria. Our experience will make [these recruits] strong. They will have the best training anyone here can give. Even army soldiers are joining us. They want to be rid of the routine and corruption that caused the defeat of the army.' The army was defeated, but the soldiers would be encouraged if they saw one or two fighters from the 'resistance' standing alongside them, he said.

The term 'resistance' had changed hands yet again, and it now referred to Shia battalions backed by Iran, all of whom brandished a variation of the Lebanese Hezbollah flag.

After two hours of waiting, I was taken to meet the boss, a turbaned cleric in a flowing black robe. Half of his dark office was occupied by a desk and bookshelves; two sofas filled the rest. He was young with delicate features dominated by wide black eyes and full lips. Behind him hung a large portrait of the smiling Iranian supreme leader Ali Khamenei. He inclined his head, and the commanders sitting on the sofas stood and filed out without saying a word.

He motioned me towards a sofa, and came to sit opposite me on the other one.

He spoke in a low voice with the hint of a Levantine accent, a relic of the time he had spent in south Lebanon working for a Shia relief agency. He told me that after studying in the religious schools of Qom and Najaf for several years, he had devoted his life to reading and writing. He had published some books on the virtues of the Shia imams and asked one of his aides to bring me a copy of his latest publication.

Then came the war in Syria, and he ended the life of contemplation to volunteer as commander of a unit fighting in the countryside, first near Damascus and then Aleppo.

'To be honest, we didn't go to defend Bashar al-Assad,' he told me. 'We [the Shia] had nothing in common with Bashar. He used to facilitate the movement of jihadis into Iraq, sending us car bombs that killed our people. We went because we, and our brothers in the Islamic Republic [Iran], had realised that this uprising was a plot to separate Syria from the Shia body and that that would weaken Hezbollah in Lebanon and eventually the "Republic" itself. It is an existential fight for the Shia and not for Bashar.'

He was a man of learning with no military experience, but he had loyalty and trust in the command of his Iranian 'brothers'. After fighting in Syria for a couple of years, he came back to Iraq and led the fighting in Baghdad's southern outskirts, an area called Jurf al-Sakhar. It sat strategically between Baghdad and the holy shrines of Karbala and had a strong presence of jihadi groups. (The vicinity had been cleansed of its Sunni inhabitants and declared a closed area by the militia.) He would spend two weeks at the front and one back home. He told me he had lost half of his men in the fighting in Syria and Iraq.

'The region is burning like a volcano, and we as a militia will go after the fire to stamp it down. In Syria, here in Iraq, tomorrow in Lebanon and with the Houthis in Yemen. Just as Daesh has a project, we too have ours. If in Syria we crushed their bodies, here in Iraq we will behead them.'

While his allies stretched from Iran to Yemen, his enemies stretched from Turkey to Saudi Arabia and to the Sunnis of Iraq.

I must have said something about IS exploiting the grievances of the Sunni community, because his smooth, kind face suddenly creased in anger.

'What legitimate demands do the Sunnis of Iraq have? How can I go fight in Jurf al-Sakhar, against Daesh, when my back is exposed here in Baghdad? We must clear Baghdad because Daesh wouldn't have existed if it didn't have local support.'

A tinge of madness crossed his eyes, and he abruptly ended the interview.

The mullah and other militia commanders, gun-toting and turban-wearing, were fundamentalist ideologues who believed that they were fighting a religious war that unfolded across the wider Middle East. The young men who were volunteering on that day were not particularly religiously observant. They joined the militia to fight in defence of the sect that was under threat. A decade after the collapse of the state, and the continuing civil wars, the 'sect' was no longer simply a set of religious beliefs and cultural practices, it came to substitute the national identity. The sect was their country, and serving it was a patriotic duty for those men. A new sectarian nationalism had emerged whose narrative was based on the myths and symbols of the sect and communal politics, rather than on a nationally inclusive narrative.

A Shia politician from the Islamic Council, a party created and nurtured in Iran, told me that they were arming and equipping a new militia force made up of young recruits. He said that he feared the Shia were becoming as extreme as the enemy they were fighting.

'We are in the process of creating Shia al-Qaeda-like radical groups equal in their extremism to the Sunni al-Qaeda. By arming the community and creating all these regiments of militias, I am scared that my sect and community will burn. Our Shia project is the building of a modern, just state but now it's been dominated by the radicals. Think twenty years ahead – what will happen to all those militias and their weapons? Where will they go when the fight is over here? They will take their wars and go to Saudi Arabia, and Yemen. Just like the Sunni jihadis migrated, so will the Shia militias.'

The new young recruits were joined by older veterans like Abu Hashem, who had fought against the army of Saddam Hussein in the 1980s and 90s, under the command of Abu Mahdi al-Muhandis. The day Mosul fell, Abu Mahdi called together his veteran Shia fighters who had fought alongside the Iranians during the eighties war.

'We met him in the Green Zone next day, he told us the Iraqi state has fallen, there is no state, I am the state now,' Abu Hashem said.

After the meeting, Abu Hashem and other veterans headed to the Taji military base north of Baghdad and began setting up a new force. Their first task was to protect the Shia shrines in Samarra and stop the ISIS militants from advancing on Baghdad.

'When we arrived at the base, we found complete chaos,' Abu Hashem said. 'Thousands of young volunteers had gathered there, and no one knew what to do with them.' They were joined by demoralised and broken soldiers, whose units had collapsed. 'We hadn't seen each other for ten years, but we'd stayed in touch, and we started work instantly. Each one of us went back to his old job. Those of us who knew how to drive a tank took over abandoned Iraqi army tanks and started forming new tank battalions and teaching the young volunteers. Others set up radio and communications networks. I had spent my life in intelligence, so I was assigned to run the security and intelligence apparatus.' Many of the veteran fighters were already in their fifties and sixties, but their younger relatives joined them. 'Each one brought two or three sons. A lot of the young had come with their fathers or uncles, and they will become the new generation.'

Abu Hashem and other commanders said that Iranian flights started delivering weapons to the newly opened airport in Najaf. 'The minister of youth and sports at that time used to be head of logistics in the Badr corps. He sat on the floor making phone calls and arranging for shipments of pickup trucks, munitions and weapons to be distributed among the different factions.' With weapons, vehicles and men came the Iranian advisers. They spread in a wide arc from Diala to the western border with Syria. Their voices could be heard on the military radio: directing mortar fire in Fallujah, installing thermal cameras in a small besieged village in the west of Mosul, and accompanying the advance of an Iraqi special forces brigade in Tikrit.

'The reality is that without the Iranians we wouldn't be able to do anything. If the Iranian advisers weren't there, the battalions wouldn't attack. Their presence gave the men confidence in the early days.'

———

Two figures were instrumental in the formation of the Hashed al-Sha'abi, or the People's Mobilisation force, and in the fight that followed: Qassem Sulaimani, the Iranian general, and his close friend Abu Mahdi al-Muhandis. However, the Hashed was never a single fighting force, but a heterogeneous umbrella for multiple militias and paramilitary units. Some were well-organised, battle-hardened companies with a clear hierarchy like Badr, Hezbollah and the Asaib; others consisted of a few dozen men hired by a local warlord or tribal sheikh.

'Sulaimani had a halo around his head, and he became the symbol that everyone was devoted to. And Abu Mahdi was negotiating these multiple factions that were unruly and difficult to control. He was like a music conductor,' Abu Hashem said.

Roughly speaking, the factions could be divided into three categories. First were the military wings of the Islamic Shia parties that had dominated Iraqi politics since 2003, and played a significant role during the civil war. Then there were smaller, more radical militias which had come of age during the war in Syria, and which closely following the Iranian leadership, religiously and politically. (Later, after the defeat of ISIS, they sent MPs to the parliament, so they became militias that owned a political wing.) The third were factions that were formed by the shrine authorities in Karbala and Najaf or by tribes, some of which were Sunni. They had no clear political agenda, beyond the preservation of their founder's interests.

'When we formed the Hashed, we tried to replicate the experience of the Basiege [the Iranian revolutionary guard], but we failed for one reason, and that is the multiplicity of factions,' Abu Hashem told me. 'Some of the battalions have just a few dozen men, but they insist on fighting under their own flag and refuse to accept the command of others.'

They bickered and argued over command, strategy and the division of loot.

'When Abu Mahdi wanted a certain faction to do something,

during the fighting, he had to convince, urge, kiss them on the shoulders, and dangle many rewards before they did his bidding,' said a member of the Hashed shura council. 'If you didn't know how the Hashed factions were run, you would make the mistake of thinking that Sulaimani is the supreme commander and he can just order people around. It is not like this, and no one can pick up a phone and order them to behave in a certain way. They are separate units, each with their own goals, beliefs and, most importantly, a leader with his own interests.'

38

Diala Front Lines

I WENT TO MEET HADI al-Amiri, the grizzled, head of the Badr corps, and the de facto war minister in those days. Like Abu Hashem, he was a close friend of Abu Mahdi al-Muhandis and General Sulaimani, and had been since the eighties when he joined the Iranians in the war against Iraq.

He lived in a villa that had belonged to a former minister from Saddam's regime and dressed in combat fatigues all the time. He told me that the Shia leadership and militia commanders were not worried about Baghdad. The Sunnis had lost Baghdad in the last war, but to protect the city they needed to cleanse the areas surrounding it.

'The Shia are worried about Diala. It's a very strategic area, the front line between the two territories [IS and Iraq], and it has to remain Shia, and that can only be achieved by pushing the fight into Sunni areas to create a Shia belt around Baghdad.'

He said that daily skirmishes were taking place between them and IS militants. 'We take a few metres, they take a few metres back; we take a village during the day, they take it back at night.'

Short and broad-shouldered with bushy eyebrows and an affinity for classical poetry, Amiri himself came from Diala and was spending most of his time there. 'I am an old man, I shouldn't be fighting, but I feel much more comfortable on the battlefield than here in Baghdad,' he said, before proceeding to explain to me how the Islamic State was an American creation because the Americans were trying to regain a foothold in Iraq to fight Iran, and had created IS as a pretext. He showed me grainy footage and assured me that these were American supplies being dropped behind IS lines. He promised he would take me to the front with him, but then never answered my calls. Instead, a friend told me that his cousin was commanding a unit with the Asaib Ahl al-Haq, fighting in Diala province and he was willing to show us the front.

A young militiaman wearing a floppy hat drove us to the front in a white Toyota pickup. The highway was deserted, and he drove at a maddening speed to avoid the IS snipers hiding in the vegetation alongside the road. The occasional military truck or Humvee sped in the opposite direction ferrying the injured and dead.

'The borders of the state of Iraq are thirty-one kilometres ahead of us,' said the militiaman. 'After that, it's the land of Islamic State. See these electricity towers in front of us? That's the town of Udhaim – it's under Daesh control.' He waved his floppy hat towards the left and added: 'They are also parallel to us now, only the Tigris River separates us.'

War debris littered the two sides of the highway: the twisted wreckage of a howitzer, a blown-up Humvee turret along with a scattering of mangled metal.

The road signs on the highway, the main artery connecting Baghdad to Kirkuk in the north, pre-dated the latest war. They declared with misplaced confidence distances that couldn't be measured in kilometres any more, but by how many men would have to die to cross them.

Small hamlets lay deserted or destroyed and what remained standing of their mud houses was occupied by military and militia units after their Sunni inhabitants had fled further north.

'All the area around us was Sunni villages whose inhabitants were displaced. Some because their villages supported Daesh, others just left because they heard we were coming,' said the militiaman with pride. 'Our name brings terror, and they fear us. They think we are like Daesh, but we are not like them. We don't kill families, and we don't attack women or children or elderly people.'

Diala, stretching from the Iranian border in the east to the Euphrates River in the west, was where the sectarian and ethnic tectonic plates of Iraq's Sunnis, Shia and Kurds crashed against each other. Hadi al-Amiri had told me that in Baghdad the front lines had to be drawn according to sectarian logic, but in Diala, like other parts of central Iraq, there were no clear lines separating the Sunnis from the Shia. The two communities had coexisted and intermarried for millennia; often Sunni hamlets and villages sat in the midst of Shia areas, and vice versa. The American invasion, Sunni jihadis and Shia militias had created sectarian fissures between the two communities that the recent war against IS had turned into a deep abyss.

Medieval-looking fortifications had risen up in recent weeks, curled between knotted villages, towns and farmlands, creating military front lines between villages. Fertile fields known for their melons, grapes, wheat and barley turned into parched wastelands when irrigation canals were destroyed by shelling or when Sunni and Shia communities cut the water that irrigated each other's land. If you don't have front lines, then you must create them, by ethnic cleansing or otherwise.

'Before separating the two communities, we need wars and demographic cleansing,' Hadi al-Amiri had said. 'We need sectarian stories to agitate the people, stories and mythologies and tragedies of how the Shia were forced to leave their lands, of how the Sunnis were killed. You need to build enough hatred until you and I can't live together any more – then the divisions become a fact.'

———

The floppy-hatted militiaman said that the military campaign against the Sunnis in Diala had started two years earlier when they began to organise Friday demonstrations and sit-ins against the sectarian policies of Nouri al-Maliki.

'For three consecutive Fridays they prayed and filled a long street with demonstrators against the government. We saw it as demonstrations against the Shia. The government is Shia and the Sunnis are allied with Daesh,' he added in a matter-of-fact tone. 'On the fourth Friday we went into the streets, we shot them, and their bodies were scattered in the streets and the demonstrations stopped . This war did us a great service. It showed our Shia people the reality of the Sunnis. The Shia moderates used to say to us, why do you kill the Sunnis? — they have legitimate demands. Look at their demands now. There is no difference between the protesters and Daesh. Now every Shia, regardless of political affiliation, is forced to support this battle.'

———

A two-metre-high berm and three lines of fortified defences separated the shrinking land of the Iraqi state from the state of the Islamic caliphate.

On the Iraqi side of the berm, a black Shia banner showing the severed head of Imam Hussein fluttered over a group of militiamen scanning the frontlines with a pair of old binoculars. On the other side, three black IS flags shimmered in the afternoon haze. Only sandy whirlwind cones and an occasional mortar bomb crossed this newly established border.

'This land is what separates the good from evil,' said one of the militiamen, pointing at the no man's land. 'Here you see the flag of Imam Hussein, and there you see the black flags of Daesh. This is history repeating itself, the camp of Imam Hussein facing the camp of Yazid,' he continued, trying to superimpose the seventh-century battle of Karbala – the most essential event of Shia Islam – onto the farmlands of Diala.

In one corner of the berm, a group of soldiers in boxer shorts and T-shirts caked with dust and sweat stood dazed under a scorching sun, flinging their M-16 rifles onto their shoulders. Instead of foxholes or shelters, they had spread mattresses and blankets on the berm, giving it the look of a giant laundry line. The soldiers were dependent on the militias to hold the front and on civilian volunteers and villagers to feed and water them. The government had forgone any attempts to supply them, they said. They had enough ammunition to last them for just a few hours of real fighting. Only one of the two ancient Russian armoured vehicles positioned nearby could fire, the other didn't function and was there simply for decorative purposes.

'They say the Iraqi soldier is a coward, but where is the government?' shouted one portly middle-aged soldier angrily. 'We haven't seen anyone here. Where are the parliamentarians who are bickering back in Baghdad? Why don't they visit the front, bring us a box of machine-gun ammo and tell us, this is from the member of parliament who is paid tens of thousands of dollars every month?'

The war resumed every night. Soldiers and militiamen opened fire at will, shooting into the darkness until the early hours of the morning.

'If they don't see us firing they will presume we have abandoned the positions and they'll start moving against us,' said a young soldier. 'We fire at everything – anything beyond the ridge is Daesh, even if it's a dog.'

———

The nearest Sunni village to the front line was deserted. Doors and windows were smashed, and many houses burned; the walls were scribbled with pro-army slogans.

A lone mortar shell had fallen in a small garden and started a fire. Palm trees burned slowly, their fronds crackled and moaned, while the heavy fetid smell of dead bodies wrapped the whole village.

'This is a village of rich farmers,' said the young militiaman with the floppy hat. 'They brought destruction upon themselves just because they hated the Shia and supported Daesh.' He looked at the village mosque that stood intact. 'It's a shame the mosque is still standing – we should have burned it.'

The militiaman was in his mid-twenties and had already spent a decade fighting Sunnis in Iraq and Syria. He had little faith in the Iraqi army's capacity to win this war.

'You can't depend on the army. Even if they put two thousand soldiers in this village I won't take them seriously or rely on them,' he said dismissively. 'When the people saw the soldiers withdrawing, driving American armoured vehicles and tanks away from the front, the Shia wanted to pull out of Diala and morale collapsed. We had to make checkpoints to detain the soldiers and prevent them from leaving. We are a resistance faction that has been fighting for eleven years. Each one of us has been sent to at least three "outside" training camps in Iran and Lebanon under supervision of Hezbollah. Each lasted for two months. Do you know what it means to go for sixty days under constant gruelling combat training by Hezbollah? You come back a new person. You can't compare us with those soldiers who joined the army for money.'

He was so enchanted by the party that he named his first son Imad Mughniyah, after the legendary Hezbollah military commander.

'Do you like Iran?' he asked me, and before waiting for an answer he carried on: 'Iran is a great nation, they have many blessings, but the best thing is that they have Wilayat al-Faqih and they are all united behind one religious leader, not like us.'

———

I spent the night with a group of militiamen, crammed into a small concrete room. The men lay half naked in the sweltering heat trying to get some rest. They had spent the previous night in the fields waiting to ambush Sunni militants. The room was a wretched place; cracks snaked across the walls and ceiling, the air reeked. White cockroaches crawled on the filthy mattresses and pillows and hopped from one sleeping fighter to the other. Many were middle-aged militiamen with paunchy bellies and salt-and-pepper beards. Brand-new machine guns, rocket launchers and Kalashnikovs were lined neatly against the wall on one side of the room that functioned like an armoury separated by wooden ammunition boxes.

The men had just returned from fighting in Syria to take charge of a sector of the front line in their home province of Diala. A one-eyed policeman who doubled as a militia fighter, planting IEDs in the surrounding fields, complained that Shia were just defending rather than attacking.

'Why are we not attacking them? Our enemy in Syria was much stronger, and there we were foreigners fighting in a strange land; now we are home, I know every village and pathway.' He had lost his eye fighting the Americans in 2005 in the same villages.

In front of him sat the commander of the unit, a quiet former school clerk who explained how the berms were bad for 'work'.

'Before, targeting them [the Sunnis] was easier, we were able to snatch the important people. Now we have walls between the two communities, and they have settled behind them,' he said.

'When I liberate an area from Daesh, why do I have to give it back to them? I would either level it or settle Shia in it. Because when I withdraw my forces, the Sunnis will come back, and they will become an incubator for Daesh again,' he added.

'If it were up to me I would start cleansing Baghdad from today,' another fighter said. 'We have not started the sectarian war, we are just trying to secure our areas, but if the "sectarian days" come back then I am sure it will be won by us. You calculate it,' he tells the men. 'In 2006 and 2007 we used to fight on three fronts, the Americans, the Sunnis and the Shia police – now it's much easier.'

'Cleansing' was something normal in the men's speech.

'We will continue in this cycle of war until the Sunnis realise that the Shia have to rule,' the school clerk said.

Like their Sunni enemies they saw themselves as warriors in a religious war that transcended borders. Diala was but a small dot in a big battlefield that stretched across the Middle East.

In their dismal poverty, devotion to war and their sadistic joy at describing how they tortured their captives – placing a tyre around their necks and lighting it was a favoured method – they were identical to the Sunni militants that they had fought for more than a decade. Both sides were the product of an American invasion, when they began their fighting life in resistance to the Americans, before turning against each other.

Three years later, and after the defeat of IS, much of what they wanted had been achieved. From Diala to Kirkuk, almost every single Sunni village along the highway had been flattened by explosives and its people driven into large refugee camps.

———

Two corpses hung from lamp posts on a large public roundabout next to the army brigade HQ in Baquba, the provincial capital of Diala.

A week earlier they had been arrested by the army. One hung upside down; his torso had turned a dark crimson brown, his head shrunk into grotesquerie. Only his military boots were spotlessly clean. The other was decapitated, his head, wrapped in an eternal mad grin, was pinned on his chest with a metal hook.

The Shia militiamen said they were IS fighters brought from the front. The local Sunnis of Diala said they were Sunni men kidnapped by the militias and murdered in retaliation for militiamen killed at the front.

'Nine men have been kidnapped in the last month; we found the bodies of three; the rest are still missing,' a terrified Sunni farmer who lived nearby told me.

Across the street from the hanging bodies, men and women waited silently for a bus, clutching their plastic shopping bags in one hand, and children in the other. They avoided looking at the corpses and pretended they didn't exist, but they hung there like an omen of the days to come.

39

The State

THE CITY.

From Baghdad, Mosul was viewed with suspicion if not outright hostility. Sitting on the road connecting Istanbul and Baghdad, Mosul's culture and history were more intertwined with those of Aleppo and Mardin than with Baghdad's or Basra's.

Its people, the Musolawis – urbane, educated, relatively wealthy and Sunni conservative – had dominated both state bureaucracy and the officers' corps since Ottoman times. In the sectarian politics of post-invasion Iraq – in which the farmers of Diala, the tribesmen of Ramadi and the wealthy merchants of Mosul were treated as a single Sunni entity and challenged to come up with a coherent political programme – Mosul was the only place where an indigenous 'Sunni' political identity took root, helped along by an old social structure that had survived the invasion relatively intact. In the civil war that followed, a brutal and highly effective urban insurgency emerged in Mosul, split between national Islamists and jihadi-Salafi factions. The strongest faction was al-Qaeda in Iraq, and its subsequent reincarnation as the Islamic State, but former Baathi and army officers also had a strong presence. For more than a decade, these factions were a fact of life in the city, vying for power among themselves, and waging a ruthless urban guerrilla war against both the Americans and the newly formed Iraqi security forces. Unlike the tribal-based insurgencies in Ramadi and Fallujah, crushed when tribal elders and commanders were bought off and converted into pro-American militias, the insurgency in Mosul was never defeated.

These factions ruled the city as shadowy gangsterly organisations; imposing taxes on businesses and kidnapping and killing those who failed to pay. Even government departments and offices had to pay them.

Azzam, a short, compact engineer with wire-rimmed glasses, working for the government's Department of Electricity told me that for more than a decade his office had allocated a fixed percentage from every contract to the militants. When I met him after the liberation of Mosul in 2017, he told me: 'Everyone from the director to the local contractor knew 8 per cent was set aside for the militants. The head of our department would get a phone call from them before every bidding process. They chose who would win and who got appointed to what job. A third of all new vacant positions were set aside for them. No one dared to disobey. Those who didn't pay were kidnapped. Every government institution was infiltrated, even the police. When Mosul fell they came to the surface.'

Maliki had worked to dismantle Sunni power and believed that demonstrations in Sunni cities in 2012/13 were a Baathi-jihadi plot financed by Turkey and Qatar to create a Sunni province. Further fuelling the animosity between Shia Baghdad and Sunni Mosul, he unleashed his police and security forces to suppress any opposition in the city. They behaved like an occupation army, detaining at will, disappearing, torturing and humiliating the people. So when the triumphant jihadis paraded their pickup trucks through the streets of Mosul in early June 2014, many saw them as liberators, or at least as the lesser evil.

To the rest of the world, these were brutal and savage bands of jihadi fighters, aided by an adept and shrewd army of internet propagandists. But they were successfully positioning themselves as saviours, freeing the 'Sunni' people of Mosul from the grip of Shia security forces.

Initially, the militants were polite and did not interfere with the population. They prevented looting, dismantled checkpoints and removed the concrete barriers the army had installed at the entrance of each neighbourhood, choking the city and limiting the movement of people. There was even confusion regarding the gunmen's identity. Were they the Tribal Revolutionaries who had been demonstrating for a year? Or were they officers from the old army attempting a comeback by exploiting different insurgent groups? Or maybe they were jihadi militants like al-Qaeda and the newly formed ISIS that were dominating Syria?

Clarity came a week after the fall of Mosul, when the militants issued a manifesto, calling it the Madina (City) Document – a reference to the treaty issued by the Prophet Muhammad when he migrated from Mecca to Madina in 622. The document – written in an archaic, flowery language, laden with millenarian references – aimed to regulate the lives of the believers, identify the new rulers and make their intentions clear. It started by congratulating the people of Mosul for '*these divine victories . . . To those who ask who are we, we say we are the soldiers of the Islamic State in Iraq and al-Sham, who took upon us the revival of the glories of the Islamic caliphate and protecting our people and brothers . . . In the end we tell you oh people you have tried all the secular regimes, from the monarchy to the republic to Safavid [Shia] government, you have tried it and been burned by its fires and here we are now in the reign of the Islamic State and the region of our imam, Abu Baker . . .*'

Although in their document they banned the sale of cigarettes and urged women to be modest and to keep to their houses, in the streets people continued to smoke, nargile cafes stayed opened until late, women came and went unchaperoned. Music played at weddings and many of the families that had fled Mosul returned.

'I have to be honest,' Ahmad, the computer business owner, said. 'When Islamic State first entered Mosul, everyone was happy. People started clapping for them, women ululating. Before they removed the army blockades, it would take an hour to go from one area to another; afterwards, the roads were open, and we felt free. They left people alone and didn't mind if people smoked, if people prayed or not. You could go anywhere, do anything you wanted as long as it didn't hurt them. I would go to the woods with a friend, sit in a cafe, smoke a nargile, and they would turn up – tall, muscled and mostly foreign – but they wouldn't dare say a word to you. In the early days, we said this was the life.'

———

IS roots lay in both the radical Islamic militancy of jihadi-Salafism and in the Islamic insurgency that came into existence after the American occupation, starting with al-Tawhid and al-Jihad of Abu Musab al-Zarqawi, which became al-Qaeda in Iraq.

After the defeat of the jihadis at the hands of a coalition of Sunni tribesmen and turncoat insurgents in 2007/8, they moved into the desert regions of western Iraq where they regrouped and reorganised. The Arab Spring and the oppression that followed gave them new impetus. Exploiting the civil war in Syria, they crossed the border, establishing themselves first in the deserts bordering Iraq and then expanding through a landscape destroyed by war and inhabited by militias.

The IS split from al-Qaeda, which had occurred in Syria earlier over the distribution of spoils, consolidated over issues of allegiance. With its disciplined and brutal forces, it quickly achieved a series of victories over the ramshackle, fragmented Syrian rebel groups. They carved a territory for themselves stretching from Raqqa and the oilfields of the east to parts of Aleppo and northern Syria along the strategic border with Turkey. Each victory brought them more weapons and more resources from captured oilfields, granaries and military depots. Tens of thousands of foreign fighters crossed the borders from Turkey and flocked to join them. All these victories paled in comparison to the capture of Mosul. The loss of its second city was a significant defeat for the government of Iraq, especially as it involved the rout of 50,000 soldiers and policemen and the capture of hundreds of tons of weapons, equipment and armoured vehicles.

Unlike in their earlier incarnations, the jihadis did not just promise the people of Mosul a Sunni resistance to the injustices inflicted on them by the American occupiers and the sectarian politics of the Shia government in Baghdad. They went further; they promised a state, with military strength, effective bureaucracy and adhering to the principles of Sunni Islam, trying to recreate the imagined perfection of the first Muslim community of the Prophet and his caliphs.

In their literature and sermons, the jihadi ideologues used different names: the Caliphate, the Islamic State in Iraq and al-Sham, Islamic State. All these names were eventually superseded by one name: the State, or al-Dawla in Arabic. It signified to the people of Mosul the nature of their new rulers, who were going to provide them with a strong, functioning and non-corrupt administration, like they had had before American intervention had destroyed it.

'They conned the people,' Ahmad told me. 'They brought prices down and reimposed order. People from the heart of Mosul, from its oldest houses, would join them because they said this is the true Islam. Doctors and university professors joined them, my son's *teacher* became a preacher for them, carrying a pistol and grenades on his belt. The whole city joined them.'

This narrative of the new State took on all the familiar qualities of the *ancien régime*: It was narrow-minded, pathologically suspicious and phantasmagorical in its call for a return to a glorious past. This wasn't because it was a conspiracy by the former regime to come back to power using Islamic State. Yes, many of its leaders and bureaucrats had served in Saddam's government, but so did many of the high-ranking generals in the new Iraqi army. Basically anyone in Iraq with decent bureaucratic experience must have been part of the state institutions during Saddam's regime.

The Baath Party was not ideologically based like the Muslim Brotherhood or the Communists, but was a Party of the State, and its members could quickly shift their allegiances to the new State power.

As the military scientist in Mosul had told me: 'Some of the Baath Party members and their followers who were once secular eventually joined al-Qaeda and later ISIS. They joined not because there was a so-called marriage or a conspiracy between Baathists and the jihadis – this is a myth and a misconception. They joined to find a position of authority for themselves. They didn't lack the money, but they missed the power. The party was everything to them and now it was gone and with it their authority and status.'

Apart from the new techniques of fear and horror disseminated by very canny use of social media networks, the jihadis had no new vision beyond that of the totalitarian regimes that ruled and still rule the region. Their newspaper read like government papers printed in Baghdad, Sana'a or Damascus: a mixture of propaganda from the latest sermon of the leader or chief ideologue on page one; delusional descriptions of victories in Syria, Iraq and Afghanistan on page two; on pages three and four statistics of how many schools and health-care centres had been opened. The last page carried stories from the glorious past designed to build morale and encourage the youth. All so familiar, repetitive and boring.

Islamic State did not unfold over Mosul in a single day. It came gradually over two months, in a series of actions and proclamations, each affecting one segment of the society at a time. And each decree brought the rulers one step closer to the eventual complete takeover of the city.

In that, they were following a 'tried-and-tested' path that many governments throughout the twentieth century had used to build their earthly utopian state, with varying degrees of failure and varying numbers of casualties.

One: Create or use a mythical narrative and a founding ideology to justify all subsequent actions.

Two: Purge the society of all undesirables, using the exclusive ideology of Step One. Preferably, conduct the purges in stages, especially if the nascent movement creating the utopia does not have numerical strength. Start the purges with those groups that could pose the highest threat, beginning with their close allies who helped them come to power, the military and organised elements in society and any inclusivity campaigners, etc.

Three: Use utmost brutality and viciousness when implementing Step Two, to strike the general society with paralysing terror that shall thwart any future resistance.

Four: Build a ruthless intelligence network. Expand that network by leveraging extreme fear from Step Three to induce members of the society to denounce and report on each other.

Five: Build a patronage system to maintain the loyalty of followers, using a mixture of perks, privileges and threats.

Six: Build a competent bureaucracy.

Seven: Begin to change society and reshape it according to the movement's own will and image. Use Step Two to justify any diversion from Step One.

In a true Stalinist way, IS moved against their former allies – aware of the long history of backstabbing and betrayals among the different insurgent factions in Iraq and Syria. They arrested anyone who might pose a threat from within, especially Baathists, and former army officers who they suspected of harbouring their own plans. In a few days, dozens of Baathists and officers were executed and disappeared.

Good information was vital for good organisation. 'They came to us and opened the big land registry ledgers, and they wanted to know which lands were owned by Christians, Sunnis or Shia,' a bespectacled clerk in the agricultural land registry told me. 'We couldn't answer, we told them these documents went back to the Ottoman times, and we only have names of the owners – there was no way to find their religion, let alone their sects.'

So they conducted a comprehensive census, so extensive and complete it would have made any Soviet or GDR apparatchik jealous. Those who had served in the army or police were registered and required to repent. Key workers such as doctors, nurses, engineers and teachers were required to provide their addresses and those of their families, and were banned from leaving the city. Every shop, factory, commercial activity and property was surveyed and marked according to the religion and sect of its owners.

A week later, the result of their meticulous and thorough property survey became evident: house doors and shopfronts were either labelled 'Sunni Muslim' or 'N'. The 'N for Nazarene' that was graffitied on properties marked them for confiscation by the State Property Office, the diwan. A decree followed demanding that all Christians should convert to Islam, or pay a levy, or be expelled from the city. The exodus of the Christians began. Families were frisked at the gates of Mosul, to prevent them from carrying anything of value on them. Some were taken as hostages and concubines. Shabak and other Muslim minorities had either fled or been killed.

After the persecution of the minorities came the prohibition of smoking and of male–female co-working and, in the universities, the purging of anything in the curriculum deemed 'un-Islamic'. A strict version of the niqab was now compulsory for women, who were no longer allowed to leave their homes without the company of a male relative.

The tools of that oppression, imposing the will of the State, were the Hisba – the State-monitoring body in charge of everything from inspecting the lengths of beards to dress code and moral behaviour – and the Amniyat – the feared security apparatus.

Ahmad, a state-approved Sunni, adapted to the new regime. He grew his beard, shortened his trousers and life continued, with his properties protected from confiscation. Even though the new State beheaded, tortured and raped, he saw freedom. 'We had been occupied since 2003, and this was the first time we were truly free.'

While the people enjoyed the new-found peace, IS leaders embarked on their most ambitious project ever, turning from a shadowy insurgency into the State, and in the process changing the society and destroying any resistance that stood in their path.

———

Totalitarian regimes can't survive on millenarial ideology and mass terror without a functioning bureaucratic system and competent administrators. Gradually, as the IS gunmen secured their position in Mosul, they turned to creating an administration for their city state and its rapidly expanding territories. They abolished all existing government structures, replacing them with ministry-like organisations, the diwans, which incorporated any directorate or institution that had existed before (health, education, electricity and water services, finance, war, judicial/security, agriculture, etc.). An emir, foreign or

Iraqi, headed each diwan. The emirs, along with their staff, oversaw every activity in the city.

'The Islamic State was a terrorist state, but it was also a modern state,' said Azzam, the engineer who worked for the Department of Electricity. 'They dressed and talked like they lived in early Islam, but administratively they were excellent and ran the state efficiently.'

Beyond the archaic names and terminologies, the commissar-like supervisors and the newly printed stationery emblazoned with their logos, the city state was a hybrid of a ruthless capitalist free market and a totalitarian regime, garnished with behaviour, social mores and manners of speech that belonged in seventh-century Arabia.

'The brilliance of Islamic State lay in its ability to bring together a world of contradictions, all for achieving the main goal: controlling the society and making money. Side issues were not important,' said Azzam, who had worked closely with IS administrators.

Like their system, the new ruling elite were also a motley mix. Azzam described an incoherent blend of different components with no common thread. Some came for financial benefit and rewards of the State and others joined out of belief; there were tribesmen from the countryside of Mosul, as well as members of the old mercantile families from the city; religious clerics and street thugs; foreign jihadis and former army officers. 'It fulfilled the desires of each one of these groups. Those who came from the countryside were given houses in the rich neighbourhoods of Mosul, something previously unimaginable. The foreigners were given women and power, and the officers were given the authority they had lost after 2003.'

Azzam's new boss at the Department of Electricity – now part of the Diwan of Services – was a French-Moroccan who had streamlined and simplified fee collections.

'The process of issuing an electricity bill used to take us almost two months; when the State came, they simplified the system – all commercial activities, factories and shops paid a fixed fee. In residential areas, they installed smart meters that provided a certain amount of electricity throughout the month. No one dared to not pay their electricity bill at the start of the month fearing the Hisba's punishments. Stealing electricity was considered theft, punishable by hand amputation.'

The same streamlined collection methods were used for everything from garbage collection to taxation. Every street in the city was handed to a certain garbage collector who was paid by its residents. Inspectors regularly came to check the streets were clean and fees were paid. Using their registry of shops and factories, they issued cards with the amounts due and again sent their Hisba enforcers to see the cards were stamped and fees paid. Terror made sure everyone paid on time.

'We in the Iraqi state couldn't draw a line without permissions and letters going back and forth to all relevant ministries, but they ran each diwan as an independent organisation. One day the new municipality decided to open a road, they brought their equipment and cut a highway through an archaeological area, the road was paved and opened in a few weeks, and it was named the Caliphate Street.'

———

Mosul's new rulers were as ingenious in envisioning new techniques to generate income as they were at devising new execution methods and torture techniques. Because Islamic State, in its essence, was a massive Ponzi scheme set up in the perfect echo chamber. It used the wealth of a captured city, or oilfield, or confiscated property, to finance further expansion and pay for its patronage network among the mujahideen and faithful. Like all aggressive states, once the expansion stopped, the Ponzi scheme crumbled.

All confiscated lands, properties, factories, along with looted wealth, in a region encompassing some of the most fertile lands in the Middle East, two of its most ancient and vibrant cities, Mosul and Aleppo, as well as the oilfields in eastern Syria, belonged to Diwan al-Mal (the Finance Department).

Extensive farmlands owned by the Shabak, Yazidis and other minorities were offered as a share-crop investment to Sunni farmers and businessmen willing to split the profits with the State. Christian houses were given to the faithful, their cars and belongings sold in auctions. The Ministry of Animal Wealth led by a short and wiry former teacher used confiscated cattle to provide meat at subsidised prices.

Crude oil extracted in Syria was sold to anyone willing to refine it. Some produced a few barrels of cheap petrol using home-made burners; others had invested in small modern refineries brought in from Turkey. The desert roads between Iraq and Syria were packed with tanker traffic ferrying oil back and forth.

'You want to produce oil, you are welcome to: they sold you the crude and you had to sell your refined product in their official selling points and pay them taxes. And it solved the problem of fuel,' Azzam said.

Trade in looted archaeological artefacts, weapons and enslaved women and children flourished. A large number of war profiteers and smugglers ensured that food products and fuel came from as far away as regime-controlled Damascus, crossing multiple front lines. Modern equipment, medical supplies and cars were smuggled across international borders from Turkey.

In matters not related to finance and security, the same centuries-old Iraqi bureaucracy prevailed. State functionaries continued to push paper, file memos, write inventories in big ledgers and refuse to take any action before receiving written orders from superiors.

People lived in a surreal universe in which they remained employees of the Iraqi state that continued to pay their salaries while answering directly to IS bosses who took a cut of their wages. They used Iraqi mobile phone and internet networks, and carried their government-issued cards with them at all times for the IS militants to inspect.

40

The People Resisting

THE CONCRETE BARRIERS THAT HAD formerly divided neighbourhoods found a new use: IS gunmen lined them up around the city, forming a high wall and turning Mosul into one giant prison. The new regime slogan 'Permanent and Expanding' hung everywhere.

The machines of oppression had turned on the Sunnis themselves, and gradually things started changing even for people like Ahmad. 'In the beginning, we were able to travel freely in and out of Mosul, but now when I think about it, I would say things started changing two or three months after they arrived, when they stopped us from moving. Then a year later, when things flipped – and what a flip – they made us tremble with terror in our own homes.' He shook his head and grinned. 'They imposed their authority, terrorising the people in simple ways, dragging them to mosques to pray, shouting into megaphones, and if you ever argued with one of them, you would be dragged into their prisons. I asked one of them one day, why are you talking to us like this, why are you treating us like inferior people? He said: we want to insult you, you doctors and engineers, we would crush your heads with our feet, because these degrees of yours are not Islamic. They brought terror into our hearts and inside our own homes. I feared my neighbour, my brother and my son. I swear I feared my own wife lest, if we argued with each other, she might go out and denounce me to them.' By 'the people' he meant,

308

of course, the State-approved Sunnis since all the undesirables were long gone.

———

Diwan al-Siha (the Health Department) like other IS diwans, implemented a two-tier system, distinguishing between the 'Brothers' – those who gave allegiance to the new regime – and the 'Awam', the commoners, or the rest of the population.

'We had two systems in the hospitals,' Wassan the doctor told me. 'Daesh members and their families were given the best treatment and complete access to medicine, while the normal people, the "Awam", were forced to buy their own medicine on the black market.' Although women were ordered to stay home, doctors and nurses were exempted. But Wassan, an idealist, had to live with the new apartheid regime imposed by the functionaries of al-Dawla. 'We started hating our work. As a doctor, I am supposed to treat all people equally, but they would force us to treat only their own patients. I felt disgusted with myself.' She couldn't resign from her job because doctors were on a special registry. 'Three days absent from work, and they arrest you for desertion.'

She tried to leave Mosul, but by then it was too late, the security around the borders of IS territory had been tightened to prevent useful people like her from leaving. She tried to escape but her attempts failed. On her third failed attempt, the smuggler – with whom she had exchanged text messages – was caught; a few days later, female members of the Hisba raided her house, confiscated her phone and told her she was being watched.

So she decided to rebel against the system from within. 'You can adjust to any condition in life, and this is how we survived the rule of Daesh. Life went on, we threw birthday and engagement parties and celebrated the weddings of female friends. We even had DJs, though they had to play the music at very low volumes. We tried to go through life as if nothing had changed. In the hospital, we would sometimes block the cameras IS installed to monitor us, and throw impromptu parties for the children in the cancer ward.' One day on her way back from work, she found one of the last pastry shops still open in the city, and asked the owner to bake her a cake in the shape of SpongeBob, a favourite character of one of her young, and terminal, patients. The owner apologised and told her that the Hisba had banned him from baking any cakes with figures drawn on them, but as a compromise, he gave her a square-shaped yellow cake.

She flipped through pictures of these parties on her phone, her eyes gleaming with tears and a big smile on her face and then she told me that half of the children in these pictures had died due to the lack of medicine during the war. She continued to plan for life after IS, studying at home for her specialist degree. 'I hoped that one day I would come out of this IS nightmare.'

In any totalitarian society, some collaborate, a few resist, and the majority bend their heads and abide by the new rules. The tall and gaunt former missile scientist, who had worked under Saddam, belonged to the majority. Every day, he left his house early in the morning and traversed the city. Riding in packed buses or walking on foot – he could not afford to buy fuel for his car or pay the fare of a taxi – he called on friends, checked on his elderly mother, and visited his sister's family. Sometimes he looked for cheap home-refined kerosene for the old heaters in his house or tried to score some contraband books and cigarettes, but mostly he just meandered aimlessly through the streets and markets, a traveller in his own city.

When he returned home, he sat at his old wooden desk, bending his bony head with its angular jaw and arched nose over one of his faux-leather notebooks, writing in meticulous detail his journal entry of the day. Most of what he wrote was trivial and banal; details of daily life, the fluctuation in prices of tomatoes, the amount of money he borrowed from his mother, how many cigarettes he cadged from a friend, the fight with his wife when he invited a friend and his family who had lost their house in an air raid to come and stay with them. At the start of each entry, he wrote his observations from the streets, his commentary on the day's news and his political analysis of events. The five volumes were the handwritten diaries of a city under occupation, a survival guide of life under the rule of jihadi-Salafi militants – charting the ascendancy of the caliphate city state, and eventually its ultimate demise.

'Life rotates around seeing friends, thinking and writing. I must live this moment and record it,' he wrote in a journal entry from August 2014. 'We live like prisoners serving a long jail sentence. Some of us will come out having finished reading dozens of books; others will be devastated and destroyed.' To survive this prison term, he made a goal of finishing all the books he had wanted to read for years but hadn't had the time: thick, leather-bound volumes of Arabic literature, Islamic history, jurisprudence, and a collection of cheaply printed classic novels.

A year into the rule of the new regime, he wrote: 'They humiliate the dignity of man, you have to eat, dress and think as they want you to. An eighteen-year-old comes and questions the length of your beard. According to his whims, he might take you to the Hisba, and there you get into the system. I fear that. I fear humiliation. I spent my life with scientists; now I have to sew a piece of elastic into the hems of my trousers to make them go above the ankle [the required trouser length according to IS regulations].'

He stopped looking into the mirror before leaving the house. It depressed him to look at his long grey scruffy beard, even trimming its edges was banned under IS rules; he acquired what he described as 'my absurd miserable look'.

Missing a prayer was a punishable crime, and although he was a devout Muslim who had never missed a prayer in four decades, he came to dread the call to prayers when he was in public. 'Under IS, the azaan became like a foreboding warning call, a shock, one immediately had to find a street corner, a mosque or a group of people gathering to pray with them.'

In an earlier journal entry, he described attending a Friday sermon, listening to the preacher who, like all mosque preachers, was appointed by the Diwan of Religious Affairs. 'I prayed the Friday in their mosque,' he wrote. 'The mullah came to the mosque carrying a Kalashnikov; he laid it against the wall and led us in prayer. After the prayers he turned and sat facing us and started a long sermon, mispronouncing half of his words and mixing his vowels. He insulted and rebuked us for not joining the jihad. He told us that this life was not worth living – "you are temporary here, and the real life is in heaven". He also told us we were fortunate to live under the shadow of the caliphate.' After that, the scientist made sure not to leave the house on Fridays so that he wouldn't be forced to attend the prayers in the mosque.

'They have a very binary mentality: either one or zero, there's no middle ground. If one argues with them they say you have a worldly mentality, we are offering to take you to heaven, and you are still obsessed with this life?'

One day, he came back home to see the street in commotion. His wife and daughters were outside comforting a weeping neighbour, whose husband had been taken by Hisba enforcers to be flogged in a nearby square. His crime was trying to intervene with the armed enforcers, on behalf of an old man who was accused of trimming his beard. Both men were taken to be flogged, and all the adult males in the street were ordered to attend the flogging ceremony. When the scientist returned home, his son, who had also attended the flogging, was furious and accused his father and the men of the neighbourhood of being cowards for not standing up to the enforcers. 'How can we let those people rule us?' the angry boy asked his father. 'But what can we do?' the scientist answered. 'We are simple people. The solution is international. It is in the hands of Obama and Putin, and who am I to them?"

As the days passed, the diary entries became those of a man struggling to maintain his sanity and his self-respect, while he and his family lived in a city ruled by mad fanatics, like one of those doomed characters in a Hans Fallada novel. 'People blame me for not attempting to leave. My young daughter said we should all move to Kirkuk, rent a room and live in it so that they could finish their education. Maybe I should have listened to her. But I was afraid of the future.'

———

At the height of their power, it was estimated that Islamic State had an annual budget of about \$2 billion, generated by oil and wheat sales, taxation and confiscations and the resale of properties. They needed to maintain their expansion to continue financing the State. By 2015, they were under military pressure both in Syria by a Kurdish-led alliance and in Iraq from the Shia militias and government forces. In that year, the government in Baghdad stopped paying the salaries of government employees in Mosul. At the same time, the US and their allies began targeting fuel trucks travelling between oilfields in Iraq and Syria. As IS expansion halted in the region they switched to attacks internationally to boost their reputation and maintain that fearful image.

In Mosul, government employees stopped showing up for work; teachers had all but abandoned their schools since most of the students had started staying home when the head of the Education Diwan changed the curriculum. Those considered essential workers, like doctors and engineers working in service departments, were ordered to show up for work and were paid one-tenth of their original salary.

The State used different tools to generate income. The salaries of the fighters were halved, and taxation increased. Fines were added to floggings; carrying prayer beads – considered a sin according to their religious teachings – was punished by a fine calculated according to the number of beads. Anyone caught selling cigarettes was sent to jail, and had to pay the price of the confiscated cigarettes on the black market as a fine. People started selling whatever they could to survive: family heirlooms, furniture, and even property. Any savings the missile scientist had were long gone. His mother supported him with $15 a month from his late father's pension, but that lasted him only a week. So he cut his family's expenses to $2 a day – food was still affordable under IS rule, but all non-essential expenses were stopped. In two years, no one in his house bought any new clothes – 'Who would you get dressed for, if you are locked in your house all the time?' But he was still short of money and then there were the cigarettes, so his daily trips around the city had a purpose now, to find a friend or an acquaintance to borrow money from.

In Azzam's Department of Electricity, he noticed that his boss was diverting electricity away from residential neighbourhoods and into the three cement factories outside the city because they generated a steady income for IS. All government cars were confiscated and sold. The air raids on the city had intensified; the university where his son was studying medicine was bombed by the US-led coalition jet fighters, gutting its elegant structures. With the bombing campaign, and the Iraqi army starting to push northward, and IS losing territory,

Azzam gradually came to realise that the collapse of the caliphate was coming and it was all too familiar; he had seen that collapse repeated many times in his life.

'Nations create a myth, and they believe in it. Our myth was the story of the Great Iraq. Saddam went to war with Iran because he wanted to maintain that myth. The repercussions from that war haven't stopped; what we see are reactions to that war. Nations dream and the people pay the price for the collapse of the dream. We used to hear about the dreams of Arab unity and saw it collapse. The Islamic State, the defender of the Sunnis, was another dream that collapsed. The Kurds have their own dream, and it just collapsed too.'

———

Wassan moved from her passive resisting to active rebellion. 'Before the start of the military operations, medicine began to run out, and I started collecting whatever I could get my hands on and stashing it at home. I built a network of pharmacists, those who I knew and could trust. I started collecting tools from the doctors and medics. Each would extract a few instruments from the hospital and give them to me until I had a full surgery kit at home. I could even perform operations with full anaesthesia, with the help of my mother who was trained as a nurse. By word of mouth, people learned that I had medicine and I was treating patients free of charge. Some started coming from the other side of Mosul, and whatever supplies I had were running out. But I knew there was plenty of medicine in our hospital to treat IS members and their families, some of which was medicine we couldn't even buy on the black market. But the storage rooms in the hospital were under the control of IS apparatchiks. I started siphoning some of that medicine under the pretext of treating IS patients. If their patient needed one injection, I would take five. After a while, they must have realised because they stopped allowing doctors to go into the storage room unaccompanied.' The punishment for stealing was hand amputation, but running an underground hospital in her house would be considered sedition punishable by death.

After the start of the government's military offensive, hospitals in Mosul were either bombed by Iraqi and coalition air forces, or turned into military installations by IS fighters, and the medicine she had stolen became a lifesaver. Her underground hospital became essential for the people in her area. She delivered more than a dozen babies on the dining table. She kicked her two brothers out of their rooms and turned one into an operating theatre and the other into somewhere for new mothers to convalesce.

——

While madness raged outside, the people of Mosul could do nothing but lock themselves into their homes and try to stay safe. First Ahmad kept his wife indoors, then the girls and later the boys, in case they were rounded up and taken to the front. Finally, he limited his own movement. 'I would rarely go out, my jobs stopped, my business stopped, the people around me disappeared, but we survived, and I'll tell you how we survived: we survived the same way we survived thirty years of Saddam's rule. By following the old Iraqi way of bending your head and walking next to the wall. They used to say Saddam's regime was brutal,' Ahmad scoffed. 'Well, Saddam was a picnic compared to them.'

People went to extremes. One man, an artist, dug a hole behind his house where he put his and his son's drawings and paintings wrapped in plastic sheets. He poured concrete into the hole and put a water tank on top, then confined his five young boys to the attic. When the boys emerged two years later, the youngest two had lost the ability to speak. A doctor, whose family had come to the attention of the local Amniyat squad twice – when he was flogged fifteen times for defending a neighbour whose beard wasn't long enough and when his son was detained and tortured for two days for listening to music – was afraid he wouldn't survive a third encounter. He built a wall around his house, cemented up his door and left only a hole through which a neighbour could pass him and his family food once a week, effectively building his own prison. 'In the end, I went mad; I just wanted to kill myself,' he told me.

Even with the self-imposed confinement Ahmad couldn't totally protect his children. In each neighbourhood IS installed 'media points'. 'They put up large TV screens and DVD players with speakers in the streets and played their propaganda films to the children who would gather and watch.' Two years into the State's rule, Ahmad tried to smuggle himself and his family out. He found someone who would take him through the desert to a refugee camp in Syria. The man asked for $10,000; when he called him a week later to say he agreed, the price had gone to $30,000.

Tens of thousands fled, not only Mosul but the whole region, starting an epic journey to Europe. Hundreds would die along the way.

41

Migration, Part 2

IN 2015, A KURDISH SCHOOL friend of mine living in northern Iraq posted a diagram on his Facebook page. With little hand-drawn arrows and stick figures and pictures of a train and a boat or two, the diagram showed you how to get from Turkey to the German border in twenty easy steps. After you've made the thousand-mile trip to western Turkey, the journey proper begins with a taxi to Izmir on the coast. An arrow points to the next stage: a boat across the Aegean to 'a Greek island', costing between €950 and €1,200. Another boat takes you to Athens. A train – looking like a deformed caterpillar – leads to Thessaloniki. Walking, buses and two more worm-like trains take you across Macedonia to Skopje, and then through Serbia to Belgrade. A stick figure walks across the border into Hungary near the city of Szeged. Then it's on to Budapest by taxi and another taxi across the whole of Austria. At the bottom of the page, a little blue stick figure is jumping in the air waving a flag. He has arrived in Germany, saying hello to Munich, after a journey of some three thousand miles, taking perhaps three weeks, at a total cost of €2,400.

Migration to Europe was the topic of almost every conversation in the cafes of Baghdad and Damascus – and in towns large and small across Syria and Iraq and beyond – and so were the pros and cons of the social aid given to migrants in different countries. The best routes were common knowledge, and information on new developments and up-to-date advice quickly spread via Viber, WhatsApp and Facebook. All you needed to reach Europe was a couple of thousand dollars and a smartphone. It was a significant change from the late 1990s, when – in Iraq at least – UN sanctions combined with the conditions of Saddam's dictatorship meant it had been barely possible to get by, your existence depending on government handouts and meagre state salaries. Hundreds of thousands of people left Iraq during the sanctions; a few reached Europe but most languished in Jordan, in dull Amman. Most people I knew wanted to leave, and most failed – for lack of funds, will or simply luck.

I was one of those who failed. I was hoping to continue my studies in Vienna or Beirut, or at least to get a half-decent job in Amman or Dubai. I was a military deserter, so I had no hope of obtaining a passport: my only way out of Iraq was by procuring fake documents or by finding a smuggler. For nine months in 1999, I tried and failed. I spent nearly $3,000 – then a fortune – on the smuggler's fees. I was lied to, betrayed and conned out of money I had borrowed. I lived with my bags packed, ready to go, and every night I made a call to the smuggler, who kept saying that the next day was the day. Eventually, I gave up and unpacked my bags and waited another five years.

———

For decades, the paths that led out of war, destruction and poverty into the safety of life in Europe were closely guarded secrets, the property of smugglers and mafias who controlled the routes and maintained a monopoly on the necessary knowledge. They conducted their illicit trade out of dingy cafes in the backstreets of Aksaray in Istanbul and – for the lucky few who reached Greece – the Omonia district of Athens. Those who got that far were handed on from one network to another, to be lied to and manipulated again and again, as they tried with their bravest faces to get any reliable assurances from the people traffickers, who just sat back and waited for the migrants to give in. After all, these people had no choice but to hand over their cash in exchange for a promise and hope.

In 2015, everything changed. A trickle of migrants had always crossed the Aegean, an undesirable route not because of choppy waters and unsound boats but because of the thuggish Greek police and the remoteness of the prospect of asylum in Athens. The trickle turned into a stream when the new Greek Syriza government rewrote the rules. 'The policy used to be: return the boats even if we put lives in danger,' a coastguard official on Lesbos told me that summer. 'With this government it's: no, let them come in, and help them if they need help.' Turkey, too, was now turning a blind eye to the migrants, and the old smugglers' networks and tightly controlled borders into Europe gave way under the weight of tens of thousands of people fleeing civil wars. Syrians previously displaced across Jordan, Lebanon and Turkey were joined by Iraqis fleeing Islamic State and Shia militias – along with a small percentage of Afghans, Eritreans and Pakistanis, all escaping their own conflicts, all seeking out the new routes in the hope of better lives. The mobilisation techniques used in the Arab Spring, which brought out thousands of demonstrators to a specific place, were now being used to organise the new waves of migration. This was no longer an exodus of the wretched and downtrodden – though many still were – but a pilgrimage, predominantly, of the young, educated and middle class. The breaking down of Europe's borders left two groups of people angry and struggling to find a way to restore the old order: the EU officials and the smugglers.

———

Early one morning on the island of Lesbos, a short grey-haired man parked his motorbike under a pine tree and sat down on a pebbly beach littered with dozens of abandoned lifejackets – orange, red and blue. The carcasses of rubber dinghies lay nearby. In the distance, on the other side of the channel, the Turkish mountains were gloomy: the day was overcast. The man came to the beach every morning and sat and waited for the migrants' boats to arrive. Occasionally he scanned the horizon with a battered pair of military binoculars. Two of his friends had set up a table a little way back, and sat drinking coffee. They were all fishermen, but now, like many others on the island, they had become scavengers, ripping the outboard motors off the arriving dinghies. The law of the sea stipulates that you can keep whatever you find drifting in.

'Sometimes they send them with bad Chinese engines,' the man said, not out of concern for the migrants' safety but for the price the find would fetch. For the three men the migrants were 'nauseating filth' from 'over there', but with each outboard motor bringing in a couple of hundred euros, they were happy to form a reception committee of sorts for the new arrivals. Businesses everywhere were flourishing thanks to the current exodus. In Karaköy, the old port area in Istanbul, outdoor supply shops that until recently were clinging on through the sale of the odd fishing rod were suddenly doing a roaring trade peddling lifejackets and dinghy motors.

As the sun climbed higher, four dots emerged on the horizon, heading out from the Turkish coast in a well-marshalled line: an operation conducted with military precision. The dots grew into boats. Three tacked to the east and one headed straight towards where the man was waiting. A single engine wasn't anything to complain about: it was still early morning and who knew how many more would come over the course of the day? But half an hour later the boat hardly seemed to have moved. 'Something's wrong,' the man told his friends. Through his binoculars, he could make out red and blue dots and arms frantically waving. 'The engine's broken,' he said.

The three men jumped on the motorbike and drove off to try to catch up with the boats that had headed to the east. By the time the bike reached the main landing site, a long train of people – men trudging under backpacks, women carrying and dragging children – was making its way into a village after climbing the cliffs below. There were at least a hundred of them and the cargo of the three boats; the fourth was being towed to shore by the Greek coastguard. The men, women and children occupied the village streets, taking over the pavements, resting on the grass, changing the landscape. Eventually, they gathered up their belongings and started their walk to Mytilene, where all migrants were required to register before being taken to Athens.

The long march into Europe had begun. This was a caravan of ethnic clusters – Arabs, Afghans, Kurds – all threaded together along the tarmac. The order of the clusters changed depending on who rested and who moved on; sometimes they spread out over a kilometre and sometimes they came together in a mass, intimidating the tourists and the locals. Two groups of walkers met each other, travelling in opposite directions: heading away from town and into the wilderness was a group of European pensioners – Germans and Brits – all dressed in bright outdoor gear, stout boots and T-shirts, and all looking anxious. In the other direction came the migrants, marching to the city, many leaving their countries for the first time, all tired from the dangerous crossing but endlessly chirpy, all talking about their plans for the journey ahead. They didn't have time to admire the scenery – green hills, blue sea. 'If I was a tourist, this would have been a great place to visit,' said a man walking with his daughter as they passed through another medieval village and its orchards. 'Maybe one day we could come back with your brother and sister?'

His name was Khaled. He had sad eyes, and his prematurely white hair was cut short. He didn't seem confident in what he was doing and kept asking his daughter if she was OK. She looked about twelve. She rarely responded but, unlike him, she wasn't fazed, and just kept going. They attached themselves to a group of Syrians, but walked a little way behind them. He said they were heading to Denmark, where his brother-in-law lived. He spoke in a thick Iraqi accent but said he was from Mayadin, a Syrian town close to the Iraqi border, where the accents are very similar. He and his family had fled after Islamic State took control of Mayadin earlier in the year, but he was uncomfortable talking about the situation in his home town. His wife, another daughter and a son were still in Turkey.

On the Greek islands, it's forbidden to transport the 'illegals'. They aren't allowed on buses or in taxis — locals are threatened with fines for people smuggling — so they have to walk the forty kilometres to the registration centres. When a tall blonde Greek girl came along to offer Khaled and his daughter a ride, he looked over sheepishly at the group of Syrians and said: 'We arrived together, it would be a shame to abandon them. We will walk on together.' After another hour under the sun, though, the daughter was growing visibly weaker, so when the Greek girl offered a ride again, he accepted. In the car, Khaled became more animated. He asked his daughter to bring out her 'Kindle', and she passed over a tablet to show the Greek some pictures of the rest of the family.

There were police at the gates of the port at Mytilene. It was early afternoon. Hundreds of migrants had settled in a queue; many had been here since the night before. Those still walking after the morning landings at the beach wouldn't arrive before dark. Here, a Libyan father and five children had made a home between two parked cars. Two dozen Somalis and Afghans were at the water's edge, though most just sat in the middle of the road. Each person had to be processed and then taken to a camp in a disused playground where they waited for their boat to Athens.

The Greek girl pushed through the crowds and talked her way past the police line. She came back a few minutes later and took Khaled and his daughter inside where a doctor from the International Organisation for Migration, a UN-affiliated body, inspected the girl. The doctor, a fifty-something Italian woman, had seen many wars and refugees, but there was something about the way the father held his daughter's hand that made her cry. She asked the father for his passport so she could expedite their claims. He froze and said they didn't have passports.

'You're Syrians, right?'

'Yes.'

'Then it won't take long.' The Greek shook hands with them and left them inside.

Soon afterwards, Khaled came back out and called to her.

'I'm sorry,' he said.

'What happened?' she asked.

'I lied. I am Iraqi, not Syrian,' he said. 'My daughter told me it was wrong to lie to people who have been helping us. I was scared. We are Shia, and the Syrians we travelled with were all Sunnis. I'm sorry.' It had been a sound decision: scuffles between ethnic groups were common. But it wasn't the only reason to lie. Syrians in Greece get preferential treatment: no one is refused an asylum claim, and they can stay in the country longer – it's one month for an Afghan, four for a Syrian.

The blonde Greek belonged to a small gang of people working to subvert EU bureaucracy. They met in a room on the ground floor of a building still under construction in a village on the outskirts of Mytilene. The gang included a florist who spent her hard-earned cash on fuel so she could ferry women and children across the hills and into the city, two doctors who had volunteered to treat the new arrivals in the morning on the beaches and smuggle them into the city at night under the cover of darkness, a coastguard official who worked in the main reception centre during the day and on the evenings when he wasn't playing volleyball would go out to help the migrants. The leader of the gang was an imposing priest with a chest-length white beard: Father Alexi Papastratis, who walked around dragging an oxygen bottle with tubes strapped to his nostrils. He was fifty-eight but looked seventy; he had hardly any use of his lungs and had had two strokes. He smoked the occasional cigarette when his son wasn't looking.

Long before the crowds in Budapest and Vienna started donating food and clothing to the refugees, and while the local government on Lesbos was still working out what to do, this gang of six was running its own unofficial reception centre, providing food, shelter and medicine to the new arrivals. The florist told me that many people on the island were descendants of refugees driven out of Turkey decades ago. She spoke while driving down from the hills with another family. On the back seat of her Renault a mother closed her eyes and fell asleep with a child on her lap; next to her were three more children between the ages of nine and fourteen. She took them into Father Alexi's reception centre, where a man had just arrived from Athens and was unloading his car, packed with pots, a stove and bags of pasta. He set up a mobile kitchen as the room filled up. Costas was an anarchist who had been feeding the homeless in Athens for a couple of years. The Marxist and the Orthodox priest made an odd team.

Unlike Father Alexi's room, the government-run reception centre in the disused playground was a miserable place, with rubbish everywhere. Fights were breaking out between Syrians, Afghans and

Somalis. Two Eritrean women were complaining of sexual harassment. The man from the coastguard – the priest's eldest son – stood in the middle of a crowd of people in the detention centre, all shouting demands at him: a Syrian family, the mother ill with cancer; two Afghans complaining that some Syrians wouldn't let them charge their phones; an Afghan woman who said her child had diarrhoea and needed pills. Everyone wanted to know when they could leave the island. 'Why are you treating us like this?' someone asked. 'What can I do?' he said. 'They want me to be their mother, their friend, their psychologist, and I'm just a coastguard: this is madness. Fuck the E U.'

———

Following the route laid out by my Facebook friend, most of these migrants would stop briefly in Athens and then travel on to Thessaloniki. It's a six-hour walk from the train station there to the Macedonian border. Next to a deserted petrol station – used by no one, since fuel is cheaper on the other side of the border – is a two-storey motel, a place to rest, buy provisions and charge your phone. Presumably, this place was once as deserted as the petrol station but now it felt like one of the busiest establishments in Greece. The lobby was stacked high with overpriced tinned food, trainers, backpacks and bottled water; it was a modern-day caravanserai. Two elderly Greek cooks were ladling out beans and rice for €10 a plate. Every table, chair and corner was occupied. A group of Syrians sat smoking and nattering away; next to them a table full of Eritreans drank beer in silence. The patron of the motel was charging round in a rage shouting orders, behaving as if his fine establishment had been invaded by vermin rather than clients. Business was so good that neighbouring tavernas and places with rooms to let had all hung out signs in misspelt

Arabic in the hope of luring in some of the new clientele. Most of the migrants had money to spend and didn't mind the prices. They had come with a few thousand euros, cash from houses and cars sold back home to fund the journey to Europe. After all, being charged €5 for a can of Coke was trivial exploitation compared to the thousand or so euros each had had to pay for a trip on an inflatable dinghy that would have cost €15 on a ferry.

From the motel, the migrants walked down a mud trail into open green fields. Thousands had been this way before, and the dirt was packed hard. Syrian and Afghan women in headscarves and ankle-length skirts trod carefully, shepherding their children. Behind them was a group of Syrian hipsters in panama hats and T-shirts, university graduates from Homs and Damascus, one of them a networking engineer who planned to go to Britain. There was a Somali in a cowboy hat, leather trousers and a necklace; he was high on hashish and spoke in gangsta English.

There was also a Syrian family: father, mother and three little girls. Bassem, the father, was carrying the youngest girl on his shoulders. He had once been a well-off merchant on the outskirts of Damascus; his family owned a large amount of agricultural land. When the revolution began in 2011, he used his money to bankroll the fighters, and in the subsequent civil war, he became a commander. 'I spent $300,000 on weapons and ammunition,' he said, 'and I lost many friends. I regret it all.' When his area was besieged he fled to the Bekaa Valley in Lebanon to lie low but he soon got into trouble with Hezbollah. His brother was detained and he was nearly captured himself. From Lebanon, he went to Turkey, where a fellow revolutionary-cum-smuggler promised to get him and his family on a ferry to Italy for €10,000. The comrade took the money and vanished. Of all the money he'd lost, he said, that hurt the most. He spoke calmly, wasn't bitter, but said he felt ashamed that he'd had to sell his wife's jewellery to get here, only to make his girls tramp through mud and sleep in fields.

The Greek police had abandoned the border, having learned early on that rather than try to stop the flow it was better to give way and let it move through as quickly as possible. After all, no one wanted to stay in Greece. It would, however, take weeks for the Macedonians to learn the same lesson. For this group of migrants, the obvious road ahead was blocked: a Land Rover and five Macedonian policemen stood in their way. So several hundred people had to move along the railway line to find a place to spend the night. Some laid out sleeping bags under a bridge, others put up improvised tents made from plastic sheets and sticks. In the morning, as more people arrived to turn the impromptu camp into a village (women from Sierra Leone, a Yemeni in a wheelchair, many more Syrians and Iraqis), a few self-appointed scouts walked up and down the border looking for a safe path. To the right of the police was an uncrossable river and to the left there were hills which, it was said, were patrolled by bandits who were demanding €200 from anyone they came across, having 'bought' the area. Two young Kurds fresh from the battles of Kobani went off into the hills to see if they could find a way through. At a bend in a track just before an abandoned Greek police post, one of them spotted a path through the bushes, leading to Macedonia. Word was sent that a way had been found.

An hour later a column of people walked through the sunflower fields towards the hills, the misery of the morning replaced by elation. When they reached the turning, the Kurdish boys helped everyone through the bushes, and then moved to the edge of the hill to watch the Macedonian police below. They spent hours rolling and lighting cigarettes. The police shifts changed twice, a dog was brought in. 'What if we all spread out in a line and run at the border in different directions?' one of the boys suggested. The idea of storming

328

international borders seemed insane to many of the older refugees behind them, but there was no other way, and when night fell the whole crowd ran down the hill into Macedonia.

And then it was downhill all the way to Gevgelija, the nearest town, where, in an absurd reversal of the game, the Macedonian police would politely process each migrant and give them the necessary papers to move freely across the country. After they had waited their turn, I bumped into the Syrian hipsters at the bus station. They were talking excitedly and looking at Google Maps on their phones. 'Next stop, Skopje,' one said. They had their route all planned out, across Serbia, Hungary and Austria. One of them was thinking of heading for Denmark. It wouldn't take them long.

I saw some of the others once more, in Lojane, a village of mostly ethnic Albanians on the Macedonian side of the border with Serbia. Here migrants would regroup and wait and try to make arrangements for the crossing of another international border, another game of cat and mouse with the police. This time, though, things were tougher: the rumour was that it wasn't safe for people to loiter. The village square was empty apart from a farmer with a stall of melons and tomatoes, and three old men in black caps sitting on a bench. Then a Syrian family came into the square, the father carrying a child and the mother holding the hands of two little boys. They were walking fast, at the heels of a teenage boy, an Arab himself, who was leading the way. They entered a narrow side street which turned into a track. They walked past a dark red Audi with no licence plates that was parked on the verge; four men sat inside, watching them. The family headed into the woods towards Serbia. At a turn in the track they vanished. It was only when I saw another family doing much the same that I understood what was happening: they were all being guided by a previous set of migrants, people who knew the tricks of this border and who could be paid to take one safely across. The old smuggling networks were still there, ready to re-emerge at any sign of tighter border controls, to take advantage of the do-it-yourself migrants who couldn't quite find their way.

———

Not all smugglers toil at the dirty tracks on the frontiers between nations. Nabil is a Swedish-Iraqi whose main talent is marketing. His job has been made difficult lately: who needs a smuggler if anyone can find their own way to Europe? So he made the decision to cater to more exclusive clients, those who want to spare themselves and their families the hardship of a long trek through the Balkans.

I met him in the lobby of a hotel in Baghdad, having told him I might need his services. His gelled hair was dyed jet black. He wore a blue shirt with white polka dots; a pair of Ray-Bans hung at his chest. He had told a friend of mine before our meeting that he dressed like a European to impress his clients.

'So, do you want to humiliate yourself by travelling to Europe on foot?' he asked me. 'Or – the salesman's pitch torquing up – 'would you prefer a guaranteed way to get a Swedish passport inside two years?' For the sum of just 'four bundles' – a bundle is $10,000 – he could arrange for one of his lady friends in Malmö to marry me. ('We have to pay her a bundle in advance.') There would be a wedding in Baghdad, with pictures. 'Then once you get your visa, arranged through a contact at the Swedish embassy in a neighbouring country, you pay us another bundle and a half. Once in Sweden you settle down and relax. The government will give you a house and a salary. Just sit and wait and they'll hand you your passport in a year or two.'

'What if I pay you the money and I don't get the passport?' I asked.

'I guarantee you a passport. I've done the same for a lot of people.'

'What if I give your friend the money and she doesn't turn up for the wedding?'

'I am your guarantor,' he assured me.

There was, he said, a cheaper option, which could be arranged through a network of corrupt officials at one of the European embassies in Baghdad, the Italian and the Polish being the best bets. 'We can get you a Schengen visa that way but we can't guarantee you a passport afterwards.' The dodgy visa would cost me a mere $18,000. I told him I'd think about it.

42

The Colonel

AFTER TWO YEARS OF FIGHTING, liberating towns and villages from IS control, Iraqi forces reached the outskirts of Mosul and stopped. Tense negotiations took place between the Americans and their coalition partners who were providing military support, the Iraqi government, Iranian-backed militias and the Kurdish regional government. For the sectarian and fractured Iraqi politics, this was a political landmark. Kurdish leadership allowed the Iraqi army to cross their territory, and even fought alongside them. Shia paramilitary units were persuaded to fight on the outskirts and not to enter the city proper, an American condition, whose jets, helicopters and special forces were active on the ground. A glimmer of hope rose in the bleak Iraqi streets; maybe this war would end the miseries of this weary nation.

The Iraqi prime minister, Haider al-Ebadi – short, round, bit of a squeaky voice – stood dressed in the black uniform of the special forces, flanked by his generals, to declare the start of Operation Restoring Hope. The battle for Mosul began in October 2016.

Thousands of Iraqi army troops, Kurdish peshmerga forces and Shia paramilitaries broke through the berms, barbed wires and concrete fortifications that stood for two years as the de facto border of the land of the caliphate. They moved swiftly to capture outlying towns and villages. With their usual delusional bravado, the generals said that Mosul would be liberated within a month. Iraqi and international media declared the imminent capture of the city. Then came the car bombs, hundreds of them in the first week, and the battle stagnated.

———

On a sunny warm day in November 2016, I arrived in Bartela, a small, deserted, once Christian town on the outskirts of Mosul. Graffiti declared that Islamic State had confiscated all properties in the town. I stood with other journalists in a car park packed with armoured vehicles, in front of a two-storey building clad with golden tinted windows and aluminium sheets, a midget imitation of an ugly skyscraper, where American and Iraqi generals were discussing the stalled battle. Large American armoured trucks were parked on one side of the lot; on the other, the black Humvees of the Iraqi special forces were mounted by swaggering black-uniformed soldiers and adorned with flags carrying pictures of Imam Hussein.

There were a dozen or so journalists milling around, and trying to get permission from the Iraqi generals huddled inside the building to go to the front, but all access had been blocked. I saw an old Iraqi friend; he was still working for the same American newspaper where I had worked as a translator in 2003. We talked about the old days of street fighting, of militias and jihadis. We looked around us, and everything in that car park was repulsively familiar. The same Humvees, the same soldiers, the same journalists, the same pictures of Imam Hussein fluttering atop the guns, and the same stink of sweat, diesel fumes and burned plastic floating in the air. Nothing had changed in Iraq over the past fourteen years. An American general, gliding on his confident smile, walked out of the building, followed by a tight group of American soldiers in the standard helmets, body armour and puffed-up air of self-importance. A tall blond captain whirled his index finger in the air, as if mixing sugar in an imaginary flipped teacup, and told a young black female soldier that he wanted the birds – helicopters – to keep circling in the sky as long as the general was on the ground.

The night before, in a cafe in Erbil, I had met a colonel who commanded a special forces battalion that was taking part in the fight. His *nom de guerre* was Folath (steel), and he was tall and heavyset. Like all officers, he was a bit vain, thought he was meant for something great, knew the solution to the problems of Iraq, and that if only he was given time and supreme authority he would fix the country. Yet unlike many officers and all the Iraqi politicians, he was honest, decent and sometimes funny. He told me that the battle was not going very well, their advance was slow, not because the fighters in Mosul were tough but because they were fighting in areas populated by civilians. 'We fought to liberate every meter of land until we reached Mosul. But now the advance has slowed, and every day we lose one or two men, which is affecting the soldiers' morale. The special forces soldiers are very close to each other, and when one of them is lost it is hard on the rest.' There was something soft about his twinkling eyes, and after many coffees and cigarettes, he agreed to take me with him to the front.

In the afternoon, the colonel summoned me. As instructed, I crammed myself into the back of a Humvee next to crates of ammunition.

The driver negotiated the tapestry of narrow residential streets, barricaded with cars, rubbish bins and tree trunks, to stop the car bombs, leaving only a single 'safe' path for the troops to move along. I found the colonel sitting on a metal bed on the roof of a house; a very young thin officer sitting next to him was sending small white drones up into the clear blue sky. On a small tablet, the colonel watched a live feed of three Humvees, and a line of his men advancing a few

334

streets away. On the other side of the bed stood a large rickety mesh cage where a dozen pigeons cooed. Three young boys watched the soldiers with awe.

An occasional bullet smacked too low overhead, sending everyone down, but the battle was at least two blocks away, and below in the street civilians and soldiers were chatting. Two parts of Iraq that had not seen each other for three years were mixing. An athletic-looking lieutenant walked up to the colonel, knelt in front of him and started giving him updates from the front. 'They are resisting very hard, sir, but we are advancing.' And then in the same tone, 'Amar has been killed.' And then he was back to talking about the fight. His shoes were covered with fresh blood. The following week he and the young officer operating the drones would be dead too.

At night, the sound of gunfire became intermittent and eventually ceased completely. Soldiers and officers climbed into their armoured trucks and Humvees and drove the few blocks back into a narrow secure residential street that had become their base. Most of the houses on the street were still occupied by civilians. In one house that had been turned into an armoury and a makeshift prison, two detained fighters, suspected IS, were squatting on the floor. One was very young with fair, almost blond, hair. The other was older and bearded. A soldier stood in front of them with a broken broomstick in his hand, taunting the younger boy, 'Oh, look at you, you are so beautiful, maybe we will fuck you later.'

'I have just joined them, I was only trained for three weeks, and I never fought,' the boy cried. The older detainee was silent and composed; he knew that they would both be dead soon.

The next morning, I could hear gunfire nearby, so I put on my flak jacket, and grabbed my camera. I was in the doorway when I saw a soldier named Rasoul standing alone in the deserted street, his half-sleepy eyes focused on a big white garbage truck that crawled slowly towards him like a giant armadillo. A few useless bullets ricocheted off its thick steel-plated armour. Rasoul looked at me and waved his arms shouting:

'Mufakhakha, mufakhakha [Car bomb, car bomb].' I ran back across the living room, and through the dark corridor. Just as I reached the back room where the officers were still sleeping, a violent explosion shook the house. It felt like the earth itself lifted and then dropped back again. Silence followed, and a thick cloud of grey concrete dust and black smoke mantled everything. I opened my eyes in the darkness, and saw the floor covered with heavy blocks of masonry. Part of the ceiling and walls had collapsed. The light was coming from where a wall was supposed to be. I touched my head, it was still there, my hands were there too, but my feet were numb. I tried to pull them up, but they were trapped under the rubble. I looked for my camera, then tried to release my feet, then went back looking for my camera, I was too confused and didn't know if my feet or the camera should be the priority. Two officers were under a layer of debris. One of them moaned, while the other let out long monotonous wails that mixed his pain with the word Allah. Soldiers came clambering through the collapsed ceiling, shouting that the house was on fire. They helped the two officers and we all climbed into a neighbouring house and slid down a slanting roof slab into the confusion and mayhem of the street below. There were fires, puddles of water, crumbled walls, and the smell of burning plastic and tyres and concrete. Everything was the colour of ash. The bomb had altered the landscape of the street. The front of the house was a pile of burning rubble, two other houses were destroyed, and four of the unit's armoured vehicles had been incinerated, melted into small chunks of black metal. One smouldering armoured vehicle perched on the roof of a house. In the middle was the crumpled wreckage of the truck bomb. Bullets flew overhead like whistling birds.

'Listen, listen, they are trying to come closer,' a soldier said.

'Let them come, my dick in their God,' answered a soldier named Ali. The two soldiers, joined by a third, still dazed and limping, scrambled to the street corner and started firing as the rest of the unit collected weapons and tended to their injured.

The civilians trickled out; a man rolling his dishdasha up ran out carrying a child, placed him in the street and went back to help a tall man with his trousers in tatters and his face covered in black ash. Another civilian, along with a soldier, helped a family emerge from a half-collapsed house, holding the mother's hand as if leading her in a dance, tiptoeing over the debris. They carried bundles of what they could salvage and filed down the street to join the tens of thousands of civilians filling the refugee camps.

'Any civilians died here?' asked one soldier.

'How should I know?' answered another. Indeed, no one knew — not even the government of Iraq knew how many civilians had been killed in this battle. Each counted their own casualties and moved on. The colonel, who stood examining the scene, listened silently to his aide's report. The truck drove through the backstreets, through liberated areas that were supposed to have been protected by other units. Rasoul inspected the wreckage of his communication-vehicle and tried to salvage his equipment. His face contorted with pain. Within forty-five minutes of the attack, he and his men drove back to the front in the two remaining vehicles, and continued their offensive. By the end of that day, another eleven soldiers and officers would be injured in the fighting, and one more would be dead.

Hundreds had exploded since the start of the Mosul operations, and they are the most lethal weapons in the IS arsenal of improvised weapons that included small toy drones dropping hand grenades, suicide bombers and home-made rockets named Jahanam, or 'Hell'.

The mere mention of the word 'mufakhakha' strikes horror. In general, you can't see bullets and shells when they come flying towards you, but a car bomb is slow enough to be seen. With its crude angular armour, fashioned from metal sheets welded together, like an eighties vision of the future, always white and with a tiny black hole for a window. The cry 'mufakhakha' is followed by a moment of disbelief, paralysis sets in, before soldiers desert their posts, vehicles and weapons and run. But run where? In what direction? Seek shelter in a house? That might collapse. Or keep running in an improbable race between man and car? Only the doomed or the very brave stand still to face an approaching car bomb.

———

On Christmas Day, I stood in a small house on a dirt road in a village on the outskirts of Mosul, waiting for one of the colonel's soldiers to pick me up and take me to see him again. The house had been converted into an emergency trauma facility. A 25-year old doctor sat on a green military cot, exhausted and dispirited. He was very suspicious at first and thought I was trying to find out the number of casualties, a major state secret in Iraq. He told me the fighting was slow today, because of the heavy rain. How did he know? I asked. He pointed at the empty cots and said there were no casualties.

The colonel's men arrived in a rickety shrapnel-ridden Humvee and we drove to the new front line. Through the cracked windscreen, I looked at the streets of Mosul that had acquired the distinctive feel of a war-torn Middle Eastern city. Bomb craters filled with mud and sewage water, the mangled wreckage of cars and armoured vehicles abandoned on the side of the street, buildings pocked with bullet holes. Civilians wrapped in thick coats to protect them from the chilling cold roamed the streets, looking for vegetables or water, scavenging for fuel, or just standing in front of their houses, in tracksuits or pyjamas chatting. Children ran along with the armoured trucks, making the victory signs taught to them by their nervous parents.

'How can you distinguish between the civilians and IS fighters?' I asked the soldier driving the Humvee.

'If they explode next to you, then you know that they're Daesh,' the soldier said.

I joined the colonel in the afternoon as he strolled in the streets glittering with fresh rain. He was stopped by a wiry old man with a bald head and spectacles.

'They have taken my son,' the old man said.

'Who took him?' the colonel asked.

'The unit that was here before you, they were also wearing black.'

'Look, I can't get back your son, but I can assure you if he is innocent then nothing will happen to him,' the colonel said. He had the strained face of a man who knows he is not telling the truth. He knew well that the old man's son would never be back. The father was trying to plead further when one of the bodyguards looked into the sky and shouted 'Drone!' The colonel and his men ran in different directions – a second later the small IS-operated drone had dropped a bomb that exploded where he'd stood.

'We fight so hard, taking so many casualties, because we want to build new relations with people, and I lose men because of that,' he said on the way back to his house. 'And then comes some shitty unit that hasn't even seen fighting, and they start detaining people and destroying all the good work we've been doing.

'I was stationed in Mosul in 2013, and I learned something about the nature of its people. They are urbanites surrounded by tribes, and they have developed this attitude in which they become meek, they only care about their houses and families. This is why the people didn't do anything when they lost their city. They didn't know that if they take your neighbour today, tomorrow they will come for you. I know I won't be able to convert all those who believed in IS – they have a strong belief, it is a new religion. Nor will I be able to kill them all, that's beyond my means. And with the corrupt politics in Baghdad, sometimes the whole war seems futile, but I still try to enhance the image of my army, save and help the civilians and convince my soldiers to do the same thing. That's the maximum of what I can achieve here. I have been at war for fourteen years, I have lost so many men. When I go home, the battle still rages in my head. I am tired, I want this war to end.'

The battle of Mosul lasted for ten months; in that time, the colonel became not only an officer but a civil servant, a policeman. For the locals these army units were the only way they could get fuel or water. 'The government had done no planning for this war,' he told me sitting on a sofa of the house he had turned into his headquarters. 'It is not my job to talk to civilians and make them feel good; my job is to fight and defeat the enemy. But in 2013 and 2014, the army behaved like an occupation here – it pressed and enslaved the people. Now, I have a responsibility to give them a better image of the army. I am a Shia, and most of my men are Shia, but there are also Sunnis and Christians among us – and I don't see this as a war between Shia and Sunnis. It's simpler: this is a city occupied by a gang that has taken its people hostage. My job is to release those hostages.'

الرُّبُعِيَّة قَصْرِ فُؤَادِ العَبَّاسِ

43

Ali's War

A COLD WIND SWEPT OVER the gutted houses and crumbling stone walls of the ruined village on the outskirts of Mosul that for the past three weeks had been the colonel's base. It was early March 2017. Four soldiers stood shivering in the predawn darkness, waiting for the colonel to wake up.

He pushed aside a curtain and emerged, groaning and in a foul mood. The soldiers ran to their armoured trucks and the convoy drove out, heading north towards Mosul. Their target was the Baghdad Circle, a bleak intersection in a grim industrial suburb, lined with small buildings, rows of shops and a scrapyard. Adorned since 2014 with a billboard, showing the black flag of Islamic State, carrying the words: Allah, Prophet, Muhammad and the seal of the Prophet beneath it, in white, along with the words: Islamic State, Wilayat al-Mosul.

Since mid-February 2017, when operations to recapture the western side of Mosul began, the colonel and his men had twice attacked the Circle, and twice they had been pushed back.

'They have formidable fortifications,' the colonel had told me the night before. 'They built a berm, with a deep trench behind it, and then built another berm, all laid with IEDs. In a whole day of fighting in this neighbourhood, we advanced no more than 150 metres.' With his thick stubby fingers, he pinched and zoomed a satellite map on his tablet. The Circle is the gateway to western Mosul, the oldest part of the city. It is a knot, where the highway

343

from Baghdad ends and an arterial north–south road begins, linking dense neighbourhoods clustered parallel to the Tigris. As long as IS held the Circle, the colonel explained, the highway to Baghdad could not be opened for traffic. Refugees and troops are forced to take a circuitous route through the outlying hills to avoid snipers and rocket launchers. For the third attack, a small unit of his special forces soldiers would cross the highway under cover of a massive barrage of fire, outflank the Circle and try to breach the fortifications from behind. Once a bridgehead was established, the rest of the troops would follow.

———

Two kilometres before reaching the Circle, the convoy turned left and followed a narrow dirt road, climbing through hills scattered with gypsum quarries and construction debris. Heavy rain had fallen the night before, and the armoured trucks creaked and moaned as they waded slowly through pools of gypsum slush and mud.

In the second vehicle, a soldier connected his phone to a large speaker and started playing dancing war music. The speaker blinked red and blue inside the dark interior of the Humvee.

When they cleared a ridge and began descending towards the city, glowing white shadows appeared in the headlights of the convoy. As they got closer, the shadows took the shape of women, children and men, terrified and caked in mud. They shuffled along the muddy cliffs, stumbling, sliding in and out of mud puddles, scurrying between vehicles, cutting through their headlights and begging the soldiers for water and cigarettes as they searched for a safe path out of the besieged city.

At the foot of the hill, the colonel's two vehicles joined a long convoy of Humvees, tanks and bulldozers. The colonel stepped out of his car to shout at a tank driver for being late. His soldiers stood by him, smoking and chatting in the darkness.

The black sky was fading into deep blue when the high-pitched voice of a general came from the radios giving the order for the attack. The soldiers climbed into their vehicles, and the column rumbled towards the Circle. Families of civilians moved in the opposite direction.

The colonel and other officers installed themselves in a house close to the front line. With radios, smartphones and tablets arrayed around them, they followed the advance of the troops. Like children playing a video game, they moved cursors, tapped in new coordinates and nudged and cajoled the men on the ground into advancing: 'Yalla, my hero, cross the street, did you cross? Do you have new coordinates?' From the distance came the sounds of explosions and gunfire.

Aides scavenged the house for a heater, gas and teacups. Over the radio, the High-Pitched General pestered the officers for progress reports. From the ground came reports of a Humvee hit by an IED, four soldiers injured, another soldier pinned down by a sniper.

Two hours into the attack, the soldiers had only managed to take a shop on the ground floor of a two-storey building that sat on the edge of the Circle. IS fighters occupied the second floor.

'Sir, sir, I am besieged,' a voice hissed on the officers' radio. 'They are on top of me.' From across the road, where the rest of the force gathered in the protection of an Abrams tank, the soldiers hiding in the shop looked small, vulnerable and hopeless. The tank turned its turret right and left scanning the highway for car bombs, but could do little to relieve the trapped men.

The soldiers and the fighters lobbed grenades at each other. IS grenades thrown from the upper window flew far into the street, while the soldiers' grenades bounced back off the building and exploded near their throwers. The colonel shouted orders for a second platoon to cross the highway to relieve the besieged unit but no one advanced.

What was a thin yellow line on an officer's satellite was on the ground a six-lane highway, barricaded on one side by a fuel tanker, a bus and earthworks, and totally exposed on the other, with bullets and RPG rockets flying unchallenged.

The soldiers squabbled and negotiated until Caesar, a thin weathered sergeant, with a large hooked nose and a goatee decided to advance. The tank bowed obligingly and turned its turret as Caesar's Humvee advanced slowly. In the middle of the road were the remnants of another Humvee, destroyed earlier that day, and further up lay the wreckage of a mangled armoured truck and a burned-out bulldozer, destroyed in previous attacks.

Caesar's vehicle started crossing the road slowly, as he chewed his gum compulsively while fixing his eyes on the road. Two rockets came in quick succession, exploding in the middle of the road a few metres short of the Humvee.

'Yalla, go,' the driver shouted.

Caesar, his face contorted into thick lines, his brow sweating, touched his colourful cap, opened the door, put his head out and then put it back again.

'Get closer,' he told the driver, who moved a few feet forward. Next to him in the car, a young soldier, his face wrapped with a green keffiyeh, stood to fire his machine gun. When he dropped it inside on the seat it filled the car with the sharp smell of gunpowder. Caesar opened the door, then slammed it shut again.

'Ya, Caesar! Either you go or we head back,' the driver pleaded. 'We are sitting in the middle of the road.'

'I want you to fuck the street with grenades,' Caesar shouted at the standing soldier, who ripped open a box and fed a long belt of copper-coloured grenades into a gun mounted on the car.

The grenades left with a quiet thud but delivered huge explosions in the distance. Encouraged by the rattle of bombs, Caesar

346

opened the door again, stepped out, clinging to the door as if his life depended on it.

'Just tell me where you want me to park the car – if I go any further they will hit us,' the driver said.

Caesar was silent, swinging back and forth by the open door. In ten years of fighting, he had crossed hundreds of these roads and had seen a dozen of his men fall and die. The sounds were not random any more, each whoosh and bang was a piece of hot metal intended to kill him and the decision to leave the protection of an armoured car and cross the street involved something more than courage. It demanded the will to ignore these flying projectiles and to trust your fate to a higher supreme power, or randomness.

'Caesar, the ammunition will run out, and you haven't crossed,' the driver said. 'Yalla, Caesar, you are a hero. Go, my brother.'

'Fire another round,' Caesar shouted.

More bombs were fired and Caesar left the car, dropping to his knees in the street. The driver rolled forward to cover him and another soldier as they started advancing in the protection of the car, until, lowering their heads, they ran across the road and jumped through the doorway of the shop. The Humvee swung quickly back and drove behind the shelter of the tank.

———

Lieutenant Ali along with a dozen soldiers were crammed inside the shop, on the Circle. Short, lean, with a large head made even larger by the helmet strapped tight to his chin, Ali was barking orders in a hoarse voice, but no one seemed to pay him any attention. By now the fighters who occupied the upper floor had either left or been killed, but heavy gunfire was coming from the side streets to his left and right. Another column of soldiers trotted across the road and gathered around Ali in the doorway of the shop. 'There are snipers on the left side,' Ali shouted at them, trying to make himself heard over the din of shooting and heavy explosions. And the column of soldiers went left. They stood behind a corner, peering into the street, until their commander, a young thin lieutenant who had deserted during an earlier battle but had been allowed to return because of a general amnesty, gave the order to advance. He was barely out of the cover provided by the corner when a burst of gunfire hit him and he fell in the street. Three soldiers ran to pull him back but they too come under fire and sheltered in a ditch in the middle of the street, unable to move, while the young lieutenant lay motionless on his back.

Ali smacked his helmet, and turned to his men. 'I told him don't go to the left.' He marched over to one of the soldiers leaning against the wall inside the shop, grabbed him by the neck and dragged him to the street, handing him a rocket launcher. 'Fire at the building,' he shouted. 'I want smoke and fire.'

The soldier stepped round the corner and fired, debris and dust filled the air, creating enough confusion for another soldier to grab the fallen lieutenant and drag him to safety, while the three soldiers crawled back to the corner.

Ali ripped off the young lieutenant's flak jacket; three holes had pierced his abdomen, and his face was yellow and motionless. His head bobbed on Ali's knees and his helmet fell and spun on the pavement. 'Alive, he is alive,' Ali shouted.

'He is dead,' a soldier cried.

'No, he is alive,' Ali insisted.

The soldier lifted the motionless body, swung it over his shoulder and ran with him back across the road, jumping over the ditches and using the wreckage as cover. The lieutenant's dangling arms flailed left and right. Minutes later, the news came through on the radio. The young lieutenant was indeed dead. The soldiers waited inside the shop, leaning against the wall, and resting their heads on the barrels of their guns, their faces grim and tired.

Over the radio, their commanding officers were ordering them to advance. One young officer, who had buried his head in his folded arms, mumbled, 'I won't go, I won't go,' and then into the radio he shouted, 'Sir, they killed the lieutenant just now, sir, they are all over us, where are you sending us?'

'What did you expect?' the commander replied. 'That they'd throw flowers at you? This is war.'

'Let him come and we will follow him,' said the young officer to his soldiers, and rested his head back on his gun, mumbling again, 'I won't go, I won't go. I am not going to kill my men.'

Ali decided to move down the street to the right. He gathered four men, formed a line and sent them one after the other. Three had gone, and the fourth was waiting for his turn when a huge explosion shook the walls. A wave of thick grey cloud wrapped the street and shrapnel fell from the sky. Up the road, a car bomb parked inside a house had gone off.

———

Later that afternoon, the High-Pitched General, accompanied by a large entourage of aides and journalists, arrived in a convoy of armoured vehicles. He was ushered into a house overlooking the Circle where he spoke to cameras in his whining voice, assuring his audience that the battle was going very well and that the Circle had been liberated. He was quickly led away when one of his bodyguards spotted a small IS surveillance drone overhead.

The colonel and other officers stayed behind, slumbering on sofas in a dark room; rays of light shafted through the shattered windows and lit their exhausted faces. Bullets flew close to the window, sometimes hitting the walls outside or just exploding in the air. Across the street, Ali and his men hadn't moved far beyond the shop.

The colonel spoke to Ali on the radio, in the tone of a tired parent trying to persuade a child to finish his homework before bedtime. 'Look, Ali, this is your sector, you will have to finish it today. Why don't you finish it while you still have daylight? Better than having to fight at night.'

'We have friendly planes in the skies,' another officer chimed in. 'Any target you spot, just give us the coordinates, and the planes will hit them.'

And so Ali moved on from building to building; whenever he encountered resistance he radioed the coordinates to the commander, who passed them to the ISOF (Iraqi Special Operation Forces) command, who passed them to the American air controllers. A few minutes later, the usual response would come through the radio: 'All units take cover, the target will be bombed in one minute.' Darkness fell outside, but Ali was still moving. Twice he and his men were outflanked and besieged. He reached the last street in his sector, moving now from house to house using the same openings in the walls made by IS fighters. In the last house in the street, a large two-storey villa that overlooked an empty scrapyard, he came face-to-face with IS fighters who opened fire, injuring his civilian guide.

'Sir, enemy position.' He radioed the coordinates.

The response came through: air strike in two minutes.

'Sir,' Ali radioed again, his voice hoarse and urgent. 'Sir, the people in the neighbourhood say there are five families hiding in the basement of that house.'

The colonel immediately radioed to the controllers again: 'ISOF, we have a problem. There are civilians in the house.'

'Operation is a go,' came the high-pitched voice of the general. 'If there is one IS fighter in the house then it's a go.'

It wasn't two minutes, but five or six long minutes later that the explosion arrived. The neighbourhood shook, windows rattled and Ali finished his sector for the day: 250 metres.

———

Early next day, the road, the Circle and the barricades were quiet, deserted and stinking of yesterday's fighting. Buildings stood with torn-off facades, metal shutters were twisted, and electricity poles, wires and debris were strewn across the road, along with charred shell casings, dried blood and the soldiers' white polyester food packets of stale rice. Soldiers guarding the intersection sat next to their vehicles. A black pot sat on a fire made out of ammunition boxes and simmered with tea. Dark grey clouds of smoke hung on the horizon.

A man with a shaggy beard, and wearing a brown shapeless tracksuit broke the stillness. He came running across the highway, holding a young girl to his chest and almost falling on his face when he reached the soldiers. A woman in a long dusty black abaya and niqab followed, clutching a plastic bag and dragging behind her a small boy. Then another family came running. Two younger men pushed a handcart on which sat an old man with dignity, his hand holding his red keffiyeh on to his head; their mother followed panting at a distance.

A constant stream of people was emerging – a woman carrying a cage of pigeons, a group of children waving white flags, a man carrying a very old woman who slipped from one shoulder to the other laughing at her exposed scrawny legs, a small boy carrying two roosters by their legs and swaying them back and forth, three cows, a flock of sheep, and all kinds of improvised wheelchairs ferrying the elderly and the handicapped. The men, all with long beards, carried stupefied grins on their faces, shouted thank you to the soldiers and begged for cigarettes. A

351

woman screaming for her children to gather around her began crying. The father, carrying many plastic bags, was trying to calm them down. She stretched out her arms and turned round, thanking the soldiers while still crying, then screaming war . . . war . . . explosions . . . She collapsed on the pavement leaning against her husband's legs and fainted. At first the tired soldiers ignored the civilians; after weeks of fighting, they were used to these scenes of misery and gratitude, but the people kept coming and soldiers started handing out water bottles to the families. When they ran out, they could do nothing but watch the masses of bodies crossing the road and occasionally help push a wheelchair or carry a child for a few metres.

The fighting resumed, and an occasional mortar exploded somewhere in the road, an air strike sent up a black column of smoke, and bursts of gunfire made the people stop for a second before running faster across the road, their dignity long gone.

———

Ali sat barefoot outside the school where he and his men had spent the night and watched the civilians walk by. He cut a plastic bottle to improvise a glass, and filled it with a sickening sweet tea, dipped some stale bread in a pot of yogurt and had his first meal in twenty-four hours.

'You know, there were civilians in the house that was bombed last night,' he said. 'I tried to stop it, I called the commander to say there were civilians, but they went ahead with the strike.'

He was watching an old man with ruffled white hair trying hard to push a wheelbarrow with his wife in it over the rubble in the street. The old man was suffering with the weight of the cart, but smiled and spoke softly to his wife, calming her and laughing with her. Ali shouted to one of the soldiers to go and help them.

'The neighbours told me that most of the people got out but three died. Did I kill the civilians?' he asked. 'Will God punish me for that?'

A huge explosion ripped through a house across the street, a black ball of cloud rose, folded and grew into a thick column of smoke. The old couple and the soldier ran and hid behind a tank. Ali sat still on his ammunition box, sipping his tea, and looked at the smoke billowing from the house; chunks of masonry and shrapnel fell around him.

'Haji, it's OK, don't worry, it's just a car bomb.' Ali laughed at the terrified old man, who walked back into the street with his wife, straightened the wheelbarrow and resumed pushing her.

'I am the intelligence officer of the regiment,' Ali said. 'I am not even supposed to fight, or lead men in street fighting.' He refilled his plastic bottle with more tea. 'But we have lost half of the officers and soldiers of the regiment since the start of the Mosul operations so I am giving them a hand.' He smiled. 'I hate wars, I hate killing. When will this be over? We are stuck in a cycle, and who knows how long we will continue fighting for. Maybe after this they will ask us to fight the Shia or the Kurds.'

Hundreds of refugees poured through the Baghdad Circle and onto the highway, sitting by the side of the road or clambering up the pickup trucks that were distributing food and aid.

'These scenes make you want to fight more,' Ali said.

'Why didn't the men of Mosul fight?' interjected a portly balding major who was the colonel's deputy. 'Why did they wait for the people of the South [Shia] to come and liberate them? Look how many they are – if each had thrown a brick at Daesh, they would have fled.'

'In ten years, people will ask, what did the Iraqis do when ISIS came, they won't ask what did the Kurds or the Shia do. They will ask, what did the Iraqis do?' Ali replied.

———

For three years, the colonel and his men had been living like modern-day nomads. Once a neighbourhood is liberated, they moved into abandoned civilian houses and set up camp. When the front lines shifted they changed houses and moved with it, sometimes every night, but often they found themselves stuck in the same house for weeks. Whether in mud huts in a village with no running water, luxurious villas, or brick houses in a narrow alleyway of a provincial town, they built a temporary nest, slept in the beds of a family that had joined a caravan of refugees, replacing the stinking blankets they had brought from a previous house with fresh ones.

That night, their base was the large, clean home of a man who had adorned his walls with family photos, some old black-and-white ones of an army officer and others more recent showing the owner in traditional Arabic dress or his sons graduating from university. The water heater was working and some took their first shower in weeks.

The colonel summoned his men to explain the objectives of the new military offensive. They sat around him in silence waiting for clues to his mood that night. He started the meeting with a self-deprecating joke about how much he feared his second wife. The men relaxed, knowing the colonel was in a good mood, and he proceeded to explain the mission: the capture of a neighbourhood with the usual narrow streets, perfect for car bombs, booby traps and IEDs, buildings that could provide cover for IS fighters. They grimaced, argued, shook their heads and shuffled out of the room. His face resumed destruction mode.

'How can you explain a battle plan, knowing very well that someone is bound to be killed?' I asked him.

'If you think of those who will die you will never move,' he replied without lifting his eye from his phone.

———

354

It was dark and cold outside when Ali and four other officers sat for dinner around a table in the kitchen. An enormous Kurdish cook ladled a watery lentil soup, fried tomatoes and some rice flavoured with spices that he had scavenged from the kitchen onto their polystyrene plates. The electric generator quivered and the feeble light eventually died. The officers placed two phones on the table to use as lights, their beams illuminating their prematurely wrinkled faces, the dark rings under their eyes and the stubble beards. The food was horrendous, but the kitchen was warm and cosy, and the men joked and laughed. After every few rounds of laughter, one of them would say, may Allah forgive us, if we laugh in the night we shall cry tomorrow. The eldest of the five, Hayder the rotund major, was in his early thirties, while the youngest was a 21-year-old lieutenant who had just finished his training. The two others and Ali were in their mid-twenties, and like other men in their twenties, they talked about women, drinks and parties. A few of the battalion soldiers and officers had managed to hook up with local girls from Mosul. Ali played a short video of a fancy bar in Erbil where he sat with a group of friends drinking Grey Goose. Ahmad, a thickly moustached captain, swore by Allah that on his next leave he would go straight to the bar in the Baghdad hotel and finish a bottle of Black Label before going home. After dinner, the cook served strong sweet tea in plastic cups and the conversation reverted to the usual reminiscing about fallen comrades and their own near-death experiences in previous battles. They told stories whose characters and protagonists had been killed or maimed, boasted of miraculous survival from snipers' bullets and car bombs, and narrated the hardships of war that raged in towns and villages spread along the road from Baghdad to Mosul. They challenged each other not with tales of courage and bravado, but chronicles of defeat and loss. These were the stories they could not share with their families, nor could they tell them in the streets or bars where the official Iraqi and sectarian media narrative had portrayed them as brave heroes and their enemies as cowards.

Here around the kitchen table in a stranger's house, they spoke openly about their fears. 'You haven't seen a real battle,' Major Hayder taunted the young officers. 'Mosul is nothing compared to Ramadi and Fallujah. There they baked us. For a year I was based in a concrete structure outside Fallujah, they attacked us again and again, day and night, and didn't let us rest. We slept for an hour at a time, and the first thing we did when we woke up was to count how many men there were still in the room.' He turned to the young lieutenant and told him to consider himself lucky because he was not married. 'When you have children, they become like heavy weights around your feet; since I had my young daughter, every time I try to cross a street during a battle, her image blinks in front of my eyes.'

Naseer, broad-shouldered and athletic, spoke about the day when he was ordered to hold an intersection north of Tikrit, was attacked by three car bombs and lost all but three of his men. 'It was a suicide mission to defend an open road with two Humvees; they had to send a tank to get us out.'

'Why didn't they give you the tank from the beginning and why would you accept a suicide mission?' I asked.

'Because it is not up to you as a junior officer to decide,' Ahmad answered on Naseer's behalf. 'The commander opens his tablet and sends you the coordinates, he tells you, these are the commands of the general, so it is your responsibility to find a way to capture that square and fulfil the order, and at the same time protect yourself and your men.' He added, laughing: 'You learn how to delay and let the day pass. You fight until noon, then it's lunchtime, and after that, you consolidate your position. By five, the day is over.'

Captain Ahmad said he was in the first column that went on the attack after IS reached the outskirts of Baghdad. He told us how they advanced from Baghdad, through the swamps, and ambushes, until they reached the Taji base, sixty kilometres north of the city, having lost many of their vehicles.

'Did you do any fighting or leave it all to the Hashed [the Shia paramilitaries]?' Hayder jeered at him.

'Yes, there were Lebanese with us, and I am not ashamed of it, I have never seen men like them. Two were snipers, and one walked ahead of our Humvees cutting IED wires in the middle of the shooting, and we followed him. The satellite map software that we are using now, it was they who taught us how to use it.'

They teased him some more but when he started talking about the the operation of the refinery in Baiji, he commanded the conversation and the table fell silent. 'They told us, we need volunteers to go to the besieged refinery for ten days, until an armoured unit arrives. We volunteered; we were twenty-five men. They took us in helicopters and dropped us there. The ten days became three months and only nine of us came back. Early in the siege, the Americans were dropping us food and ammunition, but when Daesh broke through our defences and the fighting became very close, the supplies started falling behind the enemy lines. We slept, shat and ate in the same rooms, and when one of us got injured, he died there too. The families of my dead soldiers would call and demand that I bring their sons' bodies back, but we couldn't – we buried them in shallow graves where they fell. To this day they blame me for leaving their sons behind.

'When I went home after three months, I was barefoot, with a long beard and dressed in the soiled uniform of an oil worker. I had lost my boots and uniform in a car bomb explosion. My mother wept when she saw me, as if I was dead. She swore she would never let me go back to the front. I was shocked. I saw people visiting us, they came and hugged me, but it felt as if I was watching everything from afar. Let me tell you this, it's a really funny story: the first night back home, I was sleeping next to my wife, my brother came to the house late and slammed the door, I jumped out of bed, searched for my machine gun. I couldn't find it, so I ran to the roof and crawled to the edge looking for the attackers. Then my wife came after me, asking "What are you doing on the roof?" I told her I was trying to get a better signal for my phone.'

Everyone started laughing with him.

'I went to the bar and drank for two nights; only then did I get back to my old self,' he said. 'After six weeks, I went back to the refinery and we were besieged again for forty-five days, but this time no one cared about us. The government had declared the refinery liberated and they couldn't confess that it was under siege again. We called everyone, our officers, the Shia clergy and even politicians, but no one came to our aid. We said to ourselves, they have sold us. Some men lost their minds and just wanted to run away, but run to where? To Daesh? It was more merciful to die than get caught and tortured in front of their cameras.'

In these stories, the officers said any captured fighters were executed on the spot, their bodies thrown onto rubbish heaps. 'We can't know who is a civilian and who is Daesh so anyone who is found with a weapon is executed and anyone who is accused by the locals as a Daesh member is also shot,' Ahmad said.

Wasn't it more useful to detain them to get intelligence? I asked.

'And they get released by a corrupt judicial system? No, I kill them to protect my men and the country,' Ahmad answered.

'Now we are kings,' Ali said. 'When we first started the battle against Daesh my unit had two Humvees, and one of them was broken. Things have changed now we are attacking and they are withdrawing – they have become like the Iraqi army three years ago, losing and retreating every day.'

'This whole war had been an American plot to come back to Iraq,' said Major Hayder, the deputy commander, reiterating a very common conspiracy theory in Iraq. 'We are winning now because the Americans have found a new card to play.'

Ahmad, Ali and I left the table and walked into the garden; the dark sky over Mosul shimmered with stars.

'You know, if I had a house like this,' Ahmad said, pointing back at the house with its small garden and orange tree, 'I would leave the army tomorrow. But this war is not going to end, we are being prepped for the next phase, after this we will be fighting the Shia militias – why else are they and the tribes in the south arming and buying weapons? When we started this war we would be devastated when we heard of the death of a comrade. Now we eat lunch and someone comes and says so-and-so was killed, oh peace be upon his soul, and we continue eating.'

I asked Ahmad why he went back to the refinery in Baiji. A battle that no one in Iraq even knew about.

'Because I needed my salary.'

'You could have gone to a different unit.'

'Because the Shia clergy said it's our duty.'

'But you don't even pray, Ahmad, and you drink whisky. Why did you go back really – did you miss the fighting?'

'OK, yes, maybe I went back because I missed the war. After two weeks at home I started calling my men. They told me about their situation, they spoke of the war . . . I couldn't sit home while they were there at the front. So I went back and we were besieged again.'

Ahmad, like many of the officers and soldiers of the unit, came from a poor family, and when he finished high school, he found that the realities of the new Iraq were shaped by war and murderous sectarian politics. Like many in his position, his only real prospects lay in joining the ongoing war, so (through a relative) he managed to get accepted to the military school.

'I had two unemployed brothers and a widowed mother,'

Ahmad told me that night. 'I spent my high school years with only two pairs of trousers. When I went to the military school, and they gave me my first salary — a thousand dollars — I felt like a king. I kept a hundred and I gave the rest to my mother; she replaced the corrugated-sheet roof of the house with a brick one, and married off my elder brother.'

Shortly after that evening, an IS drone dropped a bomb which killed the young lieutenant and left Ahmad with his legs severely injured. And the front line moved, at the pace of a few residential streets per day, and many, many casualties.

———

The next day Ali saw three bodies.

The first belonged to an IS fighter, killed a few hours earlier. He lay at the edge of a garden lawn, next to a gap in the wall, immaculately preserved: legs bent beneath him and arms splayed, his posture perfectly expressing a man killed in battle. He had a full brown beard; his cap was pushed back, revealing short-cropped hair. He wore a beige jacket, green combat trousers and desert boots; a smart-watch was strapped to his wrist. Early in the morning he had come through an opening in a wall without knowing that Ali and his men were on the other side waiting for him. Ali pointed at the body and walked on. It was part of the landscape of war, proof of the fighting, a measure of his men's success. It was all these things, but it was not a dead human.

The second body lay on the back seat of Ali's car, wrapped in a thin shiny trauma blanket. It was the body of a young girl, who earlier that day had run across the front lines to where Ali and his men were stationed. She'd almost reached them when a sniper shot her. She lay bleeding in the road until a civilian ran out to her and carried her to

Ali. 'She was alive – I took her to the Americans but they couldn't save her. She had a big hole in her chest,' he said.

The blanket was tied around her head and feet like a shroud, but the outlines of her small nose and mouth could be traced under it. Ali sat next to her, tired and sad, burying his head in his arms. She was all the civilians killed in this war; maybe saving her would have saved the others, for his conscience.

The third body was in Baghdad Circle. A special forces soldier was shouting at the people to move. Next to him stood a young guy working two mobiles, with a rusted metal chain wrapped around his left hand.

'And who was in the Hisba?' the young guy asked the person on the other line. 'And the Amniyat? I want names and numbers.'

I asked him what he was doing.

'That was my home.' He pointed at a half-destroyed house across the road. 'Daesh confiscated it and my family were refugees because I was in the police force. Now I won't stop until I have cleansed my city.'

'We just caught one of them [IS],' said the special forces soldier. 'He was an old man, holding the hand of a child and walking with a group of families, but once they reached us, they all pointed him out and said he was the head of the Hisba.'

'Where is he now?' I asked.

He pointed at a rusty tanker, part of the IS barricades. 'Over there, eating falafel with the Prophet,' he said, laughing.

Behind the barricades lay the old man's body, mouth open, a hole in his head. People walked past, giving him a fleeting look before moving on. Who cares about another dead body in a war that has haunted this highway for the last fifteen years?

361

By early May 2017, the afternoons were already hot, depressing and providing a taste of the coming summer. Six months into the battle and the colonel and his men were still moving from one house to another, but his unit was so depleted that they could only hold the ground after other units advanced. Even cautious Ali has been injured by a car bomb.

In Baghdad Circle, Shia volunteers from the south were distributing lunch to hungry soldiers and exhausted refugees. The smell of bean stew and rice that rose from the large blackened pot was mixed with the acrid stench of a large rotting rubbish heap. Speakers mounted on top of the tents were blasting Shia war songs. Behind them was a villa compound, surrounded by high concrete blast walls, where American Chinook helicopters landed frequently. That's where ISOF and the Iraqi and American generals were based. The Americans were not shy any more, the roar of their planes in the skies was now a welcome sound, and their large armoured trucks drove along the road in and out of Mosul frequently. They tried half-heartedly to mask their presence by painting their cars black like the Iraqis or wearing civilian clothing, but on that hot May afternoon I could see one of their more adventurous soldiers jogging along the highway. Opposite the compound there was a large parking lot, where Iraqi army trucks deposited the wretched people fleeing Mosul. They were made to squat in rows before they were loaded onto buses and taken to refugee centres that were more like detention camps. All the components of the new Iraq were there in the street – the Shia chants, the hungry refugees, the American Chinooks and the rubbish – but the Americans thought of themselves differently now: they saw themselves as saviours, not conquerors. As for the Iraqis, friend and foe alike, this was still an extension of America's war, even if it was now only Iraqis who were butchering Iraqis. Beyond the rubbish heaps and the helipad, the road to Baghdad stretched for almost five hundred kilometres, cutting through the steppes of the al-Jazeera region that sits between the Tigris and the Euphrates, and traversing the length of the Sunni heartland. One lane of the road was open for traffic, the other was still gashed by deep trenches at regular ten-metre intervals. On either side, the fortifications of IS defence lines stretched two kilometres deep. Hundreds of berms dotted the green hills, each a metre high, and from a distance identical: like an IS Maginot Line. The trenches and berms are feats of engineering that stood as monuments to wasted effort. The road was now open but war in its many incarnations – sectarian cleansing, religious purification, national liberation – had been travelling back and forth along this highway since 2003. Every inch of it has been fought over, captured and recaptured multiple times, taken and retaken.

The dead are forgotten, unknown, and their bodies are swallowed by the fertile earth, but the ruins remain: the destroyed refinery that is now a playground of mangled steel chimneys and rusting tankers; the crippled and desolate villages; the municipal buildings and schools with their flattened roofs like concrete wafers – all stand witness to the horrors. The killers – bandits, insurgents, militias, soldiers –would keep travelling, deploying new tactics, implementing new horrors under different names, but they all remain the same people – Iraqis.

44

Aftermath

IN JULY 2017, THE LAND of the caliphate in Iraq had shrunk to a tiny sliver of the Old City of Mosul squeezed between advancing columns of army and police forces and the River Tigris. Thousands of fighters – local and foreign – were trapped in a cluster of dense and circuitous streets and alleyways, with dwindling supplies of food and medicine and no water or electricity, bombed day and night by American drones and jet fighters. Caught in the siege were thousands of civilians. The few who escaped emerged emaciated, filthy and delirious from thirst and constant bombing.

The commander was trying to lose weight and had banned his cook from serving meat, not that there was much meat in the meagre army rations in the first place. But on that hot and sticky July night, there was a special occasion, and a feast of bread soaked in okra stew, roasted meat and chicken and heaps of rice flavoured with nuts and raisins was laid out to celebrate the success of the previous day's operation: the commander's unit had liberated another block of streets in the Old City without suffering any casualties. 'We have one more battle and Mosul will be fully liberated, inshallah,' the commander said as he tucked into the rice and meat. A captain, still limping from a recent injury, laughed and said: 'Our fathers used to talk about the Iran–Iraq War as the "Long War" that lasted for eight years, so soon our war against Daesh will surpass it.'

After they finished their dinner, the commander proceeded to explain the plan, showing them a map. 'Jump into this building before first light. Establish a firebase here and here at street corners.' He gave them the coordinates. 'Advance towards this high building; your flanks will be secured by other units. Once you take the building, you will dominate the whole area with your snipers, and we can reach the Tigris in a few hours.'

After dinner, Taha, a wiry young lieutenant, asked the commander: 'Sir, what do we do with the two detainees?' Squinting through the smoke of his cigarette and jutting his moustache forward, the commander said: 'What's their story?'

'They crossed the front lines last night and took shelter with a civilian who denounced them to us. We tried to hand them to the intelligence service but they refused to receive them.'

'Yes, they told me, you deal with detainees at your end. They can't hold them because of human rights organisations and Red Cross inspections,' the commander said in a thoughtful, matter-of-fact tone.

'So we brought them here, and we "worked" on them all night,' Lieutenant Taha said. 'One eventually confessed that he had been with Daesh, but he said he left them two months ago.'

Laughter from around the room.

'The other,' continued the lieutenant, 'we beat him so hard but he didn't confess, so I think he must be innocent.'

'Just finish them,' hissed a major.

'Release one and finish the other,' the commander said.

The sentence was issued; now came the question of who would receive the honour of executing it. Kifah, tall and lean, one of the commander's soldiers, stood next to the table and asked to be given the prisoner, but then Lieutenant Taha suggested that they gift him to a captain who was still grieving for his brother, killed by IS a month earlier.

'Call him and give him the detainee.'

His decision announced, the commander stood up, the officers rose swiftly and stood to attention as he made his way to the living room where tea was served.

The next day, Lieutenant Taha and two other officers headed to the Old City to scout the front line ahead of the coming battle. The streets resembled concrete dough kneaded by giant fingers. Cars and lorries lay folded and piled atop roofs of half-collapsed houses. Twists of corrugated-metal sheets filled craters left by air strikes. When they reached the end of an alleyway blocked by the carcass of a car, they heard the screams of a woman. They stopped and saw a soldier, his gun slung across his chest, appear in a side alley dragging along a thin young woman, who stumbled on the rocks, barefoot, moaning and pleading for help. Her headscarf had slid to her shoulders, revealing stringy hair flecked with white. Her shirt was torn open and her abaya fluttered behind her. She tried to resist, but the soldier pulled her effortlessly into a bombed-out house. Two other soldiers followed, and they told the officers that the woman

موصل . المربنة القريمة

was a member of IS because they had found her in possession of 'five bundles [$50,000]'.

The officers grumbled about the lucky soldier – 'And he got a woman as well!' said one. 'But did you see how ugly she was?' said the other as they turned to continue their scouting. They stopped by the Nouri Mosque – where three years earlier the Caliph Abu Baker al-Baghdadi had given his speech – climbed over its rubble and snapped selfies. The medieval Hadba Minaret with its long elegant, and distinctively curved shape, the symbol of Mosul, lay in heaps of thousand-year-old bricks, blown up by withdrawing IS fighters the day before. From behind the ruins, the refugees were pouring out – tired, gaunt and carrying their sick and injured. They were dazed, scared and delirious with thirst after months of siege and bombardment. Even by the standards of Mosul refugees, these were a wretched and dismal lot. A soldier carrying an old woman stopped in the middle of the road to rest and she desperately clung to his back, terrified he might abandon her there. Taha went to the soldier and lent him a hand, and together they carried the old woman – who swayed between them, murmuring to herself – to a shed where medics were helping other refugees. The old woman's young and very pale daughter followed them, a Quran in her hands; behind her came two soldiers carrying her injured brother on a stretcher. He was bare-chested and very thin – his bones protruding from his skinny flesh – his right leg was bandaged and he had an old scar that stretched the length of his abdomen. The soldiers who were ordered to carry him by a benevolent general left him in the shed and went back to their posts. Other soldiers took an interest in him and started asking about his injuries.

'He was trying to get water from the river when he was shot by a sniper,' cried his sister as her brother lay on the stretcher smiling faintly.

'This is the injury of a fighter,' said a soldier. 'Take him to where his brothers are.'

The women screamed, begged and wailed, but the soldiers ignored them. Two of them pulled the injured man to his feet and walked him across the street into an empty shop, where he was shot. 'You are Daesh,' one soldier said to the young girl. 'All of you in the Old City are Daesh.'

In the early stages of the battle for Mosul, the Iraqi army and police had taken extra care to preserve the lives of civilians, keen to show them a different sort of army from the exploitative sectarian one they were accustomed to. They used their vehicles to evacuate the injured, and offered water and medical help wherever they could. In the Old City, however, the last refuge of IS and their families, everyone was treated as a suspect. Locals volunteered to weed out strangers; men of fighting age from other parts of the city or those with suspicious injuries were detained on the spot. Throughout the battle for Mosul, I saw how the same men who would undertake acts of brave and selfless mercy, putting their lives in danger to save a civilian or a fellow soldier, were also capable of the worst acts of barbaric cruelty.

———

The radio crackled. Between batches of coordinates came the words: 'We caught a Daesh.'

Taha leaned forward, took the radio mouthpiece and said: 'Bring him to me.' A wave of excitement ran through the room and Taha, who had the kind face of a teacher in a provincial town, stretched his index finger, making a pistol gesture. 'We will have a party today.' The man had been sentenced even before he was led into the room.

Half an hour later, a soldier appeared, his right arm clamped around the neck of another man who was bent double with his hands tied behind his back. The soldier pushed him to the floor. The man straightened his back and looked at the faces staring at him; a wide grin on his face showed two rows of large gleaming teeth. A soldier smacked him twice on the back of his head, but Taha said that no one should touch him. The soldier who brought him in said he was spotted crossing from IS lines with the civilians but when he saw the soldiers he tried to flee back to IS areas.

The man was haggard and bony, but underneath his threadbare T-shirt his muscles were tense and strong. He had dishevelled grey hair, a bushy beard and large dark eyes, somewhat resembling a Russian revolutionary.

'Who are you?' Taha asked him in a firm voice.

'I am a hospital medic – please check my hospital card,' the man answered calmly.

'Where is your national ID card?'

'Our ID cards were taken by Daesh fighters to prevent us from

369

leaving,' the man said, as he twisted his body to try and sit more comfortably on the floor.

'Taken by Daesh, or you destroyed it to hide your name? How do we know you are not a Daesh commander?'

'But, sir, I told you I am a medic,' the man said, smiling kindly and adding: 'I am an old man, how can I join Daesh at my age?' He spoke slowly, deliberately, trying to show his patience at the ignorance of the young soldiers. This was surely just a matter of an inconvenient misunderstanding. If they would only let him go, there would be no offence taken. But the medic was appealing to a form of reason that had deserted these battlefields a long time ago.

'Why don't you just confess that you are Daesh?' Taha was shrieking now. 'If you confess, I promise, I will hand you to the intelligence service. They will take you to Baghdad, put you on trial, you will go to prison, and you know what a joke our judicial system is – in a few years you will be out like the rest of the scums. But if you don't confess,' Taha continued in a threatening voice, 'you will never leave this room. It's your choice.'

The man tilted his head from one side to the other, examining the men looking at him, grinned again, and tried to explain again that this was all a big mistake.

'I am a medic, sir, a well-known medic. Daesh forced me to go to the Old City and work in their field hospital, I was there treating injured civilians, and yes, I will be straight with you, sir, I did treat some of their fighters too because they forced me, but I am not Daesh, sir, I actually hate them.'

'You are a liar,' Taha shouted.

'I swear by Imam Abbas –' but before he had finished his oath by one of the Shia's most revered imams, Taha had leaned forward and smacked him hard across the face, sending him tumbling back into the lap of a soldier who sat behind him.

'Don't utter those names, you filthy animal.'

The medic raised himself, the look of an insulted man on his face, his eyes saying both, how can you do this to an old man? and, yet I have forgiven you this grievance. 'But I am an old man,' he said softly, gradually forcing the smile back to his face. If there had ever been a moment when he could have saved himself, it had passed.

———

Taha and the soldiers dragged the medic into the narrow street outside. A soldier who walked ahead pointed at a house with a dark marble stone facade. Through an arched doorway, the group entered the courtyard of a beautiful old house, attached to an old church, and entirely deserted. They pushed the medic through the courtyard and up a few steps into a dark room with three windows that overlooked a cemetery. Pushed to the floor, the medic sat up and leaned his back against the base of one of the windows, his head backlit by shafts of the afternoon sunlight. Taha and the soldiers stood in a semicircle around him.

'Yalla, old man, why don't you confess so we can send you away from here?' one of the young officers said.

The old man, still smiling, gently answered: 'But how can I confess something I haven't done? How can I do that to myself?'

A burly soldier picked a short metal pipe and started prodding the man's knees with it. 'Look from the window, that rotten body over there, that was one of your people, we captured him a few days ago and he too refused to confess.' The medic craned his neck and squinted through the window behind him. In the cemetery below, a bloated decomposed body had turned black under the scorching summer sun. He turned back and smiled, but was there now a hint of fear? Of loss of control? 'I am just a medic,' he mumbled.

371

Taha, bored, enraged by the heat in the room, wanted to finish this charade – the sentence had already been passed, and the whole interrogation a mere formality, to clear their own consciences, maybe. He turned his head, swung his leg back and brought it straight into the medic's face, kicking him so hard that he collapsed motionless to the floor. For a second everyone in the room thought he was dead. 'Pour water on him – he's faking death,' Taha said. One soldier pulled the man up by twisting his arms and sat him straight. The medic opened his eyes slowly; they were stunned at first, then darkened with anger and rage. He puckered his face, opened his mouth and a lump of flesh, blood and the gleaming large smiling teeth tumbled to his chest and onto the floor. He was silent and did not plead any more. He may have known that it was all over now, or maybe he didn't care any more. 'Ha? Will you confess?' said the soldier with a metal pipe.

'I have nothing to say,' hissed the medic. Blood was pouring from the darkness of his mouth. Taha nodded to the soldier, who dropped the pipe and picked up a short M-4 rifle, but another soldier told him to be careful, the bullets might ricochet in the small room. He pulled the man to his feet, his legs wobbling, and leaned him against one of the large arched windows. In one quick move, the burly soldier flipped him out of the window, but kept a grip on his feet. The old man hung swinging from the window. 'Are you going to confess now?' the soldier asked as he held on to the man's feet. 'What else is left for you?'

'How can I harm myself?' came the faint voice of the man from below.

In the dark room, the soldiers and officers looked at the two feet, dirty and cracked, for a few seconds. Then the soldier let go, and they vanished from the window. The medic fell to the yard below with a muffled thud. The soldier leaned out of the window with his rifle and fired five bullets into the body that quivered on the uneven ground.

A cloud of gunpowder filled the room, dancing in the shafts of light. The old man lay amid the rubble and debris of war, his grey clothing turning pink. The soldier then fired two more bullets. 'These two at his legs just in case he wants to walk back home,' he said, laughing.

On the way back, a young officer with a childish face asked Taha with a sheepish smile, 'I wonder if God will one day punish us for all these killings. Will we go mad, or something worse?'

'He is my number five since the start of [the battle of] Mosul,' Taha answered. 'Al-Qaeda has one good principle: if they suspect someone, or have the tiniest shred of evidence against him, they execute him, and then they say if he was guilty, he deserved it, and if he was innocent, his blood will be purged and later he will go to heaven. I follow the same principle.'

———

It was 4 a.m. In a room lit by a flickering generator light stood soldiers in tight-fitting boxer shorts and T-shirts. They were lean and young, and without their menacing black uniforms and weapons they looked harmless and even a bit vulnerable.

Like a large dysfunctional family preparing for a picnic, the soldiers bickered and argued. Someone shouted for his night-vision goggles, no one could find them, another looked for a box of smoke grenades; eventually the night visions were found but without batteries, another call went round for batteries. They jammed hand grenades and water bottles into their packs, scooped bullets from a crate and stuffed them into rice sacks, strapped ammunition magazines onto their flak jackets and tried to eat sandwiches of stale bread and cream cheese.

Finally, as the sky turned a deep crimson blue, the soldiers, armed and kitted up, formed a long line and moved in silence into the dark and ghost-haunted alleyways of Old Mosul. They walked along a winding path, climbing over stone boulders and debris, which rose and dipped in a series of jagged and slippery concrete waves that were once houses and streets. Their ammunition boxes and magazines swung and rattled like bells announcing the arrival of a herd of goats on a mountain cliff. The soldiers avoided the protruding wires of a booby-trapped school bag, skirted the lunar landscape left by an air strike and sidestepped the decomposing body of an IS fighter to descend into the basement of an old house, where they found an abandoned IS field hospital. Bottles of intravenous fluid lay scattered on the floor or hung from green marble columns. They then entered a courtyard where a large orange tree and tall elegant marble arches were bathed in the early-dawn light. At the head of the column, two men were trying to push themselves through a small gap in a thick stone wall; their guns and backpacks clanged and banged and got stuck in the stonework. The long column of soldiers stopped, sitting or leaning against walls wherever they found themselves; whether it was a living room with a flipped sofa and dusty bookshelves, a courtyard strewn with burned furniture, or the frontyard of a church. A human train passing through an urban tunnel dug through the warscape of a city. Corpses of IS fighters lay around them, a trail of putrid breadcrumbs leading to the front line. The stench announced their presence long before they were spotted: two in the cold hall of a church, another in the yard outside, one burned into a charred heap of skull and bones that sat in a black circle of flesh. An old woman lay dead under a blanket in a small house. With the rising sun, the reek of the corpses rose above the ruins, inviting swarms of flies. One young officer threw up. The men were silent; their bickering and chirpiness had deserted them, replaced by a foreboding gloom. They yearned for the reassuring sounds of bullets and explosions and feared the silence before the battle, in which their brains filled the void with horror.

'If someone is injured today, they will probably die before they reach the back line,' said one veteran soldier.

Many more grumbled.

'Why are they pushing us so fast before even securing a supply line?'

'So that the commander can reach the Tigris quickly and take selfies.'

A race was on to be the first to reach the river and declare the end of the caliphate, contested by the different special forces battalions and other army and police units. Generals were pushing their commanders hard to reach the river and claim that accolade.

———

By 7 a.m., the soldiers had climbed over the rickety skeleton of a metal bed into the back of a multi-storey building, from where they would launch their attack. The building had once housed clinics and medical labs; now it was left a gutted frame, floors piled with medical sheets of paper, X-rays, pharmaceutical boxes and a handful of decayed bodies. A piece of paper hung on the wall, instructing female doctors that by the authority of IS Moral Committee they must always wear a niqab, even when examining female patients. The building overlooked a wide road and an intersection.

When the order for the attack came, a column of men, each holding the shoulder of the man ahead, tiptoed to the front of the building and stood behind a battered metal shutter. The early-morning sunlight filtered through a thousand bullet holes, washing the soldiers' faces in a bright orange glow. The first column ran across the street, climbing a mound of debris in the middle and reaching the opposite corner. A second column followed. One by one the soldiers ran; the first crossed, the second followed, the third ran, smack came a sniper's bullet, and he fell. A fourth soldier ran to pull the fallen man back, smack came a second sniper bullet, and it hit his leg. He crawled back, and the offensive came to a halt.

The officers gathered on the upper floor called for an American air strike on the neighbouring building where they thought the sniper was hiding. It came five minutes later, and when the dust had settled, the sniper resumed firing. A couple of soldiers climbed to the upper floor of the building and opened fire with their heavy machine guns, to cover the men who were pulling back the fallen soldier, but the sniper kept firing. The officers called for a second air strike; this one was going to be closer to their positions. Soldiers and officers cowered for cover in the corridors. The building shook violently when the bomb was dropped, and filled with a thick dark cloud of dust. Smoke grenades were thrown into the street, the cloud of dust turned into orange and yellow and the dead soldier was brought in. The first casualty of the day. More air strikes were called; in the cover of their dust and smoke clouds the soldiers ran, crossing the street, stumbling over rocks and debris. Bullets fired by the enraged sniper exploded between their feet or pinged against metal bars next to their heads. He dominated the empty street with the fear of his single bullets.

———

Grenades, guns and helmets rattled against each other, as the two dozen soldiers who had crossed the street, squeezed into a small room. The alleyway outside was deserted, and there was no sign of IS resistance. The soldiers split into three groups: one headed to the right towards a large church complex, one headed to the left to take over a multi-storey building, and in the middle, Lieutenant Taha and four soldiers moved forward. They were led by a square-shouldered man with a bushy moustache. He was part of a group of local vigi-lantes helping the army, motivated by revenge for relatives killed by IS. The man walked confidently, negotiating his way in the midst of carnage as if he was walking in his garden. Crouching by the stone walls, the soldiers followed at a distance, until they came to a construction site with a rotunda of columns. Taha and his soldiers debated where their target was – the aerial maps they carried on their phones had little resemblance to the topography of destruction around them. The man pointed at a berm of earth and debris and said he used to live there. Hearing the voices, IS fighters hiding behind the berm opened fire, their bullets sounding like the cracks of metal whips. Two soldiers crawled to the edge of the berm, lifted their guns and sprayed bullets down over it. A third followed behind them: bent double, he twisted his body, pulled his arm back and swung it fast overhead. A hand grenade arced through the sky and dropped behind the berm; a few seconds of silence followed and then a fountain of debris sprouted from where it fell. But the shooting continued, bul-lets were still hitting the concrete columns. Between the shots, the soldiers could hear the faint sounds of IS fighters calling each other. 'Silence,' hissed the lieutenant. The soldiers stood and listened, and from somewhere right behind the mound they heard an IS fighter, sounding young and panicked, calling 'Abu Yussuf, Abu Yussuf, where are you?' The vigilante guide walked to the edge of the berm and shouted, 'My brother, my brother, where are you?' He pointed at a window, to the left of the mound. 'He is there,' he said.

'Give me a grenade,' said a soldier.

He was given a home-made C4 bomb to preserve their hand gren-ade supplies. He lit the fuse and crouched. 'Be careful of the sniper, don't go too close, one of the soldiers said.' He bowled it over, and there was a huge explosion. A hail of bullets followed, exploding overhead. The voice came back from behind the mound, more urgent this time, still calling for help. 'Go back and talk to him,' the lieutenant told the civilian.

'My brother, my brother, who is here?' shouted the civilian. 'Brother' was the call sign among the jihadi fighters.

'It is me, brother, come help me,' a faint voice replied. 'I am stuck here.'

'Are you alone?'

'Yes, yes, brother, I am alone, just come.'

'He is hiding across from us, behind a door, maybe trapped,' said the civilian and the soldier threw another bomb.

A cat-and-mouse game followed. After each explosion, the civilian called, the 'brother' answered, and the soldier lobbed a bomb.

The commander called on the radio and asked for progress. 'We are dealing with a trapped fighter, sir,' the lieutenant answered.

'You have been dealing with him for an hour now. Make a move,' the commander shouted over the radio. The soldiers deliberated on how to get him. The 'brother', who was growing tired of the game, fired a few more bullets and went silent but the soldiers still couldn't be sure. 'Maybe he's dead,' the vigilante said.

'Or maybe he's faking death and wearing a suicide vest,' said the lieutenant. Finally they sent the civilian and two soldiers to check. 'Be careful, one step at a time,' said the lieutenant. They descended the mound, opened a metal door and found no dead or trapped fighters.

———

'Don't cluster here, or we'll be picked off by a sniper,' said the lieutenant. 'Head to that house.' The men climbed another mound of debris, their feet slipping on pots, tiles, bits of furniture and boulders mixed with scraps of coloured fabrics. They slowly pushed open a door behind which stood a blue plastic barrel filled with old bathwater, acrid and murky. A dark film floated on top of it. In the July heat, the soldiers had run out of whatever water they had carried and were parched. They hesitated at first, but gradually yielded, crowded around the barrel, scooped water and started drinking.

'Don't drink that,' said the civilian. 'It's filthy, just wet your lips, otherwise you'll get diarrhoea.' The soldiers ignored him and drank more. The house was small, two rooms arranged above a courtyard, one had collapsed, and in the other the lieutenant, soldiers and their guide fell exhausted onto a sofa. Outside the house there was a cacophony of explosions, machine-gun fire and the whoosh of air strikes. Within the same block, at least five battles were raging and they didn't know who was firing where. 'Go down and check that the courtyard and the basement are clear,' the lieutenant said. Two soldiers dragged themselves down the rickety stairs.

'Sir,' the lieutenant said into the radio. 'Sir, are we getting any support? We are only five here, and we are waiting for other units to advance.'

'Stay put and hold your ground. Support on its way,' answered the commander.

'And water, sir, the men are parched,' added the lieutenant.

From downstairs came the clanging of furniture and pots. The courtyard was clear. The two soldiers moved towards a door leading to the basement. 'Be careful,' said the civilians from above. 'There are families still hiding in this area.'

The basement door squealed when they pushed it open slowly.

'If those families die,' joked a soldier upstairs, 'they will be martyrs in Allah's eyes.'

Silence, then bang, bang, followed by a burst of gunfire. A second burst echoed loud in the small courtyard. The two soldiers ran back up the stairs, one with his face covered in blood, clutching an injured arm and dragging his gun. 'Tie it, tie it,' he pleaded, panting as he rested the bleeding arm in his lap.

Half an hour later, there was still no news of the reinforcements, and the lieutenant decided to move.

'Boys, we can't just sit here, we will lose all our work, let's move.'

As they debated, a civilian went to investigate; he came back to say there was a narrow path and they had to move in single file. They divided up the hand grenades and prepared to move when the sound of heavy machine-gun fire came from the entrance of the house. The door was pushed open and fifteen soldiers from another column stumbled into the room. 'Disperse!' shouted their officer. 'And keep an eye on the door.' They were in a state of commotion; soldiers shouted at their officers, and the officers refused to obey orders radioed to them by their commander. A building they had captured earlier had been set ablaze by IS fighters, and two of their men had burned to death inside. 'Sir, I can't advance, we are besieged, the other battalion have an injured man and they can't even evacuate him,' the officer yelled into his radio. 'You either send us help or give us permission to retreat.'

The commanders responded by issuing orders to advance from a different corner, playing checkers on a virtual map that had nothing to do with the reality on the ground.

'Do you think they care about us?' said a soldier. 'They sit in headquarters, with the air conditioners blowing on their faces, drinking tea and cold water, and they order you to advance.'

'His platoon is besieged and he wants to advance.' The officer laughed, but he acceded, and twice he and his men tried to find a way out of the small house. Each time they opened the door, IS fighters opened fire, pinning them down and sending everyone scrambling back into the room.

'They are trying to get us killed.' The officer smacked his forehead and collapsed on the floor where men sat squeezed against each other. More stood in the doorway, unable to find a space to rest on the floor. The house was now surrounded both back and front and by the afternoon even the acrid water in the plastic barrel was running out. Some sneaked into the courtyard looking for a well or more water while the rest dozed on and off in the stifling heat. A civilian scout came back to the house saying an IS unit was moving down the lane. The officers positioned two machine guns at the windows and went back to their slumber. American jets dropped a bomb every fifteen minutes; in the silence that followed each explosion the only sounds were the flicks of lighters as the men smoked to quench their thirst.

In a moment of lull, when everyone, even those on guard at the window, was nodding off, came the tinkling sound of breaking glass and something falling just outside the room. 'What's happening?' shouted one. 'Get down, it's a grenade!' shouted another. The explosion smashed the front of the room, sending in showers of glass, shrapnel and smoke. Then bullets came screeching in, smacking hot against the ceiling or high on the walls above the soldiers' heads. Men piled on top of each other trying to seek shelter from the bullets and the shouts of 'I'm injured' were lost in the chaos. The two soldiers standing manning their heavy machine guns started firing back, their bullet casings falling with a jingle on the floor. Bullets started raining on the house from two more directions. Another grenade was tossed but exploded just outside the window.

'I need a container,' one soldier yelled and a box of ammunition was passed to him, moving from hand to hand.

'You're bleeding, let's move.' Someone crawled to the entrance and threw a smoke grenade; under the scant cover it provided the soldiers ran. 'Cross quickly, I shit on the religion of your parents, quickly, run,' the chubby officer shouted at his men. Taha and his four soldiers stayed behind, shooting bursts of machine-gun fire from the window.

'I see movement,' said Taha. 'Shoot quickly, quickly.'

'We have to leave, we have one box of ammunition left and no grenades,' said one soldier.

'If we stay here they will pick us off one by one during the night,' said another. 'We can give the coordinates of this house for it to be bombed.'

But the lieutenant didn't want to leave and lose the ground that had taken him all day to capture. He wanted to stay but his hardened fighters were pulling him; they slid over the debris, fell to the ground and stumbled across the open area in front of the house. In a few minutes they were back in the crowded room where they had started their day.

———

The soldiers collapsed – exhausted, thirsty and frustrated. There was no water or food, and no way to evacuate the injured who sat in the shade losing blood and moaning. In spite of half a dozen air strikes, the sniper still dominated the street, cutting off the only supply route.

Attempting to bring relief to the parched men, soldiers on the other side of the street stood on high balconies and tossed over plastic bottles of water. Most either cracked, spilling the precious liquid in the rubble, or fell into no man's land. Those bottles that survived were quickly snatched and drunk by the soldiers charged with collecting them on behalf of their exhausted comrades. A rope was tied across the street and two plastic bags filled with water bottles were hung on it: they slid down slowly but before reaching the soldiers, the sniper fired and severed the rope.

'This is all the chaos of the commanders pushing us on quickly without securing a supply line.'

Indifferent to all of this, the commander and his counterparts from other battalions were shouting orders over the radio, demanding that the men advance again. 'Who gave you the order to withdraw?' the commander demanded to know.

'Sir, I have four injured because of that house.'

The generals called for more air strikes; each one was preceded by the call to take cover. The men cowered and waited before a huge explosion ripped through the old city and clouds of dust, concrete and smoke blew down the street. Each air strike was churning up the earth and the concrete, creating a landscape even more difficult to negotiate. Three times the soldiers tried to attack the house, now nothing but a mound of rubble with windows sticking out of it; three times they failed.

In their rush to reach the Tigris, to declare the liberation of Mosul, the generals treated the lives of soldiers as a cheap price to be paid. At 5 p.m., as the generals were demanding the fourth attack, Lieutenant Taha called on the men to gear up and start moving. 'Water, water, we are dying of thirst,' the soldiers shouted at the lieutenant and they refused to move. He pleaded and threatened until they relented. They shuffled at crawling speed, grumbling and cursing. A boulder that in the morning was crossed in a few hops, was now taking fifteen minutes to negotiate. They were halfway to the house when they heard that a young ginger-haired new recruit who had volunteered to stay behind and collect water had been killed by the sniper. The men simply turned round and walked back, abandoning the attack and refusing to obey further orders.

In the rubble-strewn alleyway, they collapsed again, sitting on boulders, or piling up metal sheets to make a bed, and asking each other for water. The dead soldier lay under a small sheet, his feet sticking out. Two soldiers sat next to his body and wept in silence, only their shoulders shaking. A few metres away lay the rotting corpse of a dead IS fighter.

After midnight, under cover of darkness, three soldiers crawled on their bellies across the street to Lieutenant Taha and his men, braving the sniper fire. Each carried sacks with bottles of water and boxes of ammunition on their backs. They emptied their load, and returned with the body of the young soldier. The rest of the soldiers stayed to continue the fighting next day.

———

Four days later, Lieutenant Taha and the captain sat on piles of coloured underwear in a burned-out storeroom, contemplating their fate. The commander had issued his last plea for the men to advance. They knew the commander was under pressure from the generals in Baghdad, because the prime minister had arrived in Mosul and was waiting to declare victory. At the bottom of the line, all the pressure was on the few men who sat in a room of tattered bras and scorched shampoo bottles.

Since the first day of the offensive, they had manoeuvred through the rubble trying to advance but meeting fierce IS resistance at every corner. When they did manage to advance, it was for a few metres only, with an average of four suicide bombers charging at them each day. One of the suicide bombers came running in on crutches. At night, they ate and slept in burned and destroyed houses, next to the rotting bodies of fighters and civilians, sometimes separated from the jihadis by only a single wall. Only the swarms of flies crossed between them, feasting on the dead.

'I just want to see my daughter now,' the lieutenant said, looking at the captain. 'Will I ever see her again?'

'It's fine.' The captain forced a laugh. 'In a few hours this will be just another anecdote.' Between their feet, the blue, red and pink of the cheap underwear was a stark contrast to the soot-covered walls.

They stood, collected their men, and tiptoed outside, skirting around the bodies. Other units had pushed parallel to them and their snipers had killed a few IS fighters, who lay dead still strapped into their explosive vests. They started shooting at a corner building ahead of them, but before they reached it, an explosion went off: inside, the bodies of six injured fighters burned into blackened charcoal frozen in the moment of their agonising death. They took shelter in a small shop, fired, moved down an alleyway, entered a building. Two more IS fighters were killed there. They climbed through a shell hole in the wall. They looked out at the vista of destruction and the blue River Tigris, and Mosul was liberated.

———

That day the prime minister, Hayder al-Ebadi, stood in a base on the outskirts of the city, flanked by generals in crisp uniforms, and made his long-awaited victory speech, declaring that 'Mosul is liberated!' He had flown in by helicopter the night before, and the generals were pushing the soldiers to reach the river so as not to keep the PM waiting. A week of celebrations was called for and all over Iraq banners were raised in jubilation.

In the afternoon, the commander and other unit leaders headed to the river in a big convoy of armoured Humvees. They inspected the ruins where their men had fought, walked to the riverbank and stood there snapping selfies. Each officer gave his own victory speech for the accompanying TV cameras. Not far from where they stood, a lone IS sniper hiding in a collapsed building was firing desperately at a platoon of federal police stationed at the mouth of the Old Iron Bridge; the bullets hit their armoured vehicle with a loud twang. An American jet fighter descended, a rocket screeched and an explosion followed. A white plume of smoke rose into the sky before it turned to a dark cloud. Dust and debris swept over the skeleton of the bridge.

In the commander's house, exhilaration and ecstasy hung in the air as the skies outside blazed with celebratory gunfire. Officers smoked, exchanged congratulations and thrillingly told and retold the crucial moments of the battle, expanding and embellishing their own role with every retelling. Their soldiers were allowed to go back to their base to rest and shower; a week of sleeping next to decomposed bodies had given them a strange skin disease. Pockets of IS fighters continued to resist for a few more days but gradually the fighting died down and the day came in Mosul when, for the first time in many years, machine guns, car bombs and jet fighters fell silent. But then the orgy of executions began.

———

Night after night, in cells, destroyed houses or in the haunted dark streets of Mosul, those accused of being members of Islamic State – those who surrendered, or were captured, injured or denounced while fleeing with civilians – were tortured and executed. Jubilant Iraqi soldiers filmed themselves beating prisoners, before hurling them down a cliff and shooting at them. Locals, keen to extract revenge on those they held responsible for the miseries of the last three years started denouncing not only members of IS and their families, but any man of fighting age who came from the countryside, bore an injury, or simply looked suspicious. A schism between Mosul and its surrounding countryside had developed into animosity since most of the local senior leaders of IS came from the rural areas. The people of Mosul blamed them for the destruction: it remains eternally convenient to blame outsiders for any misfortune.

Men came to the commander's house every night with a flurry

of denunciations. Some were absurd: a frail man in tattered brown trousers and a white shirt came running in with a sense of urgency to denounce a family of refugees because their three young sons, he assured the commander, never left the house. A doctor denounced the brother of someone who ran a Facebook page sympathetic to IS. A man who sold vegetables and used to be a muezzin in the local mosque was dragged in by local vigilantes, though after a couple of hours of torture he was found to be innocent and released. Anyone who could be proven guilty by proximity or association was denounced. Some were beaten up but then released. Others were not so lucky.

One night when the commander was in his usual spot, perched on a sofa playing with his phone, a group of civilians entered the room pushing a man before them. They forced him to kneel on the floor, his hands in front of him, tied together with a piece of cloth ripped from his faded shirt. The locals sat around him and shouted with agitation that he was a former IS executioner.

'Remember when you stood in the middle of that roundabout and killed three men?' said one of them pointing at the man. 'He's worked with jihadis since 2005,' chimed in another.

The man said nothing. Eventually, he glanced up, the confused look of a drunk on his face, and mumbled that it had been his brother who had joined IS not him. His eyes were looking somewhere between the commander's feet.

The commander handed the man's ID card to a soldier to be burned, thus disappearing him from official records, and nodded. Kifah, the lean and tall soldier, joyfully dragged the man out into the street. Other soldiers and officers followed and locals broke into cheers of encouragement.

Kifah pushed the man up the empty street while others ran behind, kicking and punching him. When he fell, they jeered and taunted him, pulled him up and kicked him again, laughing every time he fell.

'Sing for us one of the caliphate songs,' the captain said laughing hysterically, something mad and raging in his eyes. They made him run in front of them – 'Run quickly, run, run, you are free.' He ran, stumbled, tried to pull up his falling trousers with his tied hands. They chased him, landing blows wherever they could. A soldier jumped in the air and side-kicked him in the face with the theatrical relish of a professional kick-boxer. Kifah and another soldier dragged him through a gutter flowing with thick black sewage, pulled him into a dark side street and made him kneel.

The man stared blankly at the pile of rubbish in front of him, lit by the strong lights of a Humvee. Behind him stood Kifah, stretching out an arm with an American Glock pistol at the end of it. Another soldier stood next to Kifah filming with his mobile phone. 'This is to avenge all the martyrs killed by Daesh,' said Kifah. A single shot rang out, echoing in the deserted street, a small fountain of blood squirted from the man's head and he fell instantly. Kifah flipped him onto his back with his foot, looked at him and then walked away.

'Maybe we should have checked he really died,' said the soldier filming.

'If he survived that bullet then he deserves to live,' said Kifah. He meant it.

———

The next day Kifah lounged on a mat laid between machine guns, backpacks and boots, watching the video of the execution over and over again. 'I had this filmed for an uncle of mine who wanted to come here just to execute a Daesh fighter. I told him I will kill one on your behalf.'

He told me that this was the best time to cleanse the city of IS. 'Soon the city will be divided into military sectors and we won't be able to drive around town without notifying the central command,' he explained. 'Now it's chaos and in the chaos we can work well.'

The first time Kifah executed a prisoner was in 2015, when he and two friends captured three IS fighters. They took them to a river-bank and killed them. He showed me the pictures to demonstrate how neatly his victim had been killed, compared to the clumsy jobs his two friends had managed.

He said he killed for three reasons: because he had no trust in the judicial service, rightly believing that detainees would be able to buy their way out as they had done many times before; to avenge the friends he had lost; and finally because of the Camp Speicher massacre.

We were sitting on the floor, drinking tea and playing chess. Sad Shia songs issued from his phone.

Kifah had served the last three years under the commander and followed him like a shadow: into the siege of Baiji Refinery (when they survived on rice cooked in engine oil), and marching with him to Mosul. They had survived a dozen car bomb attacks together. Kifah and his tight-knit group of friends became a sort of Praetorian Guard attached to the commander. They worshipped him and disre-spected everyone else. Kifah took special pride in picking fights and humiliating regular army and police officers; however war-hardened they were, they were always despised by the special forces men who considered themselves above the law.

'Those army fuckers, they don't fight, they just loot and oppress the people,' said Kifah contemptuously. When the officers came to the commander to complain, he would summon Kifah, look at him and burst out laughing.

Like many other soldiers in the force, Kifah survived on a mixture of drugs and alcohol. He would swallow a Captagon pill, blabber for a while with dilated eyes and saliva foaming at the edge of his mouth. When the pill kicked in, he would stay awake for the whole night. 'A pill will make you work like a donkey for three nights, carrying your machine gun and running without feeling tired,' he said. He was foul-mouthed, woke up late, and because of his exceptional courage in battles was exempted from daily duties. He would sit in his boxers holding a machine gun in his lap and wonder calmly: 'How is it that in all these years not a bullet or a car bomb has managed to kill me? What more can I do?'

———

Ammar was a fourteen-year-old student preparing for his end-of-year exams when Islamic State fighters captured Mosul in 2014 and swept through the Sunni heartland. When the fighters entered his Sunni village south of Mosul, his elder brother – who had joined them a few years earlier – told him that the years of oppression by the Shia government in Baghdad and its sectarian security forces were over. Serving the new, just and powerful Islamic State was a source of pride and good employment. Against his mother's protestation, the brother persuaded him to drop out of school and enrol in one of the new Islamic State military training camps. There, Ammar received four days of military and religious training, was handed a Kalashnikov and appointed a member of the newly established 'Religious Police'. He was assigned to a checkpoint at the entrance of his village, searching people and cars for contraband: cigarettes, alcohol, energy drinks and anything that contravened the strict new religious codes. Those caught, he detained and escorted to the Hisba, where they were flogged, tortured, imprisoned, or worse. For a few years, life was not bad: in their impoverished village, Ammar and his brother had joined the privileged members of the new regime, with regular monthly stipends and some perks. They became believers in the eternal and expanding victory of the caliphate.

In the summer of 2016, Iraqi army and Shia militias started their march towards Mosul, recapturing villages and towns along the way. Ammar's brother was killed in one of the battles, while he and his sisters and mother joined the exodus of the caliphate's faithful – fighters, local and foreign, and their families – fleeing ahead of the advancing army. They went to Mosul, moving from one neighbourhood to another until they found themselves besieged in the Old City.

The mother and sisters fled the Old City into liberated government-controlled areas. Ammar was held back by his commanders, who shot dead anyone who attempted to desert. When the Islamic State defences began to crumble, and desperate jihadis fought from one house to another in the alleyways of the old city, Ammar managed to slip through the front lines in a column of civilians. He found his mother and sisters squatting with relatives and tried to seek shelter with them, but his mother, fearing for the safety of her daughters and relatives if they were found harbouring an IS fugitive, kicked him out and told him to hand himself over to the Iraqi authorities. Desperate, scared and hungry, he roamed the war-torn city for days until he came across a group of fugitives. They hid in abandoned cemeteries and scrapyards, sleeping between the graves at night and hiding under the wreckage of trailers during the day. Every few days, one of the group, a tall, lanky former fighter called Omar, would head to a nearby market to buy food and try to find any Islamic State sympathisers who could help them flee the city. In his last trip to the market, Omar stood chatting with a shop owner in a rubble-strewn street, when two women recognised him and started screaming, 'Daesh Daesh'. Some of the commander's men were stationed nearby, and they grabbed Omar and brought him in for interrogation. They went through his wallet asking him for his ID card. 'Lost my ID card, Daesh killed my family,' he replied, his eyes darting between the soldiers and officers. They opened his phone and logged into his Facebook account; jihadi sympathisers with names like Abu Qutada al-Sudani and Afghans were chatting with him: for them, the caliphate was alive and well in the virtual world. In his wallet, they also found a scrap of paper identifying him or someone else as assistant to Brother Abu Aisha.

'I don't know whose Facebook this is. I just bought the phone and the Face came with it.'

The soldiers forced Omar to lie on his stomach and raise one leg. They fashioned whips from electrical cables and metal wires and lifted their arms high. The whips came down with horrible, frightening noise on his foot and back. Omar screamed, twisted and wailed and when he curled lowering his leg a soldier squeezed his head with his boots, and he raised his foot again. Between his cries, he insisted that he had never known IS. The captain and another officer presided over the torture.

'I swear I have never joined Daesh. Oh, people, believe me,' he cried.

'Let me punch him,' the officer pleaded.

'He will talk, he will talk, don't worry,' the captain said.

The officer punched him three times, left right left, then released his grip. Omar fell, and blood poured from his head.

'Motherfucker,' shouted the captain at the officer 'Anything you touch you break. Shit on your God, look at this blood.' The blood gushed and formed a pool around the man's head. 'Ah fuck, now the smell will be horrible, who will clean this?'

They brought him round, gave him half an hour of rest. They would often give suspects water, tea, sometimes food, for the sole purpose of prolonging the torture. Then they continued. When they started rubbing his injuries with salt, his cries became like those of an animal.

'By Allah I will kill you and shoot you in the head if you don't confess. I will kill you, do you hear me?' said the officer.

'Shoot him here?' said the captain hopefully.

'No, no, we do it in the Old City,' the other officer answered.

For five hours, soldiers and officers took shifts torturing him. After each shift he begged for water and was given short respites from pain, then made to stand up and jump on the spot, so that his feet wouldn't become numb to the agony. When the soldiers and officers were tired they called for the Yazidi cook. The soldiers goaded him: 'Those are the Daesh who raped your cousins and sisters, those are the ones who destroyed your villages.' The cook, who had lost many of his female relatives when IS attacked his village, went into a frenzy, hitting Omar so hard that the soldiers had to restrain him before he killed the man. Howls of an animal stretched Omar's hoarse voice. The wails mixed pain, desperation and anger, and when the pain was too unbearable he gave away Ammar.

Ammar was asleep between the graves when the soldiers surrounded him, flashing lights on his face. He awoke to gun barrels pointing at his head. He was brought to the officers: without needing a single slap, he told them that he had been a member of IS and he had fled the old city and that Omar was an IS fighter. His confession did not save him from torture, but it hastened the death of Omar. The two men passed each other as Ammar was taken to the torture room and Omar was dragged out into the street. They threw him into the back of a car. Two soldiers sat with him, placing their feet on his head. They drove through the dark streets of Mosul. Omar was pushed into a pile of rubble in front of a shop and made to kneel. He turned his face, watching attentively, still worried that he might be whipped again, but they ordered him to turn away. They opened fire

393

with pistols and machine guns, and after he fell, another soldier lifted a boulder and used it to smash in his head. Laughing, they drove back to where Ammar was going through his share of torture.

The heritage of torture in Iraq can be traced as a linear path, from Saddam's Mukhabarat to the Americans in Abu Ghraib and the sectarian forces of the Iraqi government and its militias. Based on the simple concept that if a man is innocent he will suffer and won't confess, but if he confesses, even if it was just to stop the harrowing pain, then he must be guilty.

In the nightmare of Mosul, torture was different: it served no investigative purpose, it achieved and demanded nothing beyond a primordial imperative to exact pain and revenge, and prove to the soldiers that they had defeated IS.

'I don't want to hear his confession,' one officer said. 'What will I do with it? I want him to suffer and die.'

For the lucky ones, death was swift and quick; for Ammar, death was a luxury that he had to wait for. The officers did not see their victims as humans let alone as fellow Iraqis, they were nothing but the ultimate enemy. It was there and then when they heard the animal-like squealing of pain, when they saw the feared and mighty IS soldiers begging for mercy, that they felt they had achieved their final victory over the caliphate. And yet perhaps, the victory of Islamic State lay in its ability to make the people adopt its own savagery. Those who were the most cruel in torturing the detainees were often the ones who had not seen actual combat: the unit cook, the logistics officers, people who spent the war in the rear and not at the front lines. Kifah left the room in disgust when he saw the torture. 'Why do they torture them? Just kill the men and get it over with.'

By midnight the soldiers were tired of Ammar and his face had been disfigured into lumps of black.

He was taken to where his friend had been lying dead for a couple of hours. There is nothing noble about death in Mosul; the flies had gathered, dogs had already taken parts of Omar's leg. Ammar was ordered to kneel a couple of meters away from his comrade's body.

When watching the footage from the Speicher massacre, I always wondered what went through the head of the man who knelt in the last row, as he watched or listened to dozens being executed before him. What happened to a person when he realised that the moment had come, that the process of negotiations, the torture, the begging, the lies, the promises were over?

A soldier who was filming asked Ammar to move a bit closer to his dead friend. Ammar obeyed, crawling on his knees closer to where Omar's body lay. He was already dead long before the bullets pierced his young skull.

———

For days the soldiers and officers drove back and forth through the streets of Old Mosul and watched the bodies they had shot disintegrate and decay, ripped apart by dogs overnight, becoming part of a rubbish heap, until eventually the bodies blended into the background, and became a permenant fixture of the landscape of urban warfare. The commander and his men had been fighting a long time. Before the Islamic State, they fought Sunni insurgents and Shia militias and before that they spent their formative years in the shadow of a civil war where many of them saw first-hand the dead relatives, car bombs, kidnappings, streets littered with bodies, and sectarian politics that enabled a handful of militiamen and politicians to loot the state in the name of protecting the sect against The Other. A decade and a half of harrowing war had become an integral part of their identity, not just as soldiers but as unfortunate citizens of the country of Iraq. They are the children of the occupation, locked in the endless cycles of violence it created.

But in the war against IS, they found a cause, the camaraderie of a close-knit tribe and something akin to patriotism. They saw themselves as the defenders of the nation, warriors of a just and pure cause against an absolute evil which allowed them to feel that they were above the state, above answering to a gang of corrupt politicians in Baghdad. They had stared death in the eye many times and they had not shied away. They felt it gave them the ultimate right to dictate the terrain of right and wrong, as well as life and death. 'Sometimes we do things and we know we are breaking the law,' the commander told me one afternoon as he sat sipping his tea. He lit a cigarette and continued. 'My commanding general told me, don't bring me any prisoners – if you know they are Daesh, then deal with them at your own end. My soldiers call me and say, we have found a man, and I tell them, kill him. I ask myself sometimes, what am I doing? Who am I to end the life of a man? I consulted a cleric, he said if the prisoner was not armed, it is better to err on the side of caution and hand him over to the state. But then who are they to pass judgement on him? What qualities does the judge have that I don't have? And who appointed the judge? You'll tell me the state, but who gave the state the right to rule on these matters? It wasn't given by God – so I have as much right to end the life of a man as the state has.' The cigarette in his hand had burned all the way down. He lit another.

He told me how early in the war, in 2005, his brother had been killed when a suicide bomber drove a car filled with explosives into the base where he was stationed. For months after, the commander formed his own death squad, driving with three other officers in an old Opel sedan with no licence plates, kidnapping and executing Sunni men who they thought were part of the insurgency.

When the soldiers and officers started counting the cost of this war, the ecstasy of battle wore off, and was replaced by bitterness, lethargic resentment and the feeling that their victory had been a hollow one.

Like many other front-line units, the commander's battalion had been decimated: half of his soldiers were killed or injured as well as many of his experienced, veteran officers (and those who came after to replace them). Those who survived carried the physical scars of two or three injuries and the mental scars of a decade of war.

Around them in Mosul, captured IS weapons were siphoned by soldiers and corrupt officers to be sold to the Kurds or one of the dozens of Shia military formations that had been established ostensibly to fight IS. Many of these now built a stockpile and waited for the next conflict. In Baghdad, the same politicians whose policies had led to the disasters of IS, like former prime minister Nouri al-Maliki, were still appearing on TV, and giving ringing speeches to their followers, while they continued to jostle, bicker and loot the wealth of the nation.

The commander and his men knew that in this ruined country the silence of guns did not mean peace, it simply indicated the absence of one kind of war and the start of another.

'I fear the end of this war – at least we know our enemy now, he is there standing in front of you carrying a gun across a front line and we fight them openly,' Lieutenant Taha said. 'What I dread most is going back to the days of sectarianism, when we didn't know who our enemy was or who our friend was. That war was hard.'

'I wonder what will come after Daesh?' asked another officer.

'It will be the militias,' the captain said, with his hoarse sarcastic laugh. 'We will finish with Daesh and they will take us down to the south. Why do you think the Hashed are hoarding all these weapons and money?' He was repeating the same words he'd uttered the winter before.

'I am afraid we will be coming back to Mosul to fight again in a few months,' said the commander without lifting his head from his phone.

'Why?' said a major angrily.

'Because there were 40,000 Daesh fighters in Mosul. Have we killed 40,000?' he asked and then answered swiftly, 'No. Then where are they?'

'Well, sir,' said Taha, 'after Mosul, we should drive to Baghdad and do to the Green Zone what we did to Daesh; only then will Iraq have peace.'

Ultimately IS was defeated because they alienated the same Sunni community that they claimed they were there to protect – to the extent that the people of Mosul yearned for the arrival of the same Shia armies that they had celebrated the defeat of three years earlier.

45

Life and Tragedy Return to Mosul

In the flat and dusty al-Baker neighbourhood, Ustad Ahmad was readying himself for dawn prayers, when his wife told him of a strange dream she'd had during the night. She was somewhere far but still able to see and hear her family, and when she woke up, she had the lingering sensation that she was still trapped in that far-away place. Ahmad laughed and assured her that at this very moment she was with him in their bedroom. After praying in the nearby mosque, Ahmad went to visit his mother. She asked him to take her to the cemetery to visit his father's grave. He said no, he was going to take the children to an amusement park, as a reward for the boys' full marks in their recent exams. Besides, he told his mother, he didn't want to be reminded of death on such a beautiful spring day.

Back home, after breakfast with the boys, Ahmad sat on a wooden chair in the bathroom and bent his large, egg-shaped head before his wife for his weekly shave.

Tall and burly, Ustad Ahmad was a very proud schoolmaster – proud of his status among the teachers, the comfort and neatness of his house, his smart and witty boys, his beautiful baby daughter and above all of his wife. He adored her to the extent that he didn't want her to take pictures of herself that strangers might see.

Ahmad was a self-confessed homebody who rarely left Mosul, while his wife had grown up in the southern city of Basra and had a passion for travelling, a trait picked up from her father, a dried-fruit merchant, who had travelled all over Iraq, and to neighbouring Syria and Turkey. To Ahmad's bewilderment, even when his wife's family didn't travel for work, they would choose to spend money on tourism trips. A week earlier, she had taken the children to Erbil, spending a considerable amount of money buying them new clothes, but he didn't mind, for things hadn't always been as neat and comfortable as they were now.

Two years ago, he was not a proud schoolmaster, but a broken, depressed and unemployed man.

When Islamic State captured Mosul in June 2014, Ustad Ahmad was categorised as an 'unreliable' and was expelled from his teaching job. For three years he was unemployed and unable to provide for his family. He sold his wife's gold and some of the furniture, borrowed money from his brother and mother, and then became dependent on whatever money his wife's family could send them from Erbil. Neighbours pestered him, told him to go out and find work as a day labourer or to get himself a cart and work in the vegetable market. But how could he? A school principal can't become a labourer, he reasoned with them. He clammed in on himself, rarely left the house, and sank into depression, arguing with his beloved wife and children, who had stopped going to school. Now, two years after the liberation of Mosul, things were back to normal. Even if the city was still in ruins and his school barely functioned, at least he was a respectable school principal again.

———

Thursday 21 March was warm and bright, with a clear, pale blue sky, after weeks of heavy rain that had swelled the Tigris. It was the start of a long Nowruz weekend, and all over Mosul, families were planning picnics and outings to the Umm Rabaen Pleasure Island and the adjacent Forests Area.

9 a.m.

Shahla woke up feeling cheerful, and she decided to take her mother to that new restaurant nearby that offered the exciting brunch menu.

Tomorrow would be her mother's seventy-second birthday and Shahla and her two sisters had bought gifts, ordered cakes and sweets, and stuffed aubergines, courgettes and vine leaves with meat and rice, stacking them delicately in a large dolma pot for the family lunch feast. Today, though, Shahla had her mother to herself.

Since her divorce, a few years earlier, Shahla and her two children had moved in with her mother, to the family's house in east Mosul. They lived like two close friends rather than a mother and daughter (Shahla didn't call her mother 'mum', or the Iraqi 'yuma', but Amoola, a diminutive of her name, Amal, meaning hope). Shahla often joked with her mother that she didn't want a man in her life any more; she was happy to live without someone controlling or dominating her life. Sometimes Shahla even thought that she loved her mother more than her children. They cooked together, went out on long walks and visited friends. Sometimes they travelled to the Kurdish city of Erbil, shopping in the flashy new malls or sitting in outdoor cafes in the shadow of the citadel. In the selfies Shahla had taken on their last trip, the two made for an odd couple: the mother in the long, dark, buttoned-up coat of the conservative women of Mosul, with a headscarf wrapped tightly around a sagging, pale face devoid of any make-up, but lit by a gentle motherly smile; and Shahla, the tall, thirty-something woman with her handsome angular face, large eyes lined with kohl, a twinkling smile, and a flair for coloured headscarves and fashionable dresses that she designed and sewed herself. The bond between them grew closer while living as virtual prisoners under the rule of the Islamic State. Their prison had been their two-storey house with its small garden that sat in a quiet, leafy neighbourhood, nestled among olive, tangerine and eucalyptus trees, not far from the eastern banks of the Tigris. Shortly after the Islamic State caliphate was declared, the thirteen Christian families that lived in the neighbourhood were expelled, their doors marked with the letter N (for Nazarenes) and their houses redistributed among the organisation's senior foreign fighters. A Chechen commander settled across the street, while a Russian woman moved in next door and shouted at Shahla and her mum to cover their faces even when walking in their own garden. She would also send her Egyptian husband to demand some of Shahla's mother's food. For three years they rarely left their house. Sometimes Shahla thought of herself as a terminal cancer patient counting the days until life was over. They never lacked food. Amal, like all the people in Mosul, stored enough rice, lentils and cooking oil to last them for a year and when the water supplies were cut off, they dug a well in the garden. When the battle to recapture Mosul began in September 2016, the houses of the foreign fighters in the neighbourhood became a target. Three were levelled in air strikes that shook the walls of Amal's house and shattered the windows. Russian snipers set up a base in the house across the street. Other fighters fired their RPGs at the approaching Iraqi armoured vehicles from barricades they had built at the end of their road. Although Amal was very scared, she refused to leave the house and stay with her other children in safer areas. In Mosul, she reminded Shahla, people say those who abandon their home, abandon their dignity.

Towards the end of the battle, as the fighting intensified and Iraqi troops grew closer, Islamic State fighters came knocking at their door in the middle of the night. They ordered the women to leave their house and come with them – they would be human shields for the retreating fighters – threatening that if they didn't, they would lock them inside the house and burn it down. The women gathered their belongings in small bags, piled food into an old wheelchair and set out under the thuds of falling mortars and bullets flying in all directions. Distant bombs exploded, shaking the ground under their feet. At the end of the street, they came across other neighbours who had been held as human shields but had slipped away from the IS fighters, and together they hid in the basement of an abandoned house. Twenty-five women and children and a few men hid in that dark basement for three nights, while above the battle raged. On the last day of fighting, they heard on the radio that their neighbourhood was liberated, but in the basement the families crouched in the darkness, silently holding their breath as fighters entered the house searching for civilian hostages to ensure their safe retreat. Not until they heard the roars of army trucks and armoured vehicles did they emerge. The first thing Shahla did, in that twilight time between the last of Islamic State fighters fleeing the street and before the Iraqi troops established full control, was to jump over the fence into the neighbouring house where the Egyptian and his Russian wife lived and siphon water from their full tanks.

A week after their liberation, Shahla met with her other siblings, all gathered in their mother's house. The simple fact of Shahla and her mother wandering outside the house without covering their faces or being shrouded in long black robes made them feel like they were living in a dream.

The war continued on the other side of the city, and one afternoon, as the mother walked up and down her long living room, looking through the open window at her favourite corner of the garden, a mortar shell – fired by IS militants in the west side of Mosul, to punish civilians who lived under government control – hit the wall outside and exploded two metres away from her. Shahla ran into the room to see her mother on the ground covered in white dust but miraculously unharmed.

All that misery was in the past. Her mother often told her that after Islamic State rule and that war, nothing worse could ever befall them.

12 noon.

Across the river, beyond the five destroyed bridges, mounds of rubble and pulverised buildings on the west side of Mosul, Aya was throwing a tantrum. Her mother – carrying her infant brother – her sister, three aunts and twelve cousins had gathered downstairs, and everyone was waiting for her to get dressed. Her mother and aunts had been planning this picnic for weeks; they were going to leave their husbands behind and take the children to Umm Rabean Island. The girls wore their best, put on make-up and struggled in their high heels, but Aya – a lean, confident and strong-headed nineteen-year-old Arabic-literature student, poet and amateur journalist – was not someone to be rushed. When her mother told her off for delaying everyone, she declared she was not going and slammed the door.

In the al-Baker neighbourhood, Ustad Ahmad wore his new blue summer blazer and a pair of jeans, and donned the new wrap-around sunglasses his wife had got him. The children, too, wore new clothes. He called a large taxi and they drove around the city looking for grilled chicken for their lunch. On that warm spring day it seemed that the whole city was planning picnics, and it took half an hour of driving around until they found a rotisserie that still had some chickens. Ustad Ahmad, who saw that the birds were large and juicy, opted for a half-chicken for his family's lunch, and they headed to the amusement park.

1–2 p.m.

After brunch, Shahla and Amal came back home. Shahla was

404

in the kitchen preparing a pot of sweet Turkish coffee, while her mother sat in the garden reading the Quran, when Um-Yussuf, a friend of Amal's, called and invited them to join her for tea on the Umm Rabean Island that afternoon. Shahla thought that on a sunny public holiday the island would be very crowded, and she didn't want to go. 'Let's not go,' she implored her mother, 'let's spend the day relaxing at home.' But her mother wanted to go, she said the weather was beautiful, and she hadn't seen Um-Yussuf for a long time. Um-Yussuf was always in a rush, so Shahla hurriedly prepared a basket of food and a flask of coffee.

Ustad Ahmad gave the two boys enough money to go on every ride in the amusement park. He even joined them for a round on the bumper cars. It was close to 2 p.m. when the family settled down to have their lunch, but there were no shady areas left in the park, and Ahmad noticed that his wife's face had turned pale. The boys suggested that they go to Umm Rabean Island: it was cooler by the Tigris and there were many trees there for shade. The wife agreed, Ustad Ahmad called another taxi, and they headed to the island.

Aya's sister, Nour, pleaded with her, told her that everyone was waiting and that if she didn't come she would spoil the picnic. She relented, got dressed, and went downstairs to join her mother, aunts and cousins in the minivan which they hired to take them to the island. And so the fates of Shahla, Ustad Ahmad and Aya were intertwined that afternoon, when each, somewhat against their will, found themselves heading to the pleasure island.

Umm Rabaen Island sits in the Tigris River, just as it takes a sharp L-shaped bend and enters the city of Mosul from the north. It resembles a parallelogram-shaped fish, 730m by 200m. Unlike other islets, which appear and disappear, depending on the water level, this one is a permanent fixture. It is connected to the east bank of the Tigris, less than a hundred metres away, by two cable-pulled, flatbed ferries.

It was first turned into a pleasure island during the late eighties, when riverside cafes, restaurants, prefabricated chalets and an elegant hotel were built as part of a large development plan for the graciously named (due to the fairly modest number of eucalyptus and pine trees) Forests Area.

The hotel, like most buildings in the city, lies a gutted and ruined shell, and most of the trees in the 'Forests' had either burned during recent battles or been chopped down for firewood.

Two years after its liberation, Mosul was still a city broken by war and corruption. The early euphoria of the release from Islamic State rule was dissolving. Pledges to rebuild the city had failed due to the negligence and corruption of the government in Baghdad and the local authorities in Mosul — government hospitals were bare and empty, the five bridges spanning the Tigris had either collapsed or remained barely strung together by military pontoons. Hundreds of thousands of people who were driven out of their homes during the fighting were still living in sprawling camps. The security situation was worsening, and Islamic State cells were reforming.

At the same time, there is something to be said about the tenacity and resilience of the people of Mosul, their love of life and entrepreneurial spirit. During the war, as the city was being recaptured block by block by Iraqi security forces, life returned quickly to liberated neighbourhoods. Families came back to their houses and teams of young volunteers cleared rubble and the wreckage of war from their streets. Someone began selling cigarettes, a grocer reopened his shop with a box of half-rotten tomatoes and canned beans, and then a restaurant was cleaned, refurbished and opened for business, albeit without water or electricity — all while the fighting still raged just a few blocks away.

Those who could raise a bit of money began rebuilding their destroyed homes, patching holes and craters made by rockets and bombs with concrete blocks and metal sheets, while still waiting for the promised government compensation. Business people who had fled the city for the safety of the Kurdish region started investing in new malls, restaurants and even private hospitals and schools.

The Forests Area, and Umm Rabaen Island facing it, embodied the mixture of ruin and resurgence that defines Mosul. Cafes and restaurants were the first things to be rebuilt and reopened. On weekends, the people of Mosul flock there, sitting at white plastic tables, drinking tea or eating kebabs. The Tigris – flowing fast and muddy – is a reassuring reminder of the enduring presence of their city, just as the vista of the ruined buildings on the opposite bank of the river evokes memories of the vicious war that they barely survived.

2.30 p.m.

It took Shahla and her mother twenty minutes to walk from their house to the Forests Area. Her mother was happy, and her cheeks were flushed red from the warm afternoon sun. When she saw the large crowd that had gathered at the riverbank, Shahla thought Mosul must be empty, everyone had come here. She didn't like crowds, and she was trying to tell her mother they should leave when Um-Yussuf, early as usual, spotted them and the two old women hugged. They made their way slowly to a gently sloping square, where a jetty stood to take the ferry to the island.

Aya and her family arrived next. Despite her earlier sulking, she was happy to be there. Ever the contemplative writer, she stood away from the rest and took pictures of the river. She thought she must at some point write a poem about it.

Ustad Ahmad was late to arrive; even so, he nudged his family closer to the jetty entrance, he wanted to be the first onto the ferry and first onto the island, to get the best spot before the rest of the crowd.

2.55 p.m.

They stood watching the ferry move from the island towards the jetty loaded with two dozen or so people standing calmly on board. It shuddered and swayed downstream tilting slightly towards the upstream side, where the water was frothing and almost lapping over the edge.

3 p.m.

The ferry docked at the jetty on the eastern bank and a single line of people disembarked, squeezing their way through the families waiting to board. The two crowds intermingled in a sea of coloured headscarves, pushing fairly gently, and moving slowly. Bodies swayed from foot to foot, heads craned left and right trying to find a clear space. Everyone was in their holiday clothes; young men and boys wore suits and bow ties and girls wore dresses with frills. A security guard in a black uniform urged the people to move quickly. A few young men jumped over the fence.

A young boy and his mother were the first to descend the set of concrete steps to the jetty. The mother was hesitant, putting her arms on the boy's shoulder, before walking across the two pieces of metal that served as the ferry's gangplank.

More women followed, their high heels protruding from beneath long black robes, their legs stretching gingerly as if they were feeling the water before they crossed. Two children carried a coolbox between them and another followed carrying a large cloth-covered pot.

Shahla walked onto the ferry carrying her bag, the food basket and her mother's handbag. She noticed that the water level was very high. Her mother and Um-Yussuf walked behind her slowly, holding hands.

Ustad Ahmad stood on the jetty, impatient, gesturing and complaining, his freshly shaven head shimmering in the light. He moved, pushing sideways, first inserting a shoulder into the crowd, and then turning his back to create a path for his wife and the pram to move along, nudging their way very slowly forward. They reached the entrance, handed over their tickets, and bent to hold one end of the pram, Ustad Ahmad going down backwards, one step at a time. He was very slow and methodical and still his feet slipped slightly. When his wife reached the edge of the metal planks, she paused. She was scared and wanted to turn back, but she couldn't, people were keen to get onto the ferry and were pushing her. So she and Ustad Ahmad lifted the heavy pram laden with food beneath their baby daughter, and walked across the planks.

Another pram was lifted down, and two men carried a large tray of food between them like a stretcher.

The back of the ferry was full, but more people pushed to board: mothers leading their children, and fathers helping their toddlers. One after the other, they shuffled to their deaths in high holiday spirits.

Aya was one of the last to board the ferry; she looked at the rushing water and thought that her sister Nour would be scared. She was always the scared one: during the war she stayed awake listening to the bombs falling, whimpering and crying while Aya slept deeply and never woke up even when the fighting was a block away from their house. 'Why wake up?' Aya, who had become so used to war, would tell her sister. 'What can I do to the planes in the skies?'

3.07 p.m.

When nearly three hundred people had climbed aboard, and the metal gate had been shut, a mother and her daughter ran to the barrier. They gestured for someone to come quickly and waited. Would they miss the ferry and survive? A moment passed before the father, holding the hand of a young boy, arrived and the operator opened the gate to let them all in. Another family came, they pleaded to be allowed aboard, but the operator had closed the gate and moved down to the boat following the passengers like a shepherd herding his flock into a slaughterhouse. Those not allowed on stood watching as the ferry started moving.

On the left side of the ferry, moored by one of the riverside cafes, was an old motorboat, whose white fibreglass coating had turned yellowish-brown with age and the sun. Omar, a short, nimble man, with alert beady eyes and withered dark bronze skin, sat in the back. He smoked slim cigarettes and leaned over to check on the engine. He had taken three families on river tours so far, and judging by the size of the crowds, he hoped that many more would follow. He was not going to allow his old engine to break down on such a busy day.

Omar came from the Old City, perched on the west banks of the River Tigris. His family had lived in its narrow alleyways for generations, and his earliest childhood memories were of the river. His father warned him against the dangers of whirlpools and swirling underwater currents but as soon as he was old enough to swim, he would accompany his elder brothers and cousins to the north of the city, where they jumped in the water, floating with the fast current downstream, past the fifteenth-century shrine of the 'Sheikh of the River', to the piers of the old, British-built Iron Bridge next to their house. When he grew up, he began working the river, just like his father and his father's father, fishing, transporting people and goods, and taking families on weekend leisure tours.

410

In the summer of 2017, when the diehard remnants of Islamic State barricaded themselves into the Old City, Omar and his family were among the thousands of trapped civilians who had to endure three months of brutal siege and daily aerial and artillery bombardment. They hid in a small room in the basement, while outside some of the most vicious urban warfare in recent decades took place. At night, Omar braved sniper fire from both sides and crawled to the riverbank to get water and collect weeds that his wife boiled to feed the kids. Eventually the hunger became unbearable, and part of their old stone house collapsed in mortar bombing, so they decided to flee. But where to? They couldn't cross the front line – IS fighters executed any civilians who tried escape, Iraqi soldiers regarded any males over the age of fifteen who came from the old city as Islamic State suspects, often detaining and torturing them. He turned to the river for help and decided to swim across it. He and his brother collected all the empty plastic jerrycans they could find and tied them together with ropes, turning them into makeshift flotation devices that they festooned around the waists of the women and children. Their neighbours, an old woman and her bedridden husband, wanted to come with them, but the old man could hardly walk, let alone swim. They tied more jerrycans to the four corners of a small metal bed, turning it into a floating stretcher. They left in the middle of the night when the fighting always subsided and crawled to the edge of the river. Omar and his brother helped the others get into the water, and they swam, pulling along the old man's bed-raft and the young children. The women followed behind. On the other bank, federal police troops spotted the movement and fired flares into the dark sky. The river lit up, and they were exposed to IS fighters who opened fire on them. They killed the old woman and one of the children, their bodies carried away by the waters.

When the war ended, they came back to see the Old City of Mosul pulverised. Their houses were mounds of rubble and Omar had lost everything. He moved into the eastern part of the city, renting a two-room apartment with his brother's family. For two years he worked at menial daily jobs, until earlier that year, when a businessman had lent him enough money to buy this boat. He hoped that with the people's renewed appetite for spring pleasure trips, he would be able to pay his debts and start rebuilding his shattered life.

Omar watched the people pile onto the ferry with a bit of unease. He knew that the owner had been informed the day before by the river police that the ferry wasn't allowed to operate due to the release upriver of large volumes of water from the Mosul dam that day. Everyone who worked or lived along the river had been informed – boatmen, cafe owners and even the farmers who raised water buffalo on the southern edge of the city. In the morning when he woke, the water level was normal, and he thought the dam authority might have been exaggerating, but in the past couple of hours it had risen quickly. The lower decks of a cafe, where he moored his boat, had been submerged and plastic tables and chairs quickly moved to higher decks.

Shahla walked to the end of the ferry and stood at the north-west corner; she got out her new iPhone to film, but she couldn't see the water because there were so many people around her. Her mother and Um-Yussuf stood beside her, having failed to find space to sit on the benches.

Ustad Ahmad stood by the rail in the middle and managed to find a place for his tired wife to rest. He took a couple of pictures, and his elder son also took selfies: they were the last images of him alive. Towards the back stood Aya next to her sister Nour and her cousin Hamada.

The ferry was a contraption made from two sections of an old pontoon bridge welded together and decorated with six open arches that rose five metres high on each side, resembling the open jaws of a carnivorous animal. Steel cables stretched between the arches above a row of benches. Two cables connected the front and the back of the ferry to motors and winches mounted on opposite sides of the river, pulling the ferry back and forth. A third, guiding cable also stretched between the two banks and was attached to the right side of the ferry, its purpose being to resist the push of the currents and maintain a straight course.

3.08 p.m.

The ferry shook and shuddered. The strength of the current pushed it downstream before the cable pulling it corrected its path and it shifted slightly upstream. Water was frothing over one corner on the upstream side, which was lower than the rest of the ferry. The broad-shouldered operator standing at the back noticed the ferry was tilting and started walking to the front, gesturing and telling people to move away from the listing right side. The current was dragging the back of the ferry further downstream than the front, pulling the ferry off its line, while it continued to list towards the right. As the ferry jerked and swayed, a few kids climbed over the right-hand railing, trying to see what was going on.

A small wave of water gushed over the deck, covering Shahla's feet. When she saw the water, her mother was anxious and said, 'Let's go back, let's sit in some other cafe,' as if they could walk away from the ferry. 'Pray upon the Prophet,' Shahla said, trying to calm her down. 'We are halfway there, and it will be OK.' But she could see that people were getting scared. Women were crying around Ustad Ahmad, too, who ignored the operator and decided to stay by the railing on the right, assuring his wife and children that the ferry would stabilise itself, while clutching the pram's handles tightly with both hands. At the back, Aya thought the water covering her feet came from a passing speedboat. She told her sister that they would take off their shoes to dry them once they reached the island, and they laughed at the thought of walking around barefoot.

Shahla was moving to the left side – holding her mother with her left hand and her mobile phone in her right, still carrying on her shoulders her bag, her mother's and the food basket. Um-Yussuf was behind them, holding on to Amal, when a second and a bigger wave of water surged in.

The ferry began listing rapidly to the right. The boys hanging on the railings threw themselves into the frothing water. Just over a minute into the crossing, the ferry had tilted so far over that one-third of the deck was under water, and people – some up to their necks in water – were clambering to the other side. But it was too late for the ferry to right itself. People were screaming around Aya. She didn't know what was happening. She fell, and the strong current sucked her away from the ferry, deep into the dark and muddy water.

When she was seven years old, her father, a military officer, had taught her to swim. Her muscle memory kicked in, she pushed and swam.

Ustad Ahmad, standing in water up to his neck still clung tightly to the pram, while trying to keep the baby above the water. He heard a loud grinding noise and saw that the ferry was turning over and people were sliding down towards him. The current was pulling the pram away, he gripped the handles tightly and pulled back, but the pram was heavy and it sank, pulling him underwater, his baby daughter disappearing in the darkness of the fast river.

At this point, the cable pulling the ferry snapped. The left side of the hull, standing almost vertical now, hit a cable stretched across the water that belonged to a second ferry. It sat on the cable for a brief three seconds, the current pushing fast at the lower right side, then it started to roll. People staggered as they lost their footing. Shahla received a sharp blow to her shoulders and was pushed into the water, still holding her mother's hand. The air was full of screams. She pushed her head above the surface but a body fell on her, she sank again and lost her mother's hand. When she got back to the surface, a woman in a black robe grabbed at her, desperate to stay afloat, and tried to climb on top of her. Shahla took a breath and sank under-water, pushing herself away from the woman and allowing herself to be dragged downstream.

The hull stood vertical; people were falling onto those below, who were trapped between the half-arches and the rods connecting them. As it turned over, the arches closed on them like giant fangs. The ferry flipped, a green-bellied whale drifting downstream, chasing after dozens of bobbing heads.

Deep under the water, Ustad Ahmad lost the pram. He paddled and reached the surface, his arms hit bags, scarves and other objects. He saw a boat nearby and swam to it and held on to its engine. He shouted for help but no one looked at him, the men inside too absorbed in pulling people from the water. The owner of the boat came down to the stern, where Ustad Ahmad was still clinging desperately to the engine. Ignoring Ahmad, the man pulled a cord to start the engine. It roared and Ahmad screamed as the blades cut into his side. The engine fluttered and died. Again the man tried to restart the engine, Ahmad cried out, but the man ignored him, and again the blades dug into his side. The third time the blades hit him, the pain became so unbearable that Ahmad let go and sank underwater. He knew he had lost his family and he decided to die, he didn't want to live any more, he just wanted to go deep and drown in the dark waters. But his body would not let him die, and involuntarily he kicked his way to the surface. He wept and mumbled, Thanks be to God, Thanks be to God, his tears sinking into the water that carried him downstream, past the riverside cafes where people stood watching and filming.

He reached another boat that had stopped next to a reed islet. Clutching the reeds he saw a young man and stretched out his hand for help. 'You have to help yourself,' the young man aboard shouted back at him. He saw two other men in the boat trying to haul a large woman to safety; twice they pulled her up but couldn't bring her into the boat and had to drop her back into the water. They left her holding the edge of the boat and came to help Ustad Ahmad. Two men grabbed him by his arms, and a third pulled him from his belt – a genuine leather belt his wife had bought him. They swung him over the edge. They went back to the large woman and heaved her onboard, but she was already dead. She lay on the bottom of the boat next to two dead children. The men rescued another woman and a child and then started the engine. To Ustad Ahmad's horror he saw that they were taking him to the island.

The current whipped Aya away from the ferry. Wrapped in the darkness of muddy waters, all sounds muffled, she thought she was dying – just a few days short of her twentieth birthday. So this is what death feels like, she thought, dark and silent, like the muddy waters of the Tigris. She had obsessed over this question since her father's death a few years earlier. Her brain was functioning on its own, anticipating death, while her body continued to resist, pushing her head above the water every time a wave tossed it down. But her hands were getting numb, her body was tired, and she wanted to give up and go down when two arms grabbed her and pulled her above the water into an old yellowing boat.

A few minutes earlier, Omar had seen the ferry capsize. He immediately drove his boat into the middle of the drowning crowd. Switching off the engine lest he hit someone, he began rescuing people. Downstream seven more fishing boats, all from the old city, lined their vessels across the middle of the river to intercept the survivors.

Sitting in Omar's boat, Aya screamed with all her voice; she couldn't believe that air was flowing back into her lungs. There was another girl in the boat; they hugged each other and wept. She watched Omar pull a small child from among the bodies floating by. He fell to the floor motionless; a young man who had been rescued before Aya bent down and revived him. A large man, with his son hanging on his back, grabbed the side of the boat and it started teetering dangerously. Aya and the other girl shouted and begged him to let go. They told him he was going to flip the boat and drown them all, but the man held on with all his might. The young man leaned across and pulled the child from the man's back into the boat. They all tried to haul the man aboard, but he was too heavy, too tired. He let go and was dragged away from the boat by the fast waters.

In the water, Shahla was bumped and rammed by objects and bodies. She looked for her mother among the screaming people around her, but the water was pushing her fast. She saw white gulls, so loved by the people of Mosul, circling overhead. Oh lord, she thought, is it possible that they're feeding on the bodies of the dead? She had been in the water for half an hour now. It was cold, and her clothes were getting heavy, her headscarf was choking her, but she clutched her phone in one hand and hung tightly to her mother's green bag. She didn't want her mother to lose her ID card and go through the hassle and the long humiliating queues – people who said their ID card had been destroyed or lost were usually suspected of being IS members.

She saw a boat, shouted and waved her arms; the man on the boat told her to come to him, he couldn't move the boat. Her chest was contracting, and she couldn't breathe, but thought she would keep swimming until she died. She grabbed the engine of the boat, threw the bag and the mobile over the side, put her feet on the propellers and called on the man to help her. She collapsed inside.

Only once aboard did she realise how exhausted she was. Her

body was shaking as she took in the extent of the disaster. Bodies floated all around them, many were children. There was a tiny boy, three or four, dressed in a onesie and floating on his back: it reminded her of the game she played as a child, with her sisters, floating their dolls in the bathtub. To her relief, she saw that the gulls were not feasting on dead bodies, but the food people had brought for their picnics.

In the boat sat a young man, bleeding and stunned, a young girl and a dead boy who lay in the bottom. The bleeding young man tried to revive the child but he couldn't, they told her he was gone. Shahla lifted the boy and threw him down on his chest, the child coughed and started throwing up – he was alive. Their boat had broken down, and they were drifting towards the bridge piers. Another boat came and pushed them towards the shore. She walked down carrying the two children and still clutching her phone and her mother's handbag.

3.30–4 p.m.

The boat dropped Ustad Ahmad on the island, where he wandered with other survivors, and watched families still enjoying their picnics. Someone gave him water; another offered him a chair. A neighbour and his wife spotted him; they took him to the island's administration office, but it had been abandoned. When the ferry sank, most of the staff had run away fearing arrest and anticipating the anger of the victims' families. The neighbours took off Ahmad's jacket and shirt and cleaned the three long cuts in his side with a piece of cloth soaked in antiseptic. At that point, he started to cry.

An officer from the Mosul SWAT police unit arrived on the island in a large civilian motorboat that he had commandeered. They promptly arrested everyone who worked there – including vendors selling coffee and burgers – but the owners and directors of the island were nowhere to be seen. The officer took pity on Ustad Ahmad and gave him a lift back to the eastern riverbank.

He stood in the street, wrapped in blankets. Shocked and unable to think, he saw an ambulance and threw himself in front of it. He forced the driver to take him to a hospital, where another of his neighbours found him and took him to his mother's house.

Omar took Aya to the headquarters of the river police – two concrete rooms positioned on the side of a large concrete yard with a small jetty that protruded into the river – and went back with his motorboat to see if he could rescue more people. Aya stood there shivering, her hair soaked in mud, and her dress dripping with water. She was surrounded by a crowd of spectators and policemen who had gathered to watch the disaster unfold, their phones pointed at her. 'My family, where is my family?' Aya screamed at a young policeman standing nearby. The bewildered policeman looked at her as if she were mad. Before her eyes, the ineptitude and failure of the Iraqi state was laid bare. In oil-wealthy Iraq, the Mosul River Police Department had one boat which had sat broken for many months. Nor did they have lifejackets, or even ropes to throw to the people drifting and drowning in front of them. While the chief of the river police had jumped into a civilian boat and gone to help with the rescue, his men just stood there staring. They didn't know what to do, most of them had never trained for such a crisis. Some didn't even know how to swim. In the highly corrupt Iraqi security services, many of those policemen had paid a bribe to be appointed to a safe and comfortable job by the river, rather than one of the more dangerous outposts outside the city. Around Aya stood wet and crying children, some injured. When she asked the policemen for blankets, they told her there were no blankets, go and stand in the sun. But whenever a high-ranking official appeared, trailed by cameramen, the helpless policemen sprang into action, declaring, Sir, by Allah, we saved all those people.

She was confused, didn't know what to do – sit with the injured children inside one of the rooms, or stay outside and look for her sister and mother among the few survivors who tumbled into the yard.

The policeman she'd yelled at had taken pity on her, seeing her shivering in her wet clothes; he went into a side room, took off his thermal underwear and gave it to her along with his heavy military jacket. 'Please don't leave me,' she said, grabbing on to him, 'please don't leave me alone.'

'I promise I won't leave you alone,' he replied. The policeman had also brought some blankets to cover the children who were sitting in their underwear. She walked among the dead bodies stacked in the yard before they were zipped into plastic bags. She saw a child, foam oozing from his mouth, and she ran away. For an hour she ran back and forth as more bodies were piled in front of her, but she couldn't see her family.

'I didn't know what had happened to them, but in my heart, I knew who would die and who would survive,' she said. 'I knew my mother and sister were dead. My mother because she was carrying my infant brother and my sister because she was always scared and couldn't do anything on her own, without me next to her all the time.'

Shahla sat on the pavement outside; a policeman had stopped a passing car and it brought her here. She had looked for her mother and Um-Yussuf, first among the living and then, with trepidation and fear, among the bodies in bags. She couldn't find them, and she still held to the hope that they were alive somewhere. She was shivering and exhausted, but she didn't want to sit in the rooms packed with crying women and children. 'There was chaos, and no one was in control, the bodies were dumped into the back of ambulances and pickup trucks like they were sacks of garbage while the policemen and the crowds filmed with their mobile phones.'

She looked at her hands and saw that she was still clutching her mother's bag and her iPhone. She clicked on it and to her surprise it worked. She called her brother and told him what had happened, told him not to worry about her but to look for their mother. She stayed on the pavement and watched people still on the way to their picnics, oblivious to the disaster that had just unfolded. Some looked at her in her wet clothes with surprise and confusion.

5–6 p.m.

Aya saw her sister being carried out of a boat. She ran towards her, screaming, 'My sister, my sister!' Someone was hitting her on the back to revive her, but she was already dead. Aya held her hands and wept, before letting go and turning away. She wanted to leave this morbid place. She asked the kind policeman to lend her his phone; she logged into her Facebook page and wrote: 'My family is dead, please help me.' A university friend found her shortly thereafter and took her to the hospital. Doctors put an oxygen mask over her face but told her that there were no bandages left in the hospital to treat the injuries to her arms and legs. Some women, who were in the hospital visiting relatives, heard there were injured children and women still in their wet clothes. Organising themselves, they collected whatever extra garments they had. Someone dressed Aya in a pink nightgown a few sizes too small; she wore it along with the policeman's thermal under-wear and oversized military jacket. Nurses escorted terrified people looking for their relatives; they had a look of horror and shock on their faces. They stared at Aya, then – disappointed – said, no, she is not ours and moved on. She was exhausted but couldn't sleep; every time she closed her eyes, she heard the screams of people drowning and saw their bodies floating in the water. She was so terrified of water she couldn't even drink from the glass at her bedside.

It was getting dark when Shahla's brother called her. He was weeping. Before he said anything, she knew their mother was dead. Shahla went home, still soaking wet, and walked into Amal's bedroom to retrieve the white shrouds that her mother had stored in her wardrobe. In Mosul, she explained, not only do people store their food but they prepare for death while they are still alive, keeping their shrouds ready so that when they die they are not dependent on anyone's charity.

At ten the next morning, Aya's uncle brought her home. They wanted her to see her mother and sister – her infant half-brother was still missing – before they were taken to the cemetery to be buried. Her mother, aunt and sister were wrapped in blankets and lay on the floor of a bedroom upstairs. She was scared of them and didn't want to go in at first, but then she knelt and felt their faces, kissed them, and promised her mother that she would take care of her two brothers. Then she started whispering to her sister. She told her how much she loved her and apologised for abandoning her. As she recalled the moment, sitting on the sofa in her grandfather's house, she wept, her chest heaving painfully. 'My mother slaughtered a sheep when the war was over – she couldn't believe that we all had survived. She didn't know that in two years she and her daughter, son and sister would be dead.'

The most organised institution in Mosul is the morgue. Two years after the war, it continues to receive black and festering remains that had remained buried under the mounds of debris and destroyed houses. The staff are efficient and thorough, comparing DNA samples with their records and trying to identify the victims from among the thousands still missing. The director, a stocky young doctor, Hassan Watheq, was having his lunch when he received a phone call from a friend to tell him about the ferry. He could hear the sounds of screaming over the phone. He hurried to the morgue, knowing that within an hour the bodies would begin to disintegrate, making identification very difficult. He knew all too well the chaos that would ensue with families pushing and shoving to try and reclaim their dead relatives. He called a police commander and asked for extra police to be stationed around the morgue and then summoned all his staff.

The bodies started arriving at the morgue: three, eight, six, four . . . Within an hour, there were sixty-five bodies in the refrigerators and hundreds of families gathering outside. Women wailing, men begged with the policemen to be allowed in. Hassan Watheq went outside. Flanked by policemen, he climbed on top of a police truck, and in his soft calm voice pleaded with the people to give him time. He then went to his office in the morgue where an overwhelming smell of disinfectant hung in the air.

The majority of the bodies that arrived were women and children, and even the hardened staff of the Mosul morgue were weeping. 'I saw a woman clutching a five-month-old child; both were dead,' Hassan said. 'And I thought of my own two girls and started crying, even though death had become normal for us.'

He began posting headshots of the victims on the morgue's gate. Where ID had been found with the body, he was able to post the names of the dead. His other priority was preventing bodies from being stolen.

'Some of the people who still had missing family members from the war were under suspicion, maybe they were IS members, and in any case Iraqi law doesn't recognise the missing as dead until five years have passed, so all this time they can't get pensions or any rights, so they tried to register their missing as dead in the ferry disaster.'

Of the 128 confirmed dead, fifty-seven were women, forty-four were children. Sixty-nine people are still missing. The most recent body was found on 11 September, almost six months after the ferry sank.

Even by the standards of a nation accustomed to murderous fanatical militias, occupying armies and mad dictators, the cruelty of death on a picnic day was shocking. 'I have seen death in this city,' Hassan, the morgue director said, 'but nothing as sad as this. People dressed for a day out lined up in body bags.' That night, the news and the images of the sinking ferry spread quickly, crossing sectarian fault lines. It hung like a giant cloud of sadness and pain over the country. A rare moment when Iraqis found themselves united in a way that only grief and calamity can achieve.

Maybe it was the raw mobile and CCTV footage, showing the ferry sinking in real time, the helplessness of young men smacking their heads as they watched the women and children struggling before they died, the macabre absurdity of the pilot who tried to hover his Russian helicopter above three drowning people but pushed them underwater with the downdraught, or the horrific scenes of families eating their lunch while people flowed down the river.

When the news emerged that the river police had issued a warning about the extra water being released from the dam, and had specifically warned against operating the ferry, grief turned to anger against the failure of the state and the recklessness of the profiteering owners.

The prime minister arrived in Mosul the same evening. He announced three days of mourning, formed an investigating committee and declared all the victims to be martyrs, to be added to the hundreds of thousands of Iraqi martyrs killed in the war. The president came the following day and was booed by a crowd protesting against political corruption. He was quickly bundled into a police pickup while crowds pressed in around it, banging on the vehicle.

A wide spectrum of local dignitaries, MPs, minor officials and tribal elders followed, thronging the jetty. They hung wreaths of plastic flowers and black mourning banners, and gave speeches vowing their continual support for the victims' families. They demanded justice. Songs and poems were composed and the Shia clergy in faraway Najaf issued a statement denouncing the general corruption in Iraq that had led to this incident. Like everything in Iraq, the ferry became a political issue.

Within days, the media was reporting that there was a connection between the owner of the island, Ubaid al-Hadidi, and a notorious militia commander. Sit-ins were organised, and on 24 March, the governor of Mosul, Nufal Hammadi, already under investigation for the embezzlement of public funds and international aid, was sacked. He was accused of enabling the militias' 'business enterprises', of raiding public funds and annexing public land. The governor told a press conference: 'I deny that I received a single cent or dinar from any party.'

I went to interview a member of Mosul city council who was on the committee formed to investigate the ferry disaster. He told me the ferry sank because it was overcrowded and sailing in very fast waters.

'The official regulations specified that the ferry was allowed to work in current speeds that do not exceed 700 metres per minute, preferably between 400 and 300 metres, with a maximum capacity of eighty people on board. On the day it sank, it was carrying 287 people, and the current was moving at 1400 metres per minute.'

He said that the owners and management of the island bore direct responsibility for the incident, having apparently ignored the safety warnings. 'Ubaid al-Hadidi [the owner] was informed by the river police the night before, and he signed the memo. But he saw a vast crowd, and he wanted to load as many people as possible. The state institution that was supposed to monitor the work of the ferry failed in their responsibility.

'That recklessness and greed of the owner and management, as well as their general disregard for official regulations, could happen because they had strong backers among some powerful men in the security forces,' said the councillor.

I asked him who these security forces were. He spent a few seconds toying with a pen, shuffled some papers and stacked them neatly on his desk. It was late in the afternoon, and we were sitting in his dark office in the heavily fortified but largely deserted city council building. His bodyguards stood by the door, and there was no one present but his secretary (a close relative) and us.

He ended the silence by replying in a barely audible voice: 'Ubaid al-Hadidi identified the Asaib as his partners and backers.'

Asaib Ahl al-Haq is one of the fiercest militias in Iraq, part of the Hashed paramilitaries and a close ally of Iran.

'Hayder al-Sa'edy and Hussein al-Shabaki, the representatives of the Asaib's Economy Office in Mosul, they are the principal backers of Ubaid al-Hadidi, the owner of the Island.'

Islamic State rule and the war that followed not only devastated the buildings and displaced a large section of the population, they also shattered the social structure of the city itself and destroyed the role of the traditional families and political elites that had long dominated the city. Shia militias – under the nominal command of the Popular Mobilisation Units, and loyal to Iran – filled the void after the war, controlling the economy and the security of the city.

These feared militias and their intelligence units settled themselves into compounds around the city. Working in parallel with the army and other security forces, they had participated in disappearing around 12,000 men since the liberation of Mosul. Many of those detained were only released after paying huge bribes. These were the same corrupt practices of the army in Baghdad and Sunni areas a decade ago which had precipitated the emergence of IS and al-Qaeda as defenders of the Sunnis.

The militias spawned 'Economy Offices', which were involved in the majority of Mosul's commercial activities. Their emergence signalled the development of the militia business model: they evolved from Kalashnikov-wielding gunmen, demanding a bribe at the gate of a port or at a checkpoint, into a more institutionalised form of corruption, in which they entered 'partnerships' with local business people or fielded their own candidates for government contracts. In the post-sectarian system, everyone shared in the looting of Mosul, from the petty Christians and Sunni militia commanders, to the more prominent and established Shia warlords. A parliamentarian fact-finding mission in early 2019 detailed how these militias/offices, working with corrupt government employees, siphoned off public funds, controlled the multimillion-dollar trade in scrap metal, were involved in oil smuggling and the takeover of public lands in the city and large swathes of agricultural lands in the Nineveh plains. They also imposed illegal taxes on commercial traffic between Erbil and Mosul as well as on other successful businesses. The Shia political parties blocked the report from being read in parliament unless all reference to these entities was removed.

Shirwan Dobadani, a member of parliament from the city of Mosul, and part of the fact-finding mission, said that the business-men who came back to rebuild the city after the war were confronted by these militias and their Economy Offices. They were forced to pay the monthly 'atawa', so many of them retreated back to Erbil.

Atawa, unlike a bribe, is paid for things not to happen, for one not to be detained, for the business not to be bombed and for the children not to be kidnapped and tortured. It does not guarantee success, but it reduces the chances of harm.

After 2003, 'atawa' was imposed on businesses in Mosul, first by al-Qaeda and later by Islamic State jihadis as well as corrupt government officials and military and security commanders. Every business from doctors and pharmacies to restaurants and factories had to pay. In the years that preceded the fall of Mosul, the 'tax' collected by the Islamic State militias amounted to millions of dollars, according to Iraqi government estimates.

Now, these militias are imposing their own atawa on the businesses in the same way, and treating Mosul like a spoil of war. 'Sometimes it feels like only the flag has changed,' said the member of the city council. 'My fear is that this behaviour, this corruption, will threaten the peace and bring back the sectarian tensions that prevailed and led to the fall of the city and the rule of the Islamic State.'

Within days of the disaster, the people in Mosul began speaking openly about the role of Economy Offices in their city. The ferry broke the fear.

'This was a disaster waiting to happen,' said a business associate of the ferry owner. 'Ubaid and his son, they became rich very quickly. Greed blinded them and they started behaving like tyrants.'

Before the fall of Mosul, Ubaid al-Hadidi was a mid-level contractor. Under the rule of Islamic State, he made a fortune by buying and selling residential and agricultural lands confiscated from the expelled Christian residents. In 2015 he bought the concession for the island from its original investor and ran it for a year and a half before he was forced to close it because of the lack of electricity and the approaching war. After the liberation of Mosul, a warrant was issued for his arrest on terrorism charges.

Enter Hayder al-Sa'edy, also known as Hayder-Ringo. A reclusive senior commander in the Asaib, he had a lean athletic body and wide shoulders, a prominent lower jaw and elongated eyes wrapped in perpetual dark circles. During the battles of Mosul he was in charge of collecting and confiscating IS assets, and since the liberation he had become the head of the Asaib military office in Mosul, in charge of the lucrative business of scrap metal, and running a few front companies that were awarded public contracts by the governor.

After Hayder's alleged intervention, the charges against Ubaid were dropped. In return, according to MPs and intelligence officers who spoke to me about the disaster, Ubaid paid a 'contribution' of 5 billion Iraqi dinars to the Asaib militia and gave Hayder a 30 per cent share of the island.

A day after the ferry sank, Ubaid claimed in a phone call to an Iraqi TV station that he and his son had not been in Mosul when the disaster occurred. The reason, he said, was that an Asaib Ahl al-Haq security representative had threatened them, and demanded a large payment. 'When we were on the island, we would shut it if the water level climbed, but we haven't been in Mosul because of the threats we received.'

Three days later Ubaid and his son were arrested in Erbil and then moved to a prison in Mosul. In an interview with an Iraqi TV network, a representative of Asaib Ahl al-Haq's political wing said: 'Even if we accept that someone connected to the movement is a partner in the island, that does not mean that Asaib are responsible for what happened.'

In a way, even before they stepped onto that doomed overcrowded ferry, the lives of Aya, Ustad Ahmad and Shahla had been woven together by their shared experience of life and death in Mosul, with the sadness and misery that resembles the stories of *Arabian Nights*, where each fable unfolds to tell another parable of grief and loss.

When they brought the body of Ustad Ahmad's wife to the house on the night of the accident, he refused to see her, though he did manage to attend her funeral the next day. The body of the elder boy was found the day after the ferry sank, trapped beneath the capsized hull. His other son and the baby girl have never been found.

'I imagine all that happened as a dream; I talk about it as if it was a story that happened to someone else,' Ustad Ahmad told me. He was sitting in his mother's house. It was as though he had collapsed in on himself, entirely bereft of his former confidence and pride. He looked old and tired, his shoulders hunched and face sagging.

Ustad Ahmad had not been back to his house since the ferry disaster. He could not stand to see his boys' toys and their school bags. 'I asked my mother to remove all their belongings and give them away. I don't want to remember them. I want to forget their memories.' His voice was breaking, and his eyes became two narrow slits. 'You know, we lost another baby girl two years ago, she was the same age, a mirror image, the same laughter, the same face.' Two years earlier, when their house was struck by an IS mortar, Ahmad had run into the street barefoot carrying the other daughter, his wife and boys following him. His brother and many neighbours rushed to help them, his brother pulling the baby from Ahmad's arms, while Ahmad and wife went back to the house to collect their valuables. Then another mortar exploded. Ahmad ran outside to find that his brother and ten of the neighbours were dead. So was his baby daughter. 'Maybe it was in our fate to die on that day, but we missed death, and it caught up with us on the ferry.'

Ustad Ahmad does not blame incompetence or corruption. He blames his wife. She was the cause, he said, she was bored in the park and didn't want to sit in the sun.

'Yes there was negligence, but what can I do with the owner, how can I get my justice from him? Is he much worse than the people who stood watching while people were floating past them? No one came to save us; no one volunteered to come down into the water; people just stood watching. No one even threw us a plastic chair or table or extended a hand. Imagine you are standing there and watching someone trying to swim, trying to swim until they drown.

430

Women were screaming and no one helped. I swam and could see the people watching us, even when they took me back to the island I saw some people sitting eating their picnics. There is callousness, maybe because of all the death the city has seen.'

'What caused the ferry to sink was corruption, negligence and treating people as if they were worth nothing,' Aya told me. 'Anything has more value than us; people are the cheapest thing in Mosul.' She spoke forcefully, articulating in her guttural countryside accent the sadness of loss mixed with the bitterness of being abandoned by the state.

'We were liberated in March 2017, and in March 2019 my mother died. I have nothing left. I used to love Mosul and love Iraq. I used to love the white gulls, the bridge and the Tigris that we crossed every day to go to university. When I see the river now, I don't see it as beautiful, but as the place where my family died. To face my sadness, first I have to learn to face the Tigris. The first time I crossed it, I cried a lot.'

She was sitting on a sofa in her grandfather's house, wearing a blue ankle-length skirt with a cardigan and a scarf. On the other end of the sofa sat her aunt; between them, a chubby five-year-old boy lay on his back, his head resting on his mother's lap and his feet on Aya's. An occasional jingling sound came from his phone every time he crushed a line of candies (in the phone game Candy Crush Saga).

'She came back from the dead,' Aya said half laughing, nodding her head towards her aunt. She was brought out of the water unconscious, put into a body bag and dumped among the dead. When medics picked her up and threw her in the back of an ambulance to take her to the morgue, she coughed and began retching. Someone heard, opened the body bag, and she was declared alive.

'I didn't feel anything,' said the aunt with a shy smile. 'I fainted the moment I fell in the water.' She had a round, kind face and didn't look much older than Aya. She smoothed the hair of the boy in her lap, who ignored her, and said in a soft voice that he had tried to save his elder brother, kept pointing him out to the men who rescued him, but he was too far away, and they couldn't reach him. 'They never found his body.'

She looked at the boy with fondness and pity and told me that a year earlier he had lost his father. I had finished our long interview, closed my notebook and was sipping tea, waiting for the rain that was hammering the street outside to stop, so I asked out of politeness, How did his father die? She told me that he was detained in a routine police round-up after the city was liberated. They gathered the men of the neighbourhood in a schoolyard. A masked informant walked among the rows of men pointing out supposed IS collaborators. He was blindfolded and taken by the soldiers. A few days later, they started receiving phone calls from officers in the detention centre where her husband was held, demanding bribes if they wanted him released. For a whole year, the family paid the officers, who came to the house to collect their bribes, but nothing happened. A neighbour introduced them to a fixer; his job was to secure the release of detainees for cash. The fixer promised he would get him released for a single payment of $5,000. The family agreed. Two days later, he called and told them that the husband had been dead for six months. He was an honourable fixer, Aya said. They found the husband in the morgue, with a death certificate pinned to his chest naming his cause of death as kidney failure. He was twenty-eight, a healthy man who had never complained of any illness. The family was not allowed to take the body until they produced an authorisation from the prison, but the officers there wouldn't issue the permit until the family signed a paper declaring that they had no grievance against the prison authority. When they came back to receive his body after signing the paper, they found the death certificate had been changed, stating that he'd died of heart failure.

'No one here cares that this happened,' Aya said. 'The ferry will be forgotten just like all this death was forgotten.' In October, Aya started receiving phone calls from prominent tribal elders, pressuring her to accept an offer of 10 million Iraqi dinars and a plot of land on the outskirts of Mosul, as blood money offered by Haji Ubaid if she dropped any charges against him and his son. The elders told her that all the other families had accepted and she was one of the last holding out. Her stepfather had already signed on behalf of her mother, but she had to sign on behalf of her sister. 'I was refusing to sign, but all the families had signed, they tell me that they won't get anything from the state and they need the money, I don't know what to do.'

I called the MP Shirwan Dobadani to ask him about these compensations. He told me that two prominent tribal sheikhs had intervened as intermediaries. 'If the families wait for the judicial system to give them justice they won't get anything. There are thousands of cases of murders and assassinations that haven't been solved, because the worst disasters in Iraq are forgotten within seventy-two hours.'

Epilogue

In October 2019, hundreds of thousands of protesters surged into the streets of Baghdad and other Iraqi cities, in what came to be known as the Tishreen Uprising, the most existential threat to the post-2003 Iraqi state. Unlike previous attempts to topple the ruling class (religious parties, regional bosses, clergy and militias) this was not a jihadi or a militant armed rebellion – since the defeat of the Islamic State, the threat of a Sunni revolt had diminished – but an uprising of young secular activists and the Shia masses from the poor suburbs of Baghdad and southern Iraqi cities. These Shia masses were the electoral backbone of the religious sectarian parties, who had used the real or imaginary threat of the 'other' as a tool to garner electoral support, empowering and enriching the ruling class, but doing little for these impoverished areas.

The majority of those demonstrators were in their late teens or early twenties, members of the so-called 'PUBG generation' after the popular computer game. They grew up in the decades of civil war that followed the toppling of the Leader Necessity. Fed up with the misrule of the sectarian parties, they came to consider elections and representative democracy as synonymous with corruption and MPs abusing their privileges. They saw themselves as the victims of a terrible con perpetrated by those professing to defend them and their sect against the 'other'.

The Iraq of this new generation is an amalgam of contradictions, born out of an illegal occupation, two decades of civil wars, savage militancy, car bombs, beheadings and torture. Men – and they were only men shaped this new metamorphosis of a country based on their own images and according to the whims and desires of their masters, with no regard to what actually may have been good for its people. From the American adventurers who dreamt of dismantling everything and building a new freedom-loving, capitalist beacon of Americana in the region – because their previous beacons have done so well – to the exiles who followed on their heels, bent on establishing a sectarian political system. And those who opposed them both, either attempting to take the country back into that imagined glorious time of the Islamic Umma fourteen centuries ago, or the time of the Leader Necessity.

Some of these contradictions were embedded into the feeble new Iraqi constitutions; others were de facto results of the civil wars. A state was created that had all the trappings of a liberal democracy – elections, free press, parliament, a free market – and yet its lethargic, inflated administration, wrapped in archaic bureaucratic rules and regulations and fossilised hierarchies, behaves like other Middle Eastern authoritarian regimes. It is a wealthy, oil-exporting country, whose citizens live in poverty without employment, an adequate health-care system, electricity or drinking water, where sectarian parties and their militias have built statelets of corruption, and fiefdoms of commercial interests within the state, and where a new class of the super-wealthy – the so-called whales of corruption – have emerged with a panache for spending fortunes in nightclubs and private gambling rooms.

The new state, whose army was trained and equipped by the Americans, while its generals and commanders served Iranian interests, maintained the ethos of violence, torture and killings inherited from the Leader Necessity. Torture in particular became the central pillar of its collective security mentality, shared among a wide range of militias, military units and intelligence services. Such was the miserable new Iraqi state that people began to yearn for a strong dictator again, someone who would storm the Green Zone, impose martial law and do away with all the corrupt party bosses and their militias.

'If they give me Iraq for one month, I will fix it,' a young Iraqi army captain told me during the battle of Mosul. We were in a small mud room in a village in the middle of the desert between the Syrian border and Mosul. He lay on a narrow bed staring at the ceiling, and explained his ideas for solving all the problems of Iraq at once.

'I will abolish the constitution and the parliament, appoint military officers as military governors, declare corruption a terrorist crime, give some good food rations to the people, and start a new war against the Kurds that will unify the Sunnis and the Shia together.'

The first signs of the popular uprising came at the end of a hot summer in 2018 in the flat plains north of Basra, not far from Qurna where the Tigris and Euphrates meet. Once this area was famous for its palm-tree groves, where large numbers of buffalo and cows cooled themselves in the muddy green waters of its canals, until a combination of drought and water salinisation wiped out most of the palm groves, and the cattle were sold. The land became parched, spattered with dry crusts of salt and thorny shrubs. Batches of palm trees – many dead headless stumps – stood isolated in the yellow-brown landscape. Local rivers dried up, and the canals stagnated, turning into sewage pits clogged with trash. Corruption and mismanagement of local and central governments, both dominated by the ruling kleptocracy of the religious parties, exacerbated an environmental disaster. With the collapse of farming, the poor and unemployed looked for work elsewhere. Many joined the police, the army or the array of Shia militias that fought in Syria and Iraq. Thousands were killed, their pictures, posing in a variety of military fatigues, hung from electrical poles or fading on building walls. Meanwhile, government

437

officials, militia commanders and tribal chiefs grew very wealthy, for this barren and dying land is home to some of the most lucrative oilfields in the world.

'It's been ten years since I last wore a new shirt. We borrow money to eat, we borrow money to teach our children. We survive on debt,' the captain of a fishing boat in Basra told me, when the demonstrations first erupted, as he tugged at the collar of his dirty torn shirt. 'When the war started in 2003 and we saw the British tanks drive through the town, we were told that life will be very beautiful. Things will change, they said, we will all be better off,' he said, with the look of someone who had been cheated in a bargain.

Around us were the reminders of the folly of war: blackened stumps stood along the water of Shatt al-Arab facing Iran where once dense palm tree plantations covered the river banks, and where tens of thousands of Iraqis and Iranians died in the eighties war. Berms, trenches and rusted coils of barbed wire from that war lay next to the decomposed Hesco barriers where once British and American bases stood.

The captain was silent for a while, the moored dhows creaked against each other giving a harsh shriek of metal against metal, then he smiled and said: 'Actually I have got one thing from the British. In the chaos after their invasion, I, along with thousands of others, became a squatter on government lands and managed to build a house for my family.'

The house was a dark box of grey cinder blocks, in a desolate neighbourhood on the outskirts of Basra. Since 2003, hundreds of these settlements had sprouted throughout Basra, Baghdad and other Iraqi cities; the concrete shacks had no running water, spewing raw sewage into canals and streets. A jungle of wires siphoned electricity from the main grid. In winter children waded knee-deep through lakes of mud and sewage to go to school. These settlements, known as Hawassim, were named after the Great Leader's last battle, the 'Hawassim', the Decisive Battle.

Standing in front of his house, one could see the glittering state-of-the-art stadium built as part of the Basra Sports City. 'I know there is money in Basra,' the captain said. 'I can see the money in this city everywhere, in malls and in big houses, but I can't touch it.'

From these settlements came the first spark of the protest in 2018. People carrying Iraqi flags filled the streets outside municipal councils, burned tyres and blocked roads. Some called for better electricity and water supplies, others demanded instant employment, but everyone denounced the corruption and nepotism of the ruling kleptocracy of religious parties. They held them responsible for all the miseries that had befallen the south. Party headquarters were attacked and ransacked. Iran, the protector of these parties, was denounced and 'Iran out, out' became the rallying cry. A picture of the late Iranian leader Ayatollah Khomeini was set ablaze. The state responded with the one thing it knew: violence. Soldiers opened fire on the demonstrators, and hundreds were detained and tortured; plain-clothes militiamen went into the street in their white pickups, shooting and kidnapping protesters.

A year later, on 1 October, much bigger protests broke out in Baghdad and other cities. The spark may have been the dismissal of a general who distinguished himself in the fight against the Islamic State, but the undercurrent was the same anger towards the corrupt religious kleptocracy, and its rotten bureaucratic regime. Security forces used tear gas and live ammunition, killing young unarmed men as they sought refuge behind concrete barriers or stood in the streets waving Iraqi flags. On 4 October, snipers positioned above buildings leading to Tahrir Square in central Baghdad opened fire, killing a dozen civilians. Iraqi forces had frequently opened fire on civilians but never before had they shot and killed poor Shia kids waving Iraqi and Shia flags who fell in puddles of blood, and never before had they then shot the young men who tried to rescue them. Those were not the 'other', jihadis or insurgents, but the poor Shia that the regime had claimed to serve and protect. Probably that was the moment when the post-2003 state lost whatever legitimacy it had. Musa, one of the organisers of the demonstrations told me many weeks later that had the government not opened fire on the demonstrators, everything would have ended the next day. But with the violent reaction, anger and rage swept through the city, and many more teenagers, mostly from the eastern suburbs of the city, took to the streets. In the first six days of demonstrations 106 were killed and more than six thousand were injured.

The day after the shootings by the snipers, I walked to Tahrir Square, the scene of all demonstrations and political upheavals in Iraq. Opened in the 1930s during the monarchy, the square was later expanded with sixties modern architecture. On the eastern side stands one of Iraq's most iconic works of art: the 'Freedom Monument'. Consisting of fourteen bronze castings hung on a white marble slab,

and created by the brilliant leftist Jawad Selim, the bas-relief figures tell the story of Iraq's 1958 revolution, from the grieving mother to the soldiers breaking the walls of the prison. The muscle contours, the faces and the symbols bring together the inspirations of Assyrian and Babylonian art, together with Picasso-influenced sculptures. On the western side of the square, the Jimhouriya Bridge spans the Tigris. Next to it is the thirteen-storey-high building known as the Turkish Restaurant. It's an ugly concrete building, erected in the seventies to house a multi-storey car park, offices and a rooftop Turkish restaurant offering panoramic views of the city. The building, which dominates the skyline of Baghdad, was targeted by the Americans in 2003; multiple rockets opened a huge gash in its side. It is still abandoned even after a partial renovation. The whole square has long been falling into neglect, ageing very ungracefully. The 'thieves market' is tucked behind it, next to a crowded bus terminal, reeking public toilets, and some of the dingiest bars and brothels. Multiple car bombs have shattered whatever grace the square had. Only the monument stands high above, withstanding all the coups and wars of the city.

There were no protests in the square on that day, as all roads leading to it were blocked by armoured vehicles and Humvees. Soldiers and policemen, armed with machine guns and hand grenades, just as they were when fighting Islamic State militants two years ago, stood ready to open fire on the unarmed civilians if they dared to come. More armoured troop carriers closed the Jimhouriya Bridge on the other side of the square, which led to the sanctum of power, the Green Zone, seat of the government, parliament, foreign embassies and many of the big politicians. Inside the square, packs of soldiers sat or lounged on mattresses splayed on the pavement in the shade of their Humvees. Behind the monument, in al-Umma Park – the 'park of the nation' – some people who had managed to pass through the barricades gathered in small groups, watched by lines of riot police. I listened to one group of a few men and two women, standing in the shade of the ageing eucalyptus trees, as they debated on how to articulate the demands of the protesters. Should they continue with their peaceful demonstrations in the face of government violence, or escalate their protests, pick up arms to defend themselves, following in the footsteps of other – tragically failed – Arab and Iraqi uprisings? 'Burning army trucks won't help us, it will only help the government accuse us of being hooligans,' said one young man. 'If I give you seventeen RPG launchers and you burn that building, how will that benefit our demands?' Another man called for the toppling of the regime and abolishing the parliament. 'Who made you a speaker?' someone else shouted, spurring the rest of the group to break into chants of 'no one represents us' and 'Iran out, out', denouncing Iraq's ruling Islamic parties and their Iranian backers.

The nature of the debate, just like the demonstrations, was chaotic, boisterous and leaderless. Groups formed, argued, shouted down speakers, disintegrated and formed again. I had watched these debates many times before in public squares in Syria, Yemen, Libya and in Iraq, and the challenges facing the earnest men and women were always the same: how to channel the demands and anger of people rising against corruption, nepotism and state brutality, into a coherent political roadmap; and in almost every single case these uprisings ended in disillusionment, fragmentation and civil war, turning the surrounding streets and buildings into battle zones roamed by mad and murderous militiamen. The difference here is that, unlike in Egypt, Syria or Tunisia, the anger was not directed at one person, a dictator figure, but at the whole of the post-2003 ruling class.

Eventually, as the setting sun filled the park with its orange glow, the small groups – most in their twenties, but among them two aged Communists wearing Che Guevara berets – agreed on a list of demands, which were read out by a young bearded and bespectacled man. 'The resignation of the government, new elections, a change in the election laws, and most importantly putting all the government officials on trial.' The crowd cheered, mobile phones were raised and the crowd called to march to Tahrir Square, which they couldn't access.

A kilometre or so to the east, under a flyover, a teenager wearing a yellow T-shirt, shorts and flip-flops, walked slowly while a policeman brandishing his Kalashnikov tried to chase him away. The boy turned his head and laughed at the policeman. Thin black strings of smoke from burning tires twisted into the sky and a handful of fellow teenagers and young men tried marching towards the square.

Policemen ran towards them, brandishing their Kalashnikovs and shooting in the air, the sound echoing in the streets emptied of car traffic. But the crowd pushed on, waving Iraqi flags and Shia banners. Two young boys brought tyres, lined them across the road and set them on fire. The men surged forward, the crackle of gunfire became continuous and the bangs of tear-gas canisters more frequent, their white gas mixing with the black fumes of the tyres. The young men surged, only to be pushed back by the heavy machine gun fire and tear gas. Amid the carnage, dozens of three-wheeled tuk-tuk motorcycle rickshaws zoomed , ferrying the injured away from the scene. A yellow one carried a man slumped in the back, unable to breathe.

Urging the men to move forward was a short thin young man with a well-trimmed ginger beard. 'Why are you standing back?' he called to the men cowering behind the bridge railing. 'Those who don't want to advance go back home.' His name was Jawdat, and he said he was a former fighter with the Hashed paramilitaries and that his brother was an officer who had been killed in the war against the Islamic State. 'I fought with the Hashed, I even went to fight in Syria, but what did I get from this government? Nothing.

While those politicians in the Green Zone are blocking any attempt to reform the state.' Ambulances joined the Tuk-Tuks darting back and forth ferrying the injured and the dead. Twenty people will be killed by the end of this day alone.

In front of the crowd stood a tall, unarmed army officer in a crisp uniform. He pleaded with the young men to disperse. 'I can let you go down and march towards Tahrir Square,' he said, pointing at the rising columns of smoke. 'But I swear by Allah the militiamen and the snipers will kill you.' The crowd responded with angry anti-Iranian chants.

Most of the demonstrators were young unemployed Iraqis, but the government, the religious parties and their militias used their media outlets to label them as plotters, former Baathists, and declared that the demonstrations had been organised by the American embassy and funded by Gulf states to topple the pro-Iranian government of Iraq.

'Look at the people around you,' said a 23-year-old lawyer, pointing at the dozens of kids who crouched in an alleyway in Sadr City, as bullets whistled over our heads. 'Do you think the American embassy even knows this alleyway exists? We are all unemployed, I finished law school three years ago and I haven't found a job yet.'

A young man was carried back by other demonstrators, his leg soaked in blood; they put him on the ground and everyone pulled out their smartphones and took pictures. A medic tried to bandage him. More injured demonstrators followed, while a pyre of burning tyres shot orange flames sky-high.

'This is the best demonstration since 2003,' said the lawyer. 'All previous demonstrations were either organised by Muqtada al-Sadr or the secularists, but this is a genuine leaderless people's uprising.'

A period of tentative calm fell on Baghdad and other Shia cities in the south that autumn, as the protesters called for a temporary halt

444

of their demonstrations while millions of people headed to Karbala to commemorate the Arba'een, marking the end of the forty days' mourning for Imam Hussein. On 25 October, when the demonstrations resumed, people began to gather in Tahrir Square from early in the morning. They stood in large groups, waving Iraqi flags and chanting 'Our soul, our blood, we sacrifice for you, Iraq'. And 'Iran out, out, Baghdad will be free'. Better services, electricity and jobs were no longer the demands, but 'We want a watan [homeland]' had become the rallying cry.

Lines of riot police were stationed at the western side of the square, at the entrance of the Jimhouriya Bridge, and in the abandoned Turkish Restaurant building which dominated the square. Their task was to prevent the protesters from crossing the bridge into the Green Zone. Young men tried to break through these police lines, pelting them with rocks, and taunting them with insults. The police, all sporting black ski masks, responded by firing stun grenades, and a volley of tear-gas canisters, which fell among the people, spinning and spewing noxious white fumes, sending the people back choking, stumbling and coughing. Volunteers and doctors sprayed faces with a milk solution and Pepsi. A red tuk-tuk stopped next to a group of young men carrying an injured teenage boy; they put him in the back and the vehicle rushed away blaring its siren. Clouds of white haze hung low over the people, and with eyes closed they rushed back towards the police lines. Others stood back, shouting encouragement.

While these skirmishes took place, crowds continued to fill the square. They came from all over the city: university and high school students, of both genders; doctors in white robes, groups of friends from middle-class neighbourhoods, families with their children; women, some with no hijab and others wrapped in a black abaya; tribesmen wearing long keffiyehs, and kids in skinny jeans and

T-shirts. It seemed that the whole city, the whole country, for similiar demonstrations had erupted all over Iraq, was out denouncing corruption, sectarianism and all that had taken place in the past two decades.

A man climbed on top of a traffic police booth and started to recite a poem, people gathered and cheered him; the poems, the speeches – all expressed a new-found pride in Iraqi patriotism, just like the waving of the Iraqi flag. Maybe, the people felt, after many years of sub-identities, they could finally revert to a larger more common identity. Or maybe, after two decades, the flag, patriotism and watan had lost their connection to the Leader Necessity, and people could own all these again. Then came another round of explosions, and the white clouds of the tear gas; people scattered, some using the Iraqi flags over their heads for protection.

By lunchtime, a shawarma stand was set up, and two men started preparing sandwiches and serving them to the long orderly queues that had formed in front of them. Others ladled rice and beans from large blackened pots placed on the back of a truck. This was a very common tradition during the big Shia festivals, when tens of thousands of people marched on foot to Karbala and Najaf, and communities organised 'Mawakeb', serving food and water to the pilgrims. It would not be the only time when protesters co-opted Shia traditions and symbols – like the martyrdom of Hussein and his uprising against oppression – in their protest, confusing their opponents in the religious parties who had claimed these same symbols, often to generate sectarian tensions between communities.

A group of young students stood under the Freedom Monument, they were wrapped in the Iraqi flag like a shroud. Next to them was a man in his mid-thirties, who had taken his shirt off. Fresh bandages covered his right arm and chest, and one circled his large belly like a sash, all from stun grenade wounds. He carried a plastic bottle with

446

the milk solution used to treat tear-gas burns in one hand, and a blanket that he used to douse the tear-gas canisters in the other. He had an angry impatient look on his face and told me that he was a teacher and the kids wrapped in the Iraqi flags were his students.

'I have a job, and I have my own business,' he said while his eyes scanned the sky for an incoming canister. 'I don't want anything from the government, but I came because when I saw my students protesting and showing so much courage I felt ashamed of myself.'

Tuk-tuks whizzed back and forth ferrying injured protesters to nearby hospitals. These red or yellow rickshaw motorcycles had become the symbol of the uprising. Driven by the most impoverished kids, they were a cheap alternative to taxis, especially in the poorer quarters of the city, and provided a little income to their owners, but the government had banned them and impounded many tuk-tuks earlier that year, so the drivers instantly joined the uprising, ferrying protesters and functioning like ambulances.

By the afternoon, as the first rains of the season pelted the filth-strewn streets, a sea of tens of thousands of people marched to the square from the Shia suburbs of Sadr City, where the maverick cleric Muqtada al-Sadr decided to support the protest to weaken the other Shia factions in power. Then a strange thing started happening that night: all over the square, a sense of community surfaced, connecting all those different peoples. Groups were organised to pick up trash, distribute blankets and food, while medics trained volunteers, and the first tents were erected. In seventeen years of fighting, I had become accustomed to seeing the cruelty of people towards each other, immersed in their selfish sectarian mentalities, and I began to process this outpouring of emotions in the streets of Baghdad. My eyes filled with tears at the acts of kindness around me, of old women in their black abayas, thrusting sandwiches into the hands of demonstrators as if they were their children, or of young medical students treating the wounded, of strangers hugging each other and crying. That moment of Tishreen had restored our dignity, and wiped out the shame of the civil war.

At first Raghad thought the protests would be like one of those organised by leftists, in which a handful of people go to the streets and quickly disperse, but she soon realised something big was taking place, and like most Iraqis these days, she began to follow the events obsessively. She tried to get news from different sources, calling friends and relatives, relying on word of mouth since the government had severely restricted access to the internet. She felt outrage when she saw footage of government forces killing unarmed protesters. 'I felt like a revolution was erupting inside me and I thought I must have a voice,' she told me when we met in Istanbul a couple of years later.

She decided to go down and join the protests, but it was not an easy decision.

'My family are very conservative, I can even say that I come from a tribal society in which the voice of a woman should always be lower than that of a man, and women should keep to their houses and definitely not go out to protest in the streets. But I had turned thirty that October, and I thought it's time for me to take a stance. My parents tried to stop me but it was my choice.'

During the civil war, her working-class neighbourhood sat near the front lines, and for a decade her only outing was when her father walked her to the nearby school and brought her back. Of all the faded memories from the past decades, she has a vivid recollection of her father weeping in 2003 when Baghdad fell to the Americans. She loved him very much, an illiterate farmer from the Shia south who moved to Baghdad during the big rural migration in the seventies, and lived in what was essentially a mud hut for years. He worked hard, built a small house for his family, and made sure that all his children and especially Raghad finished their university education, working two sometimes three jobs to support his family during the sanctions. She also remembers how one day the Shia militia that controlled their neighbourhood kidnapped her brother, a Shia, mistaking him for their cousin who was a Sunni. He was beaten and tortured but was released eventually.

One afternoon, a few days into the protests, she wrapped her father's black-and-white keffiyeh around her neck, wore a pair of loose jeans, a long shirt and a pair of trainers, and headed to central Baghdad. 'I was scared at first, I didn't want the people in my neighbourhood to know where I was going, but when they saw the keffiyeh, everyone knew I was going to the square, and they started cheering me.' She took one of the tuk-tuks that had become the ubiquitous symbol of the revolution.

'When I arrived in the square and saw all the people chanting and waving flags, I was very happy,' she told me. 'I had lost all hope that there could be a change in our situation. First, they used to tell us that we couldn't develop the country because we were at war with Daesh [IS], but Daesh was defeated in 2017, and in 2019 things had not improved. Like everyone else I could see that in sixteen years the government had done nothing for the people in terms of health care, employment or even electricity. All they'd done was patch-up jobs while the infrastructures were what the previous regime had built.'

One of the most striking things to emerge that October was the role women played in the protests. They were everywhere, not only as medics and providing logistical support, but on the front-line barricades, in the tents debating, and on the streets painting murals and revolutionary art. A space had opened wide, and they filled it, and pushed against social and religious restrictions. Solidarity, respect and a shared patriotism became the norm in an area of Baghdad where women had rarely ventured alone at night. When I asked Raghad what she made of that, she told me that woman had always had an active role in Iraqi society, but wars, sanctions and upheavals had pushed them away from the public sphere. 'Generations came that knew nothing but fear. Tishreen was our opportunity to reclaim our position and our public role. We couldn't just keep seeing ourselves as victims, we had to be active; we organised workshops to educate the women in economy, law and politics. This is how we can prepare for the future.'

The nation had two realities. One was of the 72-year-old prime minister, wearing a suit and tie, addressing the nation night after night, rarely looking at the camera and reading his speeches in a highly classical Arabic – totally detached from the vernacular of the PUBG generation. He claimed that a 'third party' opened fire on the protesters, all part of a grand plot to destabilise Iraq. In a patronising tone he told the people to go home, promising them reforms, jobs and better services. All the while, militias and security services continued to kill, maim and disappear activists. The other reality was of protesters, in the square the tent camp grew bigger, and a wall of fear had broken. It seemed that the militias had been defanged by the kids; everywhere in the city it became common to hear jibes and jokes about the beturbaned leaders.

The clashes along the Jimhouriya Bridge continued, with the protesters organising into assault squads, armed with slingshots and Molotov cocktails, and later some even carried home-made nail bombs. They wore colourful helmets and military webbing, carried shields improvised from street signs and walked with a swagger as if they were special forces fighting in Mosul. Others wore heavy gloves and were tasked with throwing tear-gas canisters back at the riot police, or snuffing them out with buckets and wet blankets. It was a very dangerous job as government troops used these military-grade canisters as weapons, shooting them straight at the protesters, aiming at their heads. One night I cowered with a group of boys and girls, as these grenades flew in front of us, in straight horizontal lines cutting through running protesters, leaving long red sparks behind.

Mussa, one of the protest leaders, was a short and portly veter-
inarian, with thick dishevelled hair, small slanting eyes and a protruding lower lip. He told me that after many of his close comrades
were killed by these grenades, they planned a large-scale attack on
the bridge, to push the lines of the police back, and on the Turkish
Restaurant building that dominated the square. 'We had to find a way
to protect the civilians in the square.'

The attack lasted for two days and nights. Hundreds of protesters ducked behind barricades of metal sheets erected on the river
embankment and began to fire volleys of metal pellets from their
slingshots. Others climbed under the bridge and lobbed Molotov
cocktails. The tear gas fired by the police was not effective any more
since almost all the protesters were wearing proper gas masks –
provided through crowdfunding by activists and business people.
Only the whooshing grenades continued to kill and injure. Finally, as
dusk fell, and thick clouds of smoke rose, and the protesters attacked
the concrete barricades on the bridge, the scene resembled a colony
of ants tearing at a large dormant cockroach. The riot police were
forced to withdraw to the middle of the bridge. Isolated and surrounded by a sea of people, police units in the Turkish Restaurant
abandoned their positions after the protesters set fire to the ground
floor to literally smoke them out. Hundreds probably thousands
flocked into the building, with everyone going up and down on the
narrow concrete stairway at once, creating such mayhem that people
climbed down through ventilation shafts and scaffolding. Below,
the streets were jam-packed, lights from tens of thousands of mobile
phones flickered, and the square looked like a large blossoming rose
in the darkness of Baghdad, while hundreds of tuk-tuks blared songs
and honked to the cheering of the crowd. And that was the height of
the euphoria of Tishreen.

Raghad became a regular to the square and the tents, which were taking a permanent shape, like that of a war camp. She and other volunteers wore Hi-Vis vests and, armed with brooms and shovels, cleared the streets of debris. The ground had become littered with tear-gas canisters, plastic bottles, torn blankets and a sticky residue of Pepsi and milk. Now the notoriously filthy Rasheed Street was cleaner than it had ever been before. The tents were made of blue tarpaulin and housed students, tribesmen or medics. In between the tents, a few sellers were peddling biscuits, fruit or small plastic replicas of the iconic tuk-tuks. At one end of the square, in a tent emblazoned with the words 'People's Theatre', there were poetry recitations and experimental theatre performances. The real cost of the two months of protest could be seen in the dozen or so 'Shrines for the Martyrs', where pictures of the dead, mostly young men in their late teens or early twenties, were placed on the ground, surrounded by plastic flowers, copies of the Quran and incense sticks. Young men and women knelt in front of them, lit candles and sat in silence; the heaving of a shoulder or a deep sob were the only indications of the sadness and grief sweeping the square.

On the bridge, the two barricades faced each other. The riot police had made theirs of blast walls, as well as prefabricated U-shapes and cylinders, topped with barbed wire looking like a formidable concrete fortress. Facing it was the protesters' own barricade, built around the abandoned riot police's early fortifications. It had arisen like a Mad Max structure, with metal sheets welded on top of each other. At night it resembled a multi-winged fanged monster. On both barricades were splayed Shia banners and Iraqi flags, and both sides used loudspeakers to taunt and insult each other.

'Front-line squads' of protesters made their home there, sleeping in grooves in the wall or underneath, jealously guarding it not only from possible government attacks but from the 'civilian' protesters. As time passed, divisions emerged between the frontliners, who had become addicted to violence and confrontations, and the residents of different tents. The leaderless nature of the protest was its power, as no one could influence the leaders and coerce them, but it was also its curse.

'My first disappointment came when I saw the protesters carrying slingshots and hitting security forces with these very dangerous metal balls and Molotov bombs. Most of those men couldn't find a job so would join the security forces,' Raghad said. 'Then I noticed the division between the protesters; they still didn't know who our true enemy was and division erupted within the tents – each tent had its leader and they failed to have a united front, a common identity.' Even the Turkish Restaurant, that bastion of resistance renamed Mount Uhud, after the mountain which the Prophet and his men captured in one of his early battles, was divided among different factions, notably the followers of Muqtada, who clashed frequently with

other protesters. When one night one of her friends was kidnapped, Raghad decided to stop going. Like all revolutions and uprisings, Tishreen eventually failed, another compromise prime minister was elected, and the domination of kleptocracy continues to this day. But Tishreen showed the power of the people when not cowed by sectarian fears, and indicates that the post-2003 state can no longer satisfy its own people. The failure of consecutive regimes that ruled Iraq – from the British mandate to the monarchy and the military dictatorships and finally Saddam – to reform and listen to the demands of their people led to their demise eventually. And now as dozens of militias cajole and compete with each other to capture a bigger share of state spoils – and whose infighting is threatening to start another round of civil war – the failure of the ruling class, the religious parties, regional bosses, the clergy and militias to heed the warnings of Tishreen will lead to their eventual demise.

Acknowledgements

On 10 April 2003, the day after Baghdad was occupied by US forces, I began my writer's journey working for the *Guardian*: first as a translator, then as a freelance contributor and finally as a staff special correspondent. I was fortunate to be inducted into the world of journalism by James Meek, who became a friend and a mentor, and whose writing I cherish.

Over the past two decades, throughout the entire timespan of this book, the *Guardian*'s unwavering commitment to provide sober and in-depth reporting allowed me to travel across the wider Middle East, telling the stories of people caught in the many civil wars plaguing the region. I am indebted to my editors at the *Guardian* for their guidance, support, patience and encouragement: Ian Katz, who believed in me and commissioned my first piece; Charlie English, Jamie Wilson, Esther Addley, Mark Rice-Oxley, Martin Hodgson, Lizzy Davies and Devika Bhat, thank you all for your painstaking labour editing my sentences. Clare Longrigg, for moulding my Mosul stories into a coherent narrative. Special thanks to Jan Thompson and Chris Elliott, and to Karen Plews, Jana Harris and Sarah Hewitt. I am specially indebted to Alan Rusbridger, who flew to Tripoli to negotiate my release from a Libyan jail. And finally, Katharine Viner, for your guidance and leadership, which has been a vital pillar of support for me. I thank you all, and please accept my apologies both for all the missed deadlines and for the sleepless nights you had to endure because of my misadventures in the various zones of conflict.

To Helen Conford, my editor at Penguin Random House, thank

you for your staunch belief in this project, and your persistence in demanding a manuscript, even at times when I was beset with doubts. I am grateful to John Freeman at Knopf, for giving thoughtful feedback that helped the book take its current shape, and to Shan Vahidy for prodigiously chiselling and honing the manuscript. Thank you all for your hard work poring over the sea of text and making sense of it.

Laurie Ip Fung Chun and Katherine Fry, thank you for your precision and meticulous attention to detail.

My agent, friend and Tavla playmate, Natasha Fairweather, thank you for your infinite patience, and for your encouragement through all the years of missed deadlines and belated deliveries.

I am grateful to Daniel Soar at the *London Review of Books*, whose gracious edits combed with effortless ease through the pages, weeding out dense sentences and redundant words. I am forever indebted to my Iraqi colleagues Ahmad, Tha'er, Tareq, Abdullah and Abdulsalam, who helped me navigate the gunmen-riddled streets of Baghdad. Without you I wouldn't have been able to travel across the city, let alone do any reporting. I am also grateful to the people who opened their doors to me and shared their stories, and who often protected and helped me. Most of their names have been changed for their protection.

Throughout the years, the invaluable insights of Iraqi writers and journalists like Sarmad al Taie, Omar al Shaher, Mushtaq el Helo and Ali al Sarai, amongst many others, have helped me untangle the mesh of Iraqi politics. Other journalists imparted their wisdom, support and encouragement: some at the *Guardian*, like Rory McCarthy, Peter Beaumont, Jonathan Steele and Ian Black, as well as Susan Sachs, Karl Vick, Philip Bennett, Raney Aronson, Christoph Reuter, Mariam Karouny, Nir Rosen, Javier Espinosa and Monica Prieto – thank you all.

Special thanks to Neil MacFarquhar for being a great teacher and a friend; Abigail Fielding-Smith, who first planted the idea of the book in my head; Joao Silva, whose stoicism and composure calmed me down even when the bullets whizzed around us; and Rania Abouzeid, whose dispatches from the Syrian war are a stellar example of journalism. But most of all, it was the late Anthony Shadid: a gentle and a great soul, with a disarming, permanent smile; a journalist of boundless humanity and an attentive eye for details, who taught me how to listen to people's stories with empathy and companionship.

In a way, the book started as a journal that I kept for my dearest friends, Nathalie Dournovo and Laurent Marion, as a record of the Baghdad they loved. Thank you for helping me discover my own city during our many long walks.

My father gave me my first book, a Toynbee, when I was a child; my great-aunt introduced me to Pushkin; and my little brother fed me very peppery pasta while I sulked in bed reading Amin Malouf. I love you all.

It took me more than ten years to write this book – during that time, many friends showered me with love, opened their homes, listened to my stories and comforted me. Ihssan and Rasheed, with whom I have been walking, debating and arguing for nearly thirty years; Sinan Antoon, who captured in his fiction the Iraqi tragedy in a way no one else could; and Razia Iqbal, with whom I shared many nourishing conversations. I owe a great debt to Melek, Zia and Shahir, who became my surrogate family – thank you, Shahir, for getting me out of incarceration, twice. To Tara Sutton, who commiserated and helped, and taught me that humour was vital for survival in the darkest of times. Bazoon and Kishmish, my cat-friends, your furry bellies were a great distraction, and eased my deadline anxieties.

But most of all, Adnan: three centuries in one man, you passed on to me your passion for collecting prayer beads and shared with me your wisdom and boundless generosity. You protected me and treated me like one of your sons. Salam pax, my lifelong and dearest friend, from the drunken debates in the squalid Red Room in Baghdad to many peaceful afternoons by the sea, staring into the horizon – thank you for your unconditional love.

Rena Effendi, my partner: you stood by me, believed in me, even when I didn't. I took shelter in your love, and you carried me through the good and the hard times over the past decade; you inspired me to draw, to cook and to write.